Assessing Capacities of Older Adults

Assessing Capacities of Older Adults

A Casebook to Guide Difficult Decisions

Edited by Jennifer Moye

American Psychological Association
Washington, DC

The opinions and statements published are the responsibility of the authors, and such opinions and statements do not necessarily represent the policies of the American Psychological Association. Any views expressed in Chapter 7 do not necessarily represent the views of the United States government, and the author's participation in the work is not meant to serve as an official endorsement.

The Editor has worked to ensure that all information in this book is accurate at the time of publication and consistent with general mental health care standards. As research and practice continue to advance, however, therapeutic standards may change. Moreover, particular situations may require a particularized therapeutic response not addressed or included in this book. For these reasons and because human and mechanical errors sometimes occur, we recommend that readers follow the advice of psychologists or other therapists directly involved in their care or the care of a member of their family.

Published by
American Psychological Association
750 First Street, NE
Washington, DC 20002
https://www.apa.org

Order Department
https://www.apa.org/pubs/books
order@apa.org

In the U.K., Europe, Africa, and the Middle East, copies may be ordered from Eurospan
https://www.eurospanbookstore.com/apa
info@eurospangroup.com

Typeset in Meridien and Ortodoxa by Circle Graphics, Inc., Reisterstown, MD

Printer: Sheridan Books, Chelsea, MI
Cover Designer: Gwen J. Grafft, Minneapolis, MN

Library of Congress Cataloging-in-Publication Data

Names: Moye, Jennifer, editor. | American Psychological Association, issuing body.
Title: Assessing capacities of older adults : a casebook to guide difficult decisions / edited by Jennifer Moye.
Description: Washington, DC : American Psychological Association, [2020] | Includes bibliographical references and index.
Identifiers: LCCN 2019051599 (print) | LCCN 2019051600 (ebook) | ISBN 9781433831546 (paperback) | ISBN 9781433831553 (ebook)
Subjects: LCSH: Decision making in old age. | Medical care—Decision making. | Older people—Functional assessment. | Capacity and disability. | Older people—Psychological testing. | Dementia.
Classification: LCC BF724.85.D44 A47 2020 (print) | LCC BF724.85.D44 (ebook) | DDC 155.67—dc23
LC record available at https://lccn.loc.gov/2019051599
LC ebook record available at https://lccn.loc.gov/2019051600

http://dx.doi.org/10.1037/0000184-000

Printed in the United States of America

10 9 8 7 6 5 4 3 2 1

For my parents, Howard and Doris Moye, with gratitude

CONTENTS

CONTRIBUTORS

Amy E. Albright, MSc, The University of Alabama, Tuscaloosa
Rebecca S. Allen, PhD, ABPP, The University of Alabama, Tuscaloosa
Brian D. Carpenter, PhD, Washington University in St. Louis, St. Louis, MO
Barry Edelstein, PhD, West Virginia University, Morgantown
Scott C. Fish, PhD, ABPP, Cognitive Neurology, Beth Israel Deaconess Medical Center, Boston, MA
Jarred V. Gallegos, MS, West Virginia University, Morgantown
Michelle M. Hilgeman, PhD, Tuscaloosa VA Medical Center, Tuscaloosa, AL, and The University of Alabama, Tuscaloosa
Kate L. M. Hinrichs, PhD, ABPP, VA Boston Healthcare System and Harvard Medical School, Boston, MA
Sean D. Hollis, PhD, The University of Alabama at Birmingham
Emma Katz, MS, West Virginia University, Morgantown
Peter A. Lichtenberg, PhD, ABPP, Wayne State University, Detroit, MI
Brian M. Ludwin, PhD, VA Boston Healthcare System, Boston, MA
Daniel C. Marson, JD, PhD, Department of Neurology and Alzheimer's Disease Center, The University of Alabama at Birmingham
Kathleen C. Matthews, PhD, VA Central Iowa Health Care System, Des Moines
C. Caroline Merz, MA, Washington University in St. Louis, St. Louis, MO
Michelle E. Mlinac, PsyD, ABPP, VA Boston Healthcare System and Harvard Medical School, Boston, MA
Jennifer Moye, PhD, ABPP, VA New England Geriatric Research Education and Clinical Center (GRECC) and Harvard Medical School, Boston, MA
Thomas A. Novack, PhD, ABPP-CN, The University of Alabama at Birmingham

Kyle S. Page, PhD, ABPP, Edward Hines, Jr. VA Hospital, Hines, IL
Ronald W. Smith, PhD, VA Boston Healthcare System and Harvard Medical School, Boston, MA
Rachael Spalding, MS, West Virginia University, Morgantown
Pamela Steadman-Wood, PhD, ABPP, Providence VA Medical Center and Alpert Medical School of Brown University, Providence, RI
Jessica V. Strong, PhD, Department of Psychology, University of Prince Edward Island, Charlottetown, Prince Edward Island, Canada
Kristen Triebel, PsyD, ABPP-CN, The University of Alabama at Birmingham
Erica Wood, JD, American Bar Association Commission on Law and Aging, Washington, DC
Stacey Wood, PhD, ABPP, Scripps College, Claremont, CA

ACKNOWLEDGMENTS

This casebook builds on the work by the American Bar Association (ABA) Commission on Law and Aging and the American Psychological Association (APA) to establish handbooks for members of their respective professional associations regarding the Assessment of Capacity in Older Adults. The handbooks (https://www.apa.org/pi/aging) were a product of a working group whose membership changed somewhat over the course of the three handbooks and also benefited from the input and review of many clinical and legal professionals. Within APA, the work was supported by the Office on Aging and the Office of General Counsel. The ABA and APA, along with the Farnsworth and Borchard Foundations, provided financial support for the handbooks. Because those handbooks lay the conceptual foundation for this edited casebook, I would like to thank all the members of the working group, reviewers, supporters, and the APA Office on Aging—in particular, Deborah DiGilio—for their contributions to the ABA/APA capacity handbook series. I also acknowledge and thank Erica Wood and Charles Sabatino from the ABA for so patiently teaching me (and all of us) about the legal perspective on capacity and guardianship.

I am so grateful to the chapter authors for the wisdom and craft they brought to writing each chapter. Each one is a gem, and each reflects the authors' commitment to ethical practice. I am also indebted to the VA Boston Healthcare System, which has been my professional home for several decades. My interest in capacity began with a desire to do the very best by the veterans we serve. I am thankful for the opportunity to have my life enriched by working with and for older veterans these many years. I have also benefitted from the community within the VA Boston Geropsychology training program, both our faculty and our trainees. In particular, I thank my colleagues for their participation in our "capacity rounds" and for being generous enough to seek my consultation on complex cases. I have learned so much for each of you and continue to learn through your work and example.

I am so appreciative of all the co-investigators who have worked with me on capacity and guardianship research projects these past 2 decades. A special thank you to the project managers on our capacity and guardianship projects, Armin Azar, Jorge Armesto, and Casey Catlin, who also helped with this book, and to my long-term collaborator and friend Michele Karel who has contributed so much to our thinking about health care values. Finally, I thank my family, especially Adam Gibbons and Ella Moye-Gibbons for their many conversations around the dinner table and for all their support.

Assessing Capacities of Older Adults

Introduction

Jennifer Moye

This casebook focuses on the clinical assessment of capacities in older adults, particularly those with late-onset neurocognitive conditions and late-life expression of lifelong neuropsychiatric conditions (e.g., schizophrenia). It is a case-based follow-up to *Assessment of Older Adults With Diminished Capacity: A Handbook for Psychologists* (American Bar Association and American Psychological Association [ABA/APA] Assessment of Capacity in Older Adults Project Working Group, 2008), which is available to download for free at http://www.apa.org/pi/aging. The psychologist handbook was one of three prepared by a working group from the ABA Commission on Law and Aging and the APA. Responding to concerns from members, the two organizations aimed to provide guidance regarding the assessment of capacity for psychologists, lawyers, and judges (the judges handbook was created in conjunction with the National College of Probate Judges). These handbooks have been extensively distributed, and much of the material within them is still current. However, translating the concepts from the handbooks into practice can be challenging. This casebook for clinicians seeks to respond to the challenge of translation by offering clinically oriented examples of challenging issues.

WHAT ARE "CAPACITIES"?

This book focuses on clinical (as opposed to judicial or legal) assessment of capacities. In this book, this term is used in a fairly specific way—meaning a clinical assessment and opinion as to whether a person has the requisite ability

http://dx.doi.org/10.1037/0000184-001
Assessing Capacities of Older Adults: A Casebook to Guide Difficult Decisions, J. Moye (Editor)

to perform a task or make a decision that is being questioned by another (e.g., can this person with dementia consent to this high-risk surgery?). What sets the assessment of capacities apart from neuropsychological assessment is that it focuses on function—mapping to the specific task not global function—and emphasizes supports and all means to enhance function, taking into account the person's values as well as the risk of the situation. Chapter 1 discusses the relationship of clinical and legal definitions and the ever-evolving use of the term *capacities* (plural) to reflect multiple task- and context-specific functions, as opposed to the broader, more all-encompassing terms *competency* (which some take to mean a global quality) or *capacity* (which some take to mean a specific task—i.e., singular). Of note, this casebook deals with *civil* matters, meaning the ability to perform tasks and make decisions germane to one's personal life—health care decisions, financial decisions, residential decisions, and relationship decisions. These are distinct from criminal matters, which arise when an individual is being prosecuted for a crime, such as competency to stand trial, to waive Miranda rights, to be held criminally culpable, and, in some states, to undergo execution.

To be clear, some of the chapters in this book do present capacities in legal contexts, such as when a change to a will made by an older adult is being disputed in a court by heirs or when criminal charges are brought for financial exploitation of an older adult. But the book's focus is on the clinician's assessment rather than the legal or the judicial finding.

HOW CAN WE SUPPORT AUTONOMY?

A common and often excruciating dilemma in clinical care is the tension between promoting autonomy and protecting from harm. This challenge is represented in the ethical principles of many professional organizations for health care providers. In psychology, the dilemma is found in Principle E: Respect for People's Rights and Dignity from APA's *Ethical Principles of Psychologists and Code of Conduct* (APA, 2017). Immediately following the endorsement of self-determination, Principle E states that "special safeguards may be necessary to protect the . . . welfare of persons or communities whose vulnerabilities impair autonomous decision making" (APA, 2017), illustrating this tension between autonomy and protection. Central to resolving the conflict between autonomy and protection is the issue of capacity. For example, consider an older woman who previously had been conservative with spending and now, with the onset of dementia and since her husband died, spends more than half of her monthly income wiring a "tax fee" to a person in advance of receiving a promised lottery winning. Is she making a bad decision but one she has the right and ability to make—a vote for autonomy? Or is she having difficulties in decision-making and subject to financial exploitation—a vote for protection? Would things change if she were provided social, emotional, and practical support? What if she refuses these? What if she spends so much on the "tax fee" that there is not enough money left for food and heat?

Often these dilemmas cannot be solved without a clear view as to the person's "capacity" to make that decision. In general, the clinical decision-making scale leans to the side of promoting autonomy and safeguarding self-determination, in line with respecting people's rights and dignity (APA, 2017, Principle E) while avoiding harm (APA, 2017, Principle A and Standard 3.04). The bar to intercede against self-determination is set high and should be approached with the utmost care. For this reason, the clinical assessment of decisional or functional abilities relevant to capacity questions is the subject of this book, in the hope of continuing to promote best practices.

IS CAPACITY EVALUATION OF OLDER ADULTS INCREASING?

Many clinicians who work with older adults find that they are increasingly asked to assess a person's decisional or functional abilities. Two trends contribute to this increased demand: the aging of our society and the growing prevalence of dementia. Regarding age, it is worth emphasizing that older age on its own does not necessarily mean a loss of decisional or functional abilities. This point is important because historically some statutory definitions of an *incapacitated person* included the term *advanced age*. The characterization of *advanced age* as a cause for legal incapacity is ageist and discriminatory. However, the expanding older population will cause almost all health service providers to see an increase in their caseload of older adults. They will likely face more questions about the decisional or functional abilities of some of those older adults in navigating circumstances in later life, such as changes in financial arrangements (e.g., wills, donations) in the context of neurocognitive disorders (i.e., dementia) or staying in a home that is increasingly hard to care for because of hoarding and self-neglect.

Regarding dementia, it is worth emphasizing that most older adults do not have dementia and that although there are normal cognitive changes with aging, these would not be expected to influence critical decision-making abilities to a significant extent. However, the risk of dementia increases strongly with age. Dementia has many causes, including Alzheimer's disease, considered the most common cause of dementia, as well as vascular dementia, dementia with Lewy bodies, and other forms. As of 2018, an estimated 5.7 million adults in the United States had Alzheimer's dementia, and by 2050, an estimated 13.8 million adults may have Alzheimer's dementia, barring medical breakthroughs (Alzheimer's Association, 2018). Dementia by definition places an individual at particular risk for decisional or functional difficulties, and thus the increasing prevalence of dementia contributes to the rising demand for assessment.

WHO SHOULD READ THIS BOOK?

As noted, this book is a follow-up to the free ABA/APA Psychologist Handbook. As such, it assumes readers have read that book or are familiar with the foundational concepts therein, particularly a conceptual framework for assessing capacities, distinctions between legal and clinical capacities, and steps to be taken in investigating referrals and planning assessment approaches. Thus, this book is aimed at health service providers with a strong foundation in psychological or neuropsychological assessment and some exposure to the assessment of capacities who are looking to enhance their assessments of capacities and to learn from others. For example, this book is relevant for a mental health clinician working in a consultation-liaison role in a medical hospital, within a rehabilitation or skilled nursing facility, or on a home-based care team. This book may also be useful to those in psychology doctoral training programs or advanced training programs in other disciplines (e.g., psychiatry, social work). This book is likely less relevant to forensic psychologists or psychiatrists who address criminal capacities practicing in the court setting with legally involved persons.

This casebook focuses on older adults with dementia and other neuropsychiatric or neurocognitive disorders but does not focus on adults with intellectual or developmental disabilities, although, of course, they may become "older adults." There are complex legal, ethical, cultural, and clinical issues relevant to persons with disabilities that are beyond the scope of the content and expertise contained herein. However, the disability community has been essential in leading a rethinking of legal concepts of capacity, as described in Chapter 1.

COMPARING VA AND NON-VA HEALTH CARE SETTINGS

This book contains 12 chapters, four of which are contributed by authors who work in the U.S. Department of Veterans Affairs (VA) health care system. This may bear some explanation for those who work in non-VA settings or for international readers. At the time that this book was written, within the United States, the structure of health care—both the ownership of hospitals and clinics and reimbursement for services—is highly complex and hotly debated. There are private and publicly owned hospitals, private (e.g., health care insurance companies) and public (e.g., Medicare and Medicaid) insurers, and the VA. The VA comprises a single payor, like Medicare, but also is an integrated health care system across the continuum of care (e.g., acute medical, rehabilitation, long-term care, home-based care), although those who receive VA-funded care also have the choice to receive care out of the VA network providing certain stipulations are met (paid for by the VA or other insurance if they have it). Without going into extensive detail beyond our purposes here, it is worth noting some similarities and differences of the VA setting versus the non-VA setting, which may inform the interpretation of cases.

Readers will find some cases presented herein set within a rehabilitation context. Here, the VA setting is fairly similar to a non-VA setting. Persons may be admitted to a rehabilitation setting after an acute hospital stay to receive rehabilitation necessary to support their return to functional independence, which is more straightforward if the acute admission was physical in nature (e.g., hip replacement) and more complex if neurocognitive changes occurred (e.g., a stroke). Unlike an acute hospital stay that may be measured in days, a rehabilitation stay is more likely to be measured in weeks. Outside the VA, the primary insurer of older adults is Medicare, which pays for approximately 3 months of rehabilitative care, although copays apply; thus, there are financial pressures to discharge within the coverage period. Within the VA, care is paid for via a capitated model (meaning the facility receives one lump sum to provide for all care for 1 year based on the individual's complexity); thus, there are financial pressures to discharge because care needs to be distributed across many persons within a fixed budget.

What is different about the VA care described in this book may be more similar to that found in other countries with single-payor or national health care systems. In the VA, as in other non-U.S. settings, individuals may move between care within the same system—for example, from medical rehabilitation to home care or from inpatient psychiatry to adult foster care, with a unified medical record, health care providers working together, a single payor, and no profit incentive. Also, when needed and for those who qualify, the VA provides long-term care akin to skilled nursing home care or long-stay psychiatric hospitals, which outside the VA in the United States are typically paid for via Medicaid. Within the VA, the provision of long-term care is integrated with other care (e.g., if a person in long-term care needs surgery, this would happen within the same health care system). Thus, for some of the VA cases presented herein, there may be care processes, settings, reimbursement, and supports not currently available within privately funded care in the United States.

HOW IS THIS BOOK ORGANIZED?

Following opening chapters on legal and conceptual foundations and on the social context for capacities, each chapter focuses on a specific type of capacity or situation. The chapter authors review the issue and present case examples.[1] A criticism of the ABA/APA Psychology Handbook is that the examples provided were completely uniform in presentation and did not reflect true-to-life variability in how different clinicians may approach these issues. In contrast, here the authors showcase their approach and reflect on their reasoning in more diverse formats. Chapter 1 reviews important foundational concepts and examines changing definitions of capacities. Chapters 2 to 4 describe assessment of capacities in diagnostic contexts: dementia, schizophrenia, and traumatic brain injury. Chapters 5 to 8 focus on assessment of capacities when there has been an allegation of elder abuse, neglect, or exploitation. Chapters 9 and 10 depict specific clinical issues that may be especially fraught with ethical

[1]Although the case examples in this book are based on the authors' real experiences, the identities of the individuals involved in these examples have been properly disguised to protect their confidentiality.

tensions: sexual consent and medical aid in dying. Chapter 11 addresses challenges that clinicians might encounter working with surrogates who may have decisional difficulties or be unfit, and Chapter 12 focuses on possible concerns when working with families in conflict. Together, this set of 12 chapters highlights key questions, ethical dilemmas, and pragmatic approaches to difficult decisions when assessing capacities.

REFERENCES

Alzheimer's Association. (2018). 2018 Alzheimer's disease facts and figures [erratum: see https://doi.org/10.1016/j.jalz.2018.04.001]. *Alzheimer's & Dementia, 14,* 367–429. http://dx.doi.org/10.1016/j.jalz.2018.02.001

American Bar Association and American Psychological Association Assessment of Capacity in Older Adults Project Working Group. (2008). *Assessment of older adults with diminished capacity: A handbook for psychologists.* Washington, DC: American Bar Association and American Psychological Association.

American Psychological Association. (2017). *Ethical principles of psychologists and code of conduct* (2002, Amended June 1, 2010 and January 1, 2017). Retrieved from http://www.apa.org/ethics/code/index.aspx

1

Understanding Legal and Clinical Capacities

Jennifer Moye and Erica Wood

KEY POINTS

- Clinical determinations of capacities are distinct from legal determinations in that they represent clinical opinions, not legal findings. However, clinical opinions can be used to inform legal determinations of capacity made by attorneys and judges.
- The term *capacities* (plural) is becoming preferable to *competency* or *capacity* (singular) because it reflects multiple areas of functioning with different levels of ability. Overly simplistic and defamatory labels such as *incompetent* or *incapacitated* should also be avoided.
- Supports and supported decision-making for older adults assist individuals to make and communicate decisions and maximize function.

THE CHANGING DEFINITION OF *CAPACITIES*

Our aim in this introductory chapter is to update the conceptual and legal information in the 2008 psychologist handbook (American Bar Association and American Psychological Association [ABA/APA] Assessment of Capacity in Older Adults Project Working Group, 2008) and to set the stage for the

http://dx.doi.org/10.1037/0000184-002
Assessing Capacities of Older Adults: A Casebook to Guide Difficult Decisions, J. Moye (Editor)

chapters to come. As noted in the Introduction, this book focuses on clinical assessment of capacities, meaning a clinical assessment and opinion as to whether a person has the requisite ability to perform a task or make a decision—if provided supports and considering their values as well as the risks of the situation. The term *clinical assessment of capacities* is often misunderstood and misused and in fact has many layers of complexity as a psycholegal construct. Building on the Introduction, we start by setting forth some basic distinctions to clarify the concept. Next, we summarize definitions of civil capacities as they are used in the law and their ongoing evolution. Finally, we will return to the assessment of clinical capacities, summarizing the ABA/APA framework and some general principles for practice.

Clinical Versus Legal Capacities

An important distinction is the clinical versus legal determination of capacities. A clinical determination refers to a clinical opinion as to whether a person has the requisite ability to perform a task or make a decision in question. For example, a clinician may consider whether an older adult with dementia has the capacity to provide informed consent for treatment or if the clinician should obtain consent from the health care agent appointed by the older adult. The clinical determination does not remove an individual's legal right to do that task or make that decision but forms the basis for clinical actions (e.g., allows the person to refuse treatment or "activates" the decision-making authority of the health care agent).

Generally, clinical opinions about these abilities enable clinical action to proceed. However, if a dispute arises, the clinician's assessment may be challenged in court through a legal action such as a guardianship proceeding. In such a legal proceeding, the clinical opinion is important evidence for the ultimate judicial determination. For example, for those who work in a health care setting, a decision to "activate" the health care proxy authority is an assessment by a clinician that enables use of the proxy and is rarely contested in court. But if there is a disagreement that brings the matter before a judge, that judge will have the final authority, taking into account the clinical statement in making judicial findings.

In contrast to a clinical assessment, when a judge makes a legal finding of lack of capacity for a certain function or decision, that finding removes a person's rights to make the decision at hand. For instance, if the judge determines the person lacks the ability to give informed consent for surgery, the consent of a surrogate would be needed for the surgery to proceed. If the judge determines the person lacks the ability to care for himself or herself or to make financial and property decisions, the judge appoints a guardian, and the person loses fundamental rights to control basic aspects of life—loses *self-determination*. Ideally, the judge writes a limited guardianship order only finding incapacity for a narrow range of functions or decisions. Nevertheless, the result is a loss of rights.

Competency Versus Capacity Versus Capacities

Historically, both legal and clinical practitioners used the word *competent*. This usage arose in the context of informed consent, defined as that which was voluntary, informed, and "competent" (Berg, Appelbaum, Lidz, & Parker, 2001). Over the years, both clinicians and legal professionals have moved away from the word *competent* to avoid the all-or-nothing status that the word conveys in the eyes of many (Moye, Marson, & Edelstein, 2013). Thus, rather than asking, "Is this individual competent?" the question has shifted to "Does this individual have the capacity to do _______, with supports?" (more on supports later).

With this shifting perception, the term *capacity* is seen not as global but as task specific and situation specific. That is why in the title of this book, as well as in this introductory chapter, we frequently refer to *capacities*—not one overall global quality. Thus, a person may have capacity for medical consent but not financial decisions, or for everyday money management but not complex business management or investments. In other words, capacity is no longer seen as a hard line but tailored to the specifics at hand, fluctuating over time and according to context. Thus, as used in this book, capacities are in sum a set of legal attributes or clinical abilities that may be described or defined in legal and clinical settings, by legal or clinical professionals. Again, the focus throughout this book is on the clinical side—the clinician assessment of clinical capacities.

Given the complexity of the term *capacity*, why not just use the word *ability* or *abilities* instead of *capacities*? Although initially appealing, calling these assessments an "assessment of abilities" may confuse a capacity assessment with cognitive and neuropsychological assessments. The latter assessments are valuable, but they may focus more on cognition, providing a diagnosis along with a detailed description of cognitive strengths and weaknesses and of recommendations. In contrast, the term *capacities* conveys something different. It conveys that this assessment will focus on a particular function that has a legal referent, with cognitive abilities bearing on that function. More important, it reflects a weighing of these abilities in the setting of supports and values to arrive at a professional clinical judgment, knowing that such a judgment may be used in evidence if the situation is adjudicated.

LEGAL DETERMINATIONS OF AND STANDARDS FOR CAPACITIES

One of the revelations in writing the ABA/APA handbook series was that legal and clinical professionals define and approach capacities issues from quite different perspectives—there are areas of overlap, distinction, and disagreement. Although this book focuses on clinical determination of capacities, such determinations, as noted earlier, may be used in legal settings, and relevant legal definitions inform clinical approaches. Thus, it is important to understand legal usage of the term *capacities* and how usage is dramatically shifting.

Attorney Determinations of Capacities

A legal determination of capacities most often occurs when an attorney in the course of representation makes a judgment, under statutory standards and rules of legal ethics, about the client's understanding in order to proceed with the legal act or transaction at hand. For example, a lawyer may consider whether a person has the capacity to enter a lawyer–client relationship or to execute or change a financial power of attorney. Such a determination is a legal determination of capacity even though it is not reviewed by a judge. If the attorney's determination comes in question or if clinicians or other professionals come to a disputed conclusion about the person's abilities, the court is the final arbiter.

Legal Capacities for Transactions

The work of attorneys frequently involves drafting and executing legal transactions for clients, such as a will, power of attorney, gift or deed. To determine capacity for such specific legal transactions, attorneys are guided by standards set out in state statute and case law. The ABA/APA (2005) Lawyers Handbook details these legal standards for a range of specific transactions. Although they differ by state, they typically fall within common patterns. In Table 1.1, we reprint the descriptions of these capacities from the ABA/APA Lawyers Handbook, as clinicians may find these helpful. For more from the Lawyers Handbook, clinicians can download it at https://www.apa.org/pi/aging.

Judicial Determinations of Capacities

Judicial determination of civil capacities may occur in a dispute over legal transactions, such as a will or in a situation in which consent for treatment is needed, but this most often occurs through a guardianship proceeding, which broadly removes rights and transfers significant authority from the individual to a guardian. A guardian is a court-appointed surrogate to make personal or property decisions (or both) for an adult. (Note that statutes provide for *guardians of the person* and *guardians of property*, often called *conservators*, but terms differ by state; for efficiency, we will use the words *guardianship* and *guardians*.)

In a guardianship proceeding, judges look to clinical assessments to determine two preliminary issues. First, they need to consider whether a less restrictive decisional option such as power of attorney might suffice instead of a guardianship, thus preserving rights. A clinical assessment as to the person's ability to name an agent under a power of attorney and execute the document will be valuable. Second, judges need to consider whether the guardianship order can be limited to only those areas in which the individual lacks ability to make decisions—called a *limited order*. Tailored, limited orders are allowed and generally preferred in most state statutes, but in practice, judges rarely write such orders, partly because they simply don't have the nuanced

TABLE 1.1. Standards of Capacity for Specific Legal Transactions

Capacities	Definition
Testamentary capacity	Typically, the testator at the time of executing a will must have capacity to know the natural objects of his or her bounty, to understand the nature and extent of his or her property, and to interrelate these elements sufficiently to make a disposition of property according to a rational plan. The terminology that the testator must be of "sound mind" is still commonly used. The test for testamentary capacity does not require that the person be capable of managing all of his or her affairs or making day-to-day business transactions, nor must the testator have capacity consistently over time. Capacity is required at the time the will was executed. Thus, a testator may lack testamentary capacity before or after executing a will, but if it is made during a "lucid interval," the will remains valid. Finally, even a testator who generally possesses the elements of testamentary capacity may have that capacity negated by an "insane delusion" (i.e., irrational perceptions of particular person or events) if the delusion materially affects the will (Parry & Gilliam, 2002).
Donative capacity	Capacity to make a gift has been defined by courts to require an understanding of the nature and purpose of the gift, an understanding of the nature and extent of property to be given, a knowledge of the natural objects of the donor's bounty, and an understanding of the nature and effect of the gift. Some states use a higher standard for donative capacity than for testamentary capacity, requiring that the donor knows the gift to be irrevocable and that it would result in a reduction in the donor's assets or estate (Mezzullo & Woolpert, 2004).
Contractual capacity	In determining an individual's capacity to execute a contract, courts generally assess the party's ability to understand the nature and effect of the act and the business being transacted (Mezzullo & Woolpert, 2004). Accordingly, if the act or business being transacted is highly complicated, a higher level of understanding may be needed to comprehend its nature and effect, in contrast to a simple contractual arrangement.
Capacity to convey real property	To execute a deed, a grantor typically must be able to understand the nature and effect of the act at the time the conveyance is made (Mezzullo & Woolpert, 2004).
Capacity to execute a durable power of attorney	The standard of capacity for creating a power of attorney has traditionally been based on the capacity to contract. However, some courts have also held that the standard is similar to that for making a will (Moye, Sabatino, & Weintraub Brendel, 2013).
Capacity to mediate	In referring a client to mediation or representing a client in a mediation, a lawyer should be familiar with the capacity to mediate. The *ADA Mediation Guidelines* name several factors to be considered by mediators: The mediator should ascertain that a party understands the nature of the mediation process, who the parties are, the role of the mediator, the parties' relationship to the mediator, and the issues at hand. The mediator should determine whether the party can assess options and make and keep an agreement (Wood, 2001).
Decisional capacity in health care	Capacity to make a health care decision is defined by statute in most states under their advance directives laws. Typical of these legal definitions is the following from the Uniform Health Care Decisions Act: *Capacity* means an individual's ability to understand the significant benefits, risks, and alternatives to proposed health care and to make and communicate a health care decision (Appelbaum & Grisso, 1988).

Note. From *Assessment of Older Adults With Diminished Capacity: A Handbook for Lawyers* (pp. 5–6), by the American Bar Association and American Psychological Association Assessment of Capacity in Older Adults Project Working Group, 2005, Washington, DC: American Bar Association and American Psychological Association.

clinical evidence on which to base the limitations. Advocates have called for limited guardianship that maximizes self-determination for decades (Frolik, 2002), and clinical assessments are a key driver.

Clinicians also can play a critical part after a guardian is appointed in determining whether the guardianship continues to be necessary or can be terminated (or at least modified) by the court, with restoration of the person's rights. Restoration may occur if the person's condition changes, if the available supports change, or if there is new evidence of the person's abilities. Restoration of rights is rare in practice (Wood, Teaster, & Cassidy, 2017). As it gains greater visibility with renewed emphasis on choice and self-determination, clinicians will face increased demand for assessments in the context of restoration of rights in guardianship.

Legal Capacities in Guardianship Law

We next discuss legal capacities in guardianship law, starting with the UN Convention, which sets a historical context for recent changes in the United States and internationally.

Legal Capacity in the UN Convention on the Rights of Persons With Disabilities

The United Nations (UN) Convention on the Rights of Persons With Disabilities (CRPD; United Nations, 2006) represents a conceptual shift from a medical model of disability (which focuses on diagnosis and inability) to a human rights model (which focuses on capability and inclusion). It is the first international law to combine human, civil, political, social and economic rights into the same document (Kanter, 2009).

Within the Convention, Article 12 seeks to counter previous manifestations of "protection" for individuals with disabilities that removed personal rights. It states that "persons with disabilities enjoy legal capacity on an equal basis with others in all aspects of life" and calls on governments to support the exercise of legal capacity (United Nations, 2006). It presents legal capacity as a human right, in which every person has the right to "engage in transactions and create, modify, or end legal relationships" regardless of abilities and limitations (Committee on the Rights of Persons with Disabilities, 2014). Article 12 is the result of many years of advocacy by the disability community to achieve a focus on the exercise of rights, so that people with disabilities can be active members of society.

In essence, the UN Convention recognizes legal capacity with support in all persons, and rejects the notion of legal incapacity. In an analogy, disability advocates assert that it is not a person's disability that is at issue, but rather a failure to accommodate needs or change the environment. The Convention breaks the link between legal capacity and clinical capacity, making it clear that clinical evaluations should not be used to deny the legal right to capacity. The "General Comment" to Article 12 states the following concerning the relationship of legal capacity to clinical capacities, which it calls "mental capacity":

> The concepts of mental and legal capacity have been conflated so that where a person is considered to have impaired decision-making skills, often because of a cognitive or psychosocial disability, his or her legal capacity to make a particular decision is consequently removed . . . A person's disability and/or decision-making skills are taken as legitimate grounds for denying his or her legal capacity and lowering his or her status as a person before the law. Article 12 does not permit such discriminatory denial of legal capacity, but, rather, requires that support be provided in the exercise of legal capacity. (Committee on the Rights of Persons with Disabilities, 2014, p. 4)

According to this perspective, legal determinations, and clinical assessments that inform them, should focus not on restricting rights but on examining a person's needs for supports in order to maximize rights.

Legal Capacity in Uniform Acts on Guardianship

The UN Convention and the concept of supports it embodies strongly influenced the most recent "Uniform Act" in the United States on guardianship. For over a hundred years the Uniform Law Commission (formerly the National Conference of Commissioners on Uniform State Laws) has developed model laws for potential adoption by state legislatures. The 1997 Uniform Guardianship and Protective Proceedings Act, derived from an earlier 1982 version, defined an incapacitated person as someone who

> is unable to receive and evaluate information or make or communicate decisions to such an extent that the individual lacks the ability to meet essential requirements for physical health, safety, or self-care, even with appropriate technological assistance. (Uniform Law Commission, 1997, pp. 2–3)

In 2017, the Uniform Law Commission approved a new act, the Uniform Guardianship, Conservatorship, and Other Protective Arrangements Act. The new act rejects the term *incapacitated person*, which, as stated in the act's Prefatory Note, the drafters determined was "demeaning and even offensive" (National Conference of Commissioners on Uniform State Laws, 2017). The act replaces a definition for *incapacitated person* with "adult subject to guardianship," which is defined as just that—an adult for whom a guardian has been appointed. Such a person may be subject to guardianship on the basis that the adult

> lacks the ability to meet essential requirements for physical health, safety, or self-care because the respondent is unable to receive and evaluate information or make or communicate decisions, even with appropriate supportive services, technological assistance, or supported decision-making; and the respondent's identified needs cannot be met by a protective arrangement instead of guardianship or other less restrictive alternative. (National Conference of Commissioners on Uniform State Laws, 2017, p. 36)

Although the second definition—and indeed the entire act—avoids the term *capacity*, the two definitions (1997 "incapacitated person" and 2017 "person subject to guardianship on the basis of") are nearly identical, with the major exception that the 2017 definition adds "supportive services" and "supported decision-making," as well as an emphasis on less restrictive alternatives. Both these definitions speak to a situation in which an individual has decisional limitations and wherein, as a last resort and after exhausting all supportive or less restrictive alternatives, a judge determines that the individual requires another person to be a sanctioned substitute decision-maker on his or her behalf. Note that this is a model act, not yet widely enacted, so state statutes for guardianship still include the terminology to define an incapacitated person, and most lack an emphasis on supports and supported decision-making, although trends in these directions are underway.

Why did the Uniform Law Commission go to such lengths to change the terminology? The removal of the term legal capacity in the 2017 Uniform Act points toward persisting societal, legal, and ethical problems with the application of the concept of legal capacity, particularly for individuals with disabilities. In brief, individuals with disabilities have in practice been subject to plenary (full) guardianship on the basis of having a disability alone—without nuanced and appropriate assessment, without adequate due process, and without use of supportive approaches. These concerns about guardianship practice and the misapplication of the legal determination of capacity have been the subject of commentary for decades (Blanck & Martinis, 2015; Horstman, 1975; Mitchell, 1978). Indeed, some of our own research showed that historically, in Massachusetts, most individuals were subject to plenary guardianship based on very limited clinical evidence, without representation or presence at the hearing (Moye, Wood, Edelstein, Armesto, et al., 2007). On the bright side, we found that states with more contemporary criteria for persons subject to guardianship had more sufficient clinical evidence and more common use of limited guardianship (Moye, Wood, Edelstein, Wood, et al., 2007).

This book is for clinicians regarding the clinical assessment of capacities of older adults, with health conditions acquired in late adulthood (e.g., dementia). Some clinicians—particularly those involved in both assessment and treatment, such as geropsychologists—might look at the new Uniform Act and see that both the older definition of a legally "incapacitated person" and the new definition of a "person subject to guardianship" rely on pillars of clinical capacities assessment that they have long used in clinical practice. These pillars include the assessment of capacities as more than just finding deficits through testing, but instead as a sophisticated recipe that includes the presumption of ability; the central role of supports and values; and the focus on function. For these clinicians, their clinical assessment framework may not change. But for legal professionals who have not followed these enlightened principles, the new model act is a more radical reconceptualization of legal capacity.

Supports and Supported Decision-Making in Legal Definitions

Essentially, Article 12 and the Uniform Act emphasize the necessity of a range of supports and of a "supported decision-making" model as an alternative to—and a paradigm shift away from—a surrogate decision-making model in which one person is designated to make decisions on behalf of another. Surrogate decision-making is said to remove "personhood" by allowing someone else to take control of basic life decisions. *Supported decision-making* has been defined as "a series of relationships, practices, arrangements, and agreements of more or less formality and intensity, designed to assist an individual with a disability to make and communicate to others, decisions about the individual's life" (Dinerstein, 2012, p. 3). These practices help an adult with a disability make his or her own decisions, by using friends, family members, professionals, and other people he or she trusts: to help understand the issues and choices; ask questions; receive explanations in language he or she understands, and communicate his or her own decisions to others (Dinerstein, 2012).

In some contexts, the term *supported decision-making* is used more narrowly as it relates to formal supported decision-making agreements, executed by an adult to identify and direct their supporters—agreements that in some states are now recognized in law. In other contexts, the phrase may be used more generally to apply to a wide range of ways in which decision-making can be maximized.

The idea is that all adults frequently need help in making decisions, and everyone uses different kinds of supports; the same should apply to adults with disabilities. Instead of enacting laws that substitute the decision of a guardian or other surrogate for the decision of the individual, the CRPD states that (a) all people have the right to make choices about their own lives and that (b) people at times may seek and need help from others, and the onus of responsibility for providing that help is on states. Thus, the UN Convention broadly promotes *personhood* and being able to be a legal actor in one's own life (Blanck & Martinis, 2015). Although the CRPD has not been ratified by the United States, its principles have strongly influenced thinking on decision-making and guardianship.

As supported decision-making is applied to older adults, particularly persons with dementia, some questions have emerged. For example, a loss of insight into deficits along with a loss of memory are clinical symptoms of dementia as the disease progresses. What, then, should a supporter do if a person with dementia no longer remembers that he or she has lost the ability to drive, and perhaps also lost a license, yet insists on driving? Is the job to support the person's decision and access to driving? Is there an obligation to others who might be hurt in an accident should one occur?

In another scenario, a substantial proportion of financial exploitation of older adults is perpetrated by family members. What if the supporter is an exploiter, using undue influence to "support" a person in a decision that financially benefits the supporter? Advocates for supported decision-making point out that although there may be risks, they may be outweighed by the benefits. By encouraging connections and building relationships, "supported decision-making can combat isolation, a major cause of abuse for people with disabilities and older adults" (Pogach, in press). Moreover, it is important to note that in supported decision-making, the supporter often is not operating alone but as part of a network of assistance and that the risk of abuse is less because the individual chooses his or her own supporters and frequently chooses more than one, which is a key safeguard (Dinerstein, 2012).

Finally, what about older adults who have outlived all their family and friends and are now alone, without "natural supporters" (Teaster, Wood, Lawrence, & Schmidt, 2007), an increasing issue for older adults, particularly the 20% without children. Although it is still possible to offer supports of course, such individuals may not be able to identify trusted others who they can name as supporters or, for that matter, in an advance directive. These are thorny issues that will be addressed as use of supported decision-making is increasingly explored for older adults with dementia.

CLINICIAN ASSESSMENT OF CLINICAL CAPACITIES

ABA/APA Framework

The ABA/APA working group's framework for clinician assessment of clinical capacities (see Figure 1.1) has nine elements (ABA/APA, 2008). The framework balances clinical factors (on the left side) with contextual factors (on the

FIGURE 1.1. Factors in a Clinical Assessment of Capacity of Older Adults

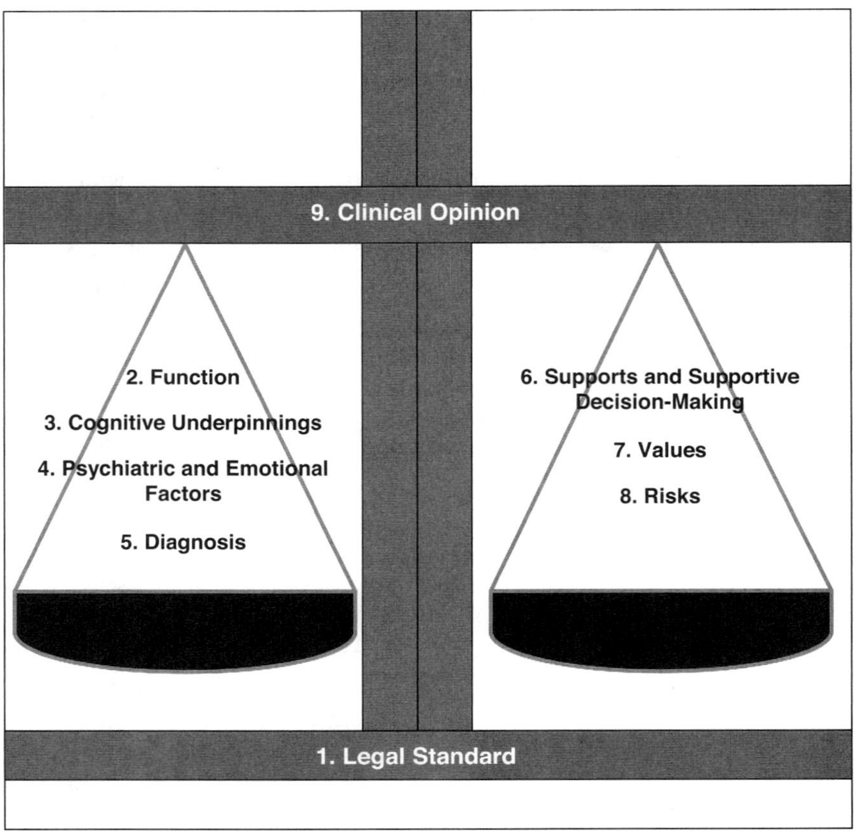

right side) in light of the legal standard (bottom). The clinical job is thus not only an assessment of abilities and supports but a balancing of these elements. A point of the framework is to avoid assessments of capacities that are inappropriately brief, that focus only on cursory assessment of a few cognitive skills that may or may not be relevant to the task (e.g., orientation, three-word memory), and to emphasize instead an approach that is focused (ask "capacity for what?"), functionally oriented, and comprehensive. This framework responds to a now classic article on pitfalls in the assessment of decision-making capacity (Ganzini, Volicer, Nelson, & Derse, 2003). These pitfalls in their reverse can be considered some of the main principles of clinical assessment of capacities, as shown in Table 1.2.

Supports and Supported Decision-Making in Clinical Application

It is worth pausing to comment more on the supports element of the ABA/APA model given the legal changes we have thus far described. We propose an adjustment to the model to give more visibility to supports as configuring the balance. In Figure 1.1, the words *supports and supported decision-making* replace the phrasing in the original ABA/APA framework, which uses the words *steps to enhance capacity*. The aim is to bring more emphasis on supports and more consistency with recent changes in thinking and the recent uniform guardianship act.

Indeed, supports are already well known in clinical practice, particularly in practice with older adults (APA, 2014), and the change in the model will simply recognize and sharpen the focus. The ABA/APA handbook includes extensive appendices focusing in detail on supports—interventions that are well known to those who work in geriatric practice, such as practical supports (e.g., bill-paying services, home health services, adult day health care, Meals on Wheels), legal instruments (e.g., advance directives, trusts), residential options (e.g., assisted living, adult foster care), and descriptions of medical conditions and possible interventions to enhance capacity (e.g., bereavement support) also including a focus on identifying and treating possible temporary causes of confusion (i.e., delirium). An emphasis on function, and enhancing function, is the cornerstone of geriatric practice; for example, for decades a defining feature of what it means to be a geriatrician (a feature learned in geriatric fellowship) is a focus not on treatment of a specific disease but on how can quality of life be improved. Such an approach is also consistent with the ethical standards of many professions including psychologists that emphasize promoting autonomy (Principle E: Respect for People's Rights and Dignity; APA, 2017).

In the case examples that follow, readers will find some supports already in place (e.g., home-based primary care) and some supports recommended, although authors may use terms such as *interventions* and *adaptions* in addition to *supports*. It is also worth noting that in the interest of space, authors may not delimit every supportive approach used, including adaptations made to maximize function during assessments (e.g., pocket talkers, enlarged type) and

TABLE 1.2. Principles of Clinical Assessment of Capacity

Rule	Explanation	Example
1. Presume capacity	All adults are presumed to have capacity.	Assessment of all adults begins with the presumption of capacity regardless of diagnosis or appearances.
2. Diagnoses do not equal inability	A specific diagnosis or "status" (i.e., disability) should never be equated with a lack of functional or decisional abilities.	A diagnosis of dementia does not mean a person cannot consent to treatment.
3. Focus on the abilities to do a specific decision and task	Do not ask "does this person have capacity?"; ask "what specific abilities or decisions are needed?" for the issue in question.	What exactly does the person need to understand to consent to a proposed treatment?
4. Support before you subtract	Do not ask "does this person lack capacity;" ask "what supports does this person need." All means to enhance and support abilities should be deployed and all less restrictive surrogate options exhausted prior to intrusive interventions such as guardianship.	When evaluating treatment consent, provide information in written or visual form, make sure the person can hear or see, address anxiety related to the situation, and consider the effects of the illness and setting on information processing.
5. Restoration is achievable	As underlying conditions change, abilities should be reevaluated and legal determinations revisited. Knowing the underlying diagnosis is therefore critical to establishing the window for reevaluation.	Does the person have delirium superimposed on dementia? Could understanding of treatment information improve once the delirium resolves?
6. Going against medical advice does not imply a lack of ability	Capacity should not be inferred from individuals going against medical advice.	Refusing a recommended treatment doesn't mean he or she lacks the capacity to make that decision, even if, for example, the person has a psychotic disorder.
7. Focus on process, not outcome	Do not ask is this decision "good or bad" with the corollary that we all have the right to make "bad" decisions; ask how the person arrived at the decision.	Spending a lot of money on fast food does not mean a person lacks the capacity to choose to do so, even if, for example, the person has moderate dementia.

knowledge of the use and limits of standardized testing consistent with APA guidelines for assessment and for psychological practice with older adults (APA, 2014) and for evaluation of dementia and age-related change (APA, 2012).

In the context of guardianship, the use of supports and a supported decision-making arrangement is an example of the principle of least restrictive alternative. State statutory provisions, as well as the new Uniform Guardianship,

Conservatorship and Other Protective Arrangements Act, call for use of less restrictive options to guardianship to the greatest extent possible. In fact, identifying such options is a central tenet of the act: Judges may not appoint a guardian unless they make a specific finding that the needs cannot be met with a less restrictive alternative. Understanding these options will help clinicians to craft assessments that consider and promote their appropriate use. Advance directives and powers of attorney have existed for decades as legal mechanisms by which people can designate and direct surrogates for future action (Sabatino, 2010), avoiding the more restrictive (and rights-reducing) approach of guardianship. The Physician Order for Life Sustaining Treatment (POLST), a set of specific actionable medical orders such as "do not transfer to an outside hospital," is another mechanism by which persons can direct and drive their care (Hickman, Keevern, & Hammes, 2015). Supported decision-making is an emergent, life-enhancing alternative to guardianship that can maximize self-determination and preserve rights.

CONCLUSION

This casebook provides detailed descriptions of common situations and conditions that may lead to a request to evaluate clinical capacities of an older adult. In approaching these evaluations, it is critical to understand the meaning of the word *capacities*, and in particular its legal usages and how that varies from clinical applications. Understanding the legal meanings of the terms *capacity* and *capacities* is indeed complex because usage varies across transactional matters and guardianship statutes and continues to evolve. We hope a high-quality, focused, and comprehensive approach to clinical assessment, with knowledge of the evolving legal climate, will promote practices that can improve the lives of older adults.

REFERENCES

American Bar Association and American Psychological Association Assessment of Capacity in Older Adults Project Working Group. (2005). *Assessment of older adults with diminished capacity: A handbook for lawyers*. Washington, DC: American Bar Association and American Psychological Association.

American Bar Association and American Psychological Association Assessment of Capacity in Older Adults Project Working Group. (2008). *Assessment of older adults with diminished capacity: A handbook for psychologists*. Washington, DC: American Bar Association and American Psychological Association.

American Psychological Association. (2012). Guidelines for the evaluation of dementia and age-related cognitive change. *American Psychologist, 67*, 1–9. http://dx.doi.org/10.1037/a0024643.

American Psychological Association. (2014). Guidelines for psychological practice with older adults. *American Psychologist, 69*, 34–65. http://dx.doi.org/10.1037/a0035063

American Psychological Association. (2017). *Ethical principles of psychologists and code of conduct* (2002, Amended June 1, 2010 and January 1, 2017). Retrieved from http://www.apa.org/ethics/code/index.aspx

Appelbaum, P. S., & Grisso, T. (1988). Assessing patients' capacities to consent to treatment. *The New England Journal of Medicine, 319,* 1635–1638. http://dx.doi.org/10.1056/NEJM198812223192504

Berg, J. W., Appelbaum, P. S., Lidz, C. W., & Parker, L. S. (2001). *Informed consent: Legal theory and clinical practice.* New York, NY: Oxford University Press.

Blanck, P., & Martinis, J. G. (2015). "The right to make choices": The National Resource Center for Supported Decision-Making. *Inclusion, 3*(1), 24–33. http://dx.doi.org/10.1352/2326-6988-3.1.24

Committee on the Rights of Persons with Disabilities. (2014). *General comment No. 1 (2014): Article 12: Equal recognition before the law.* Retrieved from http://psychrights.org/Countries/UN/140519CRPDGenCommentNo1.pdf

Dinerstein, R. D. (2012). Implementing legal capacity under article 12 of the UN Convention on the Rights of Persons with Disabilities: The difficult road from guardianship to supported decision-making. *Human Rights Brief, 19*(2), 1–5.

Frolik, L. (2002). Promoting judicial acceptance and use of limited guardianship. *Stetson Law Review, 31,* 736–755.

Ganzini, L., Volicer, L., Nelson, W., & Derse, A. (2003). Pitfalls in assessment of decision-making capacity. *Psychosomatics, 44,* 237–243. http://dx.doi.org/10.1176/appi.psy.44.3.237

Hickman, S. E., Keevern, E., & Hammes, B. J. (2015). Use of the physician orders for life-sustaining treatment program in the clinical setting: A systematic review of the literature. *Journal of the American Geriatrics Society, 63,* 341–350. http://dx.doi.org/10.1111/jgs.13248

Horstman, P. (1975). Protective services for the elderly: The limits of parens patriae. *Missouri Law Review, 40,* 215–236.

Kanter, A. (2009). The United Nations Convention on the Rights of Persons with Disabilities and its implications for the rights of elderly people under international law. *Georgia State University Law Review, 25,* 526–573.

Mezzullo, L. A., & Woolpert, M. (2004). *Advising the elderly client.* Deerfield, IL: Clark Boardman Callaghan.

Mitchell, A. (1978). Involuntary guardianship for incompetents: A strategy for legal services advocates. *Clearinghouse Review, 12,* 451–468.

Moye, J., Marson, D. C., & Edelstein, B. (2013). Assessment of capacity in an aging society. *American Psychologist, 68,* 158–171. http://dx.doi.org/10.1037/a0032159

Moye, J., Sabatino, C. P., & Weintraub Brendel, R. (2013). Evaluation of the capacity to appoint a healthcare proxy. *The American Journal of Geriatric Psychiatry, 21,* 326–336. http://dx.doi.org/10.1016/j.jagp.2012.09.001

Moye, J., Wood, E., Edelstein, B., Wood, S., Bower, E. H., Harrison, J. A., & Armesto, J. C. (2007). Statutory reform is associated with improved court practice: Results of a tri-state comparison. *Behavioral Sciences & the Law, 25,* 425–436. http://dx.doi.org/10.1002/bsl.762

Moye, J., Wood, S., Edelstein, B., Armesto, J. C., Bower, E. H., Harrison, J. A., & Wood, E. (2007). Clinical evidence in guardianship of older adults is inadequate: Findings from a tri-state study. *The Gerontologist, 47,* 604–612. http://dx.doi.org/10.1093/geront/47.5.604

National Conference of Commissioners on Uniform State Laws. (2017). *Uniform Guardianship, Conservatorship, and Other Protective Arrangements Act.* Retrieved from https://www.uniformlaws.org/viewdocument/final-act-no-comments-13?CommunityKey=2eba8654-8871-4905-ad38-aabbd573911c&tab=librarydocuments

Parry, J., & Gilliam, F. P. (2002). *Handbook on mental disability and the law.* Washington, DC: American Bar Association.

Pogach, D. (in press). Supported decision-making for older adults with age related cognitive decline, including dementia. American Society on Aging. *Generations (San Francisco, Calif.).*

Sabatino, C. P. (2010). The evolution of health care advance planning law and policy. *The Milbank Quarterly, 88,* 211–239. http://dx.doi.org/10.1111/j.1468-0009.2010.00596.x

Teaster, P. B., Wood, E. F., Lawrence, W. F., & Schmidt, W. C. (2007). Wards of the state: A national study of public guardianship. *Stetson Law Review, 37,* 193–201.

Uniform Law Commission. (1997). *Uniform Guardianship and Protective Proceedings Act.* Retrieved from https://www.uniformlaws.org/viewdocument/final-act-no-comments-35?CommunityKey=d716e47d-f50b-4b68-9e25-dd0af47a13b7&tab=librarydocuments

United Nations. (2006). *Convention on the Rights of Persons With Disabilities.* Geneva, Switzerland: Author.

Wood, E. (2001). Dispute resolution and dementia: Seeking solutions. *Georgia Law Review, 35,* 785–834.

Wood, E., Teaster, P., & Cassidy, J. (2017). *Restoration of rights in adult guardianship: Research and recommendations.* Retrieved from https://www.americanbar.org/content/dam/aba/administrative/law_aging/restoration%20report.authcheckdam.pdf

I

CAPACITIES IN DIAGNOSTIC CONTEXTS

2

Evaluating Capacities in Persons With Dementia

Kyle S. Page and Kathleen C. Matthews

KEY POINTS

- Persons with mild to moderate levels of cognitive impairment in the context of a dementia can still make many types of decisions depending on the circumstances (complexity, urgency, risk, and environment).
- Using capacity evaluations to identify cognitive and functional strengths ensures optimal engagement and reduces excessive disability for persons living with dementia.
- Emphasize ways to support the individual before subtracting rights and responsibilities.
- Advocate for the involvement of persons living with dementia in the decision-making process, even if clinically or legally judged to lack decisional or functional capacity.
- Decision-making capacity in individuals with dementia is best understood in a relational context. Clinicians often need to consider the role of caregivers or surrogates during capacity assessments.

http://dx.doi.org/10.1037/0000184-003
Assessing Capacities of Older Adults: A Casebook to Guide Difficult Decisions, J. Moye (Editor)

DEFINITION OF THE ISSUE

This chapter describes evaluating capacities in persons with dementia and discusses important points of consideration when performing these evaluations with older adults. Our goal in this first section is to clarify the context in which we are asked to perform these evaluations. We address the clinical presentation, differential diagnosis, and ethical considerations.

Many neurocognitive disorders, such as Alzheimer's and Lewy body dementias, are progressive in nature, meaning that an individual's cognitive and functional abilities deteriorate over time. Typically, an individual diagnosed with one of these degenerative diseases starts as a fully autonomous, independent being who has been his or her own decision-maker throughout adulthood. The range of disease manifestations associated with neurocognitive disorders, such as impaired memory, attention, visuospatial abilities, and judgment, can impact an individual's capacity to make safe decisions in a variety of contexts. However, the mere presence of a neurocognitive disorder does not equate to incapacity (Grisso, 1994), and capacity must be conceptualized as decision and domain specific, not as a global judgment (Moberg & Rick, 2008). With at least eight capacity domains relevant to this population (e.g., Moye & Marson, 2007), individuals with dementia often retain capacity in some areas and struggle with others.

The scope of abilities and skills required for each of the capacity domains varies greatly, and capacity in each area will be influenced by the type and degree of cognitive impairment demonstrated by the individual with dementia (Moye & Marson, 2007). For example, medical decision-making capacity is a fairly narrow domain that is heavily dependent on intact verbal conceptualization and reasoning and on verbal memory abilities (Dymek, Marson, & Harrell, 1999). If there are impairments in these cognitive abilities, even at an early stage in the dementia process, the individual may not retain decision-making capacity for more complex or high-risk medical decisions. Conversely, capacity to manage finances comprises a broad range of conceptual, pragmatic, and judgment abilities. Importantly, different components of financial capacity decline at different rates over time (Martin et al., 2019). Research has shown that within the broad domain of financial capacity, individuals with mild cognitive impairment, often a precursor to dementia, start with more focal impairments in financial judgment (Griffith et al., 2003; Martin et al., 2019), causing concern for an impaired ability to detect and protect themselves from scams. With the development and advancement of dementia, impairments in financial skills become more global and widespread (Marson, 2001). Clearly, the way that a dementia diagnosis can affect capacity varies by the type and degree of cognitive and functional impairments that are present, as well as the capacity domain under consideration.

The erosion of decisional capacity over time and associated loss of independence serves to challenge personhood and autonomy in individuals with dementia. Qualitative research has shown that individuals in the early stages of dementia often report a loss of identity and threatened perceptions of security, autonomy, and of being a meaningful member of society (Steeman, de Casterlé, Godderis, & Grypdonck, 2006). Beyond the impact of the disease itself, the appointment of a surrogate decision-maker may constitute a further considerable loss of autonomy for the individual with dementia as another person begins to make important life decisions for the individual. There is evidence that some community-dwelling and institutionalized individuals with dementia are excluded entirely from making decisions about their lives, despite having the will and desire to do so (Gilliard, Means, Beattie, & Daker-White, 2005; Smebye, Kirkevold, & Engedal, 2012; Tyrrell, Genin, & Myslinski, 2006). Such exclusions and stripping away of rights may result in depression, frustration, and anger and can create excess disability (Sabat, 2005).

Capacity assessment can serve as a vital tool for reducing such excess disability. Capacity assessments are multifaceted and comprehensive and include clinical, ethical, and legal referents (Moye & Marson, 2007; Moye, Marson, & Edelstein, 2013), as well as consideration of the individual's personal values and supports. In the clinical realm, assessment of cognitive functioning serves to identify relative cognitive and functional strengths that may be optimized, as well as weaknesses that may be compensated for, to promote the person with dementia's engagement in decision-making processes and reduce excess disability. In addition, capacity assessments evaluate a person's performance on domain-specific capacity standards as opposed to viewing capacity as a global judgment (Moberg & Rick, 2008), meaning that a person may be able to remain autonomous in one area of decision-making, even if he or she requires help in another. Regarding values, incorporation of the person's values into one's clinical determination helps differentiate between decisions that are unsafe due to cognitive impairment versus those that may seem eccentric, odd, or even foolish but are based on an individual's lifelong values and preferences. It further helps the clinician make recommendations that help support the individual's values despite an incapacity, restoring personhood to the highest degree possible.

Ethical considerations focus largely on the fundamental tension between respecting people's right to make their own decisions and the potential need to ensure the safety of vulnerable individuals. This tension often forces psychologists to balance the General Principles of Beneficence and Nonmaleficence (Principle A) with Respect for People's Rights and Dignity (Principle E) in the American Psychological Association's (APA; 2017b) *Ethical Principles of Psychologists and Code of Conduct* (hereinafter referred to as the APA Ethics Code). By conceptualizing the purpose of a capacity evaluation to be the determination of how much and what kind of supports can be provided to assist the person with dementia, the evaluator can find relief in this tension, ensuring that the person remains as autonomous as possible while also ensuring the individual's safety. Finally, by incorporating relevant legal statutes into capacity determinations, the assessor ensures that the person with dementia enjoys the full legal rights to which he or she is entitled and can also find resources provided by the state, such as guardians or conservators, that can assist a person in need.

CLINICAL PRESENTATION

The risk of developing dementia increases with age. Older adults with dementia are at further risk for multiple medical, neurologic, and mental health comorbidities, all of which may impact decision-making abilities (Moye, Armesto, & Karel, 2005). Such complicated presentations often necessitate frequent interactions with medical providers. In each health care encounter, patients make several decisions, with one study recording an average of 3.2 health care decisions per office visit (Braddock, Fihn, Levinson, Jonsen, & Pearlman, 1997). These decisions may be simple and low risk, complex and high risk, or lie somewhere in between. In their general practice, medical providers typically apply their own judgment regarding how much information to provide and how formal the informed consent process needs to be (Barbas & Wilde, 2001). They must be mindful in their presentation of information because excessive use of medical jargon, providing insufficient information, or communicating in a language in which the patient with dementia is not proficient can all contribute to pseudo-incapacity (Sessums, Zembrzuska, & Jackson, 2011).

Clinicians should take stock of the setting in which they practice and the likelihood with which they will encounter incapacitated patients. By extracting data from 43 studies that examined capacity in various contexts, Sessums, Zembrzuska, and Jackson (2011) found that incapacity to make medical decisions varied by both diagnosis and setting. Disease-specific assessment of incapacity demonstrated that only 2.8% of healthy older adult controls lacked medical decision-making capacity, whereas 20% of those with mild cognitive impairment and 54% of those with Alzheimer's disease were found to lack capacity in this domain. Regarding setting, incapacity to make medical decisions was notably higher in nursing home residents (44%) compared with those in inpatient medicine (26%; Sessums et al., 2011). Further research in nursing homes has confirmed high rates of incapacity (Moye & Marson, 2007).

In addition to considerations of the prevalence of incapacity in various settings and among different diagnostic categories, clinicians working with individuals with dementia must also take into consideration the high likelihood that they will be working with the patient's surrogate decision-maker(s) as well (Maust, Blass, Black, & Rabins, 2008). Surrogate decision-makers can take on many forms. They may be formally appointed after a legal determination of incapacity, such as a legal guardian or conservator. Surrogate decision-makers may take the form of a previously appointed surrogate (e.g., Durable Power of Attorney for Health Care) that is activated on the basis of a clinical (civil) determination of incapacity. Finally, a surrogate decision-maker may be a friend or family member who, independently or in agreement with the individual with dementia, assumes various responsibilities (e.g., paying the bills, managing medications, or hiding car keys; Moye & Marson, 2007). Clinicians should ensure that they have good understanding of local laws and facility policies to determine who will serve as the rightful surrogate decision-maker in an effort to protect the rights and welfare of the patient with dementia who is unable to make health care decisions.

An additional area of consideration relates to the neuropsychological predictors of decision-making capacity. Decision-making is an incredibly complex cognitive process that involves multiple brain systems, and the relative importance of each system varies by the capacity domain under consideration. For example, verbal conceptualization and reasoning and verbal memory abilities play a particularly important role in medical decision-making (Dymek, Marson, & Harrell, 1999), while arithmetic skills appear fundamental to financial decision-making abilities (Marson, Kerr, & McLaren, 2016). A comprehensive discussion of the neuropsychological predictors of incapacity in a variety of domains is beyond the scope of this chapter, but there are several excellent studies and reviews on this topic (see Marson et al., 2016; Moye, Karel, Gurrera, & Azar, 2006; Palmer et al., 2013, Palmer & Savla, 2007). Having this knowledge can assist clinicians in taking a strategic approach to cognitive assessment when time constraints (e.g., an urgent decision) or patient characteristics (e.g., very sick, frail, easily fatigued) preclude a more thorough cognitive evaluation. Further, there is evidence that specific areas of cognitive compromise can be supported with compensatory interventions (Rubright, Sankar, Casarett, Gur, Xie, & Karlawish, 2010), and use of such interventions during a capacity evaluation can ensure that patients with dementia are given the opportunity to perform to their highest potential.

DIAGNOSTIC STANDARDS AND DILEMMAS

Neurocognitive disorders represent a major health challenge worldwide. In the United States, an estimated 5.7 million people were living with Alzheimer's disease (AD) in 2018; this number is expected to more than double to 14 million by 2050. As a progressive disease, AD is the fifth cause of death for those who are 65 and older and the leading cause of disability and poor health (Alzheimer's Association, 2018). With the rapidly increasing prevalence of AD and other dementias, clinicians must be well versed in the current diagnostic standards in order to ensure accurate diagnosis. Per *Diagnostic and Statistical Manual of Mental Disorders* (fifth edition; American Psychiatric Association, 2013) criteria, neurocognitive disorders require a decline in at least one cognitive domain (complex attention, executive function, learning and memory, language, perceptual-motor, and social cognition) that contributes to functional impairments. Clinicians must consider the degree of cognitive decline from baseline and the impact of the disease on functioning (mild vs. major neurocognitive disorder), the degree of certainty regarding the etiology (possible vs. probable), the presence or absence of behavioral disturbances (e.g., psychosis, mood, agitation), and the severity level of the disability (mild, moderate, or severe).

Differential diagnosis is critical when working with older adults because there are multiple conditions besides dementia common in later life that can have a negative effect on decision-making abilities. When such conditions are more transient or are tractable to intervention, there is the potential for capacity to be restored. Misdiagnosis or not accounting for such conditions can lead even experienced clinicians to opine that an older adult is permanently incapacitated due to a dementia diagnosis and can unjustly strip the individual of personal liberties and the right to self-determination (Lichtenberg, 2012). A common source of diagnostic confusion in older adult populations is delirium. Delirium, which is characterized by inattention and marked cognitive impairments, is a reversible condition that can be challenging to distinguish from dementia (Fong, Tulebaev, & Inouye, 2009). It is common for clinicians to encounter older adults with delirium, with dementia, or both, and teasing apart reversible causes of incapacity (delirium) from irreversible causes of incapacity (dementia) can be challenging. Clinicians must also consider common psychiatric comorbidities that may contribute to impaired decision-making capacity, such as psychosis (Dunn, Palmer, Keehan, Jeste, & Appelbaum, 2006; Okai et al., 2007), severe depression (Hindmarch, Hotopf, & Owen, 2013), and bipolar disorder (Adida et al., 2008; Clark, Iversen, & Goodwin, 2002; Clark, Sarna, & Goodwin, 2005). Because psychiatric comorbidities are common in individuals with dementia (Carlino, Stinnett, & Kim, 2013; Ferretti, McCurry, Logsdon, Gibbons, & Teri, 2001; Hendrie et al., 2014; Lyketsos & Olin, 2002; Starkstein, Jorge, Petracca, & Robinson, 2007), they may negatively affect decision-making capacity, and they are potentially treatable conditions, clinicians must ensure that they adequately assess psychiatric symptoms as part of capacity evaluations.

Thus far, we have discussed diagnostic standards and dilemmas related to the individual with dementia. However, clinicians must also consider the important role of caregivers when conducting capacity assessments and be aware of dilemmas that may arise when working with caregivers. Unsurprisingly, research has shown that decision-making becomes increasingly caregiver-dominated as dementia severity increases (Hirschman, Xie, Feudtner, & Karlawish, 2004). However, it is important to note that several additional factors beyond the severity of a patient's cognitive impairment can interfere with patient autonomy when making decisions in a relational context, including high levels of caregiver burden (Hirschman et al., 2004), long-standing family dynamics, nefarious intent on the part of the caregiver (e.g., financial exploitation), caregiver role confusion (e.g., global perspective of incapacity or confusion about potential for capacity to be restored), or simply patient preferences to hand over decision-making to others (Smebye, Kirkevold, & Engedal, 2012). By conceptualizing decision-making as relational in nature for individuals with dementia, clinicians may determine the best way obtain and interpret collateral information and to make recommendations aimed at promoting patient autonomy in alignment with the individual's values and preferences.

CLINICAL METHODS

In this section, we review resources for the broader conceptualization of evaluating capacities and important factors to consider when determining your assessment approach. Evaluations are inherently complex given the circumstances in which they often arise, and thus we also outline common challenges and steps that clinicians can take.

Conceptual Framework

The American Bar Association (ABA) and APA's Assessment of Capacity in Older Adults Project Working Group published conceptual and practical guidance for lawyers (2005), judges (2006), and psychologists (2008) working with older adults with diminished capacities. These collective works outline a conceptual framework, promoting consideration of the following elements in a capacity evaluation: (a) relevant legal standards, (b) functional elements specific to the capacity in question, (c) medical diagnoses, (d) cognitive functioning, (e) psychiatric and emotional factors, (f) the examinee's values, (g) risks unique to the specific situation and individual, (h) means for enhancing capacity, and (i) making a clinical judgment. Regardless of the type of capacity in question (e.g., medical consent, independent living, financial), an evaluation is conceptualized best as an assessment of how much support someone may need, not whether a person does or does not have capacity. This conceptual shift helps keep the emphasis on supporting autonomy as much as possible.

Assessment Approaches

Review several pertinent resources to help guide your overall approach to an assessment in this context:

- *Ethical Principles of Psychologists and Code of Conduct* (American Psychological Association, 2017a)
- *Ethical Practice in Geropsychology* (Bush, Allen, & Molinari, 2017)
- *Multicultural Guidelines: An Ecological Approach to Context, Identity, and Intersectionality* (American Psychological Association, 2017b)
- *Guidelines for Psychological Practice With Older Adults* (American Psychological Association, 2014)
- *Guidelines for the Evaluation of Dementia and Age-Related Cognitive Change* (American Psychological Association, 2012)

In a medical or rehabilitation setting, how a clinician approaches the evaluation depends on several factors (e.g., scheduling, expected turnaround for the report, progression of the dementia, physical health, setting where the evaluation will take place). Our own approach to capacity evaluations includes several guiding steps.

Collect Information and Consider the Level of Assessment Warranted

We specifically ask the referring source what prompted the concerns (what was observed, reported, what happened). Suggested preassessment information can be found in ABA/APA (2008). We developed and apply a CURE mnemonic to help guide our planning and determine the level of formality or comprehensiveness appropriate for the capacity question (see Table 2.1). Collectively, CURE allows us to consider how much data is needed to answer the question and prioritize competing referrals.

THE CURE FRAMEWORK FOR PLANNING CAPACITY ASSESSMENTS

1. **Complexity**—How complex is the capacity in question?
    - Can range from low (a person with a mild stage of dementia and medically stable appointing a health care agent) to high (a person with dementia who is still recovering from delirium and wants to change health care agents, but there are concerns about undue influence from family).
    - Greater complexity may require additional time and data points.
2. **Urgency**—How quickly is an answer needed?
    - Can range from low (a person with vascular dementia wanting to make a usual small donation to a charity in the coming months) to high (a person with dementia on a fixed income discovered to have written large checks to a suspicious organization).
    - Urgent situations may challenge reliance on comprehensive evaluations.
3. **Risk**—How much risk is the person with dementia confronting?
    - Can range from low (consenting to a change in the timing of medication) to high (starting a new medication with serious side effects).
    - Higher risk often prompts for greater attention to the concerns and documentation of detailed discussion about these risks with the patient.
4. **Environment**—What resources are available, or potentially available, to support the person?
    - Resources may reflect family supports, community programs, and involvement of treatment team members.
    - Resources may also reflect adaptations we can make to the older individual's environment or ways we interact to promote optimal engagement.

TABLE 2.1. Framework for Levels of Assessment

Level of assessment	Features	Pros and cons	Example
Formal and comprehensive	Standardized evaluation of values, mood, cognition, decision-making, and functional aspects (if applicable) Interview with collateral informants (staff, family, etc.) May address several types of capacity (i.e., medical consent and financial management) for a larger conceptualization of the individual	*Pros*—provides the most data available for a clinical judgment; reliance on standardized measures; can provide recommendations to support the individual across domains tested; good to use when the case is complex and the level of risk is high *Cons*—can be a burden to the individual; requires a high level of patient engagement; often requires several hours of time; challenging to do in certain settings (e.g., emergency department, intensive care unit)	You are asked to complete an assessment of an individual's capacity to make medical decisions and to return to living at home alone. There are additional concerns about how the patient's advancing dementia and depression may also be factors. Your consult addresses types of supportive services and interventions that will optimize living in the community, consistent with the individual's long-held value.
Formal and abbreviated	Standardized evaluation of domains most germane to the assessment Interview with collateral informants specific to the capacity in question Abbreviated due to time constraints or pressing need for a clinical judgment	*Pros*—reliance on standardized measures; can quickly address the greatest concern; reduces burden to the patient; allows for recommendations specific to the area of concern; may incorporate assessments from other clinicians and specialties *Cons*—not a fully integrative assessment; may limit greater conceptualization of the individual's functioning	A person with vascular dementia due to stroke is referred for an evaluation of capacity to manage finances. You receive a copy of a previous neuropsychological evaluation and mood assessment. Your evaluation focuses on monetary skills, knowledge of personal finances and financial concepts, judgment, values, and history with money.

(*continues*)

TABLE 2.1. Framework for Levels of Assessment (*Continued*)

Level of assessment	Features	Pros and cons	Example
Informal or bedside evaluation	Primarily interview-based evaluation with the patient; may administer select standardized measures; discussion of values Focused consultation with available collateral informants Focused on relevant functional elements	*Pros*—quickly assess the capacity domain in question; feels less overwhelming to the patient; useful in situations when the patient is unable to engage for extended periods of time; can incorporate evaluations completed by other clinicians *Cons*—may lack standardization; may lack enough data to make a confident clinical judgment; greater challenge to personalize recommendations to promote autonomy; may not have additional information for a larger conceptualization	A person with dementia is admitted to a medical ward. After a few days, he believes the doctor is exaggerating the level of concern about his functioning and begins to assert his right to discharge. You evaluate the patient in his room, focusing on an interview using the four components of medical decision-making.
Consultation only	Discussion with referring provider about how to conceptualize capacity Education about relevant state statutes and organizational policies Direct guidance provided to referring provider about how they can approach the assessment with the patient (i.e., sample questions related to functional elements)	*Pros*—decentralizes capacity knowledge; allows referring clinicians to build confidence in addressing capacity *Cons*—reliance on referring provider's ability to follow through with recommendations and guidance on how to assess capacity; potential for hidden biases to influence the evaluation (e.g., confirmation bias)	An individual with an early stage of dementia is showing signs of progression. The physician is wondering at what point she should question the patient's ability to consent to an upcoming surgery. You provide information on decision-making ability in persons with dementia, as well as how to ask questions that address understanding, appreciation, reasoning, and expressing a choice.

Plan Your Approach and Perform the Evaluation

Create a hierarchy of the importance of data points needed for the capacity question. Consider potential barriers that may come up. Consider what cognitive and capacity measures may be helpful. This may assist with designing the sequencing of the assessment. For functional assessment suggestions, see ABA/APA (2008, p. 156). Coordinate with the treatment team on the best time to see the individual. Include in your evaluation meeting with the individual and collecting collateral information, as permissible and appropriate, from family and treatment team members.

Use the Conceptual Framework to Complete Report

It may be helpful to follow the framework outlined in ABA/APA (2008) to guide your clinical decision-making process (p. 46). A sample report structure is available in Appendix 2.1. Make a clear statement about capacity status and means for enhancing capacity (e.g., Qualls, 2007).

Provide Feedback to Stakeholders as Permitted and Appropriate

In addition to sharing this your impressions with the patient, it is often necessary to share it with the treatment team (see Standard 4.05 of the APA Ethics Code). Consider team dynamics and potential disagreements when delivering this information.

Pragmatic Concerns

Clinicians confront several challenges when assessing capacities in persons living with dementia. Obtaining informed consent is among one of the most important issues to address and starts with determining whether the patient can consent to your evaluation. This includes sharing information with the patient on the risks and benefits of participating and declining to participate, as well as confidentiality (considering APA Ethics Code Sections 4 and 9). However, as capacities are diminishing, we must also consult with professional ethics, legal counsel, and agency policies. If ability to give consent is questionable, we may consider obtaining assent or including a surrogate decision-maker relying on APA Ethics Code Standards 3.10b and 9.03b for guidance.

Often, initial referrals for a capacity evaluation will come as a single broad request ("Can this patient make decisions?") or several requests ("Can the patient make medical decisions about discharge and manage their finances after they discharge?"). The challenge will be in refining what the referring professional is concerned about and what type of capacity question is most germane. Consider prioritizing the capacity issue most at stake or presenting the greatest risk to the patient. In inpatient medical and rehabilitation settings, utilize the interdisciplinary team's available information to support your evaluation. For example, a speech pathologist may have already completed cognitive testing. Furthermore, when teams are involved, we must welcome and expect that there may be competing conceptualizations of a patient's decisional capacity. When this occurs, convene the team for open discussion on the findings, highlight the team's common value of wanting to provide a beneficial service, promoting patient autonomy, and reducing risk.

When approaching the individual, consider the length (or burden) of your planned evaluation. In inpatient medical and rehabilitation settings, patients are often fatigued, and you are competing with other professionals for the patient's time. Before your assessment, learn about the patient's abilities from a chart review and consultation with staff. This can be helpful in knowing when is the best time to speak to the patient, any motor weakness or visual impairments to account for, and other factors that are worth considering in your approach. If pressed for time, create a hierarchy of the most desired information should the patient get too fatigued or decline to continue before you are done. Importantly, when evaluating your data, consider the way in which culture influences a patient's understanding and appreciation of the issue at hand. This consideration also extends to how any caregiver–patient relationship may influence the data obtained from collateral informants. When conceptualizing and making a clinical judgment, we must be aware of and actively attend to our own values and beliefs, especially when they may differ from the patient's values (APA, 2017b). Unfortunately, normative data for capacity measures are limited for diverse populations. Consult with your peers if needed.

Situations where the individual is uninterested, disengaged, or uncooperative present their own unique challenges. Here, examine (a) how your role was introduced to the patient by the referring provider, (b) if the patient is still recovering from an acute medical condition, or (c) if the patient is suspicious about how the results are to be used. Clarify that you are providing a clinical judgment and offer direct examples of how testing can be beneficial, such as identifying appropriate resources to support the patient's functioning. If time allows, consider meeting with a patient several times to build rapport, such as conducting a brief interview, cognitive testing, and the capacity evaluation over several meetings. As a last resort, and only when additional data are available for use, consider offering consultation about decisional capacity to the referring professional (refer to Standard 9.01 of the APA Ethics Code). If warranted, consider coaching the provider on things to consider or ask so that they can assess a person's capacity should they be able to garner better engagement during their interactions.

Be familiar with state statutes related to health care decision-making, guardianship, and conservatorship. Recognize there is a lot of confusion among patients, families, and medical staff about the various forms of surrogate decision-making authority that exist. It is not uncommon to encounter a family member who is named in a durable power of attorney who believes he or she became the surrogate at signing of the paperwork, which may or may not be the case. Always ask for and read the documentation to verify the type and scope of authority. Lastly, because of the variety of medical and psychiatric conditions that may temporarily impair someone's decisional capacity, be a strong advocate for reevaluating capacity when appropriate. Offer a need for a reevaluation as a recommendation in your initial report. When known, offer evidence for when the reevaluation may be warranted (i.e., improved alertness, orientation, recall of events, functional improvement). In these instances, be sure to communicate back with the identified surrogate decision-maker about the shift in decisional authority.

CASE EXAMPLES

The following two case examples demonstrate unique complexities to performing capacity evaluations in an inpatient medical rehabilitation setting. These examples depict challenges to engaging individuals with cognitive impairment and show, using the approach and resources outlined in this chapter, how to design the assessment strategy and identify ways to support the individual.[1]

Case 1: Mr. Diemer—Lost and Found

Presentation

Hospitalized older individuals with neurocognitive impairments may experience complications during their care due to a treatment team's concerns about their capacity to make medical decisions or perform certain actions. Discharge may be delayed while surrogate decision-makers are sought and alternative living options are explored. Health care practitioners may struggle with balancing the desire to promote patient autonomy and determining whether protection is needed for safety (i.e., beneficence). Capacity evaluations can be a valuable tool in examining these complexities and offering guidance on how to proceed. This case example follows a gentleman with a suspected premorbid neurocognitive disorder who presented to a medical center with confusion and intoxication. Over the course of admission in a rehabilitation unit, his capacity to make medical decisions was questioned, with the treatment team citing his lack of engagement in care as evidence that a guardianship and higher level of care was warranted. As an integrated team psychologist, I (KSP) was consulted several times to assist in determining the patient's cognitive functioning and capacity to make decisions about his care.

History

Mr. Edward Diemer, a 79-year-old, White, non-Hispanic, recently divorced man, was found by police in a public park. Mr. Diemer was confused and was taken to a community hospital for evaluation and found to be intoxicated and suffering from hepatic encephalopathy. While in the park, he sustained a fall-related injury but did not have a fracture. After an initial period of

[1]Although the case examples in this chapter are based on the authors' real experiences, the identities of the individuals involved in these examples have been properly disguised to protect their confidentiality.

stabilization, he was transferred to a Department of Veterans Affairs (VA) inpatient physical rehabilitation unit with the goal of rehabilitation and return to his home. Table 2.2 presents relevant background information.

Once admitted to the rehabilitation unit, staff quickly learned that Mr. Diemer was uninterested in participating in physical and occupational therapy or in attending to personal hygiene and grooming. According to the patient, "I didn't ask to be brought here, I don't have to do what you say." Despite multiple attempts to engage him across several days, Mr. Diemer neither participated in nor requested to leave the rehabilitation unit. The treatment team, reviewing his records, discovered he had a suspected neurocognitive impairment of unknown etiology and was increasingly worried about his current cognitive state. A request was made for an evaluation of his capacity to make medical decisions, stating, "Please evaluate baseline cognitive functioning and decisional capacity." Initial clarification of the referral determined that staff members specifically wanted to know whether he had

TABLE 2.2. Patient Information for Case 1

Medical history	Hepatic encephalopathy
	Cirrhosis
	Orthostatic hypotension
	Gastroesophageal reflux disease
	Degenerative joint disease—knees
	Chronic obstructive pulmonary disease
	Alcohol use disorder, moderate
	Major neurocognitive disorder due to Alzheimer's disease (suspected by primary care provider prior to his admission, charted in medical record but not formally diagnosed)
Select medications	Thiamine (100 mg, daily)
	Folic acid (1 mg, daily)
	Rifaximin (55 mg, bid)
	Lactulose (30 mL, tid)
Imaging—computed tomography scan of head	Taken 1 year before admission due to falls and suspected head injury; reveals mild global cerebral atrophy and mild chronic microvascular ischemia
Psychiatric history	Seen by psychiatric prescriber for several sessions (2 decades before this admission). Notes revealed discussions about mood, nightmares, and military-related trauma. Patient declined to proceed with further treatment.
Psychosocial history	Retired (for approximately 15 years)
	History of working in corporate sales
	Divorced (within a year of this evaluation)
	One adult son in the area but limited contact
Advance directive	No record of an advance directive.

Note. bid = twice daily; tid = three times daily.

the ability to decline the offered therapies (i.e., an informed refusal). Early team discussions questioned if a guardianship was warranted to assist with placing this gentleman in a long-term care (LTC) facility. A review of community records indicated that the prior facility had not attempted to contact any family members. When the patient was approached early to involve a family member, specifically a son listed as an emergency contact, the patient refused to allow us to share any information with him. Respecting his expressed wish in the context of presumed capacity at this point, the team did not reach out to family.

Evaluation 1: Two Weeks After Admission to Rehabilitation Unit

Conducting an initial chart review, I searched available records, including any historical information on his substance use and cognitive health. No documentation regarding his capacity to make decisions had yet been entered into the medical record, and thus, at the time of his admission, he was considered his own decision-maker. Interestingly, even though the patient did not participate in therapies, he consistently took his medications aiding in his recovery. Occupational therapy administered a brief cognitive screening measure, the Montreal Cognitive Assessment (MoCA; Nasreddine et al., 2005), and noted his performance reflected dementia with a score of 9 out of 30 points.

My review of the case, using the CURE mnemonic indicated the complexity was rather high (consenting to inpatient physical therapy involved several providers conducting treatments, each with their own risks and benefits) but that the urgency was low in my opinion. Could the gentleman be allowed to stabilize before embarking on a course of rehabilitation? I suggested that the evaluation of his capacity could potentially wait, allowing him additional time to recover from the acute medical issues (specifically, his ammonia levels were elevated, which added to his confusion). I cautioned that any cognitive information obtained now would not likely represent this gentleman a few days later, as we expected him to continue to improve. However, because a decision was needed about whether he should stay on a rehabilitation unit versus be moved to an LTC unit, a clinical judgment about his capacity at that moment to make that specific decision was needed. Importantly, as the initial consult requested a broader review of decisional capacity, consulting with the team allowed for a refining of the question to the most pressing concern at that time. I internally concluded the suggestion for guardianship and LTC was too intrusive of an intervention at this stage in his care but struggled with the best way to broach this with the team members.

After an initial introduction with the patient, Mr. Diemer expressed willingness to engage in a discussion with psychology. We agreed to meet later that morning, allowing me time to coordinate schedules with nursing and therapy staff. However, upon my return an hour later, Mr. Diemer declared he no longer had an interest in speaking with psychology. Firmly, he declined an offer to discuss the issue but was tentatively open to a return visit. I spoke with the referring provider, offering a recommendation that he speak with the patient about the evaluation again and to allow me time to build rapport.

In my follow-up meeting, Mr. Diemer indicated he did not care to attend a treatment team meeting to discuss his decisional capacity and treatment plan. Feeling some pressure to share the importance of the meeting (because it did not appear that other staff members had spoken with him about these decisional concerns), I noted that the treatment team would be discussing his ability to make decisions about his medical care and ability to return home. He angrily shouted, "There is nothing that anyone can decide about my life at a meeting" and rolled over, turning his back to me. I gently offered that his input would be greatly appreciated, lest a decision be made about him without his participation or awareness of his preferences and wishes. He yelled at me to get out of his room.

As the consultant, I considered several options:

1. I could state that the patient did not engage with me and therefore I could not comment on his decisional capacity.
2. I could ask the referring provider to reconsult as needed or when the patient seemed willing to engage.
3. I could make another attempt (my fourth at this point) to visit with the patient, allowing time for more rapport.
4. I could offer consultation based on a review of the medical record, perhaps providing guidance to the team about options to consider.

I decided to offer consultation based on a review of the medical record but only after questioning if this was appropriate. I felt some discomfort offering a clinical statement about a patient, especially when he did not desire to engage in the evaluation and did not provide his consent. There was concern on my part that even an informal consultation would carry weight, and with the consequences high for this gentleman (the team was speaking of pursuing LTC placement, loss of decisional ability via court order or enacting institutional policy for a surrogate, fear he would be removed from any future discussions), I consulted with the APA Ethics Code and peers. After review, I decided there were enough data from the medical record regarding previous concerns about evolving dementia, the recent confusion that was adding an additional burden, notable cognitive impairment on screening conducted on admission, and poor understanding and appreciation evidenced during interactions with other staff members. In selecting this approach, I took the consultation as an opportunity to provide education to the treatment team on cognition, capacity, and ways to promote the patient's engagement in his care.

Even without the patient's participation, a decision was needed about what to do regarding his care. How long could a treatment team allow someone to remain on a rehabilitation unit and not engage? A rehabilitation bed could not be held for someone uninterested in therapy. Without any open dialogue and despite attempts, Mr. Diemer was not showing an ability to collaborate on what care he even wanted. With questions about his capacity, the treatment team members also felt that they could not simply discharge him from the facility. In the end, I offered that Mr. Diemer did not display the requisite functional elements needed for medical decision-making and offered several supportive data points. Furthermore, I cautioned against a finding of lack of decisional capacity as a permanent judgment, noting the expected recovery with continued abstinence and medications. Improvement in cognition and engagement warranted a reevaluation.

Because no durable health care power of attorney was on record, the referring provider was encouraged to use the medical center's policy for contacting his next-of-kin to serve as a surrogate. The son was contacted against the wish of the patient. However, due to family estrangement and dynamics where the patient's history of drinking was minimized within the family, the son felt the team was overreacting and instructed us to inform his father he should participate in rehabilitation. It was only with additional time, the son visiting, and additional meetings that the son began to see his father would need assistance once discharged.

Evaluation 2: 4 Weeks After Admission

The treatment team, patient, and son began to plan for his discharge to home as Mr. Diemer demonstrated continued improvements in physical and cognitive functioning over the month, despite inconsistent participation in rehabilitation programming during this time. Given his history of substance use and the role alcohol played in his current admission, many members of the treatment team worried he would relapse and be readmitted greatly debilitated. Specifically, they were worried about his potential dangerousness to self. To break this cycle, some members of the treatment team put forth a strong recommendation to transfer Mr. Diemer to a community-based LTC setting. The patient and son viewed this recommendation as an "overreaction" and asserted a right to discharge home. Noting the continued improvement in cognitive functioning, I spoke to the importance of a reevaluation of his decisional capacity. I narrowed the focus on the treatment of the physical health complications of his substance use. An evaluation of his capacity to live independently was addressed separately.

Interview, Examination, and Tests

Using the CURE mnemonic, I felt all categories were high and that Mr. Diemer had several supports available to him (primarily family involvement). My approach was formal and comprehensive. I prioritized (a) obtaining information on current cognitive functioning, (b) a discussion on the patient's values, (c) a capacity-focused interview on his health and course of events, and (d) administering a standardized capacity tool using a hypothetical medical decision. Mr. Diemer vaguely recalled our previous encounter but was eager to complete additional testing as staff unfortunately informed him that my evaluation was key to determining when he would be discharged. I made a mental note to go back to the treatment team and revisit how my evaluations are conceptualized and discussed with patients.

Several capacity evaluation tools are available to assist with determining decisional capacity (for a review, see Dunn, Nowrangi, Palmer, Jeste, & Saks, 2006). How does one choose which to use? In my own setting, I have the Aid to Capacity Evaluation (Etchells et al., 1999), Hopemont Capacity Assessment Inventory (Edelstein, 1999), the Assessment of the Capacity to Consent to Treatment (ACCT; Moye et al., 2007), and the MacArthur Competency Assessment Tool for Treatment (Grisso & Appelbaum, 1998). I weighed pros and cons for each in this case. For Mr. Diemer, I already had a pertinent medical issue to discuss, but I also wanted a structured way to cue myself to assess for values and to offer an additional example of his decisional abilities using a standardized method. For those reasons, I selected the ACCT.

Mr. Diemer noted overall confusion as to the exact course of events but was aware he was involved with police and was admitted to a community hospital before coming to the rehabilitation unit. He denied preadmission trouble with cognition and functioning but noted his initial "fogginess" on admission had abated, and he perceived himself at his baseline. Mr. Diemer was aware of the recommendation for transfer to a community LTC setting and strongly disagreed. He argued that the recommendation was based on testing conducted soon after his admission. He claimed his physical health was rather unremarkable, outside of the inpatient physician expressing concerns about his liver functioning. Mr. Diemer quickly related his alcohol use to his poor liver functioning and his medications to his cognitive "fog." However, he did not believe alcohol could be responsible for his own cognitive impairment. This lack of connection between alcohol and brain functioning seemed related to a lack of knowledge rather than a psychotic thought process or cognitive impairment.

A hypothetical scenario about cardiopulmonary resuscitation from the ACCT was administered. Although information was already obtained from an interview about an actual medical issue facing the patient, the vignette aided in the determination of his ability to understand, appreciate, reason, and express a clear choice. Here, I questioned how much information was needed to show decisional capacity. I opted for using the vignette as time allowed for it, the patient was willing, and I wanted to demonstrate the functional elements across two situations, given what was at stake regarding surrogate decision-making. The vignette offered me information regarding the extent of support that was needed to guide someone through a decisional process. In this instance, he had trouble remembering some of the details in the vignette, but when these were provided in a written format, rather than relying on auditory memory alone, he was able to incorporate the information into his reasoning. Mr. Diemer provided adequate responses to items assessing immediate recall of information but did need extra information on when CPR may be applied. He appropriately noted the risks and benefits associated with CPR and was able to provide examples. He identified the options available and expressed a clear choice. Regarding values, he identified his top values as living at home, thinking clearly, and having relationships with family and friends.

Finally, Mr. Diemer was administered several cognitive measures and appeared to give his full effort. He performed within expectation for his age on measures of simple auditory attention, command naming, and delayed verbal and visual recall. He performed in the borderline range on measures of verbal learning, verbal fluency, and construction. In contrast, Mr. Diemer performed in an impaired range on measures of processing speed and cognitive set-shifting.

Findings

Mr. Diemer presented remarkably different from our first encounter. Between the first and second evaluation, I remained in contact with his physician during a weekly team huddle. I learned that his ammonia level was being optimally controlled, and thus we were seeing the expected result of improved cognition, albeit with an underlying suspected dementia as his baseline. With improved physical and cognitive functioning, his participation improved, although he never fully engaged with physical and occupational therapies.

When speaking with the team, I stressed the importance of fluctuating capacities but also that the ability to make decisions can still vary within the same domain. Hence, a person living with dementia may be able to make one type of medical decision but not another. Mr. Diemer did not seem to appreciate the link between chronic problematic alcohol use and cognitive functioning; rather, he believed any cognitive changes were due to normal aging and his medications. If he lacked appreciation here, would that be grounds for a lack of capacity to make decisions about his medical care? How could I take this information and find a way to support his functioning? When considering my clinical judgment, I thought about how many other persons with concerning alcohol consumption also underappreciate, are in a precontemplative stage of change, or are just not aware of the connection to brain health. Do we seek guardianships or activate power of attorneys for all of them too?

My report summary stated,

> Hospital policy, along with current clinical recommendations on medical decision-making evaluations, support the need to examine four specific psycholegal abilities: (a) understanding, (b) appreciation, (c) reasoning, and (d) expressing a choice. On the basis of the information obtained, it is my clinical judgment that Mr. Diemer demonstrated adequate medical decision-making ability. Using a hypothetical vignette, he demonstrated adequate responses to items assessing the four psycholegal abilities when support was provided. When a more germane issue was used, he demonstrated a basic understanding and appreciation, as well as an ability to express a choice with reasoning. Of note, there does not seem to be a significant disturbance of affect or cognition that is driving his reduced ability to connect his alcohol intake to his cognitive functioning (highlighting considerations for looking at reasoning offered by Grisso & Appelbaum, 1998). On the basis of my discussions with him, this seems more related to a lack of education and a view that his behavior was not problematic. For this reason, I do not believe

his reduced appreciation of alcohol and brain functioning alone is evidence for a complete lack of decisional capacity. As there is still some cognitive compromise, he would benefit from means to support his decision-making as an intervention to enhance as much of his functioning as possible.

Recommended supports appear in Table 2.3.

Intervention and Disposition

A treatment team meeting was scheduled for all relevant stakeholders to discuss discharge plans. I spoke to the findings and means for supporting his participation, including the importance of sobriety for his overall functioning. I have since recognized that treatment team members will vary in their level of risk tolerance and understanding, but I can make a connection by highlighting our shared value of helping others and using evidence to guide our decisions.

Outcome

After the second evaluation of Mr. Diemer's capacity to make medical decisions, I saw the patient one final time for an evaluation of his independent living capacity. I offered that he had the capacity to live independently provided he accepted supportive services in the home. A final treatment team meeting was called where the patient, his son, and the team members were

TABLE 2.3. Support Strategies for Case 1

Involvement of family in medical decisions	Given level of trust between Mr. Diemer and his son, I encouraged them to discuss values regarding medical care and wishes for future care. The son may be well positioned to offer reassurance, repeat information, and to offer a structure to allow Mr. Diemer to think through a medical decision.
Attention to values	Providers were encouraged to be aware of his stated values and to include this in future discussions with him, particularly as any new information about his physical health emerged.
Presentation of information considering his cognitive functioning	Mr. Diemer's cognitive profile suggested the treatment team use the following strategies: • Important information from the treatment team should be written down in a bullet-point fashion. • Provide a simplified list of medications and provide rationale for medications at a level of his understanding. • Present information in smaller chunks at one time so as not to overload his attentional and processing capacities. • Important discussions about his medical care may wish to include a reiteration of the important parts at the end of the conversation to convey the message best.
Surrogate decision-making	Mr. Diemer was encouraged to consider completing an advance directive to formalize any care wishes and to identify a durable power of attorney for health care.

present to share their concerns about Mr. Diemer returning home. Members noted concern about his potential to consume alcohol again, but the patient assured the team he would not drink (and thus declined any referral for substance use counseling). The team was divided in that some members continued to recommend a need for LTC and others working to find ways to support him in his home. I offered that the patient was able to make reasonable decisions with support and that he was accepting of his son's offer to help and our offer for community-based services. After 8 weeks on our rehabilitation unit, Mr. Diemer discharged to home with home health care, a home health aide, a meal delivery service, and admittance to a home-based primary care team.

Case 2: Mr. Johnson—Too Tired to Reason

Presentation

Older adults with dementia are at risk for multiple medical, mental health, and neurological comorbidities that can compromise cognitive functioning and decision-making capacity in a variety of domains. It seems to be the rule rather than the exception that patients in rehab settings often present with such comorbidities. It is further not uncommon for such individuals to demonstrate fluctuations in their cognition as a delirium or frailty syndrome (which includes exhaustion, loss of weight, weakness, and difficulties with gait and balance) is superimposed on their preexisting neurocognitive disorder. Such cognitive fluctuations may also contribute to fluctuations in decision-making capacity, which poses challenges not only in assessing an individual's decision-making abilities but also for predicting ongoing abilities in the future. The following case illustrates how I (KCM) used the CURE approach (complexity, urgency, risk, and environment) to determine the most appropriate strategy for evaluating capacity in an individual who demonstrated significant cognitive fluctuations as he recovered from septic shock and subsequent medical complications. The case shows how the use of visual aids during the evaluation proved to be a fundamental cognitive prosthetic that enabled a frail, exhausted patient with vascular dementia to participate in the evaluation. Finally, this case highlights the value of integrating supported decision-making strategies as a patient recovers from an acute medical condition in an effort to promote the individual's autonomy, self-determination, and control.

History

Mr. Lyle Johnson, a 71-year-old, African American, divorced veteran was brought to the VA Emergency Department after reportedly experiencing weakness, fatigue, lower abdominal discomfort, and loose stools for 5 days. He was divorced, had no children, and had designated his sister as his preferred health care decision-maker in his advance directive. The patient was diagnosed with septic shock due to a urinary tract infection and admitted to the intensive care unit (ICU) at the VA. Mr. Johnson was intubated for

9 days and was subsequently diagnosed with dysphagia due to deconditioned swallow and length of intubation. He was followed by speech therapy on the ICU and was gradually advanced to a dysphagia I puree diet with nectar-thick liquids; a percutaneous endoscopic gastrostomy (PEG) tube was also placed for supplemental nutrition. Mr. Johnson developed a large sacral ulcer during the course of his ICU stay, eventually developing osteomyelitis at the wound site. Additionally, Mr. Johnson had a known history of HIV, mixed hyperlipidemia, hypertension, and poor nutritional status. Formerly an obese man, the patient experienced a profound, inadvertent weight loss of approximately 50 pounds in 5 years. Over the past several years, multiple providers had questioned whether he was in the early stage of a dementia process, but no one had added this diagnosis to his problem list until his current hospitalization. During his current hospitalization, Mr. Johnson was noted to be extremely fatigued, and his cognition would wax and wane considerably throughout the day. He was severely deconditioned and had four falls during his hospital stay. A computed tomography scan of the head completed after one of his falls revealed mild chronic microvascular ischemia. This information, coupled with evidence of likely premorbid cognitive and functional impairments, led his inpatient provider to add a new diagnosis of vascular dementia to his problem list (see Table 2.4).

After Mr. Johnson became more medically stable, he was transferred to an LTC environment for a 6-week course of IV antibiotics and wound care. He repeatedly voiced his dissatisfaction with his modified diet and requested to be upgraded to a normal diet. When he discussed the risks versus benefits of changing his diet with the speech therapist or the inpatient provider, he would agree it was best to remain on the modified diet so that he could work toward his goals of "getting better and going home." However, during meals, he would again request a normal diet.

The LTC treatment team members found themselves torn between the patient's safety (i.e., beneficence) and his right to self-determination (i.e., autonomy). If they respected his wishes in the moment, his intake would likely improve, helping his nutritional status and healing, but he placed himself at serious risk of harm or even death from aspiration or choking. If they denied his requests, he was unlikely to eat, harming himself in the long term, but at least he was safe in the moment. Direct care staff members tended to focus on the immediate risk to his health and safety and thus erred on the side of caution and denied his requests for regular food and water, even though he was still his own decision-maker.

Mr. Johnson's provider placed an electronic consult requesting "Cognitive evaluation with specific focus on decision-making capacity for medical decisions—do we need to enact his designated decision-maker?" So far, Mr. Johnson had been open to involving his sister, Lisa, in team discussions about his medical care, although he made it clear he did not want her to know about his HIV diagnosis.

TABLE 2.4. Patient Information for Case 2

Medical history	Diabetes mellitus, Type II Mixed hyperlipidemia Hypertension Iron deficiency anemia Vitamin D deficiency Anemia Pressure ulcer of coccygeal region Oropharyngeal dysphagia Asymptomatic HIV Mixed hyperlipidemia Mild neurocognitive disorder due to vascular disease
Select medications	Mirtazapine (15 mg, daily) Efavirenz/emtricitabine/tenofovir (1 tablet daily) Cephalexin (500 mg, qid) Ciprofloxacin (500 bid)
Imaging	Computed tomography w/o contrast completed after Mr. Johnson fell in the hospital; results showed chronic white matter ischemia
Psychosocial history	Retired (for approximately 20 years after a back injury) History of working in construction Divorced, no children, lived alone Two brothers, two sisters; close relationship with one sister, Lisa Smoked one pack of cigarettes per day for 50+ years; stopped smoking during current hospitalization
Advance directive	Advance directive completed during a previous hospital admission in 2012 identifying his sister, Lisa Goodwell, as his durable power of attorney for health care.

Note. bid = twice daily; qid = four times daily.

Interview, Examination, and Tests

I conducted an initial chart review, going back over the previous 2 years and paying special attention to historical information regarding his cognitive health, as well as reviewing primary care notes documenting concerns about the patient's self-care in the context of unintentional weight loss and poor nutritional status. Six months before his current hospitalization, the patient was seen by a psychologist in primary care after reporting increasing difficulties with memory and concentration to his medical provider. He completed a cognitive screen, which showed evidence of impairment (MoCA score 19/30). He declined the further neuropsychological testing that was recommended.

Upon his admission to the ICU and then to LTC, his providers both opined that he had medical decision-making capacity in their history and physical notes. However, the speech therapist evaluated Mr. Johnson shortly after his transfer to the LTC unit and noted that his cognition appeared to fluctuate during the evaluation. In an effort to better understand Mr. Johnson's current cognitive functioning, the speech therapist administered a brief cognitive screening test, the St. Louis University Mental Status Exam (SLUMS; Tariq et al., 2006). His total score was 16 of 30 on this evaluation, falling in a range consistent with cognitive compromise. Despite his fluctuating cognition and low score on the SLUMS, the speech therapist consistently documented that the patient "exhibited comprehension" each time they discussed his dysphagia diagnosis, treatment options, and the associated risks versus benefits of each treatment option.

Upon planning my course of action, I first considered the urgency and risks associated with the medical decision that was in question. Given that there was high risk for harm to the patient if he switched to a regular diet and that Mr. Johnson was confronted with diet-related decisions multiple times per day, I determined that the urgency was high, and this consult needed to be completed in a timely manner. I also considered the appropriate length (burden) of the evaluation in light of the knowledge that Mr. Johnson fatigued quickly, his cognitive status often fluctuated, and his wound prevented him from sitting up for more than very brief periods of time. Thus, a formal, comprehensive assessment was out of the question because it would prove overly burdensome. The decision was made to conduct a formal, abbreviated bedside evaluation. I created a hierarchy of the most desired information given the probability that the patient would fatigue as the evaluation progressed. I prioritized obtainment of information about Mr. Johnson's values and medical decision-making abilities. If he would tolerate additional testing, I hoped to obtain more data regarding his cognitive strengths and weaknesses, as well as assess for mood and anxiety symptoms. If I was unable to do additional cognitive testing, I could at least rely on the recent cognitive screening measure that the patient completed with speech therapy. I decided to attempt to complete the assessment first thing in the morning, as nursing and speech therapy reported that he tended to be most alert during the morning hours. In an effort to maximize Mr. Johnson's comprehension and minimize memory demands, I decided to type up written information regarding his dysphagia condition, recommended and alternative treatments, and risks versus benefits associated with each option. Information was brief, simple, and presented in a bullet-point format. I showed this information to the Mr. Johnson's speech therapist to confirm its accuracy.

On interview, Mr. Johnson was cooperative but fairly withdrawn and disengaged, making rapport difficult to establish. He lay in bed on his left side, with his knees drawn up to his chest, and I stood at bedside for the duration of the evaluation. He appeared fatigued but was alert at the start of the interview. However, over the course of the evaluation, his level of alertness varied significantly. At times, Mr. Johnson appeared to fall asleep, but he would awaken easily when I called out his name. His fatigue appeared to increase throughout the encounter, which likely contributed to him transitioning from discussing his condition and treatment options in his own words, to reading off of the sheet, to pointing to items at the end of the evaluation. It is noted that I assessed orientation at the end of the evaluation, and the patient was fully oriented to person, place, date and time, and situation.

I began the evaluation with the ACCT, which focuses on the values, preferences, and approaches the individual uses to make medical decisions. When assessing values, Mr. Johnson had difficulty responding to an open-ended question about what is important to him and what makes his life worth living. Instead, he began describing his daily routine at home. When provided with a list of common values, he identified the following values as currently important to him: "to walk or move around by myself, to live at home, and to have relationships with friends and family." The patient identified his sister, Lisa, and two friends as the most important people in his life, stating that he is "very close" to all of them. He indicated a preference to make medical decisions together with his doctor and his family and stated that religion does not influence his decision-making.

To assess for medical decision-making capacity, I used the ACCT Part 2 and used the real-life example of his dysphagia diagnosis. The ACCT assesses four decisional abilities, including understanding, appreciation, reasoning, and expressing a choice. Mr. Johnson was provided with the written information regarding his dysphagia diagnosis, his treatment options, and the risks and benefits of each option to reference throughout this part of the evaluation. He appeared to study this information intently during the course of our discussion. At the time of the evaluation, he was able to demonstrate adequate understanding of dysphagia but initially denied that this was a current concern, stating that it was only a problem when he was on the acute medical unit. However, over the course of the interview, the patient eventually acknowledged that he currently carries a dysphagia diagnosis, and it affected his ability to eat regular food and his overall physical health. He expressed a choice to remain on his modified diet, stating that all of the listed benefits (i.e., greatly reducing his risk of choking, reducing the chance of an infection, allowing his throat and body time to recover, the team will work with him on his food preferences, and his medications can still be taken) far outweighed the two listed risks that actually mattered to him (i.e., "The food may not look appealing" and "It takes time to adjust to this diet"). The patient denied clinically significant symptoms of anxiety or depression on screening measures, which was consistent with the interview.

Findings

I concluded that Mr. Johnson had the requisite abilities to make decisions about his health care and, specifically, about his diet. I noted that when provided with additional support (i.e., brief, simple, written information), he demonstrated adequate understanding, appreciation, reasoning, and the ability to express a choice. The decision he made during our evaluation to remain on his modified diet was consistent with his stated values.

In my report, I noted that one of the primary concerns of Mr. Johnson's treatment team was that he would agree to the modified diet after speaking with speech therapy or his provider but would then regularly request to liberalize his diet during his day-to-day care, which appeared inconsistent with his goals of care. I opined that this pattern of behavior was primarily due to two primary factors:

1. "As the patient's fatigue increases, he appears to lose the energy to put forth the necessary effort to process information and make important decisions. Instead, he appears to rely on mental shortcuts and makes quick decisions based on his emotional responses in the moment. His proclivity for making quick, emotion-laden decisions that appear inconsistent with his values and stated wishes is likely driven by medical, rather than cognitive, concerns. He is tired, making decisions takes energy, and he is using heuristics to make a quick decision and save energy."
2. "The patient appears to benefit significantly from additional supports that assist him in the decision-making process, and it may be that when he is voicing his desire not to adhere to treatment recommendations, such supports have not been in place. During my interaction with the patient, he was provided with brief, simple explanations, in writing, and given significant time to process. With such supports, the patient was able to demonstrate capacity to make medical decisions."

In regard to the first factor, research supports that as individuals become more cognitively or emotionally taxed, they may shift from a rational or "analytic" style of decision-making to using "rules of thumb" and mental shortcuts to simplify their cognitive demands (Brown, 2007; Liu & Gonzalez, 2007). The second factor is consistent with research that has shown that medical decision-making capacity in some individuals with dementia can be improved with the provision of written information (Rubright et al., 2010).

But what should team members do about the patient's fluctuating cognition? Certainly, this could influence his ability to make important medical decisions. I did acknowledge this in my report, stating,

> It is understood that the patient demonstrates fluctuating cognition, and there may be moments when he does not have capacity to make certain medical decisions, particularly those that are urgent, complex, and increase his risk of harm. Providers may reevaluate his capacity to make decisions about his diet or other health care issues as his condition changes or as new information is learned.

While acknowledging that this may be difficult in practice, I strongly encouraged the patient's provider to conceptualize his medical decision-making capacity as in need of regular reevaluation, particularly in light of his fluctuating cognition.

Interventions and Disposition

Given my conclusion that the patient would require ongoing reassessment of his medical decision-making capacity as a result of his waxing and waning cognition, I decided to list highly specific recommendations and interventions in my final report. First, I urged his provider to consider the urgency of each medical decision the patient had to make and to delay conversations about his health care until times that he appeared alert and oriented whenever possible. Under urgent circumstances when the patient was not alert or lacked capacity to make medical decisions, I noted that the provider may wish to consider activating his advanced directive. To assist the provider in making determinations regarding the patient's capacity to make decisions in a given moment, I gave specific, concrete examples of how to assess his understanding, appreciation, reasoning, and ability to express a choice, using his dysphagia diagnosis as an example. The following sample questions were embedded in the recommendations section of the patient's report:

1. Understanding: "What's the medical problem I just described?" If discussing dysphagia, look for responses that reflect actual term *dysphagia* or description of the conditions (e.g., swallowing difficulties), as well as associated risks, such as choking, aspiration, or pneumonia.
2. Appreciation: "What could happen to you or your body if you ate regular food or drank thin liquids?" The provider should try to determine whether the patient can take the information about dysphagia and find it personally relevant. Look for the patient indicating an appreciation that he personally could aspirate, develop pneumonia, and so on.
3. Choice: "What diet would you like?" Checking to see if patient can express a choice.
4. Reasoning: "What led you to that choice?" Looking to see how the patient weighed various risks and benefits of each option.

As part of this ongoing evaluation of the patient's medical decision-making capacity, I highlighted the importance of interpreting his responses within the context of his values to improve his physical health, to walk, and to go home, as well as his stated preference to make decisions about his health care with his doctor and family. Recommended supports appear in Table 2.5.

Results were shared via a formal written report in the patient's medical record, face-to-face communication with the patient's provider and speech therapist, during an evaluation feedback session with the patient, and during an interdisciplinary team meeting. Results were discussed with the patient's sister, Lisa, during the interdisciplinary team meeting, which Mr. Johnson declined to attend. During this meeting, Lisa repeatedly asked team members questions about the patient's health and prognosis that were, at times, challenging to answer due to our inability to disclose his HIV status. Lisa presented as a loving, dedicated family member who wanted to do everything she could to give her brother the best quality of life possible in the context of his declining health. She shared that she often struggled to interact with him during her visits, as his long-standing taciturn nature coupled with his fluctuating

TABLE 2.5. Support Strategies for Case 2

Involving family in medical care discussions	During our evaluation, the patient reported that he would like to make medical decisions together with his family and identified his sister as the person he would like to be involved in his care. It is emphasized that the medical decisions are ultimately the patient's until his advanced directive is officially activated.
Use of visual aids	Providing the patient with written information regarding his condition, recommended and alternative treatments, and risks versus benefits associated with each treatment option. Written information should be brief, simple, and in a bullet-point format (example was given to patient's provider). For individuals who demonstrate a strong affective component to decision-making, it is helpful to ask them to read each item presented to them aloud and slowly.
Framing	Decisions are influenced by the manner in which risks are framed with individuals being more likely to choose positively framed outcomes. For example, reminding the patient that "People with your condition who are on a dysphagia I diet tend to recover and go home more quickly," will make it more likely that he will select the modified diet than telling him, "If you're on a regular diet you could aspirate and prolong your hospital stay." Link this information to his stated values of recovering, walking, and returning home.

cognition and fatigue made her visits challenging. She requested guidance from me about how to improve the quality of these visits, and I agreed to follow-up with her, pending the patient's approval.

When meeting with the patient for testing feedback, I again used a visual aid to help promote his understanding and appreciation of the information, providing him with brief, bullet-pointed information explaining the purpose of the evaluation, what was assessed, the results, summary, and recommendations. Mr. Johnson voiced understanding of the information provided and expressed his agreement with the recommendations. When discussing my recommendations for family involvement in medical decision discussions, the patient and I spent time exploring how he wished to approach this in light of his desire to keep his HIV status from his family. I noted that during the team meeting, his sister had asked a number of questions about his health status that the team was unable to answer because of the patient's request that we not disclose his HIV status. I shared that with his sister likely increasing involvement in his medical care, it may be challenging to have comprehensive discussions with her if his HIV status could not be disclosed. I also noted that she is listed as his durable power of attorney for health care in his advanced directive, and in the event that he can no longer make medical decisions, this information would be disclosed so that she can make fully informed medical decisions. The patient was asked about his concerns about disclosing his HIV status to his sister. He replied, "I just figured that the fewer [people] that know, the better." When asked about this perspective, he stated, "It's just what I think." He acknowledged that at some point, he realized that his sister will need to know about his HIV status, but he did not want her to know right now. I affirmed that this was the patient's decision, and it is his right not to disclose this information. I asked the patient if and when he is ready to disclose this to his sister, if he would prefer to do it alone, with his doctor, or have his doctor do it without him. He stated that he would rather have his doctor tell his sister without the patient present. When informed that his sister had requested additional guidance from me regarding how to improve the quality of her visits, the patient stated that he already felt highly supported by his sister, and he did not see a need for her to change her behavior in any way. However, he agreed to have me follow-up with her because she had requested that I do so.

My final contribution to this patient's case was to contact his sister, Lisa, to discuss strategies for enhancing the quality of her interactions with her brother during her visits. Lisa expressed relief that her brother already viewed her as an important source of social support, and that he enjoyed her visits already. Lisa shared that, based on the recommendations I had made as part of the capacity evaluation, she had identified some strategies that she wanted to trial during her visits. She shared her plans to provide briefer but more frequent visits to avoid fatiguing her brother. She also wanted to trial writing down simple, brief prompts on paper to help generate conversation about his memories of their family and past experiences. Finally, she shared her plans to bring in pictures of family members to look at together to help with reminiscing, as well as to facilitate interaction even if the patient is too tired to engage in much conversation. I reinforced Lisa for the thoughtfulness of her approach and provided a few additional ideas for more task-based, rather than conversation-based, activities that she could do with her brother.

Outcomes

Approximately 2 weeks after my evaluation, the patient again requested to have his diet liberalized. His speech therapist used the visual aids I created to engage the patient in an informed consent discussion. After this discussion, the patient decided to go with a normal diet with thin liquids. He continued working with the speech therapy team on safe swallow compensatory strategies and swallow therapy exercises, and he was successfully discharged from speech therapy services. The speech therapist expressed appreciation for the detailed recommendations I had provided, stating that it greatly increased her comfort level during conversations with the patient. Further, she no longer felt ill at ease when he made a decision against her recommendations because she felt confident that he was able to do so with these supports in place.

The liberalization of the patient's diet enabled him to once again enjoy his favorite foods. His sister would often bring him home-cooked meals, which he appeared to prefer over the hospital food. Sharing these meals served as another opportunity for them to engage in pleasant, quality visits. The patient remained on supplemental nutrition via his PEG tube, and he stated that he often did not feel hungry as a result. Thus, his intake remained fairly limited, but when he did eat, it was food he enjoyed. His wound continued to slowly heal.

Despite the progress the patient had made, he remained severely deconditioned, weak, and fatigued. His cognition continued to wax and wane, and he remained dependent on staff assistance with all health care needs. The patient, his sister, and the treatment team collaborated on a discharge plan, and they are now pursuing placement in LTC where the patient can receive the support he needs. He has remained his own medical decision-maker.

REFLECTION

Across our two case studies, we illustrated challenges that can complicate the evaluation of persons with dementia. Both cases presented with medical comorbidities that influenced our approach. Using our CURE mnemonic, we reduced our own anxieties about how to approach these evaluations and identified a method that best fit the situation. Additional value was placed on the role of reassessment or monitoring of capacity status and the importance of supporting decision-making. These cases both exemplified the reality that assessment of capacity in individuals with dementia is inherently complex. Moreover, these evaluations pulled us to remain ever vigilant to the ethical and pragmatic challenges involved, as well as to the dynamic nature of these depending on the setting, urgency, and level and type of risk. With the expected growth in number of persons living with some form of dementia still ahead of us, preparing now will position us well to address these concerns.

We are fortunate to have a wealth of information on the science of decision-making, models, and theories at our disposal. However, in reality, these evaluations are messy, and the tools available to us are difficult to navigate and can be overwhelming for the clinician. After consulting published professional guidance (e.g., ABA/APA, 2008) and the literature on capacity evaluations, we found ourselves wanting to take the next step. We hope this chapter aids in your own professional development but encourage you to continually challenge yourself to expand your knowledge by incorporating relevant research from our sister disciplines of gerontology, cognitive science, and law, among others. We suggest readers consider expanding their horizons to related subjects of health literacy (e.g., Berkman et al., 2011), health care communication (e.g., Gerontological Society of America, 2016), health care decision-making (e.g., Diefenbach, Miller-Halegoua, & Bowen, 2016), and supported (e.g., Kohn, Blumenthal, & Campbell, 2012) and shared (e.g., Miller, Whitlatch, & Lyons, 2016) decision-making. Through such endeavors, you can approach your assessments with the flexibility and creativity that is necessary when putting capacity science into practice.

APPENDIX 2.1
REPORT STRUCTURE EXAMPLE

Brief patient information and reason for referral	Introduction to patient demographic information, date of admission, and provider concerns prompting the referral to psychology.
Informed consent	Explicit statement on the discussion with the patient about limits of confidentiality, as well as risks and benefits of this capacity evaluation. Discusses obtaining assent versus consent from the patient (or from the surrogate decision-maker).
Relevant legal documentation	Statement on the presence of an advance directive, identification of a health care agent, and whether the surrogate decision-maker has been activated before this evaluation.
Chart review and background information	Varies in length depending on the demands of the evaluation, time allotted, and complexity of presenting issues. Written as a description of course of events (i.e., concerns noted at home, what led to admission, course of hospitalization, observations from staff that are prompting concerns about capacity) and medical and psychiatric history.
Previous cognitive and capacity evaluations	Given the focus of my evaluation on cognitive and decisional capacity, I (KSP) offer a separate section reviewing a history of these evaluations, including those made by other disciplines (psychiatry, occupational therapy, speech therapy, admitting physician, etc.).
	Current capacity evaluation
Behavioral observations	Statement on observations and patient's level of engagement
Cognitive assessment Data summary Cognitive results summary	Summary sheet for future retesting purposes. Clinical interpretation of data
Mood evaluation	Discussion on self-report of mood during interview and results from any measures

(*continues*)

Medical decision-making Interview and assessment	Capacity-focused interview with the patient. Discussion on administration and results from capacity-specific testing (e.g., Independent Living Scales, Texas Functional Living Scale, Assessment of the Capacity to Consent to Treatment, Hopemont Capacity Assessment Interview). Information obtained from collateral informants (e.g., family, surrogate decision-maker, treatment team members).
Conceptualization and discussion	For this evaluation, I opted to include a discussion about the challenges. I often do this with an educational bent for the treatment team. I emphasize how values may conflict between patient and team, relevant state statutes, local and national policies of the organization, and ethical concerns. Shows the thought process in reaching the capacity determination.
Summary	Summary statement about my clinical judgment about the specific capacity in question, supportive data for my conclusion, and a statement about the expected length of incapacity.
Diagnostic impressions	If appropriate, provide impressions based on review of chart, interviews, and data collected.
Recommendations	Specific recommendations for the patients (e.g., those focused on psychological or cognitive health) and for the referring provider (i.e., activate a surrogate decision-maker, have another discussion with the patient using certain recommendations based on testing about how to present information). To the extent possible, offer an explicit statement about capacity status and expected status over time (i.e., if lacking capacity due to an advanced neurocognitive disorder, likely not to regain capacity in the future).
Brief points for referring clinician	Three to five points that highlight the most important information about the evaluation (e.g., extent of capacity, diagnostic impression, recommendations for the provider to act on); serves as a quick reference for the referring clinician.

REFERENCES

Adida, M., Clark, L., Pomietto, P., Kaladjian, A., Besnier, N., Azorin, J. M., . . . Goodwin, G. M. (2008). Lack of insight may predict impaired decision making in manic patients. *Bipolar Disorders, 10,* 829–837. http://dx.doi.org/10.1111/j.1399-5618.2008.00618.x

Alzheimer's Association. (2018). 2018 Alzheimer's disease facts and figures [erratum: see https://doi.org/10.1016/j.jalz.2018.04.001]. *Alzheimer's & Dementia, 14,* 367–429. http://dx.doi.org/10.1016/j.jalz.2018.02.001

American Bar Association and American Psychological Association Assessment of Capacity in Older Adults Project Working Group. (2008). *Assessment of older adults with diminished capacity: A handbook for psychologists.* Washington, DC: American Bar Association and American Psychological Association.

American Bar Association Commission on Law and Aging & American Psychological Association. (2005). *Assessment of older adults with diminished capacity: A handbook for lawyers.* Washington, DC: American Bar Association and American Psychological Association.

American Bar Association Commission on Law and Aging & American Psychological Association. (2006). *Judicial determination of capacity of older adults in guardianship proceedings: A handbook for judges.* Washington, DC: American Bar Association and American Psychological Association.

American Psychiatric Association. (2013). *Diagnostic and statistical manual of mental disorders* (5th ed.). https://dx.doi.org/10.1176/appi.books.9780890425596

American Psychological Association. (2012). Guidelines for the evaluation of dementia and age-related cognitive change. *American Psychologist, 67,* 1–9. http://dx.doi.org/10.1037/a0024643

American Psychological Association. (2014). Guidelines for psychological practice with older adults. *American Psychologist, 69,* 34–65. http://dx.doi.org/10.1037/a0035063

American Psychological Association. (2017a). *Ethical principles of psychologists and code of conduct* (2002, Amended June 1, 2010 and January 1, 2017). Washington, DC: American Psychological Association.

American Psychological Association. (2017b). *Multicultural guidelines: An ecological approach to context, identity, and intersectionality.* Retrieved from https://www.apa.org/about/policy/multicultural-guidelines.pdf

Barbas, N. R., & Wilde, E. A. (2001). Competency issues in dementia: Medical decision making, driving, and independent living. *Journal of Geriatric Psychiatry and Neurology, 14,* 199–212. http://dx.doi.org/10.1177/089198870101400405

Berkman, N. D., Sheridan, S. L., Donahue, K. E., Halpern, D. J., Viera, A., Crotty, K., . . . Viswanathan, M. (2011). *Health literacy interventions and outcomes: An updated systematic review* (Evidence Report/Technology Assessment No. 199). Rockville, MD: Agency for Healthcare Research and Quality.

Braddock, C. H., III, Fihn, S. D., Levinson, W., Jonsen, A. R., & Pearlman, R. A. (1997). How doctors and patients discuss routine clinical decisions. Informed decision making in the outpatient setting. *Journal of General Internal Medicine, 12,* 339–345.

Brown, S. C. (2007). How older adults learn medical information. In D. C. Park & L. L. Liu (Eds.), *Medical adherence and aging* (pp. 93–121). Washington, DC: American Psychological Association.

Bush, S. S., Allen, R. S., & Molinari, V. (2017). *Ethical practice in geropsychology.* Washington, DC: American Psychological Association. http://dx.doi.org/10.1037/0000010-000

Carlino, A. R., Stinnett, J. L., & Kim, D. R. (2013). New onset of bipolar disorder in late life. *Psychosomatics, 54,* 94–97. http://dx.doi.org/10.1016/j.psym.2012.01.006

Clark, L., Iversen, S. D., & Goodwin, G. M. (2002). Sustained attention deficit in bipolar disorder. *The British Journal of Psychiatry, 180,* 313–319. http://dx.doi.org/10.1192/bjp.180.4.313

Clark, L., Sarna, A., & Goodwin, G. M. (2005). Impairment of executive function but not memory in first-degree relatives of patients with bipolar I disorder and in euthymic patients with unipolar depression. *The American Journal of Psychiatry, 162,* 1980–1982. http://dx.doi.org/10.1176/appi.ajp.162.10.1980

Diefenbach, M. A., Miller-Halegoua, S., & Bowen, D. J. (Eds.). (2016). *Handbook of health decision science.* New York, NY: Springer. http://dx.doi.org/10.1007/978-1-4939-3486-7

Dunn, L. B., Nowrangi, M. A., Palmer, B. W., Jeste, D. V., & Saks, E. R. (2006). Assessing decisional capacity for clinical research or treatment: A review of instruments. *The American Journal of Psychiatry, 163,* 1323–1334. http://dx.doi.org/10.1176/ajp.2006.163.8.1323

Dunn, L. B., Palmer, B. W., Keehan, M., Jeste, D. V., & Appelbaum, P. S. (2006). Assessment of therapeutic misconception in older schizophrenia patients with a brief instrument. *The American Journal of Psychiatry, 163,* 500–506. http://dx.doi.org/10.1176/appi.ajp.163.3.500

Dymek, M. P., Marson, D. C., & Harrell, L. (1999). Factor structure of capacity to consent to medical treatment in patients with Alzheimer's disease: An exploratory study. *Journal of Forensic Neuropsychology, 1,* 27–48. http://dx.doi.org/10.1300/J151v01n01_03

Edelstein, B. (1999). *Hopemont Capacity Assessment Interview manual and scoring guide.* Morgantown, WV: Author.

Etchells, E., Darzins, P., Silberfeld, M., Singer, P. A., McKenny, J., Naglie, G., . . . Strang, D. (1999). Assessment of patient capacity to consent to treatment. *Journal of General Internal Medicine, 14,* 27–34. http://dx.doi.org/10.1046/j.1525-1497.1999.00277.x

Ferretti, L., McCurry, S. M., Logsdon, R., Gibbons, L., & Teri, L. (2001). Anxiety and Alzheimer's disease. *Journal of Geriatric Psychiatry and Neurology, 14,* 52–58. http://dx.doi.org/10.1177/089198870101400111

Fong, T. G., Tulebaev, S. R., & Inouye, S. K. (2009). Delirium in elderly adults: Diagnosis, prevention and treatment. *Nature Reviews. Neurology, 5,* 210–220. http://dx.doi.org/10.1038/nrneurol.2009.24

Gerontological Society of America. (2016). *Communication with older adults: Recognizing the hidden traps in health care decision making.* Washington, DC: Author.

Gilliard, J., Means, R., Beattie, A., & Daker-White, G. (2005). Dementia care in England and the social model of disability. *Dementia, 4,* 571–586. http://dx.doi.org/10.1177/1471301205058312

Griffith, H. R., Belue, K., Sicola, A., Krzywanski, S., Zamrini, E., Harrell, L., & Marson, D. C. (2003). Impaired financial abilities in mild cognitive impairment: A direct assessment approach. *Neurology, 60,* 449–457. http://dx.doi.org/10.1212/WNL.60.3.449

Grisso, T. (1994). Clinical assessments for legal competence of older adults. In M. Storandt & G. R. VandenBos (Eds.), *Neuropsychological assessment of dementia and depression in older adults: A clinician's guide* (pp. 119–139). Washington, DC: American Psychological Association.

Grisso, T., & Appelbaum, P. (1998). *Assessing competence to consent to treatment.* New York, NY: Oxford University Press.

Hendrie, H. C., Tu, W., Tabbey, R., Purnell, C. E., Ambuehl, R. J., & Callahan, C. M. (2014). Health outcomes and cost of care among older adults with schizophrenia: A 10-year study using medical records across the continuum of care. *The American Journal of Geriatric Psychiatry, 22,* 427–436. http://dx.doi.org/10.1016/j.jagp.2012.10.025

Hindmarch, T., Hotopf, M., & Owen, G. S. (2013). Depression and decision-making capacity for treatment or research: A systematic review. *BMC Medical Ethics, 14,* 54. http://dx.doi.org/10.1186/1472-6939-14-54

Hirschman, K. B., Xie, S. X., Feudtner, C., & Karlawish, J. H. (2004). How does an Alzheimer's disease patient's role in medical decision making change over time? *Journal of Geriatric Psychiatry and Neurology, 17,* 55–60. http://dx.doi.org/10.1177/0891988704264540

Kohn, N. A., Blumenthal, J. A., & Campbell, A. T. (2012). Supported decision-making: A viable alternative to guardianship. *Penn State Law Review, 117,* 1111–1157. http://dx.doi.org/10.2139/ssrn.2161115

Lichtenberg, P. A. (2012). Misdiagnosis of Alzheimer's disease: Case studies in capacity assessment. *Clinical Gerontologist, 35,* 42–56. http://dx.doi.org/10.1080/07317115.2011.626516

Liu, L. L., & Gonzalez, R. (2007). Judgment and decision processes in older adults' compliance with medical regimens. In D. C. Park & L. L. Liu (Eds.), *Medical adherence and aging* (pp. 201–232). Washington, DC: American Psychological Association. http://dx.doi.org/10.1037/11557-009

Lyketsos, C. G., & Olin, J. (2002). Depression in Alzheimer's disease: Overview and treatment. *Biological Psychiatry, 52,* 243–252. http://dx.doi.org/10.1016/S0006-3223(02)01348-3

Marson, D. C. (2001). Loss of financial competency in dementia: Conceptual and empirical approaches. *Aging, Neuropsychology, and Cognition, 8,* 164–181. http://dx.doi.org/10.1076/anec.8.3.164.827

Marson, D. C., Kerr, D. L., & McLaren, D. G. (2016). Financial decision-making and capacity in older adults. In K. W. Schaie & S. L. Willis (Eds.), *Handbook of the psychology of aging* (8th ed., pp. 361–388). Waltham, MA: Academic Press. http://dx.doi.org/10.1016/B978-0-12-411469-2.00019-4

Martin, R. C., Gerstenecker, A., Triebel, K. L., Falola, M., McPherson, T., Cutter, G., & Marson, D. C. (2019). Declining financial capacity in mild cognitive impairment: A six-year longitudinal study. *Archives of Clinical Neuropsychology, 34,* 152–161.

Maust, D. T., Blass, D. M., Black, B. S., & Rabins, P. V. (2008). Treatment decisions regarding hospitalization and surgery for nursing home residents with advanced dementia: The CareAD Study. *International Psychogeriatrics, 20,* 406–418. http://dx.doi.org/10.1017/S1041610207005807

Miller, L. M., Whitlatch, C. J., & Lyons, K. S. (2016). Shared decision-making in dementia: A review of patient and family carer involvement. *Dementia, 15,* 1141–1157. http://dx.doi.org/10.1177/1471301214555542

Moberg, P. J., & Rick, J. H. (2008). Decision-making capacity and competency in the elderly: A clinical and neuropsychological perspective. *NeuroRehabilitation, 23,* 403–413.

Moye, J., Armesto, J. C., & Karel, M. J. (2005). Evaluating capacity of older adults in rehabilitation settings: Conceptual models and clinical challenges. *Rehabilitation Psychology, 50,* 207–214. http://dx.doi.org/10.1037/0090-5550.50.3.207

Moye, J., Karel, M. J., Edelstein, B., Hicken, B., Armesto, J. C., & Gurrera, R. J. (2007). Assessment of capacity to consent to treatment: Challenges, the "ACCT" approach, future directions. *Clinical Gerontologist, 31,* 37–66. http://dx.doi.org/10.1080/07317110802072140

Moye, J., Karel, M. J., Gurrera, R. J., & Azar, A. R. (2006). Neuropsychological predictors of decision-making capacity over 9 months in mild-to-moderate dementia. *Journal of General Internal Medicine, 21,* 78–83. http://dx.doi.org/10.1111/j.1525-1497.2005.00288.x

Moye, J., & Marson, D. C. (2007). Assessment of decision-making capacity in older adults: An emerging area of practice and research. *The Journals of Gerontology: Series B. Psychological Sciences and Social Sciences, 62,* 3–P11. http://dx.doi.org/10.1093/geronb/62.1.P3

Moye, J., Marson, D. C., & Edelstein, B. (2013). Assessment of capacity in an aging society. *American Psychologist, 68,* 158–171. http://dx.doi.org/10.1037/a0032159

Nasreddine, Z. S., Phillips, N. A., Bédirian, V., Charbonneau, S., Whitehead, V., Collin, I., . . . Chertkow, H. (2005). The Montreal Cognitive Assessment, MoCA: A brief screening tool for mild cognitive impairment [erratum: see https://

doi.org/10.1111/jgs.15925]. *Journal of the American Geriatrics Society, 53,* 695–699. http://dx.doi.org/10.1111/j.1532-5415.2005.53221.x

Okai, D., Owen, G., McGuire, H., Singh, S., Churchill, R., & Hotopf, M. (2007). Mental capacity in psychiatric patients: Systematic review. *The British Journal of Psychiatry, 191,* 291–297. http://dx.doi.org/10.1192/bjp.bp.106.035162

Palmer, B. W., Ryan, K. A., Kim, H. M., Karlawish, J. H., Appelbaum, P. S., & Kim, S. Y. (2013). Neuropsychological correlates of capacity determinations in Alzheimer disease: Implications for assessment. *The American Journal of Geriatric Psychiatry, 21,* 373–381. http://dx.doi.org/10.1016/j.jagp.2012.11.008

Palmer, B. W., & Savla, G. N. (2007). The association of specific neuropsychological deficits with capacity to consent to research or treatment. *Journal of the International Neuropsychological Society, 13,* 1047–1059. http://dx.doi.org/10.1017/S1355617707071299

Qualls, S. H. (2007). Clinical interventions for decision making with impaired persons. In S. H. Qualls & M. A. Smyer (Eds.), *Changes in decision-making capacity in older adults: Assessment and intervention* (pp. 271–298). Hoboken, NJ: Wiley.

Rubright, J., Sankar, P., Casarett, D. J., Gur, R., Xie, S. X., & Karlawish, J. (2010). A memory and organizational aid improves Alzheimer disease research consent capacity: Results of a randomized, controlled trial. *The American Journal of Geriatric Psychiatry, 18,* 1124–1132. http://dx.doi.org/10.1097/JGP.0b013e3181dd1c3b

Sabat, S. R. (2005). Capacity for decision-making in Alzheimer's disease: Selfhood, positioning and semiotic people. *Australian and New Zealand Journal of Psychiatry, 39,* 1030–1035. http://dx.doi.org/10.1080/j.1440-1614.2005.01722.x

Sessums, L. L., Zembrzuska, H., & Jackson, J. L. (2011). Does this patient have medical decision-making capacity? *Journal of the American Medical Association, 306,* 420–427. http://dx.doi.org/10.1001/jama.2011.1023

Smebye, K. L., Kirkevold, M., & Engedal, K. (2012). How do persons with dementia participate in decision making related to health and daily care? A multi-case study. *BMC Health Services Research, 12,* 241–253. http://dx.doi.org/10.1186/1472-6963-12-241

Starkstein, S. E., Jorge, R., Petracca, G., & Robinson, R. G. (2007). The construct of generalized anxiety disorder in Alzheimer disease. *The American Journal of Geriatric Psychiatry, 15,* 42–49. http://dx.doi.org/10.1097/01.JGP.0000229664.11306.b9

Steeman, E., de Casterlé, B. D., Godderis, J., & Grypdonck, M. (2006). Living with early-stage dementia: A review of qualitative studies. *Journal of Advanced Nursing, 54,* 722–738. http://dx.doi.org/10.1111/j.1365-2648.2006.03874.x

Tariq, S. H., Tumosa, N., Chibnall, J. T., Perry, M. H., III, & Morley, J. E. M. (2006). Comparison of the Saint Louis University mental status examination and the mini-mental state examination for detecting dementia and mild neurocognitive disorder—A pilot study. *The American Journal of Geriatric Psychiatry, 14,* 900–910. http://dx.doi.org/10.1097/01.JGP.0000221510.33817.86

Tyrrell, J., Genin, N., & Myslinski, M. (2006). Freedom of choice and decision making in health and social care: Views of older patients with early-stage dementia and their carers. *Dementia, 5,* 479–502. http://dx.doi.org/10.1177/1471301206069915

3

Evaluating Capacities in Persons With Serious Mental Illness

Jessica V. Strong, Brian M. Ludwin, and Scott C. Fish

KEY POINTS

- Capacity for psychiatric treatment consent and independent living are common concerns in working with individuals with schizophrenia in an inpatient psychiatric setting.
- Core symptoms of schizophrenia, such as cognitive deficits, negative symptoms (e.g., apathy or impoverished speech), and positive symptoms (e.g., delusions or thought disorder), may compromise capacity in different ways.
- Capacity evaluations for individuals in inpatient psychiatric settings may present multiple challenges, including but not limited to assessment in the context of psychiatric instability, the establishment and maintenance of rapport, and the assessment and optimization of task engagement.

DEFINITION OF THE ISSUE

Persons with schizophrenia may experience diminished decision-making and functional capacity. Common domains of concern in this population, particularly in an inpatient psychiatric setting, include the capacity to consent to psychiatric treatment and the capacity to live independently. An evaluation of decision-making capacity in adults and older adults with schizophrenia in an

http://dx.doi.org/10.1037/0000184-004
Assessing Capacities of Older Adults: A Casebook to Guide Difficult Decisions, J. Moye (Editor)

inpatient psychiatric setting can present a range of challenges due to their complex and dynamic presentations. For the purposes of this chapter, we briefly review the clinical aspects of schizophrenia with an emphasis on findings in middle-aged and older adults and their relationship with decision-making and functional capacity. We then discuss common challenges with capacity assessments in this population and present two cases for illustration.

The reader should be aware that research into capacity evaluations, and particularly capacity evaluations in adults with schizophrenia, is an emergent area of study. The majority of our research knowledge of diminished capacity in schizophrenia is limited to stable outpatients diagnosed with schizophrenia or schizoaffective disorder. We caution our readers to apply the following findings judiciously with an inpatient population.

CLINICAL PRESENTATION

We begin by reviewing the common presentation of individuals with schizophrenia, including symptoms, onset, and prognosis and ultimately how symptoms relate to functional abilities and capacity.

Symptom Profile

Schizophrenia and its variants are distinguished symptomatically from other mental health disorders by their prominent positive (e.g., thought disorder, hallucinations, and delusions) and negative (e.g., deficits in motivation, pleasure, speech, and emotion expression) symptoms. The *Diagnostic and Statistical Manual of Mental Disorders* (fifth ed.; *DSM–5*; American Psychiatric Association, 2013) presents a commonly used classification system for differentiating schizophrenia and its variants, which include delusional disorder, brief psychotic disorder, schizophreniform disorder, schizoaffective disorder, and schizotypal personality disorder (American Psychiatric Association, 2013). Although all of the diagnoses, except schizotypal personality disorder, share an emphasis on the presence of delusions or hallucinations (or both), the diagnoses are largely differentiated from one another by the presence, prominence, or duration of these and other positive and negative symptoms.

Symptom Onset and Course

Schizophrenia occurs in approximately 4.0 per 1,000 individuals over their lifetime (Saha, Chant, Welham, & McGrath, 2005), and the prevalence in older adults may be similar to that in young adults (Meesters et al., 2012). Although schizophrenia is associated with a shorter life expectancy (Olfson, Gerhard, Huang, Crystal, & Stroup, 2015), many individuals with schizophrenia will become older adults, as the number of aging individuals with a schizophrenia diagnosis is increasing in concert with the general aging of the population (Cohen et al., 2000).

The onset, course, and outcome of schizophrenia's symptoms are heterogeneous. Symptom onset most often occurs in late adolescence or early adulthood (Tandon, Keshavan, & Nasrallah, 2008) but may occur in middle-aged or older adults in a minority of cases (Pearman & Batra, 2012). The trajectory of symptoms demonstrates significant variability across individuals and over time (Jobe & Harrow, 2005; Newman, Bland, & Thompson, 2012). For example, some people experience persistent severe symptoms, whereas others have intermittent symptoms that may partially or fully remit for variable lengths of time. Other mental health symptoms or disorders often accompany and may affect the severity and course of schizophrenia (Buckley, Miller, Lehrer, & Castle, 2009). Common comorbidities include substance abuse (47%), posttraumatic stress disorder (29%), depression (25%), obsessive–compulsive disorder (23%), and panic disorder (15%; Buckley et al., 2009).

Cognitive Abilities

There is strong empirical evidence that many individuals with schizophrenia experience cognitive deficits, largely distinct from positive symptoms and modestly related to negative and disorganized symptoms (de Gracia Dominguez, Viechtbauer, Simons, van Os, & Krabbendam, 2009). Cognitive deficits, typically of 0.25 to 0.50 standard deviation (a small-to-medium effect size), can be found before psychiatric symptom onset (Fusar-Poli et al., 2012; Woodberry, Giuliano, & Seidman, 2008). After symptom onset, deficits on the order of 0.5 to 1.5 standard deviations (medium-to-large effect size) are often found across most neuropsychological tests, with greatest deficits typically seen on measures of processing speed, complex attention and executive functions, and verbal learning and memory (Dickinson, Ramsey, & Gold, 2007; Fioravanti, Carlone, Vitale, Cinti, & Clare, 2005; Heinrichs & Zakzanis, 1998; Irani, Kalkstein, Moberg, & Moberg, 2011). Nonetheless, there is heterogeneity in the magnitude of cognitive deficits in individuals with schizophrenia (Dickinson et al., 2007; Heinrichs & Zakzanis, 1998; Mesholam-Gately et al., 2009), with about 15% to 30% performing within normal limits on neuropsychological tests (Kremen, Seidman, Faraone, Toomey, & Tsuang, 2000; Palmer et al., 1997). During the postonset period among middle-aged and older adults, there is evidence of divergent cognitive trajectories. The majority of older adults, whether community dwelling or chronically hospitalized, demonstrate stable cognition or mild decline. Sizable minorities who live in the community (10%–20%; Cohen & Murante, 2018; Thompson et al., 2013) or are chronically hospitalized (27.6%; Harvey et al., 1999) demonstrate more significant decline.

Functional Abilities

Functional deficits are common in individuals with schizophrenia across a range of domains, including interpersonal, work, academic, and independent living (Harvey et al., 2012). Functional deficits can be understood either in terms of functional capacity, defined as what an individual can do under ideal conditions, or in terms of real-world functioning, defined as what an individual does in actuality. Middle-aged and older adults with schizophrenia tend to have lower functional capacity for transportation, finances, shopping, and medication management relative to similarly aged unaffected individuals (Patterson et al., 1998, 2002) and for finances, transportation, and shopping relative to younger adults with schizophrenia (Kalache et al., 2015). When examining real-world functioning, middle-aged and older adults with schizophrenia tend to have lower rates of independent living, driving, and employment, but with significant heterogeneity such that some individuals achieve levels of functioning similar to those of unaffected adults (Palmer et al., 2002). In outpatient middle-aged and older adults, cognitive deficits are strong and consistent correlates of deficits in functional capacity (Evans et al., 2003; McClure et al., 2007; Patterson et al., 1998; Twamley et al., 2002), and the relationship of cognitive deficits and real-world functioning appears to be largely mediated by functional capacity (Bowie et al., 2008; Bowie, Reichenberg, Patterson, Heaton, & Harvey, 2006). Negative symptoms are consistently associated with functional capacity and real-world functioning, but there is mixed evidence about the relationship of positive and depressive symptoms with both types of functioning (Bowie et al., 2006, 2008; Evans et al., 2003; Harvey et al., 2003; Palmer et al., 2002; Twamley et al., 2002). Increased number of psychiatric hospital admissions also appears related to poorer performance of instrumental activities of daily living (IADLs) in the community after controlling for cognitive functioning (Lipskaya-Velikovsky, Kotler, Easterbrook, & Jarus, 2015).

Independent Living Capacity

Independent living, from the perspective of a capacity assessment, is a higher order psycholegal construct encapsulating numerous domains of functioning and involving both cognitive and procedural skills (Moye & Marson, 2007). Its primary functional elements include a conceptual understanding of what needs to be done day-to-day to care for self and home, the application of this knowledge via procedural skills—or with functional limitations, the insight into these limitations and ability to direct another agent—and sound judgment to execute these tasks in a manner that ensures one's health and safety (American Bar Association and American Psychological Association Assessment of Capacity in Older Adults Project Working Group [ABA/APA], 2008). The assessment of independent living capacity is based on multiple sources of information including but not limited to performance-based data, clinical symptoms, collateral information and preferences/values, and results in a clinical judgment classifying the individual's functioning into one of three levels (independent, semi-independent, or dependent). As described in the previous section, much is known about the functional difficulties associated with a diagnosis of schizophrenia. However, to our knowledge, there have been no research studies examining the psycholegal construct of independent living capacity in this population.

Treatment Consent Capacity

Treatment consent capacity is the ability to provide or withhold informed consent for treatment (Moye & Marson, 2007). This capacity is narrow in scope and primarily a cognitive task, involving four functional elements: understanding, appreciation, reasoning, and expression of a choice (ABA/APA, 2008; Moye & Marson, 2007). Specifically, these elements reflect an individual's ability to understand and appreciate his or her medical or psychiatric disorder(s) and the potential treatment pathways and to then reason through this information to provide a voluntary and informed treatment choice.

There has been some research into treatment consent capacity in individuals with schizophrenia. The proportion of individuals with schizophrenia who retain treatment consent capacity has varied widely across studies (e.g., 11%–100%), likely reflecting differences in sample and study characteristics (Spencer, Shields, Gergel, Hotopf, & Owen, 2017), but relative to healthy control participants, individuals with schizophrenia often demonstrate lower performance across the four domains of treatment consent (Wang et al., 2017). Reviews have suggested that cognitive abilities and insight are the most consistent and strongest correlates of consent capacity in individuals with schizophrenia, followed by negative symptoms with more modest associations and then positive symptoms with inconsistent and often attenuated associations (Palmer & Savla, 2007; Spencer et al., 2017). Minimal research has examined treatment consent capacity in older adults with schizophrenia; however, in one sample of community-dwelling middle-aged and older adults with schizophrenia, cognitive abilities, but not symptoms (positive or negative), were found to be a strong correlate of treatment consent capacity (Palmer, Dunn, Appelbaum, & Jeste, 2004).

CLINICAL METHODS

It is important to have a framework for capacity and, particularly, for how capacity may be applied with this specific population.

Conceptual Framework and Its Application

The ABA/APA Handbook (2008) provides a broad conceptual framework for assessing a wide range of civil capacities. The framework outlines how a clinician's assessment of and judgment about an individual's capacity for a specific domain is based on the relevant legal standard(s), functional elements related to the capacity domain, diagnoses, cognitive underpinnings, psychiatric and emotional factors, values, risk considerations, and efforts to support capacity. In addition, as indicated earlier, the ABA/APA Handbook provides further specifications to the framework when assessing specific capacity domains, such as treatment consent or independent living. There are several clinical considerations when implementing the ABA/APA framework in a capacity evaluation for individuals with schizophrenia.

Pragmatic Challenges

A few common, specific issues may arise when assessing capacity in individuals with schizophrenia, including presentation of psychiatric symptoms, establishing rapport, and engagement during the evaluation. We discuss how each of these issues and more should be considered to play a role in a capacity evaluation.

Psychiatric Instability

A common scenario involves the referral to evaluate capacity when an individual is not psychiatrically stable (i.e., not at their clinical baseline). Before the evaluation, a clinician should carefully weigh the risks and benefits of completing the evaluation when the patient is not psychiatrically stable versus postponing the evaluation until the person is stable. Referrals in the context of psychiatric instability typically involve treatment consent and occur in an inpatient psychiatric setting. This type of referral is appropriate because psychiatric symptoms may be interfering with the ability to provide informed consent to treatment that may improve these very symptoms, and delaying intervention may compromise the health and safety of the individual. However, there may be other instances in which it is not appropriate to assess a capacity domain when an individual is psychiatrically unstable. For decisions with potential long-term implications, such as independent living capacity, it is typically more appropriate to wait to assess this capacity until acute psychiatric symptoms have stabilized. In these cases, symptom management is the primary concern before disposition decisions should be made. One exception involves when a patient attempts to leave the hospital against medical advice (AMA), particularly when providers have significant concerns for the person's ability for self-care. In this case, assessment of aspects of independent living, with a focus on imminent and substantial safety and health risks, is appropriate. Conclusions and predictions should be qualified to reflect the presence of acute psychiatric symptoms, which may or may not resolve with a concomitant improvement in self-care abilities. Follow-up capacity evaluation after psychiatric symptom stabilization should be recommended in an effort to capture any potential recovery in functional capacity and to modify conclusions accordingly.

Emergent and Interrelated Capacity Domains

Another scenario involves the emergence of an unexpected question regarding a second capacity domain that also warrants evaluation. Careful consideration should be given, however, before proceeding with an expanded assessment. If the second capacity is directly relevant, as in the case when assessing for treatment consent capacity and capacity to name a health care proxy becomes apparent, and if additional information can be collected without impeding the initial evaluation, an expanded evaluation may be considered. However, the clinician should choose to approach this additional examination with a few caveats. First, there must be adequate understanding by the clinician of the unique framework for the second capacity, as delineated in the ABA/APA Handbook (2008). If the clinician has not had the time to reference or does not know the legal standard(s) or functional elements necessary to evaluate the second capacity, it should be considered as a second and separate evaluation. Second, the client must be able to tolerate an expanded assessment. If multiple additional information sources need to be collected or considered, the testing burden may be excessive and potentially invalidate cognitive or functional results. It may be that the clinician chooses to recommend to the referring team, court, or other source a follow-up capacity evaluation for the second capacity domain in question.

Rapport and Consent

Facilitating and establishing a sense of safety, control, and trust is important when conducting a capacity evaluation, but the presence of a thought disorder, active psychosis, affective dysregulation, and deficits in cognition and social abilities often complicate this goal. Establishing and maintaining rapport can be grounded in a person-centered approach that involves open and empathetic dialogue and normalization of unusual experiences (e.g., auditory hallucinations). We find that a critical time to build rapport occurs with the informed consent process of the requested evaluation. This discussion should include simple and clear language about its nature, purpose and potential risks and benefits, limits to confidentiality, and the examiner's role in the evaluation, which is determined by the type of capacity assessed. The importance of communicating distress related (or unrelated) to the evaluation, the opportunity for breaks, and the right to discontinue the evaluation should be emphasized, consistent with the APA's (2017) *Ethical Principles of Psychologists and Code of Conduct.*

Individuals with schizophrenia also commonly disagree with their diagnosis, descriptions of their cognitive and functional deficits, and the need for treatment and assistance. This disagreement may reflect clinical features of the illness, such as limited psychological insight (e.g., Sartorius, Shapiro, Kimura, & Barrett, 1972) or a psychotic process. However, it may also reflect an individual belief or value, and those with an active thought disorder or reduced verbal expressivity may struggle to explain their beliefs in an understandable manner. Social deficits common to schizophrenia may further contribute to such disagreements (Allen, Strauss, Donohue, & van Kammen, 2007; Pinkham, Penn, Perkins, & Lieberman, 2003). To better understand the source of an apparent disagreement over diagnosis and treatment, the examiner may consider using a person-centered approach that emphasizes the individual's way of understanding his or her experience while allowing for sharing of relevant clinical information.

Assessing and Optimizing Engagement

Eliciting and sustaining adequate engagement with a capacity evaluation is critical to the evaluation's validity and utility. Our clinical experience suggests that there is an elevated risk of poor engagement during capacity evaluations in an inpatient psychiatric setting. The factors leading to poor engagement may be wide-ranging, brief, or enduring and originate with the person, the environment, or both. These include illness-specific factors (e.g., acute psychotic and prominent negative symptoms), general clinical issues (e.g., fatigue, sedation, delirium due to polypharmacy), and, less commonly, secondary gain. We are unaware of any research examining performance validity testing in the context of civil capacity evaluations in this population. Nonetheless, there is growing evidence that individuals with psychotic presentations are more prone to failing performance validity tests (PVTs) than neurologically intact and neurologically disordered patients (Glassmire, Toofanian Ross, Kinney, & Nitch, 2016; Goldberg, Back-Madruga, & Boone, 2007; Gorissen, Sanz, & Schmand, 2005; Hunt, Root, & Bascetta, 2014; Moore et al., 2013; Schroeder & Marshall, 2011; Strauss, Morra, Sullivan, & Gold, 2015). These failure rates appear to vary across different tests, and greater failure rates are associated with common symptoms of schizophrenia, particularly negative symptoms and lower IQ scores (Glassmire et al., 2016; Gorissen et al., 2005; Moore et al., 2013; Morra, Gold, Sullivan, & Strauss, 2015; Strauss et al., 2015; Whearty, Allen, Lee, & Strauss, 2015).

We recommend the use of PVTs, particularly when cognitive and functional measures are integral to the assessment, along with careful clinical observation for signs of suboptimal or variable task engagement. In parallel with assessing engagement, clinicians should consider potential sources of disengagement and work to elicit and sustain engagement. For example, if fatigue is a concern, clinicians may complete the evaluation over multiple meetings, perform an abbreviated evaluation, or include frequent breaks. If pain or medication-related sedation is a concern, the clinician may adjust the timing of the evaluation around medication schedules or following medication reconciliation. Evaluations in the context of acute psychotic symptoms may be postponed following clinical stabilization unless there is a clinical indication for urgent assessment (e.g., refusal of antipsychotic medication, AMA discharge), as discussed earlier. Reasonable accommodations along with gentle prompting and encouragement may facilitate task engagement in the context of negative symptoms. Repetition, simplified language, frequent breaks, and extra time (when appropriate) can be useful strategies in general to enhance engagement and maximize understanding with this population.

Assessment Approaches

Evaluations of treatment consent and independent living capacity may use a variety of methods and sources (see Table 3.1). Both types of evaluations are grounded in a clinical interview and chart review and are commonly supplemented with structured interviews, self- and other-report measures, and performance measures. More specifically, treatment consent capacity is typically assessed with one of several semistructured interviews that index each of the functional elements described earlier. Independent living capacity evaluations

TABLE 3.1. Common Clinical Assessment Tools

Domains	Assessment tools
Capacity	
Treatment consent	Semistructured interviews: • Assessment of the Capacity to Consent to Treatment (Moye et al., 2007) • Hopemont Capacity Assessment Interview (Edelstein, 1999) • Capacity to Consent to Treatment Interview (Marson, Ingram, Cody, & Harrell, 1995) • MacArthur Competence Assessment Tool for Treatment (Grisso & Appelbaum, 1998)
Independent Living	Functional measures: • Independent Living Scales (Loeb & Fe, 1996) • Texas Functional Living Scales (Cullum et al., 2001)
Cognition	Global cognitive screeners: • Mattis Dementia Rating Scale—2 (Jurica, Leitten, & Mattis, 1988) • Montreal Cognitive Assessment (Nasreddine et al., 2005) • Repeatable Battery for the Assessment of Neuropsychological Status (Randolph, Tierney, Mohr, & Chase, 1998)
All domains (functional, cognition, psychiatric, emotional, medical, values, risks, enhancing capacity)	• Clinical interview with supplemental symptom ratings measures as needed (e.g., Geriatric Depression Scale, Scale for the Assessment of Positive/Negative Symptoms) • Collateral information • Chart review • Consultation with medical providers, interdisciplinary team, legal counsel

are often more comprehensive in their use of self- and other-report of real-world functioning, functional capacity measures, or neuropsychological assessment. The practitioner interprets the information, responses, and performances from these sources within the broad and specific capacity frameworks to render a clinical judgment regarding whether an individual retains capacity within a specific domain.

CASE EXAMPLES

With an understanding of the specific population, we present two cases to illustrate the common issues considered and different approaches to completing a capacity evaluation.[1]

[1]Although the case examples in this chapter are based on the authors' clinical experiences, personal details of the individuals described have been changed to protect their identities.

Case 1: Ms. April—Treatment Consent Capacity for Electroconvulsive Therapy

Ms. Laura April was a woman in her 60s on an inpatient mental health unit receiving treatment for refractory psychosis. Her attending psychiatrist referred her to psychology to determine whether she retained capacity to consent to electroconvulsive therapy (ECT). The treatment team recommended ECT, and after a week of vacillation, the patient agreed to undergo ECT. Her psychiatrist, however, expressed concerns about Ms. April's decision-making process. Ms. April was divorced with no children, and she had limited contact with a geographically distant family member. She had not appointed a surrogate decision-maker through an advance directive. In addition to her psychotic disorder, she was diagnosed with recent tonic–clonic seizures and diabetes mellitus, which are described along with additional clinical history in Exhibit 3.1.

Ms. April was administered a semistructured interview regarding her treatment consent capacity due to the complexity of the ECT procedure (see Table 3.2). Given her recent seizures and past cognitive testing results, we wanted to assess her cognition as part of the evaluation. Due to her fatigue and difficulties engaging over the course of the capacity interview, we decided first to attempt a cognitive screen with relevant age norms (APA, 2014). However, she was unable to engage effectively with the cognitive screen, and additional testing was not attempted.

Findings

During our evaluation, we found that Ms. April demonstrated limited understanding of the risks of ECT as she focused principally on the risks from the anesthesia, and despite repetition and simplification of the risks specific to ECT (e.g., headache and short-term memory loss), she was unable to learn and use this information in her decision-making. She also demonstrated variable understanding of the risks of not pursuing ECT, as well as the risks of increasing the dosage of risperidone. By contrast, she showed insight into her auditory hallucinations but not her thought disorder, and she was also able to identify and appreciate the benefits of ECT. She also expressed a clear choice to pursue ECT and stated how this decision was consistent with her value of improving her quality of life. While her choice was consistent on current evaluation, the reasoning inherent to this decision was limited because of her attentional bias toward potential ECT benefits without adequate consideration of its risks (especially more common risks), likely due to her trouble fully understanding and appreciating these risks. Furthermore, she was not able to articulate the reason for the recent change in her choice of pursuing ECT. Given all of this information, we concluded that Ms. April's preference for ECT was not well informed or reasoned and, as such, that she lacked the capacity to consent to ECT at that time.

Analysis

Ms. April's case exemplifies a few important factors to consider when completing a capacity evaluation with an older adult who is actively psychotic,

EXHIBIT 3.1

Ms. April's Clinical History

Capacity-Specific Background

- Electroconvulsive therapy (ECT)
  - Current history:
    - Before the evaluation, Ms. April initially declined due to concerns about unlikely side effects
    - After a week, she requested ECT in the context of persistent, distressing auditory hallucinations
  - Past history:
    - Indicated willingness to receive ECT in an advance directive several years ago
    - No history of ECT
  - Values:
    - Her primary value was to live an enjoyable life

Cognitive and Functional History

- Most recent neuropsychology evaluation (5 years ago while an inpatient with refractory psychosis):
  - Deficits in aspects of executive functioning (planning and conceptualization) (at least <1.5 *SD*) and memory (<2 *SD*)
  - Moderate declines in cognition and function relative to two prior evaluations spanning over the past 15 years
- Performance-based functional capacity assessment of independent living skills:
  - Total performance on Texas Functional Living Scale this admission fell in a range (t = 26; moderate impairment) suggesting that significant assistance with living skills would be required in the community

Mental Health History

- Current presentation:
  - Refractory auditory hallucinations (e.g., derogatory and accusatory) with mild-to-moderate thought disorder
  - Multiple failed medication trials (including medication washout)
- Historical presentation:
  - Chronic, fluctuating psychosis and thought disorder, and mood disruptions
- Historical diagnoses:
  - Chronic schizophrenia vs. schizoaffective disorder, bipolar type

Medical History

- During admission (6 months before evaluation):
  - Experienced tonic—clonic seizure and then postictal delirium. Diagnosed with temporal lobe epilepsy. No prior history of seizure or subsequent seizures.
- Magnetic resonance imaging scan (6 months before evaluation):
  - Mild scattered white matter hyperintensities; otherwise unremarkable
- Diabetes mellitus type II, poorly controlled

Medications

- Phenytoin, risperidone, haloperidol (as needed with regular use), divalproex, melatonin, insulin aspart and glargine, and benztropine
- Long preadmission history of numerous psychotropic medication trials with variable efficacy; history of side effects and intermittent nonadherence

(continues)

EXHIBIT 3.1

Ms. April's Clinical History (Continued)

Developmental and Educational History

- Unremarkable early medical, developmental, socioemotional, and academic history
- Graduated high school and then completed a 2-year professional degree

Social History

- Divorced
- No children

Military and Vocational History

- Worked as a health care provider for several years
- Disabled after onset of psychosis

particularly the interplay of psychosis, thought disorder, cognitive deficits, and decision-making, as well as the adjustment of capacity thresholds due to contextual risks.

An individual's decision-making abilities are intricately linked with the person's thought content and processes and affective state; active psychosis often influences and, in some cases, can significantly impair how an individual comes to a decision. Ms. April's case demonstrates an example in which long-standing cognitive deficits coupled with active psychosis and associated anxious distress influenced her decision-making. Specifically, Ms. April perceived a voice sounding like a loudspeaker that aggressively put her down and accused her of being a liar and killing her past patients and had experienced this voice for years. She experienced anxious distress related to the nature and persistence of her hallucinations. The evaluation revealed that Ms. April was motivated to seek treatment to relieve her hallucinations and associated

TABLE 3.2. Evaluation Techniques Used With Ms. April

Domain	Technique
Treatment consent capacity	Semistructured interview • Modeled on ABA/APA *Assessment of the Capacity to Consent to Treatment* (Moye et al., 2007) • Included information about purpose, procedure, benefits and risks of ECT (plus anesthesia) vs. alternative treatment (e.g., continued or augmented antipsychotic medication regimen) • Information was presented orally and on written handouts and then further simplified and scaffolded during the evaluation due to cognitive deficits
Global cognitive functioning	Montreal Cognitive Assessment (Nasreddine et al., 2005) • Widely used, brief cognitive screen with alternate forms and normative data • Patient was unable to complete

Note. ABA/APA = American Bar Association and American Psychological Association; ECT = electroconvulsive therapy.

distress to improve her quality of life. However, we found that her cognitive deficits and distress limited her capacity to attend to and learn new information. For example, she demonstrated poor learning for information about the risks of ECT, even with simplification, repetition, and provision of handouts for use as a reference in an effort to reduce working memory demands and enhance learning via multiple modalities. Even when encouraged to refer directly to the handout listing the risks, Ms. April demonstrated limited appreciation for these, likely reflecting how distress may hinder effortful, logical thinking as well as amplify the use of cognitive biases. For example, Ms. April's poor integration of information about treatment risks may have been influenced by a confirmatory bias in which she was highly motivated to find a method to reduce her distress, leading her to attend to and use information consistent with her goal of feeling better (e.g., benefits of ECT) and ignore information inconsistent with that goal (e.g., risks of either treatment choice).

Nonetheless, Ms. April's diminished understanding and appreciation of treatment risks were not inherently sufficient to determine that she lacked capacity to consent to treatment until considered within the context of the potential severity of risks specific to ECT. For example, Ms. April could have demonstrated a superficial understanding and appreciation of a blood draw's risks yet retained capacity to consent to the procedure due to the low probability of significant risks. However, ECT may result in serious side effects both from the procedure and use of general anesthesia, and the severity of some of these side effects was potentially heightened in Ms. April's case. For example, there was concern that ECT might at least temporarily worsen her already compromised short-term memory, with negative implications for her everyday functioning. Given the severity of the potential risks of ECT for her, we believed she needed to demonstrate a sound understanding and appreciation of the risks of this treatment. In essence, the threshold required for her to retain capacity was raised commensurately with the potential risk severity of this treatment.

Supports

During the evaluation, we supported Ms. April by providing empathy for her distress, repeating and simplifying information, providing information through verbal and visual modalities, and limiting the extent of the evaluation due to her difficulties with engagement. After the evaluation, we recommended that the team find Ms. April's distant family member and then assessed with the team the suitability of the family member and whether Ms. April found the individual acceptable for the role.

Recommendations

We recommended the following to the team:

- Find and activate a surrogate decision-maker for Ms. April.
- Reevaluate her decision-making capacities once psychiatrically stable in an effort to afford her the opportunity to demonstrate capacity for treatment

consent and promote independent decision-making. This recommendation was based on our prognostication that her decision-making abilities might improve to some extent with amelioration of her psychosis and distress but that her cognitive deficits may continue independently to interfere with her decision-making.

- Continue psychiatric hospitalization and treatment.

Outcome

Upon receipt of the recommendations, the team did the following:

- Invoked federal surrogacy rules and appointed a family member as a surrogate decision-maker after seeking Ms. April's assent to the appointment.
- The surrogate decision-maker provided consent for Ms. April to undergo ECT. She completed more than 10 sessions with a positive response in terms of psychotic and mood symptoms.
- Nonetheless, she remained hospitalized on a long-term care unit due to intermittent periods of worsening symptoms and function, as well as placement difficulties.

Case 2: Mr. May—Independent Living Capacity

Mr. Howard May was a man in his early 60s on an inpatient psychiatric unit with a long-standing diagnosis of schizophrenia (paranoid-type) and mood instability (a diagnosis of bipolar disorder with psychotic features has also been considered), referred for evaluation of his capacity to live independently. He had not lived in the community since the death of his wife, a few years earlier. He expressed a strong desire to discharge home from the hospital; however, providers had concerns about his ability to live independently. At the time of the referral, he was medication adherent and considered at his clinical baseline with refractory delusions.

Mr. May is widowed with no children but with close relationships with brothers, nieces, and nephews; he has not appointed a surrogate decision-maker through an advance directive. In addition to his mental health concerns, he has been treated for acute myeloid leukemia as noted with additional clinical history in Exhibit 3.2.

Mr. May completed an interview, along with cognitive and functional testing, as presented in Table 3.3. Tests were selected with relevant age norms to provide information about diverse cognitive domains within a relatively brief time period, to allow also for standardized assessment of independent living, within the context of what he could tolerate. The Independent Living Scales (ILS; Loeb & Fe, 1996) were used as a functional capacity instrument to assess skills relevant for independent living in specific domains such as home, transportation, health, and safety. Total or subtest performance is compared with community norms and classified into one of three categories: (a) high/independent—living independently in the community, (b) moderate/semi-independent—living in

EXHIBIT 3.2

Mr. May's Clinical History

Capacity-Specific Background

- Independent Living
  - During admission:
    - Medication adherent but struggled to verbalize benefits of taking medications and how medication was related to his hospitalization
    - Independent in basic activities of daily living (ADLs), with reminders and prompting from staff for hygiene-related behaviors
  - Past history:
    - Majority of his life lived in community with wife, punctuated by a handful of long-term hospitalizations precipitated by poor medication adherence
    - Wife managed all instrumental ADLs
    - Has not lived independently since death of wife

Functional History

- Total performance on functional capacity measure of independent living skills (Texas Functional Living Scales) fell in the lower end of the range observed in individuals living independently ($t = 45$; low average).

Mental Health and Psychiatric History

- Current presentation:
  - Refractory somatic and paranoid delusions about medical conditions and medication side effects, despite medical evidence to the contrary
- Historical presentations:
  - Chronic paranoia related to medication side effects
  - Persecutory and somatic delusions
  - Auditory hallucinations
- Historical diagnoses:
  - Paranoid schizophrenia versus bipolar I—severe, with psychosis
- One remote suicide attempt

Current Medications

- Acetaminophen liquid, haloperidol, lithium, lorazepam as needed, paliperidone intramuscular injection (monthly), trazodone

Medical History

- Acute myeloid leukemia (AML; type of bone marrow cancer) treated with chemotherapy without maturation
- At time of evaluation, he was medically stable with ongoing risk of AML recurrence
- Recent computed tomography scan of head: negative for acute intracranial hemorrhage, large infarction or mass

Developmental and Educational History

- Some academic difficulty
- High school graduation and some college

Social History

- Widowed
- No children
- Close family relationships with brothers, nieces, nephews
- Smoked three packs per day for 35 years

Military and Vocational History

- One tour in Vietnam
- Unknown vocational history

TABLE 3.3. Evaluation Techniques Used With Mr. May

Domain	Test
Clinical interview	Interview focused on independent living
Estimated baseline intellectual functioning	Wechsler Test of Adult Reading (The Psychological Corporation, 2001)
Cognitive functioning	Repeatable Battery for the Assessment of Neuropsychological Status (Randolph, Tierney, Mohr, & Chase, 1998), Trail Making Test A and B (Reitan, 1956), Wechsler Adult Intelligence Scale—III (Wechsler, 1997) Digit Span, Wisconsin Card Sorting Test—64 card version (Kongs et al., 2000)
Functional capacity assessment	Independent Living Scales: Healthy & Safety, Managing Home & Transportation subscales (Loeb & Fe, 1996)

supervised setting or with support, or (c) low/dependent—living in a nursing home or with full-time caregivers.

Findings

Capacity interview.

- Home—wife managed the housekeeping, grocery shopping, transportation, and finances. Mr. May shared food preparation but preferred not to use the stove. He acknowledges needing ongoing help in these areas.
- Medications—historically managed own medications, which often resulted in discontinuation and psychiatric hospitalization. He is able to provide the names of his medications and some of the purposes (i.e., "lithium is for my mood and Ativan slows my heart down and keeps me calm"). He discontinues his medication after changes in medication or providers due to suspiciousness. He is able to discuss the side effects and risks of medications, but generally unable to describe specific benefits.
- Cognitive and Functional—He denies any difficulties with cognitive functioning or basic activities of daily living (ADLs; e.g., showering, dressing).
- Mental Health—He believes he has a mental health illness, which he identifies as depression.

Neuropsychological test scores. Standardized scores below are based on age-adjusted normative comparisons available in published manual norms unless noted otherwise by an asterisk (see Table 3.4). Overall, Mr. May's baseline intellectual ability was estimated to fall in the high end of the average range. This range served as the benchmark to which all other performances were compared. In this context, he showed modest decline (1.5 *SD*) on a gross measure of neuropsychological functioning. Specifically, he showed modest impairment (i.e., 3rd–16th percentile, per *DSM–5*) in complex attention/visuomotor processing speed and verbal learning for unstructured material, and some aspects of executive functioning, specifically, set-shifting. His very

TABLE 3.4. Neuropsychological Tests and Scores by Domain

Domain or test	Raw score	Standardized score, percentile
Validity		
RBANS-A Effort Index[a] (Randolph et al., 1998)	1	Suggestive of adequate effort
Estimated baseline intellectual/cognitive ability		
WTAR (The Psychological Corporation, 2001)	36	eFSIQ = 108, 70
General cognitive functioning		
RBANS-A Total Scale (Randolph et al., 1998)	—	84SS, 14
Attention and processing speed		
RBANS-A Attention Index (Randolph et al., 1998)	—	85SS, 16
Digit Span (LDSF = 6)	9	8ss, 25
Coding (six errors)	38	7ss, 16
TMT-A (Reitan, 1956; no errors)	40	40t[b], 16
Learning and memory		
RBANS-A Immediate Memory Index (Randolph et al., 1998)	—	90SS, 25
List Learning (4,5,6,7)	22	6ss, 9
Story Memory (10,11)	21	11ss, 63
RBANS-A Delayed Memory Index (Randolph et al., 1998)	—	81SS, 10
List Recall	3	10–16 cumulative %
List Recognition (0 FPs)	17	3–9 cumulative %
Story Recall	9	10ss, 50
Figure Recall	11	8ss, 25
Executive functioning		
WAIS-III (Wechsler, 1997): DSB (LDSB)	9 (6)	24 cumulative %
TMT-B (Reitan, 1956; 1 set loss error)	122	39t*, 14
WCST-64 (Kongs et al., 2000)	Discontinued	Discontinued
Language		
RBANS-A Language Index (Randolph et al., 1998)	—	101SS, 53
Picture Naming	10	51–75 cumulative %
Semantic Fluency	22	10ss, 50
Visuospatial and construction (VS/C)		
RBANS-A VS/C Index (Randolph et al., 1998)	—	87SS, 19
Figure Copy	17	8ss, 25
Line Orientation	15	26–50 cumulative %

Note. eFSIQ = Estimated WAIS-III full-scale IQ; FP = false positives; LDSF = longest digit span forward; RBANS = Repeatable Battery for the Assessment of Neuropsychological Status; SS = standard score (*M* = 100, *SD* = 15); ss = scaled score (*M* = 10, *SD* = 3); t = t score (*M* = 50, *SD* = 10); TMT = Trail Making Test; WAIS = Wechsler Adult Intelligence Scale; WCST = Wisconsin Card Sorting Test; WTAR = Wechsler Test of Adult Reading.
[a]Silverberg, Wertheimer, and Fichtenberg (2007); see Shura et al. (2018) for a systematic review and meta-analysis. [b]Heaton et al. (2004; ethnicity, age, gender, and education corrected).

poor performance on a measure of hypothesis testing and problem-solving reflected impaired set-shifting ability or mental inflexibility. In contrast, he showed intact simple attention, working memory, visuospatial/construction, language (naming, semantic fluency), visual memory, and verbal learning/memory for structured material.

Functional capacity testing. Functional assessment (see Table 3.5) on the ILS ranged from independent (home and transportation) to dependent (health and safety).

Conclusion

We concluded that Mr. May did not have the ability to safely live independently; however, we chose to argue that he would be able to live semi-independently, departing from the classic dichotomous framework. Although we discuss the factors we weighed in detail below, briefly, we first considered Mr. May's history of serious mental illness characterized by symptoms, including limited insight, that directly contribute to treatment noncompliance and subsequent psychiatric decompensation and difficulty caring for himself in the community. Second, Mr. May has not lived independently in the community since the death of his wife, and when living in the community, his wife had performed most IADLs. Third, he showed modest cognitive impairment, particularly salient for difficulty in aspects of executive functioning. Fourth, he evidenced limited understanding of basic health and hygiene, consistent with his presentation and behavior on the ward.

We also noted Mr. May's strengths, which we believed would allow him to live semiindependently, in a less restrictive setting than the inpatient psychiatric unit but with ongoing support. We noted that while he performed below expectations in some cognitive domains, other performances were within expectations or broadly within normal limits, including basic attention, working memory, visual memory, and verbal learning and memory for structured information. He also performed within a range consistent with individuals living independently in the community on a measure of skills related to managing a home and transportation, and he showed some insight into needing assistance with some tasks and accepting of help in the home. Additionally, although his performance on a test of health and safety matters was impaired overall, there were no acute or imminent safety concerns.

Analysis of Independent Living Capacity

Functional ability and influence of medication adherence. One of the most important factors in this case was consideration of Mr. May's functional capacity

TABLE 3.5. Functional Test Scores

Independent Living Scale	Raw score	T-score, descriptive category
Managing Home and Transportation	28	53 t, high/independent
Health and Safety	31	39 t, low/dependent

(i.e., what he was capable of doing), and specifically how this may differ in the controlled inpatient test environment where he was largely psychiatrically stable versus what he had done in the community in a less structured environment and would potentially do in the future. A fundamental question to answer in this evaluation is whether Mr. May could maintain his health and safety in the community, particularly if living alone. In other words, does Mr. May have the skills necessary to live alone safely? If not, what support services would be required to ensure these conditions?

To answer the question of whether Mr. May could safely live independently, we collected a few pieces of information. First, his general neuropsychological functioning was important, with the idea that significant cognitive or intellectual impairment is predictive of functional outcome (McClure et al., 2007; Patterson et al., 1998). In regard to his neuropsychological performance, he showed modest impairment in areas of complex attention and visuomotor processing speed, verbal learning, and executive functioning, consistent with cognitive difficulties often found in schizophrenia. Although only modest in magnitude based on normative comparisons, these deficits may reflect significant declines for Mr. May given his estimated premorbid intellect (i.e., high end of average range). Baseline and serial assessments (if possible) of cognitive functioning are one important piece of information that may help to inform functional capacity deficits, which are important for determining independent living capacity. Although neuropsychological functioning may be predictive of functional outcome, there may be intervening variables (Bowie et al., 2006, 2008) that make specific neuropsychological scores less helpful at determining whether an individual can perform a specific skill directly relevant to independent living.

Therefore, the second piece of information we collected was a measure of his functional capacity—that is, his capability, under controlled conditions, to perform specific tasks and activities important for living independently in the community (Patterson & Mausbach, 2010). Functional capacity of IADLs may be divided into broad skills, such as the management of health, safety, home, and transportation, or more domain specific skills, such as the management of medications or money, or ability to cook, shop, or perform specific domestic duties (e.g., laundry). We were most interested in assessing skills relevant to his health and safety in the community. We used the Health and Safety and Managing Home and Transportation scales of the ILS. Both assess cognitive (e.g., knowledge, judgment) and procedural skills involved in either (a) ensuring one's general health and hygiene and immediate safety in a variety of potentially dangerous domestic and medical scenarios (e.g., appropriately dialing 911) or (b) ability to recognize and repair domestic problems (e.g., house is always very hot or cold) as well as use public transportation and a map. We relied on his self-report and collateral information for other IADLs (e.g., cooking, housekeeping, shopping, managing money). For basic ADLs, we questioned members of the nursing staff who had direct observations over the past few months of his ability to perform these tasks. In regard to his functional capacity,

Mr. May performed comparably to other individuals living independently in the community on matters of home upkeep and transportation (as assessed on the ILS). Although he demonstrated some concerns in terms of long-term health care management and hygiene, no imminent safety concerns were indicated in his ILS responses (e.g., he understood how to get immediate medical attention in a medical emergency and ensure his immediate safety in a potentially dangerous domestic situation).

The ability to perform a given behavior may not necessarily translate into real-world functioning for several reasons. Of relevance to this case, results were obtained when Mr. May was medication adherent and at his psychiatric and medical baseline, in a controlled environment on an inpatient unit. Thus, we had significant concerns that these results would not translate to the real-world environment (at least not for long) due to his history of poor treatment compliance. Historically, Mr. May's poor treatment compliance resulted in psychiatric and cognitive decompensation, undermining his ability to care for himself and live alone. His poor treatment compliance was likely driven by refractory psychiatric factors (e.g., poor insight and delusional thinking), cognitive deficits (particularly executive dysfunction), and the relationship between the two. Limited ability to problem-solve and consider alternatives, for example, likely contributed to his delusional beliefs about medications. Mental inflexibility may have also contributed to his difficulty adjusting to medication changes in the real world.

Our opinion that Mr. May should be able to live semi-independently was based on largely normal performance in some cognitive domains and one functional measure, balanced with self- and other-report of real-world functioning, modest impairments in key areas of executive functioning, including mental inflexibility, his chronic serious mental illness, and his current presentation, which included refractory psychotic symptoms with direct implications for medication compliance. The next step was to discharge Mr. May to a less restrictive environment, but not to an independent setting. Ultimately, we felt that Mr. May might be able to live independently in the long term if he had a trusted other who was able to help him manage his medications.

This brings us to our second question: What support services would Mr. May need to be successful in the community? We based our recommendations on historical evidence as well as his insight into needing assistance with some activities. Mr. May knew that his wife had provided him with a lot of help and support and demonstrated this insight by noting that he would likely need some help in the home. Therefore, we recommended he receive assistance with key tasks that his wife had managed, including food preparation (Meals on Wheels), finances (brother acting as fiduciary), and medication (injectable with consistent provider). Medication adherence was our biggest concern because historically Mr. May failed in the community after decompensation related to stopping his psychiatric medications. Injectables may be less triggering because they occur less frequently (i.e., monthly) compared with oral medication (i.e., daily).

Personal Values

An equally important aspect of any capacity evaluation is the personal preference of the individual. Not all individuals voice a strong preference related to the capacity in question, but in the current case, Mr. May had a strong preference for independence. This preference seemed to be tied to two factors: (a) He had lived in the community with his wife for most of his life and (b) he had a dog and was worried about the fate of his pet were he to live in an assisted or group home. Initially, when we discussed the possibility of a group home or assisted living, Mr. May was vehemently opposed. He demonstrated insight into some deficits, however, and later acknowledged that he needed some help. He was also willing and even excited to accept help into the home. Past behavior showed us that he did better with structure, consistent with his executive weaknesses and medication compliance. Therefore, when we consider his value for independence, we thought we could enhance his capacity for semi-independent living in a group home with a few targeted recommendations.

Supports

We conducted the capacity evaluation with sensitivity to Mr. May's needs by breaking the evaluation into separate sessions, with an extended break in between, which ensured that he was able to engage more fully. We also used the interview not only to assess Mr. May's appreciation of the risks and benefits of independent living but also to explore any reservations he had about a particular outcome related to his living situation. This discussion served to help him understand that we had his best interests in mind by balancing his concerns, safety, and well-being.

Recommendations

We recommended the following:

- Stepdown to a structured living environment to receive assistance with complex IADLs, including medication management, shopping, cooking, housekeeping, and finances.
- Ongoing and updated information about his medications. He will benefit from repetition and extra time to learn new information regarding medications. Clear explanations of medications he is prescribed, as well as benefits and risks (and alternatives), should be provided on a regular basis. He may benefit from assistance overcoming barriers to taking medications and finding alternatives. Additionally, he may remain more adherent if he receives a monthly injection.
- Mr. May will benefit from working with consistent providers to help him feel more comfortable. He is more trusting and has fewer delusions when interacting with the same provider.
- Mr. May was excited about the idea of having a case manager to help him adjust to living outside the hospital and provide social support and clinical oversight in the community

- Mr. May might enjoy participating in a day treatment program for social and intellectual stimulation that also offers daily structure.

Outcome

- Mr. May was discharged to a group home in stable condition.
- After a few months, Mr. May experienced an increase in delusional thinking and decided he would no longer take lithium.
- He was readmitted to psychiatric hospital and assigned a federal conservator and a guardian.
- Recurrence of acute myeloid leukemia and a second course of chemotherapy resulted in an increase in psychotic symptoms and high levels of psychiatric and emotional distress. Cancer treatment was discontinued by his guardian after discussions with the palliative care team and Mr. May.
- Patient ultimately passed away in the hospital about a year after the capacity evaluation.

REFLECTION

The interaction of psychiatric symptoms and cognition presents a unique range of challenges to a capacity assessment for an individual with schizophrenia. Some challenges include determining whether to initiate or defer a capacity assessment or examine aspects of capacity domains outside the primary ones, making judgments or individualized capacity threshold adjustments in the face of complex presentations, understanding when and how to optimize an individual's engagement with and performance on evaluation, and developing recommendations that respect an individual's values and preferences while ensuring safety (APA, 2017). In the face of such challenges, we believe knowledge of professional guides to capacity assessment, access to peer and interdisciplinary consultation, knowledge of legal standards and professional ethical codes, and flexible and judicious use of one's clinical skills (e.g., keen observation, interpersonal empathy, hypothesis testing, case conceptualization) will serve to identify these challenges and develop responses to them that will serve the best interests of all those involved in or impacted by a capacity assessment.

REFERENCES

Allen, D. N., Strauss, G. P., Donohue, B., & van Kammen, D. P. (2007). Factor analytic support for social cognition as a separable cognitive domain in schizophrenia. *Schizophrenia Research, 93*, 325–333. http://dx.doi.org/10.1016/j.schres.2007.02.008

American Bar Association and American Psychological Association Assessment of Capacity in Older Adults Project Working Group. (2008). *Assessment of older adults with diminished capacity: A handbook for psychologists*. Washington, DC: American Bar Association and American Psychological Association.

American Psychiatric Association. (2013). *Diagnostic and statistical manual of mental disorders* (5th ed.). Arlington, VA: Author.

American Psychological Association. (2014). Guidelines for psychological practice with older adults. *American Psychologist, 69,* 34–65. http://dx.doi.org/10.1037/a0035063

American Psychological Association. (2017). *Ethical principles of psychologists and code of conduct* (2002, Amended June 1, 2010 and January 1, 2017). Retrieved from http://www.apa.org/ethics/code/index.aspx

Bowie, C. R., Leung, W. W., Reichenberg, A., McClure, M. M., Patterson, T. L., Heaton, R. K., & Harvey, P. D. (2008). Predicting schizophrenia patients' real-world behavior with specific neuropsychological and functional capacity measures. *Biological Psychiatry, 63,* 505–511. http://dx.doi.org/10.1016/j.biopsych.2007.05.022

Bowie, C. R., Reichenberg, A., Patterson, T. L., Heaton, R. K., & Harvey, P. D. (2006). Determinants of real-world functional performance in schizophrenia subjects: Correlations with cognition, functional capacity, and symptoms. *The American Journal of Psychiatry, 163,* 418–425. http://dx.doi.org/10.1176/appi.ajp.163.3.418

Buckley, P. F., Miller, B. J., Lehrer, D. S., & Castle, D. J. (2009). Psychiatric comorbidities and schizophrenia. *Schizophrenia Bulletin, 35,* 383–402. http://dx.doi.org/10.1093/schbul/sbn135

Cohen, C. I., Cohen, G. D., Blank, K., Gaitz, C., Katz, I. R., Leuchter, A., . . . Shamoian, C. (2000). Schizophrenia and older adults. An overview: Directions for research and policy. *The American Journal of Geriatric Psychiatry, 8,* 19–28. http://dx.doi.org/10.1097/00019442-200002000-00003

Cohen, C. I., & Murante, T. (2018). A prospective analysis of the role of cognition in three models of aging and schizophrenia. *Schizophrenia Research, 196,* 22–28.

Cullum, C. M., Saine, K., Chan, L. D., Martin-Cook, K., Gray, K. F., & Weiner, M. F. (2001). Performance-based instrument to assess functional capacity in dementia: The Texas Functional Living Scale. *Neuropsychiatry, Neuropsychology, & Behavioral Neurology, 14,* 103–108.

de Gracia Dominguez, M. G., Viechtbauer, W., Simons, C. J., van Os, J., & Krabbendam, L. (2009). Are psychotic psychopathology and neurocognition orthogonal? A systematic review of their associations. *Psychological Bulletin, 135,* 157–171. http://dx.doi.org/10.1037/a0014415

Dickinson, D., Ramsey, M. E., & Gold, J. M. (2007). Overlooking the obvious: A meta-analytic comparison of digit symbol coding tasks and other cognitive measures in schizophrenia. *Archives of General Psychiatry, 64,* 532–542. http://dx.doi.org/10.1001/archpsyc.64.5.532

Edelstein, B. (1999). *Hopemont Capacity Assessment Interview manual and scoring guide.* Morgantown: West Virginia University.

Evans, J. D., Heaton, R. K., Paulsen, J. S., Palmer, B. W., Patterson, T., & Jeste, D. V. (2003). The relationship of neuropsychological abilities to specific domains of functional capacity in older schizophrenia patients. *Biological Psychiatry, 53,* 422–430. http://dx.doi.org/10.1016/S0006-3223(02)01476-2

Fioravanti, M., Carlone, O., Vitale, B., Cinti, M. E., & Clare, L. (2005). A meta-analysis of cognitive deficits in adults with a diagnosis of schizophrenia. *Neuropsychology Review, 15,* 73–95. http://dx.doi.org/10.1007/s11065-005-6254-9

Fusar-Poli, P., Deste, G., Smieskova, R., Barlati, S., Yung, A. R., Howes, O., . . . Borgwardt, S. (2012). Cognitive functioning in prodromal psychosis: A meta-analysis. *Archives of General Psychiatry, 69,* 562–571. http://dx.doi.org/10.1001/archgenpsychiatry.2011.1592

Glassmire, D. M., Toofanian Ross, P., Kinney, D. I., & Nitch, S. R. (2016). Derivation and cross-validation of cutoff scores for patients with schizophrenia spectrum disorders on WAIS–IV Digit-Span–based performance validity measures. *Assessment, 23,* 292–306. http://dx.doi.org/10.1177/1073191115587551

Goldberg, H. E., Back-Madruga, C., & Boone, K. B. (2007). The impact of psychiatric disorders on cognitive symptom validity test scores. In K. B. Boone (Ed.), *Assessment of feigned cognitive impairment: A neuropsychological perspective* (pp. 281–309). New York, NY: Guilford Press.

Gorissen, M., Sanz, J. C., & Schmand, B. (2005). Effort and cognition in schizophrenia patients. *Schizophrenia Research, 78,* 199–208. http://dx.doi.org/10.1016/j.schres.2005.02.016

Grisso, T., & Appelbaum, P. S. (1998). *MacArthur Competence Assessment Tool for Treatment (MacCAT–T)*. Sarasota, FL: Professional Resource Press/Professional Resource Exchange.

Harvey, P. D., Bertisch, H., Friedman, J. I., Marcus, S., Parrella, M., White, L., & Davis, K. L. (2003). The course of functional decline in geriatric patients with schizophrenia: Cognitive-functional and clinical symptoms as determinants of change. *The American Journal of Geriatric Psychiatry, 11,* 610–619. http://dx.doi.org/10.1097/00019442-200311000-00005

Harvey, P. D., Heaton, R. K., Carpenter, W. T., Jr., Green, M. F., Gold, J. M., & Schoenbaum, M. (2012). Functional impairment in people with schizophrenia: Focus on employability and eligibility for disability compensation. *Schizophrenia Research, 140,* 1–8. http://dx.doi.org/10.1016/j.schres.2012.03.025

Harvey, P. D., Silverman, J. M., Mohs, R. C., Parrella, M., White, L., Powchik, P., . . . Davis, K. L. (1999). Cognitive decline in late-life schizophrenia: A longitudinal study of geriatric chronically hospitalized patients. *Biological Psychiatry, 45,* 32–40. http://dx.doi.org/10.1016/S0006-3223(98)00273-X

Heaton, R. K., Miller, S. W., Taylor, M. J., & Grant, I. (2004). *Revised comprehensive norms for an expanded Halstead–Reitan Battery: Demographically adjusted neuropsychological norms for African American and Caucasian adults.* Lutz, FL: Psychological Assessment Resources.

Heinrichs, R. W., & Zakzanis, K. K. (1998). Neurocognitive deficit in schizophrenia: A quantitative review of the evidence. *Neuropsychology, 12,* 426–445. http://dx.doi.org/10.1037/0894-4105.12.3.426

Hunt, S., Root, J. C., & Bascetta, B. L. (2014). Effort testing in schizophrenia and schizoaffective disorder: Validity indicator profile and test of memory malingering performance characteristics. *Archives of Clinical Neuropsychology, 29,* 164–172. http://dx.doi.org/10.1093/arclin/act069

Irani, F., Kalkstein, S., Moberg, E. A., & Moberg, P. J. (2011). Neuropsychological performance in older patients with schizophrenia: A meta-analysis of cross-sectional and longitudinal studies. *Schizophrenia Bulletin, 37,* 1318–1326. http://dx.doi.org/10.1093/schbul/sbq057

Jobe, T. H., & Harrow, M. (2005). Long-term outcome of patients with schizophrenia: A review. *Canadian Journal of Psychiatry, 50,* 892–900. http://dx.doi.org/10.1177/070674370505001403

Jurica, P. J., Leitten, C. L., & Mattis, S. (1988). *DRS-2 Dementia Rating Scale-2 professional manual.* Retrieved from https://www.parinc.com/Products/Pkey/90

Kalache, S. M., Mulsant, B. H., Davies, S. J., Liu, A. Y., Voineskos, A. N., Butters, M. A., . . . Rajji, T. K. (2015). The impact of aging, cognition, and symptoms on functional competence in individuals with schizophrenia across the lifespan. *Schizophrenia Bulletin, 41,* 374–381. http://dx.doi.org/10.1093/schbul/sbu114

Kongs, S. K., Thompson, L. L., Iverson, G. L., & Heaton, R. K. (2000). *WCST-64: Wisconsin Card Sorting Test–64 Card Version.* Odessa, FL: Psychological Assessment Resources.

Kremen, W. S., Seidman, L. J., Faraone, S. V., Toomey, R., & Tsuang, M. T. (2000). The paradox of normal neuropsychological function in schizophrenia. *Journal of Abnormal Psychology, 109,* 743–752. http://dx.doi.org/10.1037/0021-843X.109.4.743

Lipskaya-Velikovsky, L., Kotler, M., Easterbrook, A., & Jarus, T. (2015). From hospital admission to independent living: Is prediction possible? *Psychiatry Research, 226,* 499–506. http://dx.doi.org/10.1016/j.psychres.2015.01.027

Loeb, P. A., & Fe, R. (1996). *ILS: Independent Living Scales manual.* San Antonio, TX: The Psychological Corporation.

Marson, D. C., Ingram, K. K., Cody, H. A., & Harrell, L. E. (1995). Assessing the competency of patients with Alzheimer's disease under different legal standards: A prototype instrument. *Archives of Neurology, 52,* 949–954. http://dx.doi.org/10.1001/archneur.1995.00540340029010

McClure, M. M., Bowie, C. R., Patterson, T. L., Heaton, R. K., Weaver, C., Anderson, H., & Harvey, P. D. (2007). Correlations of functional capacity and neuropsychological performance in older patients with schizophrenia: Evidence for specificity of relationships? *Schizophrenia Research, 89,* 330–338. http://dx.doi.org/10.1016/j.schres.2006.07.024

Meesters, P. D., de Haan, L., Comijs, H. C., Stek, M. L., Smeets-Janssen, M. M., Weeda, M. R., . . . Beekman, A. T. (2012). Schizophrenia spectrum disorders in later life: Prevalence and distribution of age at onset and sex in a Dutch catchment area. *The American Journal of Geriatric Psychiatry, 20,* 18–28. http://dx.doi.org/10.1097/JGP.0b013e3182011b7f

Mesholam-Gately, R. I., Giuliano, A. J., Goff, K. P., Faraone, S. V., & Seidman, L. J. (2009). Neurocognition in first-episode schizophrenia: A meta-analytic review. *Neuropsychology, 23,* 315–336. http://dx.doi.org/10.1037/a0014708

Moore, R. C., Davine, T., Harmell, A. L., Cardenas, V., Palmer, B. W., & Mausbach, B. T. (2013). Using the repeatable battery for the assessment of neuropsychological status (RBANS) effort index to predict treatment group attendance in patients with schizophrenia. *Journal of International Neuropsychological Society, 19,* 198–205. http://dx.doi.org/10.1017/S1355617712001221

Morra, L. F., Gold, J. M., Sullivan, S. K., & Strauss, G. P. (2015). Predictors of neuropsychological effort test performance in schizophrenia. *Schizophrenia Research, 162,* 205–210. http://dx.doi.org/10.1016/j.schres.2014.12.033

Moye, J., Karel, M. J., Edelstein, B., Hicken, B., Armesto, J. C., & Gurrera, R. J. (2007). Assessment of Capacity to Consent to Treatment: Challenges, the "ACCT" approach, future directions. *Clinical Gerontologist, 31,* 37–66. http://dx.doi.org/10.1080/07317110802072140

Moye, J., & Marson, D. C. (2007). Assessment of decision-making capacity in older adults: An emerging area of practice and research. *The Journals of Gerontology: Series B. Psychological Sciences and Social Sciences, 62,* P3–P11. http://dx.doi.org/10.1093/geronb/62.1.P3

Nasreddine, Z. S., Phillips, N. A., Bédirian, V., Charbonneau, S., Whitehead, V., Collin, I., . . . Chertkow, H. (2005). The Montreal Cognitive Assessment, MoCA: A brief screening tool for mild cognitive impairment [correction: see https://doi.org/10.1111/jgs.15925]. *Journal of the American Geriatrics Society, 53,* 695–699. http://dx.doi.org/10.1111/j.1532-5415.2005.53221.x

Newman, S. C., Bland, R. C., & Thompson, A. H. (2012). Long-term course and outcome in schizophrenia: A 34-year follow-up study in Alberta, Canada. *Psychological Medicine, 42,* 2137–2143. http://dx.doi.org/10.1017/S0033291712000177

Olfson, M., Gerhard, T., Huang, C., Crystal, S., & Stroup, T. S. (2015). Premature mortality among adults with schizophrenia in the United States. *JAMA Psychiatry, 72,* 1172–1181. http://dx.doi.org/10.1001/jamapsychiatry.2015.1737

Palmer, B. W., Dunn, L. B., Appelbaum, P. S., & Jeste, D. V. (2004). Correlates of treatment-related decision-making capacity among middle-aged and older patients with schizophrenia. *Archives of General Psychiatry, 61,* 230–236. http://dx.doi.org/10.1001/archpsyc.61.3.230

Palmer, B. W., Heaton, R. K., Gladsjo, J. A., Evans, J. D., Patterson, T. L., Golshan, S., & Jeste, D. V. (2002). Heterogeneity in functional status among older outpatients with schizophrenia: Employment history, living situation, and driving. *Schizophrenia Research, 55,* 205–215. http://dx.doi.org/10.1016/S0920-9964(01)00218-3

Palmer, B. W., Heaton, R. K., Paulsen, J. S., Kuck, J., Braff, D., Harris, M. J., . . . Jeste, D. V. (1997). Is it possible to be schizophrenic yet neuropsychologically normal? *Neuropsychology, 11*, 437–446. http://dx.doi.org/10.1037/0894-4105.11.3.437

Palmer, B. W., & Savla, G. N. (2007). The association of specific neuropsychological deficits with capacity to consent to research or treatment. *Journal of the International Neuropsychological Society, 13*, 1047–1059. http://dx.doi.org/10.1017/S1355617707071299

Patterson, T. L., Klapow, J. C., Eastham, J. H., Heaton, R. K., Evans, J. D., Koch, W. L., & Jeste, D. V. (1998). Correlates of functional status in older patients with schizophrenia. *Psychiatry Research, 80*, 41–52. http://dx.doi.org/10.1016/S0165-1781(98)00060-2

Patterson, T. L., Lacro, J., McKibbin, C. L., Moscona, S., Hughs, T., & Jeste, D. V. (2002). Medication management ability assessment: Results from a performance-based measure in older outpatients with schizophrenia. *Journal of Clinical Psychopharmacology, 22*, 11–19. http://dx.doi.org/10.1097/00004714-200202000-00003

Patterson, T. L., & Mausbach, B. T. (2010). Measurement of functional capacity: A new approach to understanding functional differences and real-world behavioral adaptation in those with mental illness. *Annual Review of Clinical Psychology, 6*, 139–154. http://dx.doi.org/10.1146/annurev.clinpsy.121208.131339

Pearman, A., & Batra, A. (2012). Late-onset schizophrenia: A review for clinicians. *Clinical Gerontologist, 35*, 126–147. http://dx.doi.org/10.1080/07317115.2011.642943

Pinkham, A. E., Penn, D. L., Perkins, D. O., & Lieberman, J. (2003). Implications for the neural basis of social cognition for the study of schizophrenia. *The American Journal of Psychiatry, 160*, 815–824. http://dx.doi.org/10.1176/appi.ajp.160.5.815

The Psychological Corporation. (2001). *Wechsler test of adult reading*. San Antonio, TX: Harcourt Assessment.

Randolph, C., Tierney, M. C., Mohr, E., & Chase, T. N. (1998). The Repeatable Battery for the Assessment of Neuropsychological Status (RBANS): Preliminary clinical validity. *Journal of Clinical and Experimental Neuropsychology, 20*, 310–319. http://dx.doi.org/10.1076/jcen.20.3.310.823

Reitan, R. M. (1956). *Trail Making Test: Manual for administration, scoring and interpretation*. Indianapolis: Indiana University.

Saha, S., Chant, D., Welham, J., & McGrath, J. (2005). A systematic review of the prevalence of schizophrenia. *PLoS Medicine, 2*, e141. http://dx.doi.org/10.1371/journal.pmed.0020141

Sartorius, N., Shapiro, R., Kimura, M., & Barrett, K. (1972). WHO international pilot study of schizophrenia. *Psychological Medicine, 2*, 422–425. http://dx.doi.org/10.1017/S0033291700045244

Schroeder, R. W., & Marshall, P. S. (2011). Evaluation of the appropriateness of multiple symptom validity indices in psychotic and non-psychotic psychiatric populations. *The Clinical Neuropsychologist, 25*, 437–453. http://dx.doi.org/10.1080/13854046.2011.556668

Shura, R. D., Brearly, T. W., Rowland, J. A., Martindale, S. L., Miskey, H. M., & Duff, K. (2018). RBANS Validity Indices: A systematic review and meta-analysis. *Neuropsychology Review, 28*, 269–284. http://dx.doi.org/10.1007/s11065-018-9377-5

Silverberg, N. D., Wertheimer, J. C., & Fichtenberg, N. L. (2007). An effort index for the Repeatable Battery for the Assessment of Neuropsychological Status (RBANS). *The Clinical Neuropsychologist, 21*, 841–854. http://dx.doi.org/10.1080/13854040600850958

Spencer, B. W. J., Shields, G., Gergel, T., Hotopf, M., & Owen, G. S. (2017). Diversity or disarray? A systematic review of decision-making capacity for treatment and research in schizophrenia and other non-affective psychoses. *Psychological Medicine, 47*, 1906–1922. http://dx.doi.org/10.1017/S0033291717000502

Strauss, G. P., Morra, L. F., Sullivan, S. K., & Gold, J. M. (2015). The role of low cognitive effort and negative symptoms in neuropsychological impairment in schizophrenia. *Neuropsychology, 29*, 282–291. http://dx.doi.org/10.1037/neu0000113

Tandon, R., Keshavan, M. S., & Nasrallah, H. A. (2008). Schizophrenia, "just the facts": What we know in 2008. Part 1: Overview. *Schizophrenia Research, 100,* 4–19. http://dx.doi.org/10.1016/j.schres.2008.01.022

Thompson, W. K., Savla, G. N., Vahia, I. V., Depp, C. A., O'Hara, R., Jeste, D. V., & Palmer, B. W. (2013). Characterizing trajectories of cognitive functioning in older adults with schizophrenia: Does method matter? *Schizophrenia Research, 143,* 90–96. http://dx.doi.org/10.1016/j.schres.2012.10.033

Twamley, E. W., Doshi, R. R., Nayak, G. V., Palmer, B. W., Golshan, S., Heaton, R. K., . . . Jeste, D. V. (2002). Generalized cognitive impairments, ability to perform everyday tasks, and level of independence in community living situations of older patients with psychosis. *The American Journal of Psychiatry, 159,* 2013–2020. http://dx.doi.org/10.1176/appi.ajp.159.12.2013

Wang, S. B., Wang, Y. Y., Ungvari, G. S., Ng, C. H., Wu, R. R., Wang, J., & Xiang, Y. T. (2017). The MacArthur Competence Assessment Tools for assessing decision-making capacity in schizophrenia: A meta-analysis. *Schizophrenia Research, 183,* 56–63. http://dx.doi.org/10.1016/j.schres.2016.11.020

Wechsler, D. (1997). *WAIS–III administration and scoring manual.* San Antonio, TX: The Psychological Association.

Whearty, K. M., Allen, D. N., Lee, B. G., & Strauss, G. P. (2015). The evaluation of insufficient cognitive effort in schizophrenia in light of low IQ scores. *Journal of Psychiatric Research, 68,* 397–404. http://dx.doi.org/10.1016/j.jpsychires.2015.04.018

Woodberry, K. A., Giuliano, A. J., & Seidman, L. J. (2008). Premorbid IQ in schizophrenia: A meta-analytic review. *The American Journal of Psychiatry, 165,* 579–587. http://dx.doi.org/10.1176/appi.ajp.2008.07081242

4

Evaluating Capacities After Traumatic Brain Injury

Kristen Triebel, Sean D. Hollis, and Thomas A. Novack

KEY POINTS

- Traumatic brain injuries (TBIs) are common across the life span, but the highest rates occur in persons aged 2 to 5, 15 to 24, and over age 75 years (Thurman, 2016).
- Areas of the brain particularly vulnerable to a closed TBI are the frontal and temporal regions of the brain, which are areas critical for memory, judgment, and problem-solving. These cognitive abilities are correlated with various capacities.
- Severity of injury and time since injury are related to capacity; individuals with moderate and severe TBI are more likely to experience enduring impairments in cognition and decision-making.
- The most rapid phase of recovery of capacity after moderate to severe TBI occurs during the first year postinjury, although some recovery can occur afterward.
- Return to work and ability to drive are two common capacity questions that arise in the inpatient rehabilitation setting. Comprehensive assessments of these capacities that include an actual driving evaluation are ideal but not always practical or cost-efficient. Clinicians in these settings play a significant role of assessing recovery of these capacities following TBI.

http://dx.doi.org/10.1037/0000184-005
Assessing Capacities of Older Adults: A Casebook to Guide Difficult Decisions, J. Moye (Editor)

DEFINITION OF THE ISSUE

Traumatic brain injuries (TBIs) can result from open or closed head injuries, although the majority are closed head injuries (Centers for Disease Control and Prevention [CDC], 2016). Not all head injuries result in TBI. The difference is that TBIs involve brain damage or dysfunction. Brain injuries can occur as the result of acceleration-deceleration forces, blunt trauma, penetrating trauma, or a mixture (CDC, 2016). Traumatic (or diffuse) axonal injuries occur due to whiplash-like injuries that involve axonal shearing (Lezak, Howieson, Bigler, & Tranel, 2012). Permanent impairment can occur from a single moderate or severe TBI. In addition, repeated mild TBIs, especially those that occur close in time, may produce cognitive and behavioral changes (Lezak et al., 2012; Nguyen et al., 2016).

Consideration of decision-making capacities is particularly relevant in moderate and severe TBI or in persons with repeated mild TBIs (Steward et al., 2016; Triebel et al., 2012, 2014). Persons with a single mild TBI typically do not experience capacity impairments unless it is a complicated mild injury (i.e., abnormal imaging findings; Triebel et al., 2012). Consideration of capacity after TBI differs in several ways from that for other acquired brain injuries. Perhaps the primary difference is the possibility of a dynamic recovery process in TBI, which may occur at a more accelerated pace than in conditions such as stroke or tumor. In this regard, serial assessment of capacity in TBI is essential. In our clinical experience, capacities that are particularly vulnerable to becoming impaired include driving capacity, vocational capacity, financial capacity, and medical decision-making capacity. This chapter highlights two of these capacities (i.e., return to driving and return to work) in depth as they are most often encountered in the acute rehabilitation setting. The assessment of these capacities is somewhat unique, whereas the assessment of financial capacity and medical decision-making capacity in TBI is similar in process to those described for other populations in this volume.

CLINICAL PRESENTATION

TBI is a significant and growing challenge for the health care field. Estimates of prevalence range as high as 1.4 million to 1.7 million TBIs annually in the United States (CDC, 2016; Langlois, Rutland-Brown, & Thomas, 2004; Nguyen et al., 2016). Additionally, there are 50,000 fatalities, 235,000 hospitalizations, and 1.1 million people treated and released from emergency departments annually due to TBI (Langlois et al., 2004). TBI is related to 30.5% of all injury-related deaths in the United States (CDC, 2016). As many as 12% of adults in developed countries have a history of TBI (Nguyen et al., 2016).

TBI is 1.5 times more common in males than females, particularly after age 3 (Langlois et al., 2004). Those at highest risk for TBI are within the age ranges of 0 to 4, 15 to 19, and 75+ (Langlois et al., 2004). Additionally, following a TBI, an individual's risk for a subsequent TBI is greatly increased. The reported incidence of TBI has been climbing in recent years, possibly related to improved awareness of mild TBI, as well as falls in an increasingly older adult global population and greater use of motor vehicles in developing countries (Faul, Xu, Wald, & Coronado, 2010; Maas, Stocchetti, & Bullock, 2008; Roozenbeek, Maas, & Menon, 2013). Falls and motor vehicle collisions (MVCs) are the leading causes of TBI (Faul et al., 2010), followed by work injury, assault, and sports-related injury. MVC is the leading cause of TBI in adolescents and young adults, while falls are the most common cause among older adults. Use of alcohol is frequently associated with TBI as well. Mild TBI is most common (75%–80% of all TBIs; Nguyen et al., 2016) with a small proportion falling into the moderate and severe range (less than 10% each; CDC, 2016). Mild injuries, even seemingly trivial events, can have negative consequences for older people due to the development of chronic subdural hematoma and other problems. A mild trauma for which a younger person might receive outpatient care can result in an older person being hospitalized and requiring rehabilitation (Dams-O'Connor et al., 2013). In general, the outcome after TBI, of any severity, is not as good for older individuals as for those who are younger (Coronado, Thomas, Sattin, & Johnson, 2005; Cifu et al., 1996), in part due to age-related comorbidities (Mas, Mathews, & Gilbert-Baffoe, 2017). The number of older people with TBI is steadily increasing with the aging of the North American population in general (Dams-O'Connor et al., 2013). Although most clinicians would not confuse cognitive impairment associated with a recent TBI for dementia as a careful history would reveal the occurrence of the TBI, a history of TBI increases the risk for dementia (LoBue et al., 2019).

There are 5.3 million people in the United States (2% of the entire population) who require long-term assistance with activities of daily living (ADLs) due to TBI (Crooks, Zumsteg, & Bell, 2007; Heegaard & Biros, 2007). The economic burden of TBI is estimated at $76.5 billion (Finkelstein, Corso, & Miller, 2006), with severe TBI accounting for 90% of that cost (Thurman, 2016). Individuals who sustain a TBI are less likely to achieve milestones such as completing high school or college and obtaining and maintaining employment (Finkelstein et al., 2006; Schwab, Gudmudsson, & Lew, 2015). They are also at higher risk for medical and mental health comorbidities and report a lower quality of life (Finkelstein et al., 2006; Schwab et al., 2015).

Recovery after TBI is determined by multiple factors, including location and severity of cerebral dysfunction and medical care received. Other factors contributing to outcome include premorbid health and personality, intelligence, age, substance use, and socioeconomic status (Hessen, Anderson, & Nestvold, 2008; Ketchum et al., 2012; Lezak et al., 2012; Schwab et al., 2015). Family support is an important factor but seems to be more related to behavioral than cognitive outcomes.

A particularly important functional consequence of TBI is the effect it may have on driving ability. Driving is considered an instrumental ADL (IADL; Fisk, Schneider, & Novack, 1998). Driving can also be considered an occupation enabler, allowing for participation in ADLs, IADLs, work, education, and desired social activities (Schwab et al., 2015). A key focus of rehabilitation is return to driving to empower people to regain independence and increase social engagement (Rapport, Bryer, & Hanks, 2008; Ross, Di Stefano, Charlton, Spitz, & Ponsford, 2018). Approximately 10% of those experiencing mild TBI do not return to driving (Andersson, Bedics, & Falkmer, 2011), and half of those with moderate–severe TBI return to driving within 2 years of injury (Novack et al., 2010). Some studies have raised concerns about people with TBI exhibiting higher rates of general driving difficulty, near misses, and road rage, as well as higher rates of crashes (Bivona et al., 2012; Brooks & Hawley, 2005). However, many people with moderate-to-severe TBI do not return to driving (Labbe, Vance, Wadley, & Novack, 2014; Novack et al., 2010). All states have statutes restricting driving following neurological events, typically for 6 to 12 months after the event or until cleared by a medical professional.

Like driving, return to employment activities is a milestone in recovery after TBI. This affects both the injured person and family members who otherwise might be home providing supervision and companionship. While those with mild TBI generally return to work after a brief period of recovery (Cancelliere et al., 2014), those with moderate–severe TBI often must contend with physical, cognitive, emotional, or behavioral changes that can affect the capacity to return to a former job or, in some cases, any job (Cuthbert et al., 2015). Multiple studies indicate that 30% to 50% of those with moderate–severe TBI return to employment (DiSanto et al., 2019; Grauwmeijer, Heijenbrok-Kal, Haitsma, & Ribbers, 2017; Ponsford & Spitz, 2015), although often with altered job responsibilities or a different job altogether. Those employed in white-collar settings and who have higher education are more likely to return to work, perhaps related to greater cognitive reserve, greater likelihood of employer accommodations, differing financial incentives, and greater injury risk in manual labor employees (Walker, Marwitz, Kreutzer, Hart, & Novack, 2006). Individuals who were not employed before injury (Andelic, Stevens, Sigurdardottir, Arango-Lasprilla, & Roe, 2012), who are female (Cuthbert et al., 2015), or who are of minority status (Arango-Lasprilla et al., 2011) are less likely to return to work. After 2 years, the prospects of returning to work diminish precipitously. Return to work is complicated by several factors. After this level of injury, many people become eligible for disability benefits, such as that sponsored by Social Security (in the United States) or a job-based policy. Once a steady income, albeit less than earned previously, is established, it is understandably difficult to risk that support by chancing a successful return to work. Fortunately, Social Security has in place a transition program that lessens the risk. Transportation to work is also an issue in this situation (Kreutzer et al., 2003), underscoring the importance of return to driving. Finally, there is the perspective of the employer. Employers vary considerably with respect to accepting the risk of having someone with (even mild) physical and cognitive difficulties on the premises and their willingness to provide a transition back to work, such as by arranging "light duty" and supervision for a period of time. In general, employers who expect return to full duties immediately

TABLE 4.1. Common Traumatic Brain Injury Classification System

Severity classification	Duration of loss of consciousness	Glasgow Coma Scale (Teasdale & Jennett, 1974) Score	Duration of posttraumatic amnesia
Mild	< 30 min	13–15	< 24 hr
Moderate	30 min–24 hr	9–12	1–7 days
Severe	> 24 hr	3–8	> 7 days

upon return to work preclude this activity for those with moderate–severe TBI. That being said, there is evidence that those who are able to work in some capacity exhibit greater life satisfaction (Franulic, Carbonell, Pinto, & Sepulveda, 2004), fewer difficulties with mood (Garrelfs, Donker-Cools, Wind, & Frings-Dresen, 2015), and more community involvement (O'Neill et al., 1998). Even part-time work, which is possible when receiving Social Security disability benefits, can be beneficial.

DIAGNOSTIC STANDARDS AND DILEMMAS

One of the challenges for clinicians is that there are no uniform diagnostic criteria for classifying TBI. As shown in Table 4.1, TBI severity is typically categorized using the Glasgow Coma Scale (GCS; Teasdale & Jennett, 1974), duration of loss of consciousness (LOC), and duration of posttraumatic amnesia (PTA, which recently is being reframed as an extended confusional state).

As described in Table 4.2, the GCS is the most widely used screening instrument to determine injury severity. It evaluates three components of arousal, including stimulus required to make the eyes open, best motor response, and best verbal response. GCS severity classifications are *mild* = 13 to 15, *moderate* = 9 to 12, and *severe* = 3 to 8. The GCS score used is defined as the lowest GCS score obtained 30 minutes or more postinjury as performed by a neurosurgeon or trauma surgeon.

Although not as objective or clear as the GCS score, severity guidelines for LOC and PTA have also been established (Iverson & Lange, 2011a, 2011b).

TABLE 4.2. Glasgow Coma Scale Score, Range 3 to 15 Points

Stage	Range	Scoring
Eye opening	1–4 points	*Spontaneously* = 4, *to speech* = 3, *to pain* = 2, *no response* = 1
Best verbal response	1–5 points	*Fully oriented* = 5, *confused* = 4, *inappropriate* = 3, *incomprehensible* = 2, *no response* = 1
Best motor response	1–6 points	*Obeying* = 6, *localizes pain* = 5, *withdraws from pain* = 4, *flexion* (pain) = 3, *extension* (pain) = 2, *no response* = 1

The duration of PTA has been increasingly recognized as a strong predictor of long-term outcome among those with moderate-to-severe TBI.

Several comorbidities and risk factors increase the chance of capacity impairments in TBI.

COMORBIDITIES AND RISK FACTORS FOR CAPACITY IMPAIRMENTS IN TBI

- Prior TBI
- Substance abuse
- Other medical conditions, such as infections, delirium, or chronic medical conditions
- Preexisting dementia
- Psychiatric comorbidities, such as mania or delusions, attention-deficit/hyperactivity disorder

CLINICAL METHODS

Assessment Approaches

The approach for assessing capacity in TBI depends on the clinical setting. For example, inpatient assessments of capacity may be performed at the bedside and may involve shorter evaluations. In addition, during the acute stages, repeated assessments may be needed. Capacity assessment for moderate–severe TBI often occurs within the context of sequential neuropsychological evaluations that can document progress across time. A thorough evaluation will involve assessment of physical, cognitive, behavioral, and emotional status. As shown in the nine-step process for evaluating capacities, input is obtained from multiple perspectives: objective testing, interview of the injured person, separate interview of family members, review of medical records, and collateral information (e.g., employer, school).

STEPS TO TAKE WHEN EVALUATING CAPACITY

1. Consider the referral source.
2. Identify the specific capacity questions to address (e.g., capacity to drive, manage finances, return to work, make treatment decisions, live independently).
3. Review medical records.

4. Review imaging records if available.
5. Interview patient and family or other collateral informants.
    a. Specific interview questions
    b. Current functional status
    c. Family perspective
6. Cognitive assessment
7. Functional assessment
    a. Interview with patient and family
    b. Direct functional assessment
8. Report
9. Feedback

Assessment Instruments

As a clinician, it is important to choose test instruments that are either developed to assess the relevant capacity or are cognitive tests that measure abilities known to be relevant to the specific capacity. In working with an older population, it is essential to use measures that are appropriately normed for older adults (American Psychological Association [APA], 2014). Global measures, such as the Dementia Rating Scale and the Repeatable Battery for the Assessment of Neuropsychological Status, are also helpful in determining level of functioning. Examples of commonly used measures are presented in Table 4.3.

The ability to return to driving and work are common capacity questions clinicians in rehabilitation settings are asked to evaluate (Rao et al., 1990; Ross, Ponsford, Di Stefano, & Spitz, 2015). We briefly discuss each of these capacities and highlight key questions to ask. Finally, we present two actual clinical cases of a driving capacity and a work capacity evaluation.

Driving Capacity

Despite the importance of driving and the risks involved to those experiencing TBI, evaluation of driving capacity is still evolving. In many instances (some studies indicate the majority of cases; Ortoleva, Brugger, Van der Linden, & Walder, 2012; Rapport et al., 2008) there is no assessment after TBI that addresses return to driving. People with TBI may rely on their own perception of ability, advice of family members, or a brief interaction with a health care provider (Tamietto et al., 2006). Obviously, this is not optimal. On-road assessment is considered a gold standard (Fox, Bowden, & Smith, 1998; Schanke & Sundet, 2000), but such evaluations take place under optimal conditions, are expensive (and not covered by insurance in many

TABLE 4.3. Neuropsychological Measures Commonly Used in Capacity Evaluations

Neuropsychological measure	Cognitive skills measured
Return to driving	
Unified Field of Vision Test (Fisk, Novack, Mennemeier, & Roenker, 2002)	Visual processing speed, selective and divided visual attention
Neuropsychological Assessment Battery (NAB; Stern & White, 2003) Driving Scenes Subtest	Visual attention, identification of driving hazards
NAB Map Reading Subtest	Visuospatial, executive abilities
Stroke Drivers' Screening Assessment (SDSA; Nouri & Lincoln, 1994)	Visuospatial problem-solving, multitasking, road sign recognition
Trail Making Test (TMT; Reitan, 1956) A and B	Processing speed, executive functioning
Symbol Digit Modalities Test (SDMT; Smith, 1973)	Processing speed
Return to work	
Grooved Pegboard Test, Grip Strength Test	Fine motor abilities
Wisconsin Card Sorting Test—64 (Kongs et al., 2000), Wechsler Adult Intelligence Scale—IV: Matrix Reasoning Subtest (Wechsler, 2008)	Problem-solving; executive functioning
TMT A and B (Reitan, 1956), SDMT (Smith, 1973), Paced Auditory Serial Addition Test (PASAT; Gronwall, 1977)	Processing speed
Boston Naming Test (Kaplan, Goodglass, & Weintraub, 1983), Controlled Oral Word Association Test (Benton, Hamsher, et al., 1994)	Language
California Verbal Learning Test, 2nd ed. (Delis et al., 2000); Wechsler Memory Scale—IV: Logical Memory Subtest (Wechsler, 2009), Rey Complex Figure Test (Meyers & Meyers, 1995)	Memory
	Position-specific evaluations

Note. It is also important to consider additional referrals, such as a formal driving evaluation, sensory evaluation (e.g., vision), or a work-hardening evaluation. These may include an evaluation of real or simulated physical job responsibilities or strength and physical stamina. These evaluations are typically completed by an occupational therapist or physical therapist.

instances; Tamietto et al., 2006), and focus on operational skills without addressing strategic and tactical component of driving (Coleman et al., 2002). Simulators are increasing in sophistication and use but have not supplanted on-road assessments and have drawbacks as well, such as nausea induced by the assessment (Carlozzi, Gade, Rizzo, & Tulsky, 2013). In this situation, there is still room for cognitive, emotional, and behavioral assessment to contribute substantially.

Common cognitive deficits that occur in TBI that are associated with driving ability include slowed processing speed, divided attention deficits, and dysexecutive functioning, in addition to other focal and diffuse deficits (Lundqvist, 2001). Visual deficits are another important possible factor. Slowed processing in particular is a significant problem due to the time pressures of driving (van Zomeren, Brouwer, & Minderhoud, 1987). Processing of information is needed to obtain input from the driving environment, responding to that information, adjusting response as needed, and developing alternative responses (Fisk et al., 1998; Innes et al., 2007). Coordination, strength, and range of motion are also necessary for the physical actions of driving (Fisk et al., 1998; Innes et al., 2007). Communication skills are also important for interacting with other drivers. Poor insight may lead to an inability to accommodate for deficits (Korteling & Kaptein, 1996). Given the cognitive skills assumed to be important for driving safety, neuropsychological evaluations of driving safety tend to focus primarily on selective and divided attention, processing speed, working memory, perceptual motor skills, visuomotor speed, and executive functioning (Brouwer, Waterink, Van Wolffelaar, & Rothengatter, 1991; Coleman et al., 2002; Lundqvist, 2001; Schanke & Sundet, 2000), as well as efficient detection of hazards (Elander, West, & French, 1993). Emotional control is also an important factor in avoiding negative outcomes such as road rage (Tamietto et al., 2006). Social responsibility can be considered another factor, along with conscientiousness (less risky driving style; Bogg & Roberts, 2004). Important questions to ask during a clinical interview for a return to driving evaluation are listed in the following box.

KEY QUESTIONS TO ASK REGARDING DRIVING CAPACITY

1. Has the individual attempted return to driving?
2. Issues with driving (e.g., crashes, traffic citations)
3. Driving history
4. Valid license
5. Perception of readiness to return to driving
6. Family perception of readiness
7. State guidelines, including the need to report

There is support for the efficacy of neuropsychological evaluation of cognitive abilities, emotional status, and behavior related to driving, but (as might be expected) no single measure has been shown to reliably predict safe return to driving (Brooks & Hawley, 2005). A small group of tests, however, have proven to be related to driving, at least in terms of correlation (Meyers, Volbrecht, & Kaster-Bundgaard, 1999). In particular, the Stroke Drivers' Screening Assessment (SDSA; Nouri & Lincoln, 1994), Trail Making Test–B (TMT; Reitan, 1956), and Unified Field of Vision Test (UFOV; Fisk, Novack,

Mennemeier, & Roenker, 2002; Novack et al., 2006) have been effective in this regard.

Capacity to Return to Work

Due to an increasing focus on quality of life and concerns about financial stability, there is growing interest in continuing employment past what has traditionally been considered retirement age. As a result, return to employment after TBI is of interest to some older people. Given the breadth of cognitive and physical abilities necessary to perform a job, no single test will justify a release to return to work. Knowledge of the job duties is essential to tailor the assessment to the situation as much as possible. In most cases, a broad assessment of cognitive abilities is appropriate, in part to establish a need for accommodations that can be addressed by a vocational counselor and a flexible employer. It is important that the assessment also focus on emotional status and behavioral changes because both have been demonstrated to correlate with successful return to work. Employers in many settings have made significant progress in adapting work sites and jobs for those with physical limitations, but not so much those with cognitive or behavioral deficits. Behavioral difficulties, such as temper outburst and impulsive behavior, are particularly difficult to tolerate in an employment setting. Several key questions to ask when assessing the capacity to return to work are as follows.

KEY QUESTIONS TO ASK REGARDING RETURN TO WORK CAPACITY

1. What are the specific job duties?
2. What are the physical requirements (e.g., sitting, standing, lifting)?
3. What is the work setting (e.g., indoor, outdoor, climate controlled)?
4. What is the work schedule (e.g., part-time or full-time, days, nights, weekends)?
5. Is supervision available?
6. Is a transitional period a possibility?
7. Are there possible risks of returning to work, both to the patient and to those he or she is working with and for?
8. What are the financial considerations for the person?
9. Are there laws, licensing boards, or other rules that must be considered?

Pragmatic Considerations

There are several pragmatic considerations for clinicians working with TBI populations. Several examples are presented in this section, with tips for addressing the problems.

Seeking Consent From a Person Whose Capacity Is in Question

- The determination of capacity to consent is ultimately a clinical judgment that can either be determined through dialogue between the clinician and the person with TBI or can be assisted with the use of semistructured interviews or standardized capacity tests.
- It is likely in the case of TBI that capacity to consent may fluctuate or change during the course of recovery. In cases when the person has a severe TBI and is clearly incapable of consenting, clinicians can obtain permission from a legal guardian, power of attorney, or family.
- Further discussion of important factors in obtaining informed consent from someone who may lack capacity is found in the Standards 3.10b and 9.03b of the APA's (2017) *Ethical Principles of Psychologists and Code of Conduct.*

Seeking Consent From a Person Who Is Not Medically Stable

- Typically, neuropsychological testing is not conducted until the person is medically stable or is not in a state of posttraumatic amnesia.

Length of Assessments

- This depends on the setting. Inpatient evaluations are typically shorter in length and may be broken into multiple sessions if testing is to be worked around other therapy services.
- In outpatient settings, testing can take several hours.
- If there is a forensic or legal question, the assessments are usually longer and involve more in-depth interviews with both patient and knowledgeable informants, and relevant documents are reviewed in more detail.

Who Is Paying for the Service?

- If the assessment is for medical purposes, then insurance is billed, and the patient only pays for the portion not covered by insurance.
- If the purpose of the assessment is for a legal purpose (e.g., guardianship or conservatorship proceedings; personal injury litigation) then clinicians are usually retained by legal counsel who is responsible for paying the clinician. It is important in these cases not to do a contingency fee arrangement (i.e., pay is determined by the outcome of the trial) because this is seen as unethical and biased. Insurance is not billed in these cases. Importantly, if the attorney is paying for your services, then the attorney is the client, not the examinee; the attorney may not be representing the client but, for example, may be representing the employer. Therefore, the examinee may not receive feedback or a copy of the report. This needs to be discussed before the evaluation.

- Further discussion of third-party requests for services is found in the APA (2017) Standards 3.07 and *Specialty Guidelines for Forensic Psychology* (APA, 2013).

How to Structure the Report

- Again, this depends on the referral source, setting, purpose of the evaluation, and personal preferences of the clinician. The authors of this chapter have different styles of report writing. One of the authors (TN) puts his summary and recommendations at the beginning of the report because it is the most important section and the one most likely to be read by the referring physician. Another author (KT) sticks with a more traditional approach to report writing but keeps the report brief, includes a test summary sheet, and does not repeat all the test scores but discusses them in the impressions. KT also usually has two separate sections for these types of reports: The first section is for the clinical impressions (e.g., diagnosis, etiology, mood), and the second section is for the forensic impressions (the specific legal capacities being evaluated).

How Much Time Is Spent on Capacity Cases (Including Record Review, Testing, Scoring, Writing)?

- Inpatient consultations may be brief, such as bedside mental status screening to document progress, while outpatient assessments may be much longer, ranging from 4 to 15 hours depending on the specific capacity questions being assessed.

Repeat Assessment

- TBI differs from other neurological disorders in that many individuals can experience full or at least partial recovery of capacity over time; therefore, repeat assessment is often useful. Recovery from TBI is often a more accelerated and complete process compared with recovery from other acquired brain injuries (Cullen, Park, & Bayley, 2008). Most of the recovery from TBI occurs during the first year after injury, so the reevaluation may occur at a year or so after injury or at important milestones (e.g., return to work, return to driving, possible return to independent living).

Accommodations for Driving and Work Capacity

- Certain areas of diminished ability may be compensated for with accommodations. Environmental alterations are particularly useful for addressing physical limitations. Examples may include hand controls and altered steering wheels for driving and voice dictation software or workspace alterations for employment. Unfortunately, at this time it is difficult to compensate for cognitive deficits in driving because deficits such as slowed processing speed or poor attention preclude safe operation of a motor vehicle.

Supporting Decision-Making in Persons With Diminished Capacity

- Capacity to consent to treatment and to research are two key areas in which clinicians can provide support to maximize capacity. For individuals with memory impairments, information should be written down so that it can be referred back to. Comprehension may be affected so information should be explained in a discrete, easy-to-understand manner. In addition, clinicians can check in with individuals and have them repeat what they have heard them say about their treatment or research options so that they can correct any errors and ensure the individual truly understands the information. Because many individuals with TBI experience slowed processing speed, monitor the pace of the dialogue and allow time for them to process the information and to ask questions.

CASE EXAMPLES

In our clinical experience, we tend to see a greater number of return to work and driving capacity assessments in younger and middle-age populations after TBI.[1] Although older adults certainly experience TBI, they are less likely to present with a desire to return to work or driving, possibly due to retiring or being more open to relying on family members to provide transportation. Therefore, one of our cases presented here is an example of a capacity evaluation for a younger adult. However, the capacity assessment process would be similar in an older adult with similar injuries.

Case 1: Mr. Smith—Return to Driving After a Severe TBI

Mr. Howard Smith, a 60-year-old Caucasian man with 13 years of education, was initially seen in the context of admission to an inpatient rehabilitation unit. He sustained a severe TBI in an MVC 2 weeks before admission. No GCS was available in his medical record; however, on emergency department admission, he exhibited altered mental status but was moving all extremities. Imaging revealed brain injury, specifically bifrontal and temporal lobe contusions, tentorial subdural hematoma and subarachnoid hemorrhage, and a diffuse axonal injury. He also sustained multiple orthopedic

[1]Although the case examples in this chapter are based on the authors' real experiences, the identities of the individuals involved in these examples have been properly disguised to protect their confidentiality.

fractures, including vertebral fractures. Mr. Smith exhibited agitation and altered mental status throughout his acute care hospitalization and was administered an antipsychotic medication to manage his agitation. He also exhibited consistent left-side weakness. While in the acute care hospital, he underwent surgical procedures including cervical spinal fusion and halo placement. He was then admitted to an interdisciplinary inpatient rehabilitation unit, where he completed 2 weeks of rehabilitation. Before his injury, he was auditing classes at a college and worked part time as an attendant at a golf course. There was no known history of learning or psychiatric difficulties and no history of substance abuse.

Mr. Smith completed an initial neuropsychological evaluation 3.5 weeks after injury. On this evaluation, he demonstrated full orientation, intact attention, and functional language abilities. Motor and sensory functioning was intact. He exhibited slowed processing speed (Symbol Digit Modalities Test [SDMT], TMT) and variable memory performance, with significant difficulty on a high-load list learning task (California Verbal Learning Test—II; Delis et al., 2000). Overall, his performance was consistent with mild frontotemporal dysfunction. Given his cognitive deficits, Mr. Smith was advised not to return to driving and informed that state statutes required a 6-month driving restriction period after a neurological event. Approximately 4 weeks after his injury, he was discharged home to the care of his family, with instructions to continue with outpatient follow-up care, including speech and physical therapy.

Mr. Smith returned for a follow-up neuropsychological evaluation at 3 months postinjury. He had recently returned to work but had not yet returned to driving. At this point he reported physical and cognitive difficulties including vertigo, hearing loss in right ear, impaired left side fine motor ability, impaired strength bilaterally, and slow but variable processing speed. His cognitive performance was otherwise intact. This assessment included several measures thought to be relevant for return to driving, including SDMT (oral—low average; written—borderline impaired), UFOV (very low risk; normal on visual processing speed, divided attention, and selective attention), TMT (Trails A—low average; Trails B—mildly impaired), Neuropsychological Assessment Battery (NAB; Stern & White, 2003) Driving Scenes (average), NAB Map Reading (low average), and the SDMT (pass). Although his performance on these measures was variable, he was overall deemed to have exhibited sufficient cognitive recovery to attempt to resume driving. Despite the difficulty on some measures (Trails B, SDMT), overall the balance of his cognitive performance led us to conclude that his cognition was sufficient to return to driving. Table 4.4 lists the results of his evaluation.

Mr. Smith had exhibited strong improvements and was believed to be nearing his cognitive baseline. He exhibited good awareness of his deficits and expressed openness to a gradual supervised return to driving once physically able. Mr. Smith also recognized the need to resolve his continued physical and sensory deficits before resuming driving. Thus, he was cleared to return to driving from a cognitive standpoint, pending clearance from a medical

TABLE 4.4. Neuropsychological Evaluation Results of Case 1

Test	Type of score	Score	Classification
Grooved Pegboard Test, dominant hand	Std	93	Average
Grooved Pegboard Test, nondominant hand	Std	67	Mildly impaired
Grip Strength Test, dominant hand	Std	79	Borderline impaired
Grip Strength Test, nondominant hand	Std	72	Mildly impaired
Wechsler Abbreviated Scale of Intelligence—II Matrix Reasoning Subtest (Wechsler, 2011)	Std	103	Average
Wechsler Abbreviated Scale of Intelligence—II Full Scale IQ-2 (Wechsler, 2011)	Std	95	Average
Symbol Digit Modalities Test (Smith, 1973)			
Oral	Std	83	Low average
Written	Std	75	Borderline impaired
Useful Field of View Test (Fisk et al., 2002)			Very low risk
Processing speed	Raw (m/s)	16.7	Normal central vision and/or processing speed
Divided attention	Raw (m/s)	20	Normal
Selective attention	Raw (m/s)	30.1	Normal
Trail Making Test Part A (Reitan, 1956)	Std	83	Low average
Trail Making Test Part B (Reitan, 1956)	Std	73	Mildly impaired
Frontal Systems Behavior Scale—Family (Grace & Malloy, 2001)			
Before injury			
Apathy	T	37	Clinically insignificant
Disinhibition	T	43	Clinically insignificant
Executive dysfunction	T	55	Clinically insignificant
Total	T	44	Clinically insignificant
After injury			
Apathy	T	35	Clinically insignificant
Disinhibition	T	33	Clinically insignificant
Executive dysfunction	T	42	Clinically insignificant
Total	T	34	Clinically insignificant

(*continues*)

TABLE 4.4. Neuropsychological Evaluation Results of Case 1 (*Continued*)

Test	Type of score	Score	Classification
Stroke Drivers' Screening Assessment (Nouri & Lincoln, 1994)			
Square matrix: directions	Raw		—
Square matrix: compass	Raw	32/32	Pass
Road sign recognition	Raw	6/12	Pass
Neuropsychological Assessment Battery (Stern & White, 2003)			
Map reading subtest	Std	89	Low average
Driving scenes subtest	Std	97	Average

Note. Std = Standard score (Mean of 100); T = T score (Mean of 50).

professional in regard to his physical deficits, such as vertigo. This appeared to be a motivating factor for him to continue engaging in continued outpatient rehabilitation to maximize his recovery and to avoid mild symptoms of depression and frustration that were beginning to arise due to his lack of functional independence. He also was encouraged to continue increasing his level of independence by taking on more responsibilities within the home, engaging in cognitively stimulating activities, and resuming a regular exercise routine.

On the basis of the results of this evaluation, Mr. Smith was cleared to return to driving from a cognitive standpoint. However, vertigo and his physical deficits, including impaired range of motion secondary to cervical and collarbone fractures, remained as physical barriers to his returning to driving. It was recommended he continue follow-up with physicians and therapists and begin gradual return to driving when physically released to do so. Upon receiving that release, he was advised to resume driving in a gradual fashion, beginning in lightly trafficked areas in ideal driving conditions with another adult in the car to supervise, and later progressing to more challenging driving situations as he and his family felt comfortable. With this advice, he continued engagement in interdisciplinary rehabilitative care, which was particularly important in his recovery, given his constellation of symptoms. He continued to attend therapies for the vertigo and limited range of motion. Once these issues resolved, in addition to his improved cognitive performance, his physiatrist formally cleared his return to driving.

Mr. Smith returned for a follow-up neuropsychological evaluation at 6 months postinjury. At this point, he had returned to classes and employment and was driving without difficulty. He was working with a state-run vocational rehabilitation program. His processing speed had improved and fell within the low average to average range (SDMT oral and written—low average; Trails A—average; Trails B—low average). He exhibited otherwise cognitively intact performance. He noted continued occasional subjective memory lapses, but his performance was intact on formal testing. He was mildly impulsive. He had not experienced any seizure activity. The vertigo and physical weakness had resolved. No mood or behavioral issues were reported.

Case 1: Pragmatic and Ethical Challenges

1. Guidelines differ somewhat by state, but in the state where we practice, guidelines require a 6-month period after a neurological event without any further events before returning to driving. In other states, statutes may range from a 6-month to a 1-year period, and specificity of the type of neurological event may vary. The way our state statute is written, theoretically this applies to any event resulting in altered mental status, such as a concussion. Thus, it poses a dilemma when an individual appears to be sufficiently recovered to drive before the 6-month window. In this case, the patient was informed of the statute but also cleared from a cognitive standpoint pending further physical clearance from a physician.
2. Despite the state statute restricting driving, it was felt that returning to driving would be in the patient's best interest once he had adequately recovered. Returning to driving would allow the patient to increase his level of independence by returning to work and social engagements. This would also serve to potentially improve his symptoms of depression by increasing his engagement in activities and getting him out of the house.
3. Providing supports is key. Further easing concern about his resumption of driving, Mr. Smith's family was highly supportive and invested in assisting his recovery. They were willing to provide close supervision as he returned to driving in a gradual fashion. This included returning to driving in a similar manner to individuals with a learner's driver permit. Initially, he was encouraged to drive in low-traffic areas, such as an empty parking lot, and in ideal driving conditions. As the driver and supervisors increased in their level of comfort and confidence, driving could progress to higher traffic areas and more challenging driving situations (e.g., bad weather, rush hour, nighttime driving).
4. Input from multiple health care providers was necessary for providing clearance to return to driving. Given Mr. Smith's constellation of symptoms, he required neuropsychological clearance in regard to his cognitive status and medical clearance given his physical difficulties, such as vertigo and weakness.
5. If Mr. Smith's recovery had been insufficient to return to driving, it would be critical to intervene to develop alternative methods of transportation and provide support for associated consequences. This is particularly important

for older adults because driving cessation in older populations is associated with declines in physical, social, and cognitive health as well as with depression (Chihuri et al., 2016). Additionally, in many cases, referrals to occupational therapy may be in order to arrange vehicle accommodations to address residual physical deficits even if an individual is cognitively able to return to driving.

Case 2: Mr. Jones—Return to Work After Severe TBI

Mr. Al Jones, a 62-year-old man, was admitted to an acute rehabilitation program for injuries sustained when he fell about 6 feet onto concrete in late 2016. He briefly lost consciousness, followed by altered mental status and agitation. A complete Glasgow Coma Scale score was not available because Mr. Jones had been sedated before arrival at the hospital, but there was an extended period of confusion and PTA (more than 7 days) consistent with a severe TBI. Head computed tomography (CT) scan revealed right subdural hematoma, left intracranial hemorrhage, and subarachnoid hemorrhage. He did not require neurosurgical intervention. An electroencephalogram did not show seizure activity but did reveal diffuse encephalopathy. A follow-up CT scan 11 days after the event showed increased hemorrhage in the left frontal and temporal lobes with 2 mm midline shift. Two weeks after his injury, he was able to follow commands, but verbal output was confused. He exhibited significant receptive and expressive aphasia during his brief stay in acute rehabilitation, which began 2 weeks after his injury. There were no significant motor limitations, and he was able to participate in ADLs. Mr. Jones was insistent on being discharged; it was not clear whether he was aware of his deficits. With assurance that his wife could provide supervision, he was discharged with plans for follow-up 6 weeks later.

At the time of his injury, Mr. Jones was residing with his wife of 25 years. Mr. Jones completed a general associate's degree with an A–B average. He had served as a school resource officer for 15 years, walking the hallways while interacting with staff and students. He was responsible for locker and backpack searches with cause, but he had not physically confronted a student or come close to drawing a weapon. Medical history included obstructive sleep apnea, osteoarthritis (c-spine and hips), and mild cardiomyopathy. There was no reported history of psychiatric difficulties. There was no history of alcohol, tobacco, or illicit drug use.

Ms. Jones was contacted by phone 2 weeks after discharge and reported that her husband was doing well. Being home had calmed him, and his language abilities were improving. He was participating in outpatient speech therapy. A month later, Ms. Jones called to express concern about her husband's anger outbursts and general level of agitation. He was confused at times and argumentative. She was counseled about behavioral interventions and steps to take if she felt endangered. She mentioned that during a visual exam, a right upper quadrantanopia was noted, but otherwise intact visual abilities were found. It was agreed to meet in the office, which occurred 3 days later, 2 months after his injury. His language was much improved, and he was able to participate in an interview. He was fully oriented. Mr. Jones was performing all ADLs independently. He attended speech therapy twice a week and was performing a home program recommended by his therapist. He was able to stay at home alone when his wife returned to work. He was engaging in maintenance and animal care activities on his farm. He admitted to having driven a couple of times without any mishaps. He was taking his own medications. He was eating regularly and could make his own meals. He was receiving sick leave benefits from his job and expressed concern that physically and mentally, he would not be capable of performing as a school resource officer, particularly if there were an emergency. His hope was to continue working as a resource officer for another 5 years, which would entitle him to a pension, and then focus on his farm.

During the session, Mr. Jones admitted that earlier in his recovery he had "dark days" when he was depressed and frustrated over his inability to work, inactivity, and communication difficulties. Things had improved substantially for him. He denied suicidal or homicidal ideation. He was still having angry thoughts at times, but these were diminishing. His wife noted that he had displayed his anger overtly to the point that he would raise his voice and exhibit profanity, which was not characteristic of him before his injury. He was not violent, and things were improving. Ms. Jones was provided a handout regarding managing behavioral difficulties after TBI, and they agreed to meet again in 2 months for a neuropsychological evaluation. In the interim, Mr. Jones was to continue with his recovery program, and Ms. Jones was advised to call if further behavioral problems arose.

Neuropsychological evaluation took place 5 months after the injury. During the interview, there were intermittent word retrieval difficulties that did not interfere with communication. Comprehension was not a problem. Mr. Jones was spontaneous in his discourse and seemed able to recall recent events. His mood was euthymic, and affect ranged appropriately. Ms. Jones, in a separate interview, indicated that anger outbursts had resolved. Mr. Jones, in her opinion, had no problems with attention, memory, or problem-solving skills. She had no concerns about his judgment. Mild language difficulties, such as difficulty retrieving a word or with syntax, were evident but did not interfere with communication. He was interacting normally in social situations. She expressed no concerns about his returning to driving or working as a resource officer. The neuropsychological evaluation focused on multiple cognitive domains, physical abilities, emotional status, and behavioral issues. Table 4.5 lists the results of Mr. Jones's evaluation.

The right upper quadrant visual defect was not having a significant impact on his functioning. There were no significant motor limitations. He was also doing relatively well cognitively. He performed within average limits for his age with respect to basic attention skills, spatial and constructional abilities,

TABLE 4.5. Neuropsychological Evaluations Results of Case 2

Test	Type of score	Score	Classification
Neglect screening	—	—	No evidence of neglect
Grooved Pegboard Test, dominant hand	Std	89	Low average
Grooved Pegboard Test, nondominant hand	Std	87	Low average
Grip Strength Test, dominant hand	Std	90	Average
Grip Strength Test, nondominant hand	Std	99	Average
Wechsler Adult Intelligence Scale—IV Digit Span Subtest (Wechsler, 2008)	Std	90	Average
Useful Field of View (UFOV; Fisk et al., 2002) Test			
Processing speed	—		Normal
Divided attention	—		Normal
Selective attention	—		Difficulty
Token Test (De Renzi & Vignolo, 1962)	Std	113	High average
Benton Sentence Repetition Test (Spreen & Benton, 1963)	Std	90	Average
Boston Naming Test (Kaplan, Goodglass, & Weintraub, 1983)			
Correct	Std	80	Low average
Correct with phonemic cues		4/10	
Controlled Oral Word Association Test (Benton, Hamsher, et al., 1994)			
FAS	Std	78	Borderline impaired
Animal naming	Std	83	Low average
Benton Visual Form Discrimination (Benton, Sivan, et al., 1994)	Std	113	High average
Rey Complex Figure Test (Meyers & Meyers, 1995)			
Copy	Std	>120	Superior
Immediate reproduction	Std	108	Average
Delayed reproduction	Std	113	High average
Recognition	Std	98	Average

TABLE 4.5. Neuropsychological Evaluations Results of Case 2 (*Continued*)

Test	Type of score	Score	Classification
California Verbal Learning Test—II (Delis et al., 2000)			
Trials 1–5 total	Std	109	Average
Short delay free recall	Std	122	Superior
Long delay free recall	Std	130	Superior
Intrusions (all recall trials)	Std	78	Borderline impaired
Recognition hits	Std	115	High average
Recognition false positives	Std	115	High average
Recognition discriminability (*d′*)	Std	122	Superior
Trail Making Test Part A (Reitan, 1956)	Std	72	Mildly impaired
Trail Making Test Part B (Reitan, 1956)	Std	77	Borderline impaired
Wisconsin Card Sorting Test—64 (Kongs et al., 2000)			
Categories		2	
Perseverative responses	Std	84	Low average
Wechsler Test of Adult Reading (The Psychological Corporation, 2001)	Std	84	Low average
Full-scale IQ estimate	Std	95	Average
Patient Health Questionnaire (Spitzer et al., 1999)	Raw	4	Minimal depression
Frontal Systems Behavior Scale—Family (Grace & Malloy, 2001)			
Before injury			
Apathy	T	45	Clinically insignificant
Disinhibition	T	45	Clinically insignificant
Executive dysfunction	T	47	Clinically insignificant
Total	T	45	Clinically insignificant
After injury			
Apathy	T	44	Clinically insignificant
Disinhibition	T	47	Clinically insignificant
Executive dysfunction	T	53	Clinically insignificant
Total	T	48	Clinically insignificant

(*continues*)

TABLE 4.5. Neuropsychological Evaluations Results of Case 2 (*Continued*)

Test	Type of score	Score	Classification
Stroke Drivers' Screening Assessment (Nouri & Lincoln, 1994)			
Square matrix: directions	Raw	32	—
Square matrix: compass	Raw	27	Pass
Road sign recognition	Raw	10	Pass
Neuropsychological Assessment Battery (Stern & White, 2003)			
Map reading	Std	115	High average
Driving scenes	Std	130	Superior

Note. Std = Standard score (Mean of 100); T = T score (Mean of 50).

and memory for new information. Performance within average limits on tasks assessing language comprehension and expression was particularly impressive given his earlier aphasia. Mr. Jones had mild difficulty with speed of response, but he was persistent and accurate. He was capable of independent reasoning as long as speed was not expected. Results were considered to reflect mild left hemisphere disorder. Mr. Jones was not exhibiting signs of emotional distress, and there were no behavioral issues of note.

The results were discussed with Mr. Jones's physiatrist, who saw him on the same day as the neuropsychological evaluation. It was agreed that he had reached a level of recovery that participation in a driving evaluation was reasonable. A gradual, supervised resumption of his duties as a school resource officer was also considered reasonable. Mr. Jones was provided with a letter to present to the sheriff's department indicating "a gradual and supervised resumption of job duties is reasonable, specifically focusing on his duties as a school resource officer. The most suitable plan is for Mr. Jones to join the officer who has been substituting for him to ensure that he can manage his duties as a resource officer." Mr. Jones was advised to contact the office if there was further need for information or documentation or if problems arose. He was also advised that the sheriff's department would have specific performance expectations (e.g., regarding use of his weapon) that he would have to meet. He subsequently underwent a driving evaluation with the sheriff's department and a weapons check, both of which he passed. Three months later, Mr. Jones was driving without restriction and had not experienced any mishaps. He was working full time as a school resource officer. Further follow-up after another 3 months did not indicate any changes in his circumstances.

Case 2: Pragmatic and Ethical Challenges

1. Mr. Jones demanded discharge even though he was obviously cognitively impaired and could not manage his life independently. The decision to

discharge him was based on several factors. First, his hospitalization was voluntary; there was no commitment proceeding. This could have been challenged, but that would not have furthered any rehabilitation goals. He was not willing to attend therapies, so extending his inpatient stay would not have added to his treatment benefit. It was established that his wife would be present, and she had demonstrated a good capacity to deal with him. Being in familiar surroundings at home would potentially benefit his recovery and prospects for improvement were good. Arrangements for outpatient therapies were made. Needless to say, this required a lot of discussion among the treatment team.

2. Mr. Jones was already driving when he returned 2 months after his injury, albeit just a couple of times (although experience suggests it was likely more than that). The state places a 6-month hiatus on driving after an altered mental state. He could have been reported to the Medical Advisory Board, which might have initiated the process of suspending his license. However, it can take several weeks to complete the process, by which time Mr. Jones may have been beyond the 6-month restriction. Experience has also demonstrated that once suspended, it is burdensome to get the license reinstated. Thus, he was notified of the state statute and advised to desist in driving.

3. As with the first case, providing supports is key. Mr. Jones participated in rehabilitation services on an inpatient and outpatient basis. His family supported him in his adjustment and encouraged him to participate in meaningful activities on his farm. In addition, supportive services were provided to the caregiver to assist her in managing his recovery.

4. When is there sufficient recovery to return to driving and to work? When there is a confluence of reports indicating that the time is right. The neuropsychological results lined up with the report of Mr. Jones and his wife. He demonstrated adequate physical capacity based on daily activities and an examination of job duties. Cognitive abilities were sufficient to allow communication, recall of information, and reasoning at a level consistent with job demands. There were no behavioral problems that might affect job performance. Admittedly, this was a judgment call, but it was bolstered by data and information. Consultation with other members of the treatment team, in this case, the physiatrist, was also essential.

5. It is important to work with community resources and employers. Although not involved in this case, state vocational rehabilitation services can be a valuable partner. It was known that the sheriff's department was going to evaluate Mr. Jones with regard to driving (under more challenging circumstances than a typical driving evaluation) and weapon safety. Often, police and fire departments also impose physical strength and conditioning requirements for those returning to patrol duty. This was not required, presumably because of the nature of the job.

6. Finally, if Mr. Jones had not been able to return to work because of insufficient recovery, it would be important to consider potential effects on his health and mental health and to provide additional supports as well as information on opportunities for supplemental income (Mandal & Roe, 2008). Barring a return to work, it would be important to assist Mr. Jones to find activities that maximize his independence and allow him to remain active throughout the day. Options could include engaging in volunteer opportunities, finding new hobbies, or working with supports, such as vocational rehabilitation services.

REFLECTION

TBIs are common across the life span. Although uncomplicated mild TBI usually does not result in impaired capacity, persons with more severe injuries may experience cognitive and physical changes that can impair their capacity to function independently. Two common capacities assessed in a rehabilitation setting include the ability to return to driving and employment. When combined with other sources of data, neuropsychological testing can be useful in helping determine the capacity to return to driving and employment. In this chapter, we provided an overview of TBI and assessment of capacity in this population focusing on two important areas of capacity: return to driving and return to employment. We presented two case examples of these two capacities to provide the reader with a better understanding of how these evaluations are conducted, what tests to include, and important information for clinicians to cover in their reports. We also provided practical advice and the potential challenges that may occur when performing these types of evaluations.

REFERENCES

American Psychological Association. (2013). Specialty guidelines for forensic psychology. *American Psychologist, 68,* 7–19. http://dx.doi.org/10.1037/a0029889

American Psychological Association. (2014). Guidelines for psychological practice with older adults. *American Psychologist, 69,* 34–65. http://dx.doi.org/10.1037/a0035063

American Psychological Association. (2017). *Ethical principles of psychologists and code of conduct* (2002, Amended June 1, 2010, and January 1, 2017). Washington, DC: American Psychological Association. Retrieved from http://www.apa.org/ethics/code/index

Andelic, N., Stevens, L. F., Sigurdardottir, S., Arango-Lasprilla, J. C., & Roe, C. (2012). Associations between disability and employment 1 year after traumatic brain injury in a working age population. *Brain Injury, 26,* 261–269. http://dx.doi.org/10.3109/02699052.2012.654589

Andersson, E. E., Bedics, B. K., & Falkmer, T. (2011). Mild traumatic brain injuries: A 10-year follow-up. *Journal of Rehabilitation Medicine, 43,* 323–329. http://dx.doi.org/10.2340/16501977-0666

Arango-Lasprilla, J. C., Ketchum, J. M., Lewis, A. N., Krch, D., Gary, K. W., & Dodd, B. A., Jr. (2011). Racial and ethnic disparities in employment outcomes for persons with traumatic brain injury: A longitudinal investigation 1–5 years after injury. *PM & R, 3,* 1083–1091. http://dx.doi.org/10.1016/j.pmrj.2011.05.023

Benton, A. L., Hamsher, K. de S., & Sivan, A. B. (1994). *Multilingual Aphasia Examination*. Iowa City, Iowa: AJA Associates.

Benton, A. L., Sivan, A. B., Hamsher, K., Varney, N. R., & Spreen, O. (1994). *Contributions to neuropsychological assessment: A clinical manual* (2nd ed.). New York, NY: Oxford University Press.

Bivona, U., D'Ippolito, M., Giustini, M., Vignally, P., Longo, E., Taggi, F., & Formisano, R. (2012). Return to driving after severe traumatic brain injury: Increased risk of traffic accidents and personal responsibility. *The Journal of Head Trauma Rehabilitation, 27,* 210–215. http://dx.doi.org/10.1097/HTR.0b013e31822178a9

Bogg, T., & Roberts, B. W. (2004). Conscientiousness and health-related behaviors: A meta-analysis of the leading behavioral contributors to mortality. *Psychological Bulletin, 130,* 887–919. http://dx.doi.org/10.1037/0033-2909.130.6.887

Brooks, N., & Hawley, C. A. (2005). Return to driving after traumatic brain injury: A British perspective. *Brain Injury, 19,* 165–175. http://dx.doi.org/10.1080/02699050410001720004

Brouwer, W. H., Waterink, W., Van Wolffelaar, P. C., & Rothengatter, T. (1991). Divided attention in experienced young and older drivers: Lane tracking and visual analysis in a dynamic driving simulator. *Human Factors, 33,* 573–582. http://dx.doi.org/10.1177/001872089103300508

Cancelliere, C., Kristman, V. L., Cassidy, J. D., Hincapié, C. A., Côté, P., Boyle, E., . . . Borg, J. (2014). Systematic review of return to work after mild traumatic brain injury: Results of the International Collaboration on Mild Traumatic Brain Injury Prognosis. *Archives of Physical Medicine and Rehabilitation, 95*(3, Suppl.), S201–S209. http://dx.doi.org/10.1016/j.apmr.2013.10.010

Carlozzi, N. E., Gade, V., Rizzo, A. S., & Tulsky, D. S. (2013). Using virtual reality driving simulators in persons with spinal cord injury: Three screen display versus head mounted display. *Disability and Rehabilitation: Assistive Technology, 8,* 176–180. http://dx.doi.org/10.3109/17483107.2012.699990

Centers for Disease Control and Prevention. (2016, 01/22/2016). *Basic information about traumatic brain injury and concussion*. Retrieved from http://cdc.gov/traumatic braininjury/basics.html

Chihuri, S., Mielenz, T. J., DiMaggio, C. J., Betz, M. E., DiGuiseppi, C., Jones, V. C., & Li, G. (2016). Driving cessation and health outcomes in older adults. *Journal of the American Geriatrics Society, 64,* 332–341. http://dx.doi.org/10.1111/jgs.13931.

Cifu, D. X., Kreutzer, J. S., Marwitz, J. H., Rosenthal, M., Englander, J., & High, W. (1996). Functional outcomes of older adults with traumatic brain injury: A prospective, multicenter analysis. *Archives of Physical Medicine and Rehabilitation, 77,* 883–888. http://dx.doi.org/10.1016/S0003-9993(96)90274-9

Coleman, R. D., Rapport, L. J., Ergh, T. C., Hanks, R. A., Ricker, J. H., & Millis, S. R. (2002). Predictors of driving outcome after traumatic brain injury. *Archives of Physical Medicine and Rehabilitation, 83,* 1415–1422. http://dx.doi.org/10.1053/apmr.2002.35111

Coronado, V. G., Thomas, K. E., Sattin, R. W., & Johnson, R. L. (2005). The CDC traumatic brain injury surveillance system: Characteristics of persons aged 65 years and older hospitalized with a TBI. *The Journal of Head Trauma Rehabilitation, 20,* 215–228. http://dx.doi.org/10.1097/00001199-200505000-00005

Crooks, C. Y., Zumsteg, J. M., & Bell, K. R. (2007). Traumatic brain injury: A review of practice management and recent advances. *Physical Medicine and Rehabilitation Clinics of North America, 18,* 681–710, vi. http://dx.doi.org/10.1016/j.pmr.2007.06.005

Cullen, N. K., Park, Y. G., & Bayley, M. T. (2008). Functional recovery following traumatic vs non-traumatic brain injury: A case-controlled study. *Brain Injury, 22,* 1013–1020. http://dx.doi.org/10.1080/02699050802530581

Cuthbert, J. P., Pretz, C. R., Bushnik, T., Fraser, R. T., Hart, T., Kolakowsky-Hayner, S. A., . . . Sherer, M. (2015). Ten-year employment patterns of working age individuals after moderate to severe traumatic brain injury: A National Institute on Disability and Rehabilitation Research Traumatic Brain Injury Model Systems study. *Archives of Physical Medicine and Rehabilitation, 96,* 2128–2136. http://dx.doi.org/10.1016/j.apmr.2015.07.020

Dams-O'Connor, K., Cuthbert, J. P., Whyte, J., Corrigan, J. D., Faul, M., & Harrison-Felix, C. (2013). Traumatic brain injury among older adults at Level I and II trauma centers. *Journal of Neurotrauma, 30,* 2001–2013. http://dx.doi.org/10.1089/neu.2013.3047

Delis, D. C., Kramer, J. H., Kaplan, E., & Ober, B. (2000). *California Verbal Learning Test—II.* San Antonio, TX: Pearson.

De Renzi, E., & Vignolo, L. (1962). The Token Test: A sensitive test to detect receptive disturbances in aphasics. *Brain, 85,* 665–678.

DiSanto, D., Kumar, R. G., Juengst, S. B., Hart, T., O'Neil-Pirozzi, T. M., Zasler, N. D., . . . Wagner, A. K. (2019). Employment stability in the first 5 years after moderate-to-severe traumatic brain injury. *Archives of Physical Medicine and Rehabilitation, 100,* 412–421.

Elander, J., West, R., & French, D. (1993). Behavioral correlates of individual differences in road-traffic crash risk: An examination method and findings. *Psychological Bulletin, 113,* 279–294. http://dx.doi.org/10.1037/0033-2909.113.2.279

Faul, M., Xu, L., Wald, M., & Coronado, V. (2010). *Traumatic brain injury in the United States: Emergency department visits, hospitalizations and deaths, 2002–2006.* Atlanta, GA: Centers for Disease Control and Prevention, National Center for Injury Prevention and Control. http://dx.doi.org/10.15620/cdc.5571

Finkelstein, E., Corso, P., & Miller, T. (2006). *The incidence and economic burden of injuries in the United States.* New York, NY: Oxford University Press. http://dx.doi.org/10.1093/acprof:oso/9780195179484.001.0001

Fisk, G. D., Novack, T., Mennemeier, M., & Roenker, D. (2002). Useful field of view after traumatic brain injury. *The Journal of Head Trauma Rehabilitation, 17,* 16–25. http://dx.doi.org/10.1097/00001199-200202000-00004

Fisk, G. D., Schneider, J. J., & Novack, T. A. (1998). Driving following traumatic brain injury: Prevalence, exposure, advice and evaluations. *Brain Injury, 12,* 683–695. http://dx.doi.org/10.1080/026990598122241

Fox, G. K., Bowden, S. C., & Smith, D. S. (1998). On-road assessment of driving competence after brain impairment: Review of current practice and recommendations for a standardized examination. *Archives of Physical Medicine and Rehabilitation, 79,* 1288–1296. http://dx.doi.org/10.1016/S0003-9993(98)90277-5

Franulic, A., Carbonell, C. G., Pinto, P., & Sepulveda, I. (2004). Psychosocial adjustment and employment outcome 2, 5 and 10 years after TBI. *Brain Injury, 18,* 119–129. http://dx.doi.org/10.1080/0269905031000149515

Garrelfs, S. F., Donker-Cools, B. H., Wind, H., & Frings-Dresen, M. H. (2015). Return-to-work in patients with acquired brain injury and psychiatric disorders as a comorbidity: A systematic review. *Brain Injury, 29,* 550–557. http://dx.doi.org/10.3109/02699052.2014.995227

Grace, J., & Malloy, P. (2001). *Frontal Systems Behavior Scale: Professional manual.* Lutz, FL: Psychological Assessment Resources.

Grauwmeijer, E., Heijenbrok-Kal, M. H., Haitsma, I. K., & Ribbers, G. M. (2017). Employment outcome ten years after moderate to severe traumatic brain injury: A prospective cohort study. *Journal of Neurotrauma, 34,* 2575–2581. http://dx.doi.org/10.1089/neu.2016.4846

Gronwall, D. M. A. (1977). Paced auditory serial-addition task: A measure of recovery from concussion. *Perceptual and Motor Skills, 44,* 367–373.

Heegaard, W., & Biros, M. (2007). Traumatic brain injury. *Emergency Medical Clinics of North America, 25,* 655–678, viii. http://dx.doi.org/10.1016/j.emc.2007.07.001

Hessen, E., Anderson, V., & Nestvold, K. (2008). MMPI–2 profiles 23 years after paediatric mild traumatic brain injury. *Brain Injury, 22,* 39–50. http://dx.doi.org/10.1080/02699050701846179

Innes, C. R., Jones, R. D., Dalrymple-Alford, J. C., Hayes, S., Hollobon, S., Severinsen, J., . . . Anderson, T. J. (2007). Sensory-motor and cognitive tests predict driving ability of persons with brain disorders. *Journal of the Neurological Sciences, 260,* 188–198. http://dx.doi.org/10.1016/j.jns.2007.04.052

Iverson, G. L., & Lange, R. T. (2011a). Mild traumatic brain injury. In M. R. Schoenberg & J. G. Scott (Eds.), *The little black book of neuropsychology: A syndrome based approach* (pp. 697–719). New York, NY: Springer. http://dx.doi.org/10.1007/978-0-387-76978-3_22

Iverson, G. L., & Lange, R. T. (2011b). Moderate and severe traumatic brain injury. In M. R. Shoenberg & J. G. Scott (Eds.), *The little black book of neuropsychology: A syndrome-based approach* (pp. 663–696). New York, NY: Springer. http://dx.doi.org/10.1007/978-0-387-76978-3_21

Kaplan, E. F., Goodglass, H., & Weintraub, S. (1983). *The Boston Naming Test* (2nd ed.). Philadelphia, PA: Lea & Febiger.

Ketchum, J. M., Almaz Getachew, M., Krch, D., Baños, J. H., Kolakowsky-Hayner, S. A., Lequerica, A., . . . Arango-Lasprilla, J. C. (2012). Early predictors of employment outcomes 1 year post traumatic brain injury in a population of Hispanic individuals. *NeuroRehabilitation, 30,* 13–22.

Kongs, S. K., Thompson, L. L., Iverson, G. L., & Heaton, R. K. (2000). *WCST-64: Wisconsin Card Sorting Test–64 Card Version*. Odessa, FL: Psychological Assessment Resources.

Korteling, J. E., & Kaptein, N. A. (1996). Neuropsychological driving fitness tests for brain-damaged subjects. *Archives of Physical Medicine and Rehabilitation, 77,* 138–146. http://dx.doi.org/10.1016/S0003-9993(96)90158-6

Kreutzer, J. S., Marwitz, J. H., Walker, W., Sander, A., Sherer, M., Bogner, J., . . . Bushnik, T. (2003). Moderating factors in return to work and job stability after traumatic brain injury. *The Journal of Head Trauma Rehabilitation, 18,* 128–138. http://dx.doi.org/10.1097/00001199-200303000-00004

Labbe, D. R., Vance, D. E., Wadley, V., & Novack, T. A. (2014). Predictors of driving avoidance and exposure following traumatic brain injury. *The Journal of Head Trauma Rehabilitation, 29,* 185–192. http://dx.doi.org/10.1097/HTR.0b013e3182795211

Langlois, J., Rutland-Brown, W., & Thomas, K. (2004). *Traumatic brain injury in the United States: Emergency department visits, hospitalizations, and deaths*. Atlanta, GA: Centers for Disease Control and Prevention, National Center for Injury Prevention.

Lezak, M., Howieson, D., Bigler, E., & Tranel, D. (2012). *Neuropsychological assessment* (5th ed.). New York, NY: Oxford University Press.

LoBue, C., Munro, C., Schaffert, J., Didehbani, N., Hart, J., Batjer, H., & Cullum, C. M. (2019). Traumatic brain injury and risk of long-term brain changes, accumulation of pathological markers, and developing dementia: A review. *Journal of Alzheimer's Disease, 70,* 629–654. http://dx.doi.org/10.3233/JAD-190028

Lundqvist, A. (2001). Neuropsychological aspects of driving characteristics. *Brain Injury, 15,* 981–994. http://dx.doi.org/10.1080/02699050110065637

Maas, A. I., Stocchetti, N., & Bullock, R. (2008). Moderate and severe traumatic brain injury in adults. *The Lancet Neurology, 7,* 728–741. http://dx.doi.org/10.1016/S1474-4422(08)70164-9

Mandal, B., & Roe, B. (2008, December). Job loss, retirement and the mental health of older Americans. *Journal of Mental Health Policy and Economics, 11,* 167–176.

Mas, M. F., Mathews, A., & Gilbert-Baffoe, E. (2017). Rehabilitation needs of the elder with traumatic brain injury. *Physical Medicine and Rehabilitation Clinics of North America, 28*(4), 829–842. http://dx.doi.org/10.1016/j.pmr.2017.06.014

Meyers, J. E., & Meyers, K. R. (1995). *Rey Complex Figure Test and Recognition Trial*. Lutz, FL: Psychological Assessment Resources.

Meyers, J. E., Volbrecht, M., & Kaster-Bundgaard, J. (1999). Driving is more than pedal pushing. *Applied Neuropsychology, 6*, 154–164. http://dx.doi.org/10.1207/s15324826an0603_3

Nguyen, R., Fiest, K. M., McChesney, J., Kwon, C. S., Jette, N., Frolkis, A. D., . . . Gallagher, C. (2016). The international incidence of traumatic brain injury: A systematic review and meta-analysis. *The Canadian Journal of Neurological Sciences, 43*, 774–785. http://dx.doi.org/10.1017/cjn.2016.290

Nouri, F. M., & Lincoln, N. B. (1994). *The Stroke Drivers Screening Assessment*. Nottingham, England: Nottingham Rehab.

Novack, T. A., Baños, J. H., Alderson, A. L., Schneider, J. J., Weed, W., Blankenship, J., & Salisbury, D. (2006). UFOV performance and driving ability following traumatic brain injury. *Brain Injury, 20*, 455–461. http://dx.doi.org/10.1080/02699050600664541

Novack, T. A., Labbe, D., Grote, M., Carlson, N., Sherer, M., Arango-Lasprilla, J. C., . . . Seel, R. T. (2010). Return to driving within 5 years of moderate–severe traumatic brain injury. *Brain Injury, 24*(3), 464–471. http://dx.doi.org/10.3109/02699051003601713

O'Neill, J., Hibbard, M. R., Brown, M., Jaffe, M., Sliwinski, M., Vandergoot, D., & Weiss, M. J. (1998). The effect of employment on quality of life and community integration after traumatic brain injury. *The Journal of Head Trauma Rehabilitation, 13*, 68–79. http://dx.doi.org/10.1097/00001199-199808000-00007

Ortoleva, C., Brugger, C., Van der Linden, M., & Walder, B. (2012). Prediction of driving capacity after traumatic brain injury: A systematic review. *The Journal of Head Trauma Rehabilitation, 27*, 302–313. http://dx.doi.org/10.1097/HTR.0b013e3182236299

Ponsford, J. L., & Spitz, G. (2015). Stability of employment over the first 3 years following traumatic brain injury. *The Journal of Head Trauma Rehabilitation, 30*, E1–E11. http://dx.doi.org/10.1097/HTR.0000000000000033

The Psychological Corporation. (2001). *Wechsler test of adult reading*. San Antonio, TX: Harcourt Assessment.

Rao, N., Rosenthal, M., Cronin-Stubbs, D., Lambert, R., Barnes, P., & Swanson, B. (1990). Return to work after rehabilitation following traumatic brain injury. *Brain Injury, 4*, 49–56. http://dx.doi.org/10.3109/02699059009026148

Rapport, L. J., Bryer, R. C., & Hanks, R. A. (2008). Driving and community integration after traumatic brain injury. *Archives of Physical Medicine and Rehabilitation, 89*, 922–930. http://dx.doi.org/10.1016/j.apmr.2008.01.009

Reitan, R. M. (1956). *Trail Making Test: Manual for administration, scoring and interpretation*. Indianapolis: Indiana University.

Roozenbeek, B., Maas, A. I., & Menon, D. K. (2013). Changing patterns in the epidemiology of traumatic brain injury. *Nature Reviews. Neurology, 9*, 231–236. http://dx.doi.org/10.1038/nrneurol.2013.22

Ross, P. E., Di Stefano, M., Charlton, J., Spitz, G., & Ponsford, J. L. (2018). Interventions for resuming driving after traumatic brain injury. *Disability and Rehabilitation, 40*, 757–764. http://dx.doi.org/10.1080/09638288.2016.1274341

Ross, P. E., Ponsford, J. L., Di Stefano, M., & Spitz, G. (2015). Predictors of on-road driver performance following traumatic brain injury. *Archives of Physical Medicine and Rehabilitation, 96*, 440–446. http://dx.doi.org/10.1016/j.apmr.2014.09.027

Schanke, A. K., & Sundet, K. (2000). Comprehensive driving assessment: Neuropsychological testing and on-road evaluation of brain injured patients. *Scandinavian Journal of Psychology, 41*, 113–121. http://dx.doi.org/10.1111/1467-9450.00179

Schwab, K. A., Gudmudsson, L. S., & Lew, H. L. (2015). Long-term functional outcomes of traumatic brain injury. *Handbook of Clinical Neurology, 128*, 649–659. http://dx.doi.org/10.1016/B978-0-444-63521-1.00040-6

Smith, A. (1973). *Symbol Digit Modalities Test.* Los Angeles, CA: Western Psychological Services.

Spitzer, R. L., Kroenke, K., Williams, J. B. W., & Patient Health Questionnaire Study Group. (1999). Validity and utility of a self-report version of PRIME-MD: The PHQ Primary Care Study. *JAMA, 282,* 1737–1744.

Spreen, O., & Benton, A. L. (1963). *Sentence Repetition Test: Administration, scoring, and preliminary norms.* Unpublished manuscript, University of Iowa.

Stern, R. A., & White, T. (2003). *Neuropsychological assessment battery.* Lutz, FL: Psychological Assessment Resources.

Steward, K. A., Gerstenecker, A., Triebel, K. L., Kennedy, R., Novack, T. A., Dreer, L. E., & Marson, D. C. (2016). Twelve-month recovery of medical decision-making capacity following traumatic brain injury. *Neurology, 87,* 1052–1059. http://dx.doi.org/10.1212/WNL.0000000000003079

Tamietto, M., Torrini, G., Adenzato, M., Pietrapiana, P., Rago, R., & Perino, C. (2006). To drive or not to drive (after TBI)? A review of the literature and its implications for rehabilitation and future research. *NeuroRehabilitation, 21,* 81–92.

Teasdale, G., & Jennett, B. (1974). Assessment of coma and impaired consciousness: A practical scale. *The Lancet, 304,* 81–84. http://dx.doi.org/10.1016/S0140-6736(74)91639-0

Thurman, D. J. (2016). The epidemiology of traumatic brain injury in children and youths: A review of research since 1990. *Journal of Child Neurology, 31,* 20–27. http://dx.doi.org/10.1177/0883073814544363

Triebel, K. L., Martin, R. C., Novack, T. A., Dreer, L. E., Turner, C., Kennedy, R., & Marson, D. C. (2014). Recovery over 6 months of medical decision-making capacity after traumatic brain injury. *Archives of Physical Medicine and Rehabilitation, 95,* 2296–2303. http://dx.doi.org/10.1016/j.apmr.2014.07.413

Triebel, K. L., Martin, R. C., Novack, T. A., Dreer, L., Turner, C., Pritchard, P. R., . . . Marson, D. C. (2012). Treatment consent capacity in patients with traumatic brain injury across a range of injury severity. *Neurology, 78,* 1472–1478. http://dx.doi.org/10.1212/WNL.0b013e3182553c38

van Zomeren, A. H., Brouwer, W. H., & Minderhoud, J. M. (1987). Acquired brain damage and driving: A review. *Archives of Physical Medicine and Rehabilitation, 68,* 697–705.

Walker, W. C., Marwitz, J. H., Kreutzer, J. S., Hart, T., & Novack, T. A. (2006). Occupational categories and return to work after traumatic brain injury: A multicenter study. *Archives of Physical Medicine and Rehabilitation, 87,* 1576–1582. http://dx.doi.org/10.1016/j.apmr.2006.08.335

Wechsler, D. (2008). *Wechsler Adult Intelligence Scale—Fourth Edition.* San Antonio, TX: Pearson.

Wechsler, D. (2009). *Wechsler Memory Scale—Fourth Edition.* San Antonio, TX: Pearson.

Wechsler, D. (2011). *Wechsler Abbreviated Scale of Intelligence—Second Edition.* San Antonio, TX: Pearson.

II

CAPACITIES IN THE CONTEXT OF ELDER ABUSE AND EXPLOITATION

5

Assessment of Financial Exploitation

Peter A. Lichtenberg

> **KEY POINTS**
>
> - Some older adults are more vulnerable than others, but all of us are vulnerable to financial exploitation.
> - Reduced financial decision-making skills are often a key element of cases with exploitation.
> - Onset of cognitive decline and early dementia are prime times for financial exploitation.
> - Financial exploitation often intersects with issues of diminished capacity and susceptibility to undue influence.

SETTING THE STAGE FOR CLINICAL AND PSYCHOLEGAL WORK

This chapter explores how signs of financial exploitation (defined in Table 5.1) emerge and how to recognize it when we are asked to consider possible cases of financial capacity and/or undue influence. It also presents information about new instruments to assess financial exploitation, specifically three scales I developed to assess key contextual and intellectual factors that influence financial decision-making: the Lichtenberg Financial Decision-Making

http://dx.doi.org/10.1037/0000184-006
Assessing Capacities of Older Adults: A Casebook to Guide Difficult Decisions, J. Moye (Editor)

TABLE 5.1. Financial Capacity, Decision-Making, and Exploitation Definitions

Financial capacity	A quality of an individual, here defined through psychological research	1. Financial execution 2. Financial decision-making
Financial incapacity	A legal characteristic of an individual, here defined through conservatorship statutes	1. Inability to manage money and property due to a neurocognitive or mental health condition 2. High risk of waste or dissipation of property without intervention
Financial decision-making (Part 2 of financial capacity, as shown in right column)	An aspect of financial capacity	1. Communicating a Choice 2. Understanding 3. Appreciation 4. Reasoning
Financial exploitation	A relationship between two persons	1. Improper use of funds, property, or resources by another 2. A form of elder abuse 3. Diminished financial capacity increases risk for financial exploitation

Screening Scale (LFDSS; Lichtenberg, Ficker, et al., 2016), the Lichtenberg Financial Decision Rating Scale (LFDRS; Lichtenberg, 2016), and the Lichtenberg Financial Decision Rating Scale—Friends and Family (LFDRS–FF; Campbell, Lichtenberg, et al., 2019). In addition, this chapter presents suggestions when working as an expert witness in cases of financial exploitation.

Until recently, few psychologists received a referral or consultation request asking for a determination of whether an older adult was financially exploited or were asked to determine whether an older adult was vulnerable to financial exploitation. There are three related yet separate terms important to understand in this area: *financial incapacity*, *financial capacity*, and *financial exploitation* (see Table 5.1). In 2007, Moye and Marson noted that few working models of financial capacity were available. Financial capacity, a psycholegal construct, deals with two major aspects of financial transactions: financial execution and financial decision-making. Financial execution is the management part of finances—paying bills, managing a checking account, managing debt and credit card payments, for example. *Capacity* refers to the ability to perform these activities. Clearly, many people have the ability (capacity) to manage their money but make decisions that negatively affect their financial well-being.

Financial decision-making is the second major category of financial capacity. This is discussed in greater detail later but is defined as the ability to make informed decisions (i.e., communicate choice, understanding, appreciation, and reasoning). Assessment (both experimental and clinical) of financial execution has long been a study of applied and clinical gerontology and geropsychology, but financial decision-making research has largely been confined to experimental studies of applied cognitive aging and until recently has not led to assessment tools for financial decision-making. In 2008, the American Bar Association and American Psychological Association (ABA/APA) workgroup produced the *Assessment of Older Adults With Diminished Capacity*. In the chapter on financial capacity, the work group confirmed that unlike real-world clinical judgment scales for the assessment of capacity for medical treatment, no in-depth instruments existed for measuring real-world (i.e., the actual decision(s) the older adult is making) financial decision-making capacity.

Financial incapacity, a legal construct (as in a conservatorship), is often determined by a two-prong test:

1. Does the individual demonstrate an inability to manage money and property due to a neurocognitive or mental health condition?
2. Is there a high risk of waste or dissipation of property without intervention?

The dearth of instruments for assessing financial decision-making was keenly felt by those investigating financial exploitation. Financial exploitation often occurs alongside of other forms of elder abuse. Most elder abuse multidisciplinary teams do not have psychologists on their teams or use psychological evaluations. One exception to this is the L.A. County Forensic Center (see Wood et al., 2014). Wood and colleagues (2014) reported that financially exploited older adults had worse cognitive scores than did a community control group and that these worsened scores were linked to the cases being prosecuted. Despite this outstanding work, psychologists are not often involved in financial exploitation work—or at least they weren't in the past. With financial exploitation affecting an increasing number of older adults, the number of psychologists who encounter these cases in their practices will likewise increase. To be effective in this new realm, psychologists must go beyond traditional methods of cognitive and financial assessment and seek out information specific to the case and the legal questions that are being asked.

FINANCIAL EXPLOITATION: WHAT IS IT?

Financial exploitation is the improper use of a person's funds, property, or resources by another individual. It is commonly discussed in terms of theft, scams, and abuse of trust (Conrad, Iris, Ridings, Langley, & Wilber, 2010). Financial exploitation is the second most common form of elder abuse (after emotional abuse), with an estimated prevalence rate of 5% each year (Acierno et al., 2010). Focusing on elder mistreatment, Pillemer, Connolly, Breckman, Spreng, and Lachs (2015) emphasized that Alzheimer's disease renders older adults more susceptible to all types of elder abuse. Conrad and colleagues

SIX DOMAINS OF FINANCIAL EXPLOITATION[1]

1. The Exploitation Event: Thefts and Scams (e.g., Has anyone misused your ATM card?)

Mechanisms of Exploitation

2. Abuse of Trust (e.g., Has anyone convinced you to sign over your property to them?)
3. Financial Entitlement (e.g., Are family members fighting over your money?)
4. Coercion (e.g., Has anyone isolated you and suggested he/she is the only one who cares about you?)

Risk Factors for Exploitation

5. Signs of Possible Financial Exploitation (e.g., Do you feel pressured to help others in your household with finances?)
6. Money Management Difficulties (e.g., Do you forget to pay bills? Or pay them late?)

(2010) defined six domains of financial exploitation, as shown in the box. Conrad et al. created a self-report Older Adult Financial Exploitation Measure. However, this tool does not measure decision-making or financial judgment.

There is a growing consensus that financial exploitation in older adults is an increasing problem (Acierno et al., 2010; Lichtenberg, Sugarman, et al., 2016), and yet estimating its actual prevalence is fraught with difficulties, underreporting being, by far, the most serious. Nevertheless, as mentioned earlier, in population-based random sample survey studies, financial exploitation has been found to be the second most common form of elder abuse, after psychological, or emotional, abuse. Other vulnerabilities go hand in hand with financial exploitation and increase susceptibility. These include activities of daily living, disabilities, lack of social support, depression, and what my colleagues and I have termed *psychological vulnerability*—a combination of depression and a low sense of social status. Those with psychological vulnerability were 2 to 3 times more likely to report financial exploitation, even when the psychological vulnerability occurred up to 4 years before the exploitation (see Lichtenberg et al., 2013; Lichtenberg, Sugarman, et al., 2016).

[1]From "Conceptual Model and Map of Financial Exploitation of Older Adults," by K. J. Conrad, M. Iris, J. W. Ridings, K. P. Fairman, A. Rosen, and K. H. Wilber, 2011, *Journal of Elder Abuse & Neglect, 23,* p. 317. Copyright 2011 by Taylor & Francis. Reprinted with permission.

DIAGNOSTIC ISSUES: THE INTERSECTION OF ALZHEIMER'S DISEASE, FINANCIAL DECISION-MAKING, AND FINANCIAL EXPLOITATION

By definition, the clinical diagnosis of probable Alzheimer's disease is to have an insidious onset. This means that unless you were to happen upon an older adult at just the right time, his or her dementia symptoms would remain hidden from view. Some symptoms are cognitive, others are functional, and still others are psychological. Trouble remembering, repetition of stories, or missing appointments are some of the more common cognitive symptoms in early dementia. Reduced abilities in financial management (paying bills late or forgetting to record checks one has written), failing to take medications properly (skipping doses or taking the wrong amounts), and problems with driving (accidents or difficulty locating familiar destinations) are the most common functional deficits in instrumental activities of daily living in early dementia. In one 6-year longitudinal study, Martin et al. (2019) found that financial judgment of hypothetical scenarios declined the most in a group of participants with mild cognitive impairment (MCI). Lack of initiative, anger and irritability, or depression are some of the most common early psychological symptoms changes associated with early dementia. Of course, there are other illnesses that cause dementia, such as Lewy body, frontotemporal, Parkinson's disease, and vascular disease; however, this brief literature review focuses mostly on Alzheimer's disease as an exemplar of dementia and vulnerability to financial exploitation.

Financial exploitation, like all forms of elder abuse, occurs more often in older persons suffering from dementia. Psychologists are more likely to be asked to evaluate financial capacity in the context of Alzheimer's disease, but such evaluations often uncover the unfortunate reality of financial exploitation. It doesn't take the full onset of Alzheimer's disease for this risk to begin, however. There is evidence that financial decision-making deficits may precede cognitive decline and make an older adult vulnerable to financial exploitation much earlier than previously believed (Han et al., 2016). Here I review some of the literature on financial management skills, decision-making, and undue influence—all in the context of cognitive decline such as in MCI or dementia.

In Marson's (2001) clinical research with persons with dementia, he created the Financial Capacity Inventory (FCI) to measure financial capacity across eight domains. Further, Marson (2016) categorized his own approach as a clinical model for financial capacity. He argued that these eight domains of financial capacity are necessary for independent functioning (e.g., examples of the domains include basic monetary skills, checkbook management, bill payment, financial judgment). His research provided supporting evidence that the progression of age-related dementia (e.g., Alzheimer's disease) is one of the biggest challenges to intact financial capacity—most notably, FCI scores were strongly linked to the person's stage of Alzheimer's disease, as shown in

TABLE 5.2. Summary of Relationship Between Financial Abilities and Alzheimer's Stage

Stage of Alzheimer's	Study participants considered "fully capable" in the following areas (percent)		
	Basic monetary skills	Financial concepts	Financial judgment
Mild	53	47	13
Moderate	10	5	0

Note. From "Loss of Financial Competency in Dementia: Conceptual and Empirical Approaches," by D. C. Marson, 2001, *Neuropsychology, Development, and Cognition: Section B. Aging, Neuropsychology and Cognition, 8*, p. 174. Copyright 2001 by Taylor & Francis. Reprinted with permission.

Table 5.2. In fact, 50% of those with mild-stage Alzheimer's disease were judged capable or marginally capable of financial judgment.

Sherod et al. (2009) extended Marson's work by investigating the neurocognitive predictors of financial capacity domains across a group of elders ranging from healthy (no impairment) to mild Alzheimer's disease, inclusive of MCI participants. It was found that arithmetic ability was the single best predictor of FCI scores, accounting for 27% of the variance in healthy elders and 46% in those with mild Alzheimer's disease. Financial judgment, however, remained an area in which even those with MCI were as accurate in assessing their abilities as healthy control participants. Sherod et al.'s findings demonstrate that impaired cognition, even as early as MCI, affects financial capacity in certain domains and that neuropsychological tests are significantly related to these financial capacity domains. Taken together, these studies strongly suggest that the ability to execute financial capacity domain tasks successfully is highly related to cognitive functioning and that declines in this ability are prevalent early in neurocognitive disorders. Clinicians need to understand these broad trends, but not simply rule those with MCI or those with early Alzheimer's disease to have incapacity. One of the important aspects of this work is that there is a good deal of variability; some people with cognitive impairment do well on one or more financial domains. Clinicians need to assess the specific skills of the individual in their office and not use a broad brush and "overprotect" older adults by assuming they no longer have financial capacity.

Belbase and Sanzenbacher (2017) provided further support for a decline in financial capacity with the onset of dementia. Using data from a variety of sources, including the Health and Retirement Survey, they found that healthy adults in their 70s and 80s are just as likely to be able to pay bills, manage debt, and maintain good credit as are people in their 50s and 60s. The authors did recognize, however, the impact of cognitive impairment on these financial abilities: 95% of older adults with no cognitive impairment could manage their finances well; in contrast, only 82% of those with MCI could do so, and a scant 20% of those with dementia. On the basis of these results, Belbase and Sanzenbacher argued that cognitive impairment can rapidly erode financial capacity.

Financial decision-making ability is emerging as a separate construct from cognition and from financial management skills. Hsu and Willis (2013) examined financial decision-making in their 10-year study of couples in the Health and Retirement Survey and were able to assess real-world decision-making in areas such as how participants managed their retirement funds. Overall, those with declining cognition were no longer the primary financial respondent for their household. Even so, a surprisingly high number of cognitively impaired individuals continued in this role. These findings highlight the importance of financial decision-making as an area of assessment. The FCI, described earlier, has only a small emphasis on decision-making, and it is based on hypothetical situations. As is explored more in depth later in the chapter, financial decision-making is a key domain and improvements in assessing it are imperative.

Financial decision-making may well be a construct that is related to, but separate from, cognition. Boyle and colleagues in the Rush University Memory and Aging Project (see Boyle et al., 2012, 2013; Han et al., 2016) examined financial decision-making and cognition longitudinally in a sample of more than 400 older adults (Boyle et al., 2012); the authors found that even modest cognitive decline (i.e., outside the range of actual cognitive impairment) is related to a decline in financial decision-making ability. Further, they speculated that decision-making and cognition are related but independent constructs. Han et al. (2016) tested the discrepancy between cognition and decision-making in a sample of 689 older adults and found that in 13% of cases, decision-making scores were more than 1 *z*-score below cognition; in 11% of cases, cognition scores were lower than decision-making scores. Thus, Han et al.'s work illustrates that sometimes decision-making declines precede cognitive decline, and sometimes they follow after cognitive decline—although in the majority of cases, they decline together.

One chief concern: Does a decline in financial decision-making skills lead to increased vulnerability and to financial exploitation? Boyle et al. (2012) found that reduced decision-making ability was related to increased susceptibility to scams. Despite advances in our understanding of the relationships among financial capacity domains, cognition, and financial decision-making ability, scant research has focused on what Marson (2016) termed *financial function in the real world*. This need for real-world financial decision-making assessment led to the creation of a new assessment tool and conceptual model.

A NEW MODEL OF FINANCIAL DECISION-MAKING

Noting the lack of assessment tools for real-world financial decision-making, I set out to create a new assessment tool. I approached Ken Conrad and Micki Iris, who created the Financial Exploitation model and measure, and they agreed to help lead a Concept Mapping method. The Concept Mapping method made extensive use of 20 experts comprising two groups and a variety of mental health, social service, financial service, and legal professionals. Together we created a new model and instrument (see Lichtenberg et al., 2015). Our conceptual model of financial decisional capacity combines key contextual and intellectual factors that influence financial decision-making. The final model included both contextual factors (defined subsequently) and intellectual factors. The conceptual frameworks used in creating this model (and new scale) were the Whole Person Dementia Assessment model (Mast, 2011) and the decision-making model of Appelbaum and Grisso (1988), which elaborates on what Lichtenberg et al. (2015) termed the *intellectual factors* involved in capacity assessment: choice, understanding, appreciation, and reasoning. The Whole Person Assessment model is described in some depth in Lichtenberg et al. (2015) and applies person-centered principles of deep respect for individuality and personhood to the standardized psychological assessment process. This includes focusing on actual decisions instead of hypothetical vignettes.

These key intellectual factors have been reiterated as fundamental aspects of decisional abilities (ABA/APA 2008). Although articulated originally for medical decision-making, the same intellectual factors apply to financial decisions. First, the older adult must be capable of clearly *communicating* his or her choice. *Understanding* is the ability to comprehend the nature of the proposed decision and provide some explanation or demonstrate awareness of its risks and benefits. *Appreciation* refers to the situation and its consequences and often involves the impact on both the older adult and others. Appelbaum and Grisso contended that the most common causes of impairment in appreciation are lack of awareness of deficits or delusions/distortions. Reasoning includes the ability to compare options—for instance, different treatment options in the case of health decision-making. It also includes the ability to provide a rationale for the decision or explain the communicated choice.

We (Lichtenberg et al., 2015) also included *contextual factors*—that is, information about an individual that helps gain better understanding of issues of financial stress, vulnerability, and susceptibility. The contextual factors are as follows:

CONTEXTUAL FACTORS IN FINANCIAL DECISION-MAKING

- Financial situational awareness
- Psychological vulnerability (which includes loneliness and depression)
- Susceptibility to undue Influence, and to financial exploitation

Contextual factors are viewed as having a direct impact on the intellectual factors associated with financial decisional integrity for a significant financial transaction (see Figure 5.1).

FIGURE 5.1. Conceptual Model for Financial Decision-Making

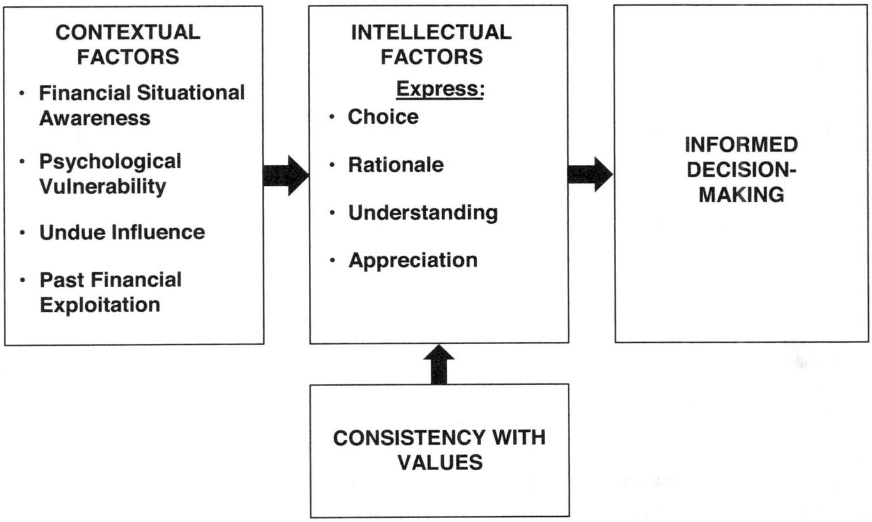

Intellectual factors refer to the functional abilities required for financial decision-making capacity. These include the ability to do the following:

INTELLECTUAL FACTORS IN FINANCIAL DECISION-MAKING

- Express a choice
- Communicate the rationale for the choice
- Demonstrate an understanding of the choice
- Demonstrate an appreciation of the relevant factors involved in the choice
- Ensure that the choice is consistent with one's values

In the decisional capacities framework, the intellectual factors—along with the contextual factors' impact on them—determine financial capacity.

Together, the contextual and intellectual factors are useful in determining the integrity of an individual's decision or related set of decisions. In other words: Is it an informed decision?

EMPIRICAL EVIDENCE FOR THE LICHTENBERG SCALES

Based on the original 68-item scale, we developed three additional scales, selecting the best items: a 10-item screening scale, a 34-item full scale, and a 14-item informant scale. All three scales can be found at http://www.olderadultnestegg.com. The entire 68-item scale can be found in Lichtenberg

TABLE 5.3. Reliability and Validity Studies of the Lichtenberg Scales

Study	Findings
Lichtenberg Financial Decision-Making Screening Scale (LFDSS)	
Lichtenberg, Stoltman, Ficker, Iris, and Mast (2015)	Convergent validity: risk score is significantly related to cognition and money-management skills
Lichtenberg, Sugarman, Paulson, Ficker, and Rahman-Filipiak (2016)	Financial decision-making risk scoring higher in both cases for capacity and cases for financial exploitation
Lichtenberg et al. (2018)	Factor analysis, item response theory, area under the curve Scale found to be internally consistent, one factor, and all 10 items contributing to the scale Receiver operating curve found the risk scoring system to be good–excellent
Campbell, Gross, and Lichtenberg (2019)	Cross-validation study of cutoff score using a new sample of 105 adult protective services cases Cutoff score supported in cross-validation
Lichtenberg Financial Decision Rating Scale (LFDRS)	
Lichtenberg et al. (2015)	Scale creation using concept mapping, conceptual model, and interrater reliability
Lichtenberg, Ficker, et al. (2016)	Convergent validity in sample of urban African American older adults; correlations with cognition and financial management
Lichtenberg, Teresi, Ocepek-Welikson, and Eimicke (2017)	Factor analysis, internal consistency Support for conceptual model of three contextual subscales Convergent validity with cognition and money-management skills
Lichtenberg, Gross, and Ficker (2018)	Clinical utility of the risk scoring system for decision-making abilities and financial exploitation Excellent discriminability for decision-making and good for financial exploitation
Lichtenberg, Gross, and Campbell (2018)	Short-form (34 items) of the LFDRS; based on factor analysis, demonstrating convergent validity and good clinical utility
Lichtenberg Financial Decision Rating Scale—Friends and Family (LFDRS-FF)	
Campbell, Lichtenberg, et al. (2019)	Factor analysis, clinical utility of a 14-item informant scale

et al. (2018). The empirical studies supporting the original scale, conceptual model, the screening scale, and informant scale are found in Table 5.3. Briefly, we have found good evidence for reliability and validity for all three scales.

USING THE SCALES IN CASES OF FINANCIAL EXPLOITATION (AND CAPACITY)

Financial exploitation, the dark side of many capacity cases, is often revealed in cases involving contested legal matters within the probate court system. Thus, some introduction to capacity assessment is necessary here. The growth in interest about capacity assessment followed the significant changes in laws determining competency. At one time, the mere presence of one or more mental health diagnoses was the legal standard for incompetence across the United States (for review, see Appelbaum & Grisso, 1988). Functional tests and the presence of neurocognitive and mental health diagnoses have now replaced that standard. Geropsychology, which focuses on how older adults' mental health and neurocognitive disorders apply to specific situations, is a discipline well suited for contested legal cases within the probate system.

On the basis of practice guidelines (ABA/APA, 2008; Baker et al., 1998) and clinical experience, capacity evaluations must include assessments that address five criteria involved in determining capacity.

CRITERIA ASSESSED IN DETERMINING CAPACITY

1. To determine whether an older adult suffers from a mental health condition, neurocognitive disorder or decline, or both; in other words, a cause for the diminished capacity must be established.
2. The mental health or neurocognitive disorder must affect functional abilities. The term *functional abilities* is used here as legal terminology, which differs from how geropsychologists typically use the term. In legal terms, functional abilities refer to intact decisional abilities. These include evidence of choice, understanding, reasoning, and appreciation (Appelbaum & Grisso, 1988).
3. Older adults' awareness of any deficits and whether compensatory strategies would be useful for them.
4. Older adults' decisions must be of their own free will and not subject to undue influence (termed *coercion* in Conrad's domains of financial exploitation).
5. Best practice requires integrating the legal standards for incapacity with the findings from any assessment.

Consistent with this framework, the methods and procedures used in an evaluation often include the following:

METHODS FOR CAPACITY EVALUATION

- Interview of the individual older adult whose capacity is in question and of key informants
- Cognitive testing
- Decisional ability assessment, which is often accomplished with specific assessment of the skills in question (e.g., financial decision-making for cases of wills, contracts, gifts)
- A process to identify needed adaptations and environmental support
- Integration of the findings with the relevant legal standards.

WORKING AS AN EXPERT: EVALUATOR AND EXPERT WITNESS

Clinicians who evaluate for financial exploitation should be prepared to testify as an expert witness because when exploitation is found, criminal complaints may follow. Following are some general tips for expert testimony as it pertains to financial exploitation (for additional guidance, refer to APA, 2013). Who qualifies as an expert and what is involved in doing expert work? To some degree, we each must self-define whether we have enough experience and training to be an expert. During my more recent experiences, there is considerable variability in how much scrutiny the court gives to reviewing the proposed expert's credentials.

Some 30 years and 250 cases later, I have developed a list of qualities (in addition to geropsychology expertise) needed to be an expert. First, it is important to be able to assert oneself comfortably; even when one's findings are not what the hiring attorney wants to hear. Being a "straight shooter" is an important principle in expert work. I would estimate that in nearly 30% of cases I have worked on I have told the attorneys that, based on the evidence, I cannot give an opinion that supports their case. Assertiveness also is necessary to request additional documents and records that were not initially divulged or given to you. Second, be objective but not neutral. To me, neutral opinions are ones offered with a lack of conviction. Let the evidence determine what you can and cannot say as an expert, but once you have a firm opinion, be prepared to clearly provide support for your conclusion in a way that the judge (and jury, if there is one) can understand it, then vigorously defend it. Working on legal cases is about advocacy, and if you firmly believe your conclusions, then advocate for those by giving strong and determined opinions in your report and testimony at deposition or trial.

An expert should expect to know the nuances of each individual case and not rely on overgeneralizations from the research literature. For example, many psychologists overgeneralize from cognitive deficits to financial incapacity. I often see in reports a claim that a person, due to his or her executive

QUESTIONS FOR DETERMINING EXPERT WITNESS STATUS

1. Do I believe I have the training and clinical experience needed to be an expert in this particular case?
2. Do I have the assertiveness skills necessary to work with attorneys who often have a certain position they want supported?
3. Can I be an advocate for the older person's best interests in cases where I am able to form an opinion?
4. Can I handle the scrutiny and defend my position without losing my composure?

dysfunction and memory deficits, lacks financial capacity. I help attorneys question conclusions such as these by asking the following: What specific aspects of financial capacity? How were the specific aspects assessed? What evidence is there that you can predict an individual's ability to perform the specific capacity based on these cognitive tests? An expert should expect to have all of his or her work scrutinized and be prepared to defend the ideas in that work without being defensive. In sum, before agreeing to be an expert, clinicians should ask themselves several questions.

If the answers to the preceding questions are "yes" or "I'm going to get to yes," then the journey of being an expert begins. There are several things to attend to before and in the early part of any evaluation.

1. *Negotiating referral.* A court representative or attorney advocating for one side may approach an expert. The expert must determine (a) what capacity is in question; (b) whether it is a forensic assessment (i.e., using medical records only, as if the older person died), or will it require a new assessment; (c) what legal standards (i.e., state court case law) are germane to the specific capacity; (d) the time frame for which the analysis is needed; (e) whether the hiring party understands that the assessment is impartial and, regardless of who hires the expert, that the conclusions are not mutable; and (f) that a fee has been agreed on.
2. *Obtaining records and setting the evaluation.* An expert often must persistently push to get both medical and legal records. These allow the expert to create a timeline of relevant events. The medical records serve as a fundamental source of unbiased information, often including notations about cognitive decline or dementia. Being able to view the absence or presence of progressive decline is essential to establishing the correct diagnosis. When scheduling the evaluation, the expert must explain who will be involved (e.g., family caregiver or other informants interviewed). The expert must also clarify that no one except the examiner and the older person can be present.
3. *Obtaining informed consent.* Strikingly, unlike in other evaluations, no protection is provided for patient confidentiality with respect to medical facts. Thus, before the interview and formal assessment, the person must give informed consent or (if not possible) assent. The expert must explain to the older adult that unlike most health procedures, results of the capacity assessment are shared with all parties in the legal proceedings. This lack of confidentiality is a glaring, underappreciated contrast between a clinical and a legal capacity assessment. See also Standard 3.10, Informed Consent, in the APA's (2017) *Ethical Principles of Psychologists and Code of Conduct.*

CASE EXAMPLES

These case examples illustrate three things: (a) the intersection of deficits in financial decision-making and financial exploitation, (b) vulnerability to undue influence, and (c) the devastating impact of financial exploitation.

In the first case, a stranger scams the older adult out of hundreds of thousands of dollars; despite this, the older adult demonstrates a lack of understanding of the decision to send monies. In the second case, a man with early dementia is influenced by a friend to hand over $100,000 in cash.[2]

Case 1: Mr. Daniels—A Romance–Inheritance Scam

This case of a scam victim found its way to probate court, and indeed the dark side to this capacity evaluation was a case of deep financial exploitation. Mr. Robert Daniels, an 86-year-old White man who was widowed and a retired account executive, was referred to me for a capacity evaluation. Not only did the family suspect financial exploitation, but Mr. Daniels expressed much resistance to learning and believing the truth about the exploitation. He lived in New York City and had been used to a busy social lifestyle and considerable status to go along with it. His two children lived out of town but visited frequently. On one visit, they noticed that he received 15 phone calls within an 8-hour period from what was presumed to be young women. On the next visit, a month later, they found Mr. Daniels a bit disheveled, and his water was shut off due for failure to pay his bill. A review of his bank account revealed that he had already wired more than $500,000 to overseas accounts.

It turned out that Mr. Daniels believed he was engaged to be married to two young women, although he had never actually met them in person. But they did talk over the phone and corresponded by text and email. They not only called him but sent him pictures, several of which were pornographic. The women told Mr. Daniels they needed to be married to receive the $10 million inheritance they were entitled to from their families—and of course, as their husband, he would share in that wealth. However, before anything else could proceed, they needed money wired to them for "initial processing fees." As the scheme became more and more elaborate, Mr. Daniels's children, respectful of his pride and independence, brought in not only his bank president but also an FBI agent to discuss the situation with Mr. Daniels. It was to no avail. Mr. Daniels still thought he and his future brides were going to inherit a great deal of money. At this point, I was brought in, and I agreed to perform an evaluation. But before we could even schedule it, the matter took a significant turn.

Mr. Daniels, without telling anyone, decided to drive all night from New York to Florida, where he believed one of these young women lived. He was desperate to find her and prove to everyone that he knew what he was doing. He ended up driving his car the wrong way down a one-way street

---

[2]Although the case examples in this chapter are based on the author's real experiences, the identities of the individuals involved in these examples have been properly disguised to protect their confidentiality.

and hitting a street pole. The police, recognizing his confusion, had him hospitalized. After this, he went to live with his son in Atlanta, Georgia. At his son's home, he began eating well, sleeping well, and, after a few weeks, was feeling much better. He felt so good, in fact, that he no longer believed he needed any help. However, his son had already begun a request for guardianship, and thus this case became a contested matter.

The Evaluation

In an evaluation and case like this, it is not enough to simply assess the individual's current condition, nor can you rely on historical facts alone. Hearing the history, one might be tempted to think that of course this older man needs protection and should have a conservator. However, to complicate matters, the attorney representing Mr. Daniels wrote that one of his children was only interested in trying to ensure a substantial inheritance and that the child had been willing to let his father do as he wanted so long as he first gave the son several million dollars. When a case is contested, things can get very muddied and unclear. This is where the details of the case and the preciseness of the interview and decisional ability assessment become extremely important.

With so many facets to this case, what to focus on in the interview? Judges (and juries) best understand descriptions of functional deficits and tangible evidence of life problems. I chose to spend 3 hours interviewing Mr. Daniels and 2 hours giving him cognitive tests. Given my understanding of the events, I wanted to assess three major things in my interview:

1. accuracy of his own report,
2. awareness of impact, and
3. decisional abilities.

Accuracy. During our interview, Mr. Daniels took the position that he was a wealthy man and could afford spending money on his pursuit of these women. He stated that he only spent about $30,000 when in fact he spent more than $500,000 (as per the financial records that I reviewed and an independent accountant reviewed). He believed the "investment" would pay off in the end. He was inaccurate both in remembering how much he gave these women and in estimating his ability to afford these kinds of gifts. He was no longer wealthy. His liquid investments were gone. He didn't even pay his most basic bills, such as utilities and taxes, because he couldn't gather the cash to do so.

Awareness. I was particularly struck by how catastrophic the situation could have been. He could have lost his home to foreclosure—and it was worth millions (much of it as equity). He was completely, or largely, unaware of any of the impact of his spending. He finally admitted during the interview that, yes, he could have become homeless and due to his lack of cash, if his children had not stepped in, he would have lost his home.

Decisional abilities. I administered the LFDRS to him. On the LFDRS, he reported that he was supremely confident of his abilities. He reported that he did not regret any recent financial decisions and that he was rarely asked for money by anyone. In analyzing his choices, he communicated that he knew what he was doing and that his children clearly just wanted to take his money. Interestingly, when asked if he ever lost money due to a financial scam, he only related that, yes, a decade ago a contractor had scammed him. He expressed a lot of conflict with his children about his expenditures on the young women. Finally, he stated emphatically that there were no possible risks to his financial well-being if he were to take back complete control of his finances.

What Did I Glean From My Interview in These Three Areas?

Mr. Daniels was extremely well spoken. In addition, he was cooperative and engaged readily in conversation. But when it came to how accurately he understood his finances, there was a clear deficit. He was inaccurate not only in the amount he expended but also about the amount he was able to pay out without consequence to his life and lifestyle. This inaccuracy raised concerns about his lack of awareness. These expenditures came close to leaving him homeless and functionally destitute. He displayed no awareness of this whatsoever. In his mind, these matters were both looking backward. In other words, maybe he once had these problems but was now recovered from them. That is why the LFDRS was so important. It revealed his lack of both understanding and appreciation, but even more, it raised red flags that coercion was involved and that this was indeed a romance–inheritance scam.

Coercion—Evidence of Undue Influence

To dig deeper, I applied the SCAM method of analysis to examine issues of undue influence in this matter (see ABA/APA, 2008). SCAM takes into account four major risk factors:

S: Susceptibility. Cognitive testing revealed that Mr. D. was extremely high functioning on visuospatial tasks, numeracy, and verbal learning and memory. Where he displayed deficits was in executive functioning as demonstrated by poor scores across verbal fluency tasks and the Stroop Interference task. There was no evidence of any progressive dementia but a lot of evidence for vascular cognitive impairment. This evidence included a long history of heart disease and artery blockages relieved by stents and MRI scans revealing extensive cerebellar and cerebral atrophy and extensive white matter disease.

C: Confidential relationship. The scammers had him believing that the young women were not only in love with him but totally dependent on him for their well-being; without him, they would drop into severe poverty. The scammers also convinced him that his children were simply greedy and did not care about his well-being. By poisoning the relationships he had with his children, the scammers got Mr. Daniels to rely solely on them for major decisions.

A: Active procurement. The scammers requested money daily and sometimes multiple requests in a day. During a single 2-month stretch, Mr. Daniels made more than 100 separate money transfers from his bank to the scammers.

M: Monetary loss. As stated earlier, Mr. Daniels lost half a million dollars in cash to these scammers and almost lost his home to foreclosure.

Deposition and Court Testimony

Mr. Daniels's attorney held an important dual role—equivalent of a guardian ad litem (court appointed representative) and an advocate for Mr. Daniels. The attorney was open to guardianship as long as it was limited in its reach. Thus, my deposition was relatively straightforward. I was asked to detail all of these findings and concluded that Mr. Daniels was unable to make informed decisions relative to his property and to his personal well-being (e.g., choosing where to live, what supports he needed) and thus needed a guardian. By the time the court hearing came 4 months later, however, the matter was hotly contested.

To testify effectively as an expert witness in a probate hearing, you must be able to tie the findings of the case to the legal standards being applied. In other words, you, the clinician, must come outside of the clinical jargon and integrate your findings with the legal wording and meaning. The legal standard issues for most guardianship and conservatorship cases are (a) mental deficiency, (b) inability to use information to make an informed decision, and (c) inability to manage property to the extent that without intervention the wealth may be dissipated and lost.

Despite low scores in executive functioning, Mr. Daniels did score incredibly well on most of his cognitive tests. Although it is much easier to argue that there is mental deficiency when there is evidence of a dementia, it is not the only factor. I was able to make a case for mental deficiency by contrasting some of his outstanding skills with his difficulty in problem-solving and lack of mental flexibility, for example. I did this by tying the deficits again to those issues of inaccuracy and limited awareness. The LFDRS findings gave empirical evidence that Mr. Daniels could not make informed decisions about his finances without certain restrictions. Further, the coercion and undue influence evidence was the key to explaining why Mr. Daniels could not keep his property from being dissipated and wasted. In the end, the judge ruled that a guardian should be assigned but also specified that Mr. Daniels be given a generous monthly allotment to spend at his own discretion to enjoy some of the finer things in life.

Postscript

Mr. Daniels did well—in large part because he never returned to living alone. He lived with the guardian (his daughter), and she was able to provide the structure and support that made him feel he had control of his own life. He continued to want to find these young women and twice had to have his cell phone number changed, but, behaviorally, he never did anything more than verbalize this desire. He never again wired money to anyone.

Case 2: Mr. Elliott—Unjust Enrichment

In this situation, my evaluation was part of a criminal case. The most critical part of the State of Michigan legal standard for this case was "A person shall not through fraud, deceit, misrepresentation, coercion, or unjust enrichment obtain or use or attempt to obtain or use a vulnerable adult's money or property to directly or indirectly benefit that person knowing or having reason to know the vulnerable adult is a vulnerable adult." Key issues for this case are the following:

1. Did the person who benefitted know or have reason to know that the adult in question was indeed a vulnerable adult?
2. Was there an issue of coercion or undue influence?

Evaluation and Brief History

I was asked by the prosecutor's office to perform an evaluation 18 months after the event in question occurred. It was explained that this gentleman, Mr. Leonard Elliott, was diagnosed with dementia and lived near several of his brothers. While the man had been known to loan small amounts of money to various family members, he was also meticulous in his record keeping and successful in getting the loans repaid. Mr. Elliott had a history of heart disease (he had a pacemaker inserted) and Type 2 diabetes. During the winter, he was hospitalized related to those conditions and was also diagnosed with dementia at that time. Following that diagnosis, he promptly retired from his business. He also gave up total control of his finances, to his wife of 50 years, after it was discovered that he had written multiple checks to the same charity thinking it was a single payment (i.e., forgetting that he already had sent in a contribution). Two months before the alleged crime event, Mr. Elliott had alerted his wife that he was headed to a town 90 miles away to pick up "his sweepstake winnings." At the time he spoke with his wife, he was at his friend's house (this friend would later be charged with unjust enrichment). Mr. Elliott's wife called the friend, explained Mr. Elliott's dementia and that she was sure he was being scammed. The friend intervened and stopped Mr. Elliott from making the trip—preventing an unfortunate financial loss. Two months later, this very friend took Mr. Elliott to Mr. Elliott's bank so that he could withdraw $200,000 from an IRA. Mr. Elliott then gave this money to the friend to pay off the friend's mortgage.

Neuropsychological Assessment

Following is in excerpt from my report on the neuropsychological assessment. Note that my description is much more cursory than a typical clinical evaluation. This was purposeful—I wanted each section of the report (neuropsychological, decisional abilities, awareness, and undue influence) to receive roughly equal weight and thus did not want to take up a lot of space with neuropsychological jargon. This section of the report read as follows:

> On a test of reading, Mr. Elliott scored in the average range; consistent with his education, he is functioning at or slightly above the mean scores for individuals his age. On a test of aural comprehension, he scored in the mildly impaired range, indicating that he sometimes gets confused by what is being said to him and does not comprehend it accurately. On a test of orientation, he scored in the unimpaired range. On a test of confrontation naming, Mr. Elliott scored in the severely impaired range with several semantic paraphasia errors and word-finding difficulties. On tests of basic attention, Mr. Elliott scored within normal limits.
>
> On a test of basic cognitive functioning, Mr. Elliott scored in the moderately impaired range with significant deficits in initiation and executive functioning, mild–moderate deficits in abstract reasoning, and moderate–severe memory deficits.
>
> On tests of paragraph recall, Mr. Elliott scored in the moderately impaired range on immediate recall and severely impaired range (0% recall) on delayed recall.
>
> On a variety of tasks of executive functioning and reasoning (verbal, nonverbal, motoric, nonmotoric), Mr. Elliott scored in the moderate–severely impaired range.

Overall, Mr. Elliott demonstrated problems with language, executive functioning, and memory for new information—all consistent with dementia and likely similar to his status 18 months earlier when he was diagnosed. I opined that the results were similar to what they would have been 18 months earlier because his medical history was more consistent with Vascular Dementia and his functioning had remained stable throughout the 18-month interview period as evidenced by interviews with law enforcement and descriptions by his wife.

Decisional Abilities Interview

Similar to the first case study, if the gift was based on an informed decision-making process, then it would not necessarily be a crime for the friend to receive the money. I again used the LFDRS to dig deeper into the specifics of the transaction. Mr. Elliott expressed clearly that he gave his friend a gift of money from his own account and that he wanted to help his friend. However, Mr. Elliott demonstrated no ability to reason through alternatives to this action, or to appreciate the potential consequences to his own financial status. Thus, although he showed some aspects of informed decision-making (e.g., choice, rationale), he demonstrated a greater lack of understanding and appreciation for the transaction.

Awareness. Awareness in this case, as in Case 1, was important to my assessment. The ability to compensate can help one cope with cognitive deficits by using strategies such as notebooks, calendar reminders, or other memory aids and thus overcome cognitive deficits. Conversely, the lack of awareness can lead an individual to a false sense of competence. My report read as follows:

> Mr. Elliott's self-assessment of his cognitive functioning indicated that he lacks any awareness of his deficits, making him extremely susceptible to influence

and unjust enrichment because he does not compensate for his lack of awareness by checking decisions with a trusted other.

Undue influence. I assessed coercion, synonymous in my mind for this case with undue influence, by again using the SCAM model. My report highlighted each aspect of the report as follows:

Susceptibility: The combination of Mr. Elliott's dementia (especially the combination of memory and executive functioning problems), decisional ability deficits, and his lack of awareness of deficits make Mr. Elliott highly susceptible to influence.

Confidential Relationship: The friend had a history of borrowing smaller sums of money from his friend Mr. Elliott. In addition, he saw Mr. Elliott almost daily as Mr. Elliott liked to walk down to his friend's place but was often too tired to walk home and so got rides from his friend. Finally, the friend kept the transaction a secret despite knowing that Mr. Elliott had dementia.

Active Procurement and Monetary Loss: The friend took active steps to procure the money from Mr. Elliott. First, he initiated the discussion of the need to pay off his mortgage and then took Mr. Elliott to the bank where Mr. Elliott could withdraw the money from an IRA. Deception was also a key part of the tactics that the friend used. Despite directly knowing that Mr. Elliott was susceptible when others asked him for money (i.e., the sweepstakes experience), the friend kept the $200,000 "gift" secret; he never told Mr. Elliott's wife about the money.

Summary

Financial exploitation is frequently found in cases where the primary issue appears to be capacity. For older adults, issues of informed decision-making and undue influence have as much relevance in financial exploitation cases as they do in probate cases about wills and trusts. In the case studies I presented, both involved financial transactions and "gifting." Although one case demonstrated how susceptibility to scams can lead to the need for guardianship, the second case demonstrated how financial exploitation can lead to criminal charges, even when the older adult states that he wanted to make the transaction.

Postscript

Three weeks before the trial was set to begin, the defendant (perpetrator of the financial exploitation) pleaded guilty to unjust enrichment; agreed to have a lien placed on his property to reimburse the entire amount of the fraud; and, if there were no further troubles across a 12-month period, his charge would be lessened (not the lien, however), and he would not have to serve jail time. If there were further problems, he would be immediately sentenced for unjust enrichment.

REFLECTION

The combination of the sheer volume of older people suffering from cognitive impairment, along with property and wealth accumulation among older adults means that financial exploitation of older adults will continue to rise. This chapter focused on how deficits in financial decision-making are often key to cases of incapacity and financial exploitation. The Lichtenberg rating scale was introduced and its conceptual and empirical properties reviewed. Case studies highlighted how decision-making ability assessment played a key role in a case of incapacity and one of unjust enrichment. In both cases, financial exploitation was present. The cases illustrate how exploitation can come from strangers skilled at scamming older adults, or the closest family members or friends whose own financial strains can lead to theft. In both cases, the importance of demonstrating "mental deficiency" (i.e., cognitive impairment or dementia) was illustrated, along with the relevance of awareness of deficit. Both cases showed the critical role that data from the LFDRS can play in analyzing whether the actual decision or transaction in question was an informed one.

REFERENCES

Acierno, R., Hernandez, M. A., Amstadter, A. B., Resnick, H. S., Steve, K., Muzzy, W., & Kilpatrick, D. G. (2010). Prevalence and correlates of emotional, physical, sexual, and financial abuse and potential neglect in the United States: The National Elder Mistreatment Study. *American Journal of Public Health, 100*, 292–297. http://dx.doi.org/10.2105/AJPH.2009.163089

American Bar Association and American Psychological Association Assessment of Capacity in Older Adults Project Working Group. (2008). *Assessment of older adults with diminished capacity: A handbook for psychologists*. Washington, DC: American Bar Association and American Psychological Association.

American Psychological Association. (2013). Specialty guidelines for forensic psychology. *American Psychologist, 68*(1), 7–19. http://dx.doi.org/10.1037/a0029889

American Psychological Association. (2017). *Ethical principles of psychologists and code of conduct* (2002, Amended June 1, 2010, and January 1, 2017). Washington, DC: Author. Retrieved from http://www.apa.org/ethics/index.aspxcode

Appelbaum, P. S., & Grisso, T. (1988). Assessing patients' capacities to consent to treatment. *The New England Journal of Medicine, 319*, 1635–1638. http://dx.doi.org/10.1056/NEJM198812223192504

Baker, R. R., Lichtenberg, P. A., & Moye, J. (1998). A practice guideline for assessment of competency and capacity of the older adult. *Professional Psychology: Research and Practice, 29*, 149–154.

Belbase, A. B., & Sanzenbacher, G. T. (2017). Cognitive aging and the capacity to manage money. *Center for Retirement Research at Boston College, 17*(1), 1–7. http://crr.bc.edu/wp-content/uploads/2017/01/IB_17-1.pdf

Boyle, P. A., Wilson, R. S., Yu, L., Buchman, A. S., & Bennett, D. A. (2013). Poor decision making is associated with an increased risk of mortality among community-dwelling older persons without dementia. *Neuroepidemiology, 40*, 247–252. http://dx.doi.org/10.1159/000342781

Boyle, P. A., Yu, L., Wilson, R. S., Gamble, K., Buchman, A. S., & Bennett, D. A. (2012). Poor decision making is a consequence of cognitive decline among older persons without Alzheimer's disease or mild cognitive impairment. *PLoS ONE, 7*(8), e43647. http://dx.doi.org/10.1371/journal.pone.0043647

Campbell, R. C., Lichtenberg, P. A., Hall, L., Ocepek-Welikson, K., & Teresi, J. (2019). Assessment of financial decision-making: An informant scale. *Journal of Elder Abuse and Neglect, 31*, 115–128. http://dx.doi.org/10.1080/08946566.2018.1556762

Campbell, R. J., Gross, E., & Lichtenberg, P. A. (2019). Cross-validation of the screening scale in an adult protective services sample. *Journal of Elder Abuse & Neglect, 31*, 25–37. http://dx.doi.org/10.1080/08946566.2018.1531098

Conrad, K. J., Iris, M., Ridings, J. W., Langley, K., & Wilber, K. H. (2010). Self-report measure of financial exploitation of older adults. *The Gerontologist, 50*, 758–773. http://dx.doi.org/10.1093/geront/gnq054

Han, S. D., Boyle, P. A., James, B. D., Yu, L., Barnes, L. L., & Bennett, D. A. (2016). Discrepancies between cognition and decision making in older adults. *Aging Clinical and Experimental Research, 28*, 99–108. http://dx.doi.org/10.1007/s40520-015-0375-7

Hsu, J. W., & Willis, R. (2013, April 1). Dementia risk and financial decision making by older households: The impact of information. *Journal of Human Capitol, 2013*, 45.

Lichtenberg, P. A. (2016). Financial exploitation, financial capacity, and Alzheimer's disease. *American Psychologist, 71*, 312–320. http://dx.doi.org/10.1037/a0040192

Lichtenberg, P. A., Ficker, L., Rahman-Filipiak, A., Tatro, R., Farrell, C., Speir, J. J., . . . Jackman, J. D. (2016). The Lichtenberg Financial Decision Screening Scale (LFDSS): A new tool for assessing financial decision making and preventing financial exploitation. *Journal of Elder Abuse & Neglect, 28*, 134–151. http://dx.doi.org/10.1080/08946566.2016.1168333

Lichtenberg, P. A., Gross, E., & Campbell, R. (2018). A short form of the Lichtenberg Financial Decision Rating Scale. *Clinical Gerontologist*. Advance online publication. http://dx.doi.org/10.1080/07317115.2018.1527424

Lichtenberg, P. A., Gross, E., & Ficker, L. (2018). Quantifying risk of financial incapacity and financial exploitation in community-dwelling older adults: Utility of a scoring system for the Lichtenberg Financial Decision-Making Rating Scale. *Clinical Gerontologist*. Advance online publication. http://dx.doi.org/10.1080/07317115.2018.1485812

Lichtenberg, P. A., Ocepek-Welikson, K., Ficker, L. J., Gross, E., Rahman-Filipiak, A., & Teresi, J. A. (2018). Conceptual and empirical approaches to financial decision making in older adults: Results from a financial decision-making rating scale. *Clinical Gerontologist, 41*, 42–65. http://dx.doi.org/10.1080/07317115.2017.1367748

Lichtenberg, P. A., Stickney, L., & Paulson, D. (2013). Is psychological vulnerability related to the experience of fraud in older adults? *Clinical Gerontologist, 36*, 132–146. http://dx.doi.org/10.1080/07317115.2012.749323

Lichtenberg, P. A., Stoltman, J., Ficker, L. J., Iris, M., & Mast, B. T. (2015). A person-centered approach to financial capacity assessment: Preliminary development of a new rating scale. *Clinical Gerontologist, 38*, 49–67. http://dx.doi.org/10.1080/07317115.2014.970318 JGP.0b013e318157cb00

Lichtenberg, P. A., Sugarman, M., Paulson, D., Ficker, L., & Rahman-Filipiak, A. (2016). Psychological and functional vulnerability predicts fraud cases in older adults: Results of a longitudinal study. *Clinical Gerontologist, 39*, 48–63. http://dx.doi.org/10.1080/07317115.2015.1101632

Lichtenberg, P. A., Teresi, J. A., Ocepek-Welikson, K., & Eimicke, J. P. (2017). Reliability and validity of the Lichtenberg Financial Decision Screening Scale. *Innovation in Aging, 1*(1), 1–9. http://dx.doi.org/10.1093/geroni/igx003

Marson, D. (2016). Conceptual models and guidelines for clinical assessment of financial capacity. *Archives of Clinical Neuropsychology, 31*, 541–553. http://dx.doi.org/10.1093/arclin/acw052

Marson, D. C. (2001). Loss of financial competency in dementia: Conceptual and empirical approaches. *Neuropsychology, Development, and Cognition: Section B. Aging, Neuropsychology and Cognition, 8,* 164–181. http://dx.doi.org/10.1076/anec.8.3.164.827

Martin, R. C., Gerstenecker, A., Triebel, K. L., Falola, M., McPherson, T., Cutter, G., & Marson, D. C. (2019). Declining financial capacity in mild cognitive impairment: A six-year longitudinal study. *Archives of Clinical Neuropsychology, 34,* 152–161. https://doi.org/10.1093/arclin/acy030

Mast, B. T. (2011). *Whole person dementia assessment.* Baltimore, MD: Health Professions Press.

Moye, J., & Marson, D. C. (2007). Assessment of decision-making capacity in older adults: An emerging area of practice and research. *The Journals of Gerontology: Series B. Psychological Sciences and Social Sciences, 62,* P3–P11. http://dx.doi.org/10.1093/geronb/62.1.P3

Pillemer, K., Connolly, M.-T., Breckman, R., Spreng, N., & Lachs, M. S. (2015). Elder mistreatment: Priorities for consideration by the white house conference on aging. *The Gerontologist, 55,* 320–327. http://dx.doi.org/10.1093/geront/gnu180

Sherod, M. G., Griffith, H. R., Copeland, J., Belue, K., Krzywanski, S., Zamrini, E. Y., . . . Marson, D. C. (2009). Neurocognitive predictors of financial capacity across the dementia spectrum: Normal aging, mild cognitive impairment, and Alzheimer's disease. *Journal of the International Neuropsychological Society, 15,* 258–267. http://dx.doi.org/10.1017/S1355617709090365

Wood, S., Rakela, B., Liu, P. J., Navarro, A. E., Bernatz, S., Wilber, K. H., . . . Homeier, D. (2014). Neuropsychological profiles of victims of financial elder exploitation at the Los Angeles County Elder Abuse Forensic Center. *Journal of Elder Abuse & Neglect, 26,* 414–423. http://dx.doi.org/10.1080/08946566.2014.881270

6

Assessment of Undue Influence

Stacey Wood

KEY POINTS

- *Undue influence* (UI) refers to excessive or unfair persuasion of a weaker party by a stronger party who has a special relationship with that individual.
- UI is a legal argument that typically arises in will contests and contract disputes but can also be used in other cases of financial exploitation.
- UI is a separate concept from capacity.
- Risk factors that increase undue influence include age, illness, dependency, isolation, emotional distress, disability, cognitive impairment, and education.
- Assessment of UI requires a comprehensive approach that includes an assessment of psychological, medical, and cognitive factors.

DEFINITION OF THE ISSUE

Undue influence (UI) is unfair persuasion of a party who is under the domination of the person exercising the persuasion or who by virtue of the relation between them is justified in assuming that person will not act in a manner inconsistent with his or her welfare (American Law Institute, 1981).

http://dx.doi.org/10.1037/0000184-007
Assessing Capacities of Older Adults: A Casebook to Guide Difficult Decisions, J. Moye (Editor)

UI is most frequently evoked in cases involving wills or trusts, but it can also be used in civil cases related in general to financial exploitation. As a clinician, one may be asked to provide an opinion regarding susceptibility to UI for a specific transaction or asked about future susceptibility.

CLINICAL PRESENTATION

UI is a specific type of financial exploitation that involves a relational dynamic. Different definitions and state statutes defining UI can make it difficult to estimate overall prevalence. However, it is possible to glean some relevant information from financial elder abuse regarding prevalence. Overall, elder financial abuse including both stranger-initiated fraud and financial exploitation from a trusted other is estimated at 5% to 10 % of the senior population (Wood & Lichtenberg, 2017). A True Link Financial (2015) report estimates annual losses from financial abuse to seniors in the United States of $36.48 billion per year based on a survey of 2,096 respondents, of whom 467 indicated some responsibility caring for an older adult. On the basis of these responses, estimates of subtypes of elder financial abuse and subsequent losses were calculated. The subcategory of *caregiver abuse* fits best with current definitions of UI. This category of financial exploitation had "abuse of a trusting relationship" as its defining feature and included items such as "theft by family members or caregivers," and "rewritten wills or powers of attorney." True Link Financial estimates $6.67 billion per year in losses to seniors as a result of this type of abuse.

Other work suggests that minority groups are at increased risk overall for financial exploitation, which can include both UI type situations and third party–initiated fraud (Lichtenberg, Ficker, & Rahman-Filipiak, 2016).

DIAGNOSTIC STANDARDS AND CONCEPTUAL FRAMEWORKS

UI is not a diagnosis per se but rather refers to an uneven relational dynamic that places senior victims at increased risk for excessive persuasion and causes them to act against their own self-interest. A number of conceptual models have been developed in psychology to explain the power dynamic of UI in general (Blum, 2012; Brandl, Heisler, & Stiegel, 2005; Quinn, 2001). Most of these models emphasize that UI can occur in individuals who retain capacity. Further, they highlight themes such as presence of a confidential relationship, isolation, and dependency. Overall, the models tend to emphasize victim characteristics, relational elements, and potential tactics employed.

Additionally, the work of Margaret Singer (Quinn, 2001) has been influential in the field for identifying common tactics used by influencers. Singer identified the following six factors that are present in relationships marked by UI and noted that they may be sequential: (a) creating isolation, (b) fostering a siege mentality (us against them), (c) inducing dependence, (d) promoting a sense of powerlessness, (e) manipulating existing fears, and (f) keeping the victim unaware.

Quinn, Goldman, Nerenberg, and Piazza (2010) reviewed these clinical models as well as state definitions from across the country and concluded: "Despite wide variations in the contexts and circumstances in which UI and coercive persuasion in general have been explored, the findings are remarkably similar in terms of the salient features. Psychologists, sociologists, criminologists, victimologists, legal experts, and courts have focused on the following factors:

COMMONALITIES IN UI FRAMEWORKS

1. **Characteristics of the victim** that may be contributing to a vulnerability. These can include medical, cognitive, psychological, and functional vulnerabilities.
2. **Descriptions of the influencer's power.** Undue influence occurs in a relationship where the influencer has power and has a confidential or trusting relationship. The authority can be formal, such as a physician or financial advisor, or informal, such as a caregiver or neighbor.
3. **Improper action or tactics.** Influencers often take steps to actively take advantage of the alleged influenced individual. These may range from isolating the senior from others, reinforcing dependency, initiating or actively procuring legal documents, among many others. There may also be an element of secrecy or inappropriate timing (same day as a hospitalization, shortly after a loss) that favors the influencer.
4. **Unfair, unequal, or "unnatural" financial outcomes.** UI results in financial losses for the victim and financial gain for the influencer. An unfair outcome may be a transaction that is below market value benefiting the influencer. However, an uneven outcome that is a clear deviation from previously stated preferences in the context of suspicious circumstances may rise to the level of UI." (Quinn et al., 2010, pp. 10–12)

In summary, there is broad consensus now among conceptual models. In my own work as a researcher and clinician with adult protective services (APS), I have found these four elements to be a useful framework in which to understand and assess UI. UI occurs when a powerful person who has a confidential relationship with a vulnerable individual takes advantage of that relationship for financial benefit at the expense of the vulnerable senior.

These four elements have been codified into the California legal standard for UI. The California standard provides a helpful framework for assessment and analysis in cases of UI. The wording and identification of UI varies significantly from state to state. I recommend asking an elder law attorney for all relevant codes in specific jurisdictions. Clinicians are also advised to consult the following link at the Department of Justice, which provides a searchable database for civil and criminal elder financial abuse codes by state: https://www.justice.gov/elderjustice/prosecutors/statutes.

CALIFORNIA LEGAL STANDARD FOR UI

"Undue influence" means *excessive persuasion* that causes another person to act or refrain from acting by overcoming that person's free will and results in inequity. In determining whether a result was produced by undue influence, all of the following shall be considered:

1. **The vulnerability of the victim.** Evidence of vulnerability may include, but is not limited to, incapacity, illness, disability, injury, age, education, impaired cognitive function, emotional distress, isolation, or dependency, and whether the influencer knew or should have known of the alleged victim's vulnerability.
2. **The influencer's apparent authority.** Evidence of apparent authority may include, but is not limited to, status as a fiduciary, family member, care provider, health care professional, legal professional, spiritual adviser, expert, or other qualification.
3. **The actions or tactics used by the influencer.** Evidence of actions or tactics used may include, but is not limited to, all of the following:
   A. Controlling necessaries of life, medication, the victim's interactions with others, access to information, or sleep.
   B. Use of affection, intimidation, or coercion.
   C. Initiation of changes in personal or property rights, use of haste or secrecy in effecting those changes, effecting changes at inappropriate times and places, and claims of expertise in effecting changes.
4. **The equity of the result.** (California Welfare and Institutions Code section 15610.70)

In terms of the first element, susceptibility, a range of disorders can increase the vulnerability of an older adult. They may be neurocognitive disorders that impair cognition and decision-making but are not so severe that they render the older adult incapacitated. Common neurocognitive disorders seen in cases of UI include both mild neurocognitive disorder, such as mild cognitive impairment (MCI), and major neurocognitive disorders, such as dementia. Etiologies can span a range of disorders and symptom severity and can include Alzheimer's disease, Parkinson's disease, traumatic brain injury, Lewy body dementia, or any diagnosis that may result in cognitive impairment. Diagnoses such as Parkinson's, which can have mild cognitive symptoms, may increase risk due to declines in function and key decisional domains.

Individuals with other mental health concerns may have symptoms that increase "emotional distress," including depression, anxiety disorders, substance use disorders, dependent personality disorders, delusional disorders, and paranoia. Medical conditions that cause temporary fluctuations in cognitive status and decision-making are important to note. Medical conditions such as untreated diabetes and urinary tract infections may worsen a preexisting, relatively mild cognitive impairment, increasing risk of UI. Some experts in the field (Plotkin, Spar, & Horwitz, 2016) have expressed their opinion that mental health professionals should primarily emphasize the first element of the standard (characteristics of the alleged influenced individual) and refrain from addressing the other elements. In some cases, this may be the best approach, particularly if you are working in a clinic setting versus where one's ability to access additional information is limited. However, if information is available regarding the other elements, an ability to understand the tactics used by the alleged influencer and the dynamic can be especially useful. I would also agree that in cases of fraud, the use of experts, such as forensic accountants, may be best suited to address questions of the fairness of a financial outcome.

CLINICAL METHODS: ASSESSMENT APPROACHES

Organizing the Assessment

Cases involving potential UI elements may include those with a living alleged victim and those that require a retrospective determination of UI of a decedent. Cases involving a contemporaneous assessment are often around questions of some type of contractual agreement. Retrospective assessments are typically related to will contests, although they may also relate to a transaction that was made in the past.

A general tip for approaching UI cases is that comprehensive investigation and organization of materials is key. In general, at the start of a case, I create a timeline of important events and transactions involved in the case. For example, the key dates may be related to the dates a contract was signed. Next, I work to fill in available social, cognitive, psychological, deposition, collateral medical, financial, and legal information as it becomes available. The timeline can help form a framework for making sense of the copious records that often come to light in these cases and can help with the organization of the main body of your report. For example, consider the example of Mr. Barnes, the decedent in a trust contest between his second wife and his daughters from a previous marriage. Exhibit 6.1 illustrates organization of a timeline.

UI cases involve a comprehensive assessment of the whole person, consistent with principles of geropsychology and the use of a biopsychosocial approach.

EXHIBIT 6.1

Example of Timeline for Case of "Mr. Barnes"

1945 Birth
1966 Graduation from college
1967 Marriage to Ms. Barnes
1970 Birth of Daughter 1
1972 Birth of Daughter 2
1995 Initial estate planning, Revocable Trust documents drafted
2008 Ms. Barnes diagnosed with Alzheimer's Disease
2014 Ms. Barnes dies
2015 Remarriage to Ms. Shaw
2016 Change in all estate planning documents favoring Ms. Shaw
2016 Death of Mr. Barnes
2017 Daughters challenge validity of the revised Trust

While reviewing records, be mindful of the elements from the California legal standard that map on fairly well to the conceptual models and research on risk for financial exploitation. That is, review available records while looking for *evidence of incapacity, illness, disability, injury, age, education, impaired cognitive function, emotional distress, isolation*, or *dependency*. At the same time, be mindful of the client's strengths and values, and include these as well in your consideration.

Sources of Data

Medical and psychiatric records can provide insight into changes in cognitive and functional abilities during the time frame of interest. Visiting nurses and hospice notes can provide a wealth of information regarding daily functioning, declines, pain medication use, and isolation. Records need to be reviewed for the following information.

RECORD REVIEW CHECKLIST

1. Medical diagnoses and dates
2. Descriptions of cognitive impairment, presence of MCI, or a dementia syndrome
3. Medications
4. Delirium: changes in mental status, sleep, sleep-wake cycles
5. Hospitalizations
6. Hospice notes
7. Rehab and senior nursing facility stays
8. Psychological diagnoses and therapy records

Even if you are fortunate enough to have a case with a neuropsychological or neuropsychiatric report, specific capacity issues are rarely addressed. However, often there is relevant information that is helpful for your analysis. Calculation, executive functioning, new learning, financial literacy, and language issues may all be important to consider if the client has evidence of diminished capacity. These domains have been associated with financial capacity and declines can signal an erosion in financial skills and judgment that can set the stage of UI (Griffith et al., 2003; Wood & Lichtenberg, 2017).

Because UI specifically refers to a relational dynamic, an evaluation of the client's social context is critical. In the timeline in Exhibit 6.1, key dates regarding relationships, births, and deaths can be helpful to map out current and past social relationships. For many reasons, a high percentage of cases in my experience involves blended families. Mapping out these relationships and fluid dynamics through collateral interviews and deposition review can add information to address many of the elements described in the checklist. These interviews and sources of information may also be helpful in gleaning cultural information and values that are critical to this particular family.

Of special note for these assessments are the issues of dependency and isolation. Virtually every clinical framework (Quinn et al., 2010) has emphasized the role that these two factors have with increasing risk of UI. Therefore, any factor that increases dependency or isolation (or both) should be considered.

FACTORS THAT MAY INCREASE DEPENDENCY AND ISOLATION

1. Driving
2. Vision and hearing impairment and access to aids
3. Mobility issues or changes
4. Change in activities of daily living and instrumental activities of daily living
5. Change in environment or moving to a new location

These are factors that can be assessed using collateral interviews, home visits, or in person interviews. Potential collateral interviews include relatives, caregivers, neighbors, and friends, for example. In cases of alleged influence, there can be reports of decreased contact by other family members. Tactics of the influencer to increase isolation may include attempts at intimidation or more passive strategies, such as not returning calls or brushing off concerned others by indicating the elder is "not well," can "no longer use the phone," or "does not care for visitors at this time," for example.

Financial decision-making can be an area necessary to explore, particularly in contemporaneous cases where there may be consideration of a fiduciary or conservatorship to protect the victim from future losses. In complicated cases of UI, financial professionals may be brought in to conduct a technical analysis of the accounting (e.g., forensic accountant, securities expert). As clinicians, it can be helpful to collect information regarding clients' financial knowledge and understanding of their general financial situation as well as the events in questions at present. The Lichtenberg Financial Decision Rating Scale (LFDRS) covers general financial decision-making as well as psychological vulnerability to UI and provides helpful areas of inquiry to guide investigation. The LFDRS is a validated scale (Lichtenberg et al., 2016; see also Chapter 5, this volume).

Working With Attorneys, Courts, and Protective Services

One factor to consider in working with the courts is the court of jurisdiction and the legal standards relevant to that court. For example, in California, UI is a legal standard in the civil code but does not apply in criminal matters. Many states do have criminal as well as civil codes that make explicit and implicit references to UI (coercion). Even in states without explicit UI statutes, criminal cases and APS cases may still benefit from highlighting particular client vulnerabilities to develop care plans and guide efforts to protect the individual. Further, civil litigation may follow criminal proceedings. UI as a legal argument is used commonly in civil and probate matters (e.g., conservatorship and guardianship).

UI in Probate Court

Arguments of UI may arise in will and trust disagreements but can also arise from other contractual disputes. In my experience, cases in probate court (wills, trusts, and conservatorship matters) tend to be less intense overall. In general, these cases are less adversarial, require less time, and typically are in front of a judge who has experience dealing with the legal issues at hand. Often (although not always) there is a shared sense that the proceedings should result in an outcome that is in the best interest of the elder client. Testifying still requires a direct examination and cross-examination, and there can be less formal interactions as well, with the judge interrupting to ask questions and gain clarifications. Cross-examination will usually focus on weaknesses of the case and often emphasize capacity issues versus UI issues. There may also be other parties in the court (court-appointed attorneys, guardians ad litem) who can ask questions as well. Most of the time, an expert's submitted report and administrative forms will suffice for these cases, with an appearance requested occasionally. I personally have never been deposed before a contested conservatorship type appearance, although I imagine that it could happen.

UI in Civil Court

Arguments of UI in civil courts can include will and trust disagreements, as well as other contractual issues and general claims of financial elder abuse. These cases are more intense, require more time, and will almost certainly result in a deposition being required of the expert. Typically, an expert will be contacted by an attorney and discuss the essentials of the matter. If the fit is good with the expert's knowledge, training, and experience and there are no conflicts, the attorney may retain the expert at that point. Once retained, all notes, reports, and correspondence become discoverable to opposing counsel and may have to be turned over at some point. In these cases, there is an expert disclosure date before the trial (the deadline can vary; check with your attorney), where your information (e.g., curriculum vitae) and the scope of your opinion, together with other work you have relied on (such as this chapter), are turned over to the other side. The specific requirements vary among states and between state and federal courts. In some cases, you may inform the attorney that you do not have an opinion regarding UI, either because there is a lack of information or the facts do not support such an opinion. In these cases, the attorney may choose not to disclose you as a testifying expert, and you may instead have a role as a consulting expert. More commonly, the attorney will disclose you and your scope of opinion. It is important that the expert review the expert disclosure statement for accuracy and ensure that the expert and attorney are on the same page regarding the scope of the expert's opinion. For example, on a case I consulted on, there was strong evidence of physical neglect (e.g., malnutrition, pressure ulcers) as well as UI, which was included under my scope of opinions. Instead, I recommended that the attorneys remove that element from my disclosure and seek a different expert who would be better positioned to discuss the medical issues related to that particular case of neglect. Once disclosed, you will be contacted to set up a deposition date. These cases usually settle, but I have found that it is often after the deposition and before trial. Once you have prepared for and survived a deposition, you will be fairly well prepared for trial.

STEPS FOR SUCCESSFUL TRIAL TESTIMONY

1. Establish your credibility through voir dire and credentialing.
2. Convincing the courts that UI is a "real thing" and that is possible to prove through a discussion of conceptual models and relevant legal standards.
3. Prepare with the attorney to determine the best way to obtain all the evidence you will need to support your opinion (e.g., medical records).
4. Go through timeline and talk about "significance" of each part of your case. Try to make the presentation a narrative rather than simply a collection of facts.
5. Voice clear opinions.

Understand that these cases are often built on circumstantial evidence and so the ability to put it all together for the court is critical. An example of this is found in *Lintz v. Lintz* (2014). In this case, an action was brought by the decedent's daughters against the defendant, the decedent's third wife. The court of appeal found that circumstantial evidence was sufficient to support a finding that the execution of the testamentary instruments had been obtained by UI. The court found that the widow exerted UI specifically "to procure estate plans and control over assets, according to her wishes and contrary to the wishes of decedent" (http://cclawyer.cccba.org/2014/04/undue-influence-defined-new-statutory-definition-and-recent-case-law/).

Pragmatic Considerations

By their nature, UI cases are complicated. Much of the time, experts are involved in retrospective analyses. Our ability to express opinions relates to the quality of records and information from the timeframe of interest. Explain to your referral that you may need to review records before being able to state whether you can even form an opinion. It is also helpful to have a list of records that you would like to review during this initial stage (see the assessment tips earlier in the chapter). Retrospective analyses often take more time to complete than contemporaneous assessments, so plan accordingly. The transactions at issue are not occurring in a vacuum. Chances are the elderly alleged victim may have made many decisions or transactions at the same time as the contested decision. I would recommend taking some time to clarify the scope of your expertise at the beginning of the cases so that it is clear to all parties exactly what decision is at issue.

SUGGESTIONS FOR ORGANIZING YOUR REPORT

1. Consider using timelines to assist readers in understanding your argument. Also consider using tables to track key information (e.g., medications), if relevant.
2. Make a clear statement regarding your opinion in conclusion to bridge from clinical findings to legal issues.
   A. Not just "Memory and executive functioning were mild to moderately impaired and the client was dependent on others"
   B. but "The client was significantly susceptible to undue influence during the time period because . . ."
   C. Be as direct as possible with your clients and the attorneys as well: "significant cognitive deficits"—"Yes, but did she have capacity to do X?"
3. Avoid addressing the ultimate legal issue but instead focus on gathering, organizing, analyzing, and presenting facts.

CASE EXAMPLE

Mrs. Joy Smith: Validity of a Trust and Will

Following a hospitalization in 2014, Joy Smith[1] moved in with her daughter. Shortly thereafter, she changed all her estate planning documents from a 50–50 split between her daughter and son to a 100% share to her daughter. She also changed her power of attorney from her son to her daughter and placed her daughter on all of her accounts. After her death, when the trust was discovered, her son sued his sister for elder financial abuse and UI. The following is a timeline of key dates in this example:

1995: Original trust was developed
2014: New trust was developed
2016: Mrs. Smith's death
2018: Date of the trial

Presentation

I was initially contacted in 2016 by a local civil attorney representing the son in this matter. The attorney asked me to complete a record review regarding issues related to capacity, UI, and financial elder abuse. In this case, the alleged victim was deceased. Ethical issues regarding this case could include (a) conflict of interest, (b) role on the case, (c) privacy and confidentiality.

To address the first issue, conflict of interest, I had to ask the attorney for the name of the case. With cases in my community, there is a possibility that I may have a personal conflict (know the family) or a contractual conflict (if the client had an APS history with my office), or it's possible that the opposing attorney could have already contacted me. After this step, I was able to ascertain that I had no conflicts. Next, we discussed my potential role in the case, including the scope of my opinion. In this case, records were still being gathered, and the attorneys wanted an analysis of capacity issues, UI, and financial elder abuse. This case would involve a retrospective determination of capacity and require a review of medical records. These records would need to be obtained through the attorney (the discovery process) and through deposition testimony with treating physicians; they could not be obtained through traditional means.

History

Mrs. Smith was a divorced, Caucasian woman who grew up in Minnesota and moved to California after she was married. She was married one time (for approximately 22 years) and had two children, Frank and Karen. She did

[1]Although the case examples in this chapter are based on the author's real experiences, the identities of the individuals involved in the examples have been properly disguised to protect their confidentiality.

not remarry. Per available records, Mrs. Smith obtained a master's degree in education after completing her bachelor's at the University of Minnesota. She worked at Alta Vista High School in the Los Angeles area for most of her career. She retired in 1997.

Mrs. Smith lived in her own home from approximately 1963 until October 2014. In August 2014, she was hospitalized for a fall. After the hospitalization, she was discharged home with recommendations for home health support, a caregiver, or assisted living setting. Mrs. Smith moved to her daughter's home in a town approximately an hour away. In October 2014, a few days after moving to her daughters' home, Mrs. Smith changed her estate documents with a new attorney that her daughter had located through a friend. Mrs. Smith lived at her daughter's home until her death in 2016.

Medical records were reviewed from 2006 through 2016. The records included some past medical history. These records indicated that Mrs. Smith had a large number of medical conditions during the time frame of interest. The following list is a summary of her medical history and conditions based on available medical records:

- Long-standing: heavy smoker, approximately 40 years; alcohol use, moderate to heavy
- 2009: Cataracts
- 2010: Coronary artery disease, chronic pain, arthritis, hypertension
- 2012: Dementia, diabetes
- 2014: Incontinence
- 2016: Advanced Alzheimer's disease

A medical record analysis from the timeframe of interest, 2007 through 2016, is summarized in more detail in what follows, where I used a timeline to organize information. These have been changed and abbreviated for confidentiality reasons and for ease of comprehension.

- Medical records from Dr. Snouffer (primary care physician; 2012):

  Dr. Snouffer's notes indicated a history of a memory deficit, and a prescription for Aricept, a medication prescribed for individuals with mild to moderate Alzheimer's disease.

- Medical records from Dr. Linworth (specialist; 2013):

  These records noted, "She is having trouble with her memory—whether she has done things and needs to recheck. She is still driving, and she has gotten lost even in her hometown. She has acknowledged that she hasn't had a memory loss workup." Recommendations included "consider using Meals on Wheels" to help with weight loss. Further, the note indicated "Patient need to follow-up with Dr. Snouffer regarding her hypertension, weight loss, and what appears to be advanced memory loss." "She is very concerned about her memory, is still driving, and lives alone." The records indicated urinary incontinence.

- *Medical records from community hospital (2013 admission date).* At this visit, it is noted that

> the patient has chronic hip pain and gradually deteriorated functionally over the past couple of years. The patient is now having difficulty at her house and her caregiver left . . . she is having to do some activities in which she is concerned about her balance and ability to do some of the chores of her house.

The records noted a strong recommendation to consider assisted living or hiring another caregiver given her functional deterioration.

- *Evaluation to assist with discharge planning including an assessment of her home environment (2013).* The client reported that she lived alone at home and reported no significant relationships with anyone. She is described as able to ambulate within the household with an assistive device (rolling walker), with ambulation distance noted as "household." Mrs. Smith reported that her daughter or neighbors go shopping for her. She is noted to be able to toilet, dress, and bathe with assistive devices. She is noted to be able to communicate without difficulty.
- *Medical records from community hospital (2016 admission date):* These records indicated the following diagnoses (1) Alzheimer's dementia, (2) kidney failure, dehydration. The note indicated, "Briefly, Mrs. Smith has a known history of advanced Alzheimer's dementia [and] was transferred to Riverdale Hospital. Discharge planning was consulted for placement as well as physical therapy and occupational therapy. She is expected to be discharged today to a skilled nursing facility." At this point, Mrs. Smith is oriented to person only. The note indicated that she requires total assistance with sitting and rolling in bed.

Interview, Examination, and Tests

This retrospective assessment did not include additional tests. In cases of UI when the client is living, I would include an assessment of cognitive and psychological functioning as well as a tool like the LFDRS. Record reviews, including collateral interviews with friends and neighbors, were completed. An interview with a friend and former colleague revealed that Mrs. Smith had noted functional declines beginning in 2012. For example, she saw Mrs. Smith with unkempt hair and clothing, which was very unlike her. She also noted that her home was poorly kept. Her friend tried to stay in touch but reported her phone calls and cards were never answered, and she herself was unable to drive out to visit.

I was also able to interview the pastor from her church where Mrs. Smith had been a very active member before her move. He reported that Mrs. Smith had become increasingly housebound and reclusive over time. He indicated that her home was exceedingly full of objects, papers, and magazines from years and years, accumulated very high. He noted that her appearance was not as neat recently as in the past. The pastor indicated that Mrs. Smith expressed an interest in moving to an assisted living with a church affiliation. However, whenever he tried to plan a visit, she backed out. After Mrs. Smith moved in with her daughter, he had no further contact with her, to the best of his recollection.

Findings

For the purposes of this chapter, I describe the findings related only to UI, which have been modified for clarity and to preserve confidentiality, but otherwise stated as I might in a report. As I summarize in Exhibit 6.2, Mrs. Smith was susceptible to UI by her daughter. I am hesitant to present a

---

EXHIBIT 6.2

Example of Findings

Statement of conclusion

It is this examiner's opinion that Mrs. Smith had been significantly susceptible to undue influence in the time period of interest.

Restatement of legal standard

"Undue influence" means *excessive persuasion* that causes another person to act or refrain from acting by overcoming that person's free will and results in inequity. In determining whether a result was produced by undue influence, all of the following shall be considered:

Statement of findings relevant to legal standard

1. **The vulnerability of the victim.** In the current matter, Mrs. Smith demonstrated an extensive number of vulnerabilities that seriously increased her risk for undue influence. In terms of illness, Mrs. Smith was quite ill and had a large number of medical conditions including a recent hospitalization. In terms of cognitive impairment, Mrs. Smith demonstrated significant vulnerability. Mrs. Smith had a diagnosis of dementia and had reported concerns regarding her memory loss to physicians starting in 2012 when she was placed on Aricept, a drug prescribed for Alzheimer's disease. She also reported getting lost while driving in her area as early as 2011 and appeared to stop driving in 2012. In terms of emotional distress, Mrs. Smith demonstrated some vulnerability. Mrs. Smith was described by her pastor as becoming increasingly reclusive and had a history of alcohol dependence. In terms of isolation, Mrs. Smith was noted to become more withdrawn and reclusive over time by her pastor. After her move, she became more isolated. In terms of dependency, Mrs. Smith was significantly vulnerable.
2. **The influencer's apparent authority.** Karen Smith, the alleged influencer, had a confidential relationship and apparent authority serving as a caregiver, POA and as a family member (daughter) at the time of the execution of the documents. Ms. K. Smith had complete control over all necessities of life.
3. **Actions or tactics used by the influencer.** Once at her daughter's home, her daughter indicated in deposition that she assisted with all ADLS and IADLs, rarely left her alone, and accompanied her whenever she left the home.
4. **The equity of the result.** In the new trust, Mrs. Smith changed her preferences from a 50–50 split between her two adult children, to a 100% distribution to Ms. Karen Smith. All previous testamentary instruments speak to her long-standing preferences for equal treatment of her natural heirs.

Note. ADLs = activities of daily living; IADLs = instrumental activities of daily living; POA = power of attorney.

UI analysis as an "adding up" of factors. The expert can provide information on many of these factors, but it is up to the trier of fact to make the ultimate legal opinion. Each case is unique and requires individual analysis. As such, I do not state that Mrs. Smith was unduly influenced but rather state that she was susceptible to UI and then provide an objective analysis of the factors that were present during the transaction in question in this case. In this case, we have a vulnerable client who is engaging in estate planning changes that disproportionately benefit one heir, with whom she has a confidential relationship and who appeared to be actively initiating the changes. The new will represents a shift from previous dispositions. These types of factors are reflected in many jurisdictions and can support a finding of UI.

Outcome

In this case, the judge ruled that there was a clear preponderance of evidence that the respondent exerted UI over the decedent. Therefore, trusts and will were made as a direct result of the UI exercised over respondent and are invalid.

REFLECTION

Cases of UI are complex and require a comprehensive approach to their analysis. However, they are also fascinating cases to investigate. Developing skill and expertise in UI cases takes time and exposure to these cases. Broadening one's own assessment approach, for example, adding in some items from the LFDRS where appropriate with clients may help a clinician become more familiar with the key issues and their assessment.

REFERENCES

American Law Institute. (1981). *Restatement of the law (second): Contracts.* Philadelphia, PA: Author.

Blum, B. (2012). *Undue influence.* Retrieved from http://www.bennettblummd.com/undue_influence.html

Brandl, B., Heisler, C. J., & Stiegel, L. A. (2005). The parallels between undue influence, domestic violence, stalking, and sexual assault. *Journal of Elder Abuse & Neglect, 17,* 37–52. http://dx.doi.org/10.1300/J084v17n03_03

Griffith, H. R., Belue, K., Sicola, A., Krzywanski, S., Zamrini, E., Harrell, L., & Marson, D. C. (2003). Impaired financial abilities in mild cognitive impairment: A direct assessment approach. *Neurology, 60,* 449–457. http://dx.doi.org/10.1212/WNL.60.3.449

Lichtenberg, P. A., Ficker, L. J., & Rahman-Filipiak, A. (2016). Financial decision-making abilities and exploitation in older African Americans: Preliminary validity evidence for the Lichtenberg Financial Decision Rating Scale (LFDRS). *Journal of Elder Abuse & Neglect, 29,* 14–33. http://dx.doi.org/10.1080/08946566.2015.1078760

Lintz v. Lintz, 222 Cal. App. 4th 1346 (2014).

Plotkin, D. A., Spar, J. E., & Horwitz, H. L. (2016). Assessing undue influence. *Journal of the American Academy of Psychiatry and the Law, 44,* 344–351.

Quinn, M. J. (2001). Friendly persuasion, good salesmanship, or undue influence. *Marquette Elder's Advisor, 2*(4), Article 8.

Quinn, M. J., Goldman, E., Nerenberg, L., & Piazza, D. (2010). *Undue influence: Definitions and applications.* Salt Lake City, UT: The Borchard Foundation for Law and Aging. http://dx.doi.org/10.1002/bsl.2370130307

True Link Financial. (2015). *The True Link report on elder financial abuse.* Retrieved from http://documents.truelinkfinancial.com/True-Link-Report-On-Elder-Financial-Abuse-012815.pdf

Wood, S., & Lichtenberg, P. A. (2017). Financial capacity and financial exploitation of older adults: Research findings, policy recommendations and clinical implications. *Clinical Gerontologist, 40*, 3–13. http://dx.doi.org/10.1080/07317115.2016.1203382

7

Assessment of Independent Living Capacity in the Context of Elder Self-Neglect

Michelle E. Mlinac and Pamela Steadman-Wood

KEY POINTS

- Elder self-neglect (ESN) is a complex, multifactorial syndrome
- ESN may impact the ability to live independently
- Concerns for ESN may trigger an evaluation of independent living capacity
- Best practices involve interdisciplinary approaches to assessment and intervention
- Requires interface with regulatory agencies

DEFINITION OF THE ISSUE

This chapter deals with several related and intersecting clinical concepts. To assist with distinguishing their use, the definitions as they are used in this chapter appear in Table 7.1.

---

http://dx.doi.org/10.1037/0000184-008
Assessing Capacities of Older Adults: A Casebook to Guide Difficult Decisions, J. Moye (Editor)

TABLE 7.1. Key Terms

Term	Definition as used in this chapter
Elder self-neglect (ESN): a set of behaviors of an individual	The behavior of a person that threatens his or her own health or safety. Self-neglect generally manifests itself in an older person as a refusal or failure to provide oneself with adequate food, water, clothing, shelter, personal hygiene, medication (when indicated), and safety precautions (National Center for Elder Abuse, 2019).
Independent living capacity: an opinion of a clinical professional about a characteristic of an individual	Abilities to care for self or home (or both), providing all means of support, as assessed by 1. understanding: Does the individual understand day-to-day requirements of taking care of self and home? 2. application: Does the individual understand general requirements of living independently? 3. judgment: Does the presence of a cognitive, emotional or thought disorder affect the individual's judgment as it relates to self or home care?
Capacity related to guardianship: a legal term defined in guardianship laws and adjudicated in the court	Lacking the ability to meet essential requirements for physical health, safety, or self-care because the respondent is unable to receive and evaluate information or make or communicate decisions, even with appropriate supportive services, technological assistance, or supported decision-making; the respondent's identified needs cannot be met by a protective arrangement instead of guardianship or other less restrictive alternative (National Conference of Commissioners on Uniform State Laws, 2017).
Hoarding: a diagnosis of a clinical condition by a clinician	A specific condition in which an individual experiences persistent difficulty discarding or parting with possessions because of a perceived need to save them and accumulates items excessively, regardless of actual value and despite associated negative consequences.

Providing home-based services to older adults who are unable to meet their own needs raises challenging clinical and ethical issues. In this chapter, we discuss the concept of elder self-neglect (ESN) as it relates to capacity evaluations in the home setting. Determining exactly what constitutes ESN can be puzzling because it is a complex multifactorial syndrome that lacks a formal definition. Given that many older adults and their families value maximizing independence and a desire for the older adult to remain living in their home for as long as possible, ethical issues of autonomy versus protection are often at play. Best practices involve interdisciplinary approaches to assessment and intervention, including interface with local community and state regulatory agencies. This chapter discusses salient issues related to addressing ESN. Case examples are included to illustrate some of the issues we grapple with related to our work with older adults at risk for ESN.

CLINICAL PRESENTATION

According to the Institute on Aging (2018) in 2010, nearly one third of community-dwelling older adults (11.3 million) live alone. The likelihood of living alone increases with age, and almost half of older adults over age 75 live alone. Older women are twice as likely as older men to reside alone. Living arrangements differ by race and ethnicity with older non-Hispanic White and Black women most likely to live alone compared with women of other races. Older adults living alone are often at risk for self-neglect. ESN is the most frequently reported form of elder abuse reported to adult protective service (APS) agencies. ESN is 3 times more common than physical abuse or caregiver neglect (Iris, Conrad, & Ridings, 2014) and can increase mortality risk by 16-fold (Hildebrand et al., 2014). In the United States alone, there are approximately 1.2 million cases of reported ESN annually (Dong, Simon, & Evans, 2010), and rates of reporting are on the rise according to National Association of Protective Services Administrators. Literature on ESN describes risk factors as demographic, social, and physiological in nature, and ESN subtypes have been proposed to capture the scope of the problem. A population-based study of more than 4,600 adults in greater Chicago found that ESN was more prevalent in men than women (Dong et al., 2012). Demographic risk factors include older age, lower income, and being African American (Dong et al., 2010, 2011). Social factors include having less social engagement and support (Dong et al., 2010), being less trusting (Naik, Kunik, Cassidy, Nair, & Coverdale, 2010), and having substance abuse issues (Spensley, 2008). Physiological factors include medical, psychological, and cognitive comorbidities. Having served in the military also appears to be a risk factor for ESN (Moon, Lawson, Carpiac, & Spaziano, 2006). As the population ages, concern about ESN is projected to have a significant impact on individuals, families, communities, health care systems, and insurers. As such, having an awareness of the signs and symptoms of ESN and the tools required to assess and intervene are paramount in this population.

DIAGNOSTIC STANDARDS AND DILEMMAS

As home care providers, we have a bird's eye view into how an older adult is functioning in the home. We are often the first responders when issues of self-neglect become a concern. Having a framework to address ESN is important in our clinical practice, and to our knowledge, few evidence-based models exist. ESN is a complex, multifactorial syndrome that lacks a unified definition. ESN is not considered a clinical diagnosis and thus is not in the *Diagnostic and Statistical Manual of Mental Disorders*. The National Center for Elder Abuse (2019) defines *self-neglect* as neglecting one's own health or safety in a way that leads to illness or injury. Self-neglect generally manifests in an older person as a refusal or failure to provide oneself with adequate food, water, clothing, shelter, personal hygiene, medication (when indicated), and safety precautions.

Researchers have proposed clinical criteria, conceptual frameworks, and ESN subtypes to help operationalize ESN, as follows.

CLINICAL CRITERIA, CONCEPTUAL FRAMEWORKS, AND ESN SUBTYPES

Pavlou and Lachs's (2008) Criteria for Elder Self Neglect

- Persistent inattention to personal hygiene or environment
- Repeated refusal of some or all indicated services that can reasonably be expected to improve quality of life
- Self-endangerment through manifestation of unsafe behaviors (e.g., persistent refusal to care for a wound, creating fire hazards in the home)

Conceptual Framework for Elder Self-Neglect and Risk Factors (Iris et al., 2014)

Psychological Factors

- Physical health
- Mental health
- Cognitive impairment
- Social network
- Personal endangerment (e.g., noncompliance, help refusal)

Environmental Factors

- Physical living conditions
- Financial situation
- Personal living conditions (e.g., hoarding, blocked pathways)

Burnett et al.'s (2014) Subtypes of Elder Self Neglect

- Physical and medical neglect
- Environmental neglect
- Global neglect
- Financial neglect

In our clinical experience, ESN occurs most often in the context of neurocognitive disorders and other cognitive impairments that are clinically significant but do not meet criteria for neurocognitive disorder (e.g., processing speed, executive functions, memory), anxiety disorders, depressive disorders, posttraumatic stress disorders, substance use disorders, hoarding disorder, serious and persistent mental illness (e.g., psychotic disorders, bipolar disorders), chronic pain and physical disability related to comorbid medical conditions. Psychosocial factors at play often include refusal of assistance, lack of resources available to provide the assistance needed, perceived burden, familial discord, and medical regimen complexity.

Hoarding disorder is often a risk factor for ESN due to the functional consequences associated with the accumulation of excessive amounts of clutter (e.g., impairment in activities of daily living [ADLs] and quality of life, safety concerns, and hazardous living conditions). Although not all older adults with hoarding disorder have issues with self-neglect, comorbid conditions and contributing factors such as cognitive impairment, anxiety, and mood and trauma-related disorders increase the risk. As such, older adults with hoarding disorder should be assessed for ESN.

Overall, in the absence of a formal definition or diagnosis of ESN, clinicians rely on use of risk factors and warning signs to guide the assessment of ESN and related capacity issues. In ESN, issues of capacity for independent living, finance management, health care management, and medical decision-making are quite common. In some cases, it may be necessary to assess more than one decision-making capacity domain when ESN is in question.

Ethical dilemmas of autonomy versus protection are often present in cases of suspected ESN and require an analysis of the risk of harm and the level of supervision needed to ensure safety. It is important to assess warning signs, collaborate with all parties involved including, but not limited to, families, caregivers (formal and informal), interdisciplinary team members, and community and other state agencies (e.g., APS) to implement interventions that optimize safety, consider all means to enhance capacity, and maximize independence and respect for the individual's personal values in the least restrictive manner. In addition to ethical responsibilities, such as those outlined in the American Psychological Association's (APA's; 2017) *Ethical Principles of Psychologists and Code of Conduct* (e.g., Principles A and E), it is important for psychologists to be familiar with local and state laws and regulatory statutes where they practice, as these vary by state.

CLINICAL METHODS

We next discuss a clinical strategy that can be used to evaluate ESN in the context of decision-making capacity evaluations. Whenever possible, these types of evaluations benefit from the input of providers of several disciplines (e.g., nursing, social work), and we discuss how that information can be elicited and incorporated into the report in the following sections. We recognize that in some cases, providers may be working independently and not have the opportunity for an interdisciplinary assessment, but we hope that this strategy can provide suggestions for referrals or recommendations to make the evaluation as patient-centered and robust as possible.

Conceptual Framework

We approach the issue of ESN from our experience as clinical psychologists in the Home-Based Primary Care (HBPC) program in the Department of Veterans

Affairs (VA). Within the VA, HBPC is a comprehensive interdisciplinary care model for complex, chronically ill individuals (Beales & Edes, 2009). VA HBPC teams typically comprise nurse care managers, social workers, primary care providers, dieticians, pharmacists, physical and occupational therapists, psychologists, and psychiatrists. All disciplines work together to provide patient-centered care for veterans enrolled in the program (Beales & Edes, 2009; Karlin & Karel, 2014; Zeiss & Karlin, 2008). When an individual's ability to function safely at home becomes a concern, mental health providers in this setting are often asked to conduct an assessment and assist with intervention. As noted earlier, there are few evidence-based models to guide an assessment of ESN, although algorithms to assess ESN and related decision-making capacities have been adopted.

Mosqueda and Dong (2011) developed an algorithm for clinicians to approach when self-neglect is suspected that is used widely in APS agencies. In this model, once a warning sign for ESN is identified, decision-making capacity is assessed informally, and efforts to enhance capacity are put forth. In some cases, a formal decision-making capacity assessment is required and a referral is placed. In other cases, a referral to APS is made to conduct the assessment and assist with interventions. The precise decisions and referrals are made on the basis of a team's resources, specialties, and relationships with community and state regulatory agencies.

In HBPC, the team likely has a longitudinal relationship with the person suspected of ESN and may implement a screening and management process that differs from what APS may use. Feng, Murphy, and Mlinac (2017) developed a dynamic risk assessment and intervention model that integrates the process of what to do after the risk of ESN has been identified and managed by largely by the interprofessional team, referring to APS, as needed (see Figure 7.1). According to this model, a risk assessment is conducted informally by each provider at every home visit with the patient. Risks and needs are reviewed formally by the interdisciplinary team at quarterly care planning meetings. Modifications to treatment plan are made and adjusted on the basis of the level of risk, along with the patient's goals and needs over time. A report or concern by APS of ESN may trigger an assessment of independent living capacity; an assessment of capacity may trigger a report to APS of ESN.

Assessment Approaches

Assessing ESN is a complicated and often difficult task because there is no agreement regarding evidence-based risk factors, nor is there a psychometrically sound screening tool for clinicians. Screening tools have been used by APS agencies to assess elder abuse (e.g., Client Assessment and Risk Evaluation) and the Self-Neglect Severity Scale, but none are specific to ESN. Moreover, the U.S. Preventative Services Task Force does not recommend or discourage screening for elder abuse. Overall, most assessment

FIGURE 7.1. Dynamic Risk Assessment and Intervention Cycle in Home-Based Primary Care

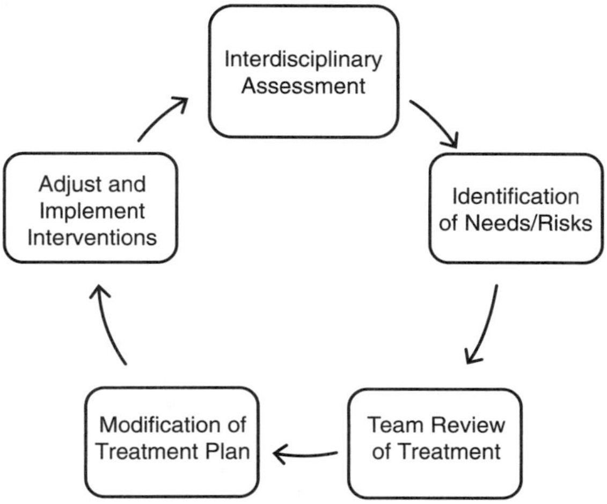

From "Independent Living Capacity Evaluation in Home-Based Primary Care: Considerations and Outcomes of a Quality Improvement Project," by M. C. Feng, M. R. Murphy, and M. Mlinac, 2017, *Clinical Gerontologist, 40*, p. 54. Copyright 2017 by Taylor & Francis. Reprinted with permission.

tools are self-developed and minimally supported by research. In our home-based practice, we generally integrate the aforementioned models developed by Feng, Murphy, and Mlinac (2017) and Mosqueda and Dong (2011) by identifying ESN, conducting an assessment, providing intervention, monitoring and evaluating the effectiveness of the intervention, evaluating decision-making capacity, and referring to APS as clinically indicated.

Clarify Concern of Self-Neglect

When working with interdisciplinary teams, community and state agency workers, families, and caregivers, each may have different training backgrounds, philosophical views, and ways of viewing behavior. It is important to clarify whether there is a true self-neglect issue. This may require monitoring for a period of time before conducting any formal assessment(s).

Assessment and Intervention

Once a self-neglect issue is identified and a formal risk assessment has been completed, the team works together to devise an intervention with the potential to increase supports and minimize risk. The plan is implemented with frequent monitoring from various team members and community agencies to determine effectiveness, then it is modified as needed until either the individual's needs are met or a more comprehensive decision-making capacity is required or a referral to APS is warranted.

Consider Decision-Making Capacity

If interventions to minimize risk are unsuccessful, the next step typically involves determining whether the individual's decision-making capacity is impaired. In many cases, we are considering independent living capacity, but other capacity domains may be in question and should be assessed separately. If a formal decision-making capacity assessment is required, we use the following steps.

ASSESSMENT STEPS

1. Historical information. Consider a medical record review and information from collateral sources such as team members, family, caregivers, community agency providers.
2. Clinical interview. Conduct a clinical interview to determine the individual's current situation, concerns, symptoms, and mental status.
3. Functional assessment. Assess everyday abilities, including home-based assessment.
4. Cognitive assessment. Consider to what extent will cognitive deficits affect the individual's ability to live alone.
5. Psychiatric and emotional assessment. Consider to what extent psychiatric conditions affect the individual's ability to live alone.
6. Values. It is important to become familiar with an individual's culture, religion, and belief system to accurately assess whether the current behaviors and judgments are consistent with longstanding beliefs.
7. Risks. It is necessary to weigh the risks of the individual continuing to live independently without supervision or a guardian versus the benefits of a supervised living situation and imposing restrictions on autonomy.
8. Steps to enhance capacity. The level of assistance required will vary depending on a variety of cognitive, social, emotional, and physical factors. (American Bar Association [ABA]/APA, 2008)

When possible, a home-based assessment is ideal to see exactly how the person functions in their environment. A general framework appears in Table 7.2, with additional detail in Table 7.3.

Observations of the home also afford a view into strengths, personal experiences, and values that can inform clinical recommendations. Examples include family photos, awards, hobbies, pets, and religious and cultural symbols. In addition, we assess ADLs required for survival and instrumental ADLs. There are a variety of functional instruments in the field, with some

TABLE 7.2. Home Assessment

Factors to consider	Understanding: Does the individual understand day-to-day requirements of taking care of self and home? Application: Does the individual understand the general requirements of living independently? Judgment: Does the presence of a cognitive, emotional or thought disorder affect the individual's judgment as it relates to self or home care? When possible, environmental observations should be included in a report.
Functional instrument examples	The Katz Index of Independence in Activities of Daily Living (ADLs; Katz, Ford, Moskowitz, Jackson, & Jaffe, 1963) is one of the most commonly used tools to asses basic ADLs (bathing, dressing, toileting transferring, continence, and feeding). The Physical Self-Maintenance Scale (PSMS) and Instrumental ADL (IADL) scale (Lawton & Brody, 1969) is an informant-report measure. Each of six ADLs (toilet, feeding, dressing, grooming, ambulation, and bathing) is rated as dependent or independent and has more descriptors than the Katz. Other instruments such as the Texas Functional Living Scale (Cullum et al., 2001) and Independent Living Scales (Loeb, 1996) use performance-based measures of daily activities and can address self-care more broadly (e.g., identifying the benefits of regular personal hygiene). However, they mainly evaluate IADLs rather than ADLs.

examples provided in Table 7.2 A more comprehensive overview on assessment of ADLs appears in Mlinac and Feng (2016).

Clinical Decision

Once the assessment is complete, the psychologist will need to integrate the data and come to a clinical decision about the individual's capacity for independent living. Overall, it can be helpful to think about categorizing

TABLE 7.3. Assessing Home Safety Risks

Area observed	Issues to observe
Garage and driveway	Yard maintenance; dings, dents, or scratches on car; exterior lighting; entryway stairs and path
Kitchen	Poor sanitation, evidence of bugs or rodents, adequate food supply (check fridge, cupboards, freezer), working appliances
Living room or bedroom	Working phone and personal alarm, fall risks, stairs, walkable paths, medication storage and pill planners, calendars
Bathroom	Sanitation, grab bars, ease of access to tub, shower, and toilet

interventions as targeting (a) older adults with diminished capacity but who can remain living independently with adequate supports (e.g., home health aides, Meals on Wheels, family or caregiver supports) or (b) older adults who lack capacity and are unsafe to remain living independently despite extensive supports in place and need to be relocated to a more supervised setting.

Interventions

Working collaboratively with an interdisciplinary team, families, caregivers, and community and state agencies often leads to the most fruitful outcomes.

Working With Attorneys, Courts, and Protective Services.

In this section, we offer several suggestions to consider when working with various social and legal parties involved in the individual's care.

Be Aware of Applicable Privacy Policies That Operate in Your Clinical Setting

Cooperation with APS regarding specific individuals over time may depend on their relationship with the medical facility. In our locations, we have standing letters to allow communication relevant to individual safety with elder protective services when necessary for the care of the individual. However, when the concern is under investigation, the agencies may or may not be able to provide information back to the clinical team. In some cases, we may not find out the specific determination of the case until after it has been found to be substantiated (or not). When these are chronic issues, over time multiple protective reports may end up being filed until the situation comes to a head.

Collaborate With Relevant Agencies

For cases where hoarding or hazardous conditions exist, providers may end up collaborating with building or facility management or the Department of Public Health (DPH; or building management, assisted living facility staff, etc.) with housing issues. Privacy regulations may be different, but if the individual is agreeable, it may be helpful to work with these authorities to prevent homelessness or eviction, or to identify alternate housing. In cases where animal hoarding is a concern, interfacing with animal protective agencies may also come into play. See Table 7.3 for an overview of specific areas of the home where common safety issues may be assessed. It can also be useful to collaborate with elder law attorneys (for a listing, see the National Association of Elder Law Attorneys website: https://www.naela.org).

Be Aware of the Local Protective Statutes in Your Jurisdiction

Further, we recommend fostering a collaborative learning process with local elder law attorneys and APS. Psychologists and other clinical providers can offer education around capacity evaluations and psychiatric disorders that can affect capacity, while in return they may learn more about the role elder law attorneys play in these cases. It can be useful to understand the process for APS referrals, the general timeframe in which these referrals are investigated, and how the triage process works. In specific cases when communication with individual APS workers seems challenging, consider reaching out to the person's supervisor. As with any busy government agency, roles can change quickly, and the supervisors may be best able to coordinate effectively.

Pragmatic Considerations

Self-neglect can occur when functioning declines to the point that a person cannot complete ADLs and instrumental ADLs. On one hand, these can lend themselves to remediation if services and supports are available, but at times we have found that the person is not willing to accept them. In these cases, a protective services referral is made, yet often APS is not yet warranted or the case is screened out. In these instances, things will most likely get worse before they get better. Relying on others for help is not an easy transition for many older adults. They may rightly fear being placed in a nursing home or having their rights taken away. We may frame these functional supports as opportunities to remain in place as long as possible rather than the first step toward a feared outcome. There may be some small area where the person is willing to begin accepting help—perhaps having a friendly visitor or someone to help fill a pillbox. Over time, a trusting relationship can be built and in-home services can be augmented if functioning further worsens. When conducting independent living capacity evaluations, it is crucial to have a clear understanding of available formal and informal supports so that individuals can remain in place when possible. This again calls the importance of team collaboration in identifying, enlisting, and partnering with these available supports. Ideally, the person would have providers who know the individual well and who can be involved longitudinally (so supports can be trialed in the home), although we recognize this may not always be the case. Sometimes these situations come to a head in a crisis.

We advocate that whenever possible, independent living capacity evaluations should be done within the person's home environment. Although not always possible or practical (for example, when determining a safe discharge plan back home from a skilled nursing facility), consider that the environment in which the capacity testing is done may not correlate well to the home environment. In other words, although individuals may or may not be able to tell you what they do in a home situation, it may or may not translate into practice. For example, during a capacity evaluation, individuals can tell you they know it is important to call 911 if there is a fire. Yet when in their home they would not actually do so in the moment. Similarly, they may be unable to provide a correct verbal response during testing in the clinic, but in their own environment, they may in fact carry out these activities.

Finally, collateral information can be key in determining independent living capacity, although caregivers and family members known to the individual may not be free from bias themselves. They may be burnt out or have other reasons for wanting the person to either remain in the home or to have a higher level of care. They may also over- or underestimate the person's functional abilities (Mlinac & Feng, 2016). Seek objective functional data from nursing, dieticians, or physical or occupational therapists to ensure a robust representation of the person's functional strengths and weaknesses. This data can also be crucial to developing a workable set of recommendations within the report.

CASE EXAMPLES

The following two case examples[1] illustrate the complex nature of performing capacity evaluations in instances of self-neglect. There can be complexities including overlapping service providers with competing interests, unclear histories, and unavailable or misinformed collateral sources. It is important to be aware of your own personal reactions to these often-challenging evaluations and consult with colleagues as needed.

Case 1: Mr. Jacob Young—Self-Neglect, APS, and Guardianship

In the context of ESN, APS or other concerned parties may request evaluation of the older adult's independent living capacity. The first case is of an older adult who is engaged in self-neglect behaviors marked by an inability to maintain personal hygiene, adhere to health care recommendations, and manage the upkeep of his home. Although self-neglect was evident, what was less clear was how the HBPC team and APS should proceed.

Mr. Young was a Caucasian man in his 90s who was widowed and estranged from children and lived alone in his own single-family suburban home. After outpatient neuropsychological testing in which he was diagnosed with major neurocognitive disorder, this individual was referred to the interdisciplinary HBPC team by his home telehealth nurse. While he had been sending his vital signs to his telehealth nurse daily for several years, this had become much more sporadic. He was also noted to be frequently missing clinic appointments and needing assistance with medication management. A few months earlier, she also referred him to APS for concerns about self-neglect and financial exploitation by a neighbor. Protective services resolved the financial exploitation concern but were also concerned about his overall well-being in the home and ability to continue to live independently in context of self-neglect.

Our first visit with Mr. Young was a brief initial introduction done jointly with his ongoing protective services case manager to build rapport as he could be guarded around strangers but had developed trust in the case manager. Mr. Young often would not answer his front door and would sleep at various

[1]Although the case examples in this chapter are based on the authors' real experiences, the identities of the individuals involved in the examples have been properly disguised to protect their confidentiality.

times during the day and take the phone off the hook. To get him to answer the door, the case manager would walk into the side yard and knock on the bedroom window to alert him. Although this generally was successful, Mr. Young did keep a baseball bat nearby in case of intruders and could be easily startled.

History

Mr. Young had an elementary school education and operated a small business for 30 years. He had been widowed for 10 years before the referral. He reported having three children from prior brief sexual relationships, but he noted he had never wanted to be part of their lives and did not choose to keep in contact with them over the years. His niece was his primary source of emotional and instrumental support. From the outpatient neuropsychological testing a few weeks before the capacity evaluation, he had been diagnosed with unspecified major neurocognitive disorder. Testing at that time indicated severe impairments in learning and memory and several aspects of executive functioning (e.g., visual divided attention and organization), borderline to mild impairments in processing speed, semantic fluency and working memory, and intact performances across the domains of orientation simple attention, phonemic fluency, and constructional ability. Other medical concerns included heart failure and anemia. He denied depressive symptoms, although he was not sleeping well.

Interview, Examination, and Tests

Behavioral observations. Self-neglect was evident in his appearance. The individual's hygiene was poor (e.g., unshaven, long toenails), and his clothing was unkempt. He was oriented to person and place but not to all aspects of time. He was generally agreeable and friendly, cooperating with all aspects of the evaluation. He indicated he could see and hear the examiners and clearly see the testing materials. Although his speech was normal in tone and rate, his responses were often tangential and confabulatory.

Environmental observations. His home was cluttered and unclean (suggestive of a long pattern of self-neglect) and was in foreclosure due to failure to pay mortgage and taxes. His late parents had been hoarders, and he noted he never really cleaned out what was important to them. He had piles of old mail, including bank statements and magazines from months earlier. Additionally, he had many duplicate appliances (e.g., five televisions). He stated that he alternates between using one of five coffee makers each morning. On the day we saw him for the capacity evaluation, we found one of the coffee makers plugged in and sitting in the damp kitchen sink. The car outside of his home had many dents and makeshift repairs (e.g., repairs with masking tape).

Clinical interview. Mr. Young expressed a clear preference for remaining in his current living environment because he had been living there since 1939 and wanted to stay as independent as possible. With regard to ADLs, he denied any difficulty completing household tasks and he repeatedly stated, "I don't need help. I'm my own person." He reported that he often cooks even though he receives home-delivered meals. He noted that he has never left the stove on by accident (although other team members had found his oven left on during their visits). He also noted that he still drives occasionally. He reported that he takes "six pills once/day" (seven pills were on his medication list), and he could identify one of the pills by name, stating "I take metoprolol for my heart." He was unable to spontaneously recall additional medical problems or medications without significant cueing (e.g., he said, "Yes, I think I have heart failure, but it does not bother me"). He expressed appreciation for the services he received at home but was unable to describe the types of help he had been receiving. Although he could express a choice when asked questions about his medical care, he was limited in his ability to weigh the risks and benefits of various medical treatments and health-related behaviors. When discussing his wishes for a health care proxy, he clearly stated that he would want his niece to help with medical decisions if necessary. He did not feel he needed additional help at home, and he lacked insight about his functional impairments.

Functional measures. We assessed Mr. Young with the Health and Safety subscale of the Independent Living Scales (Loeb, 1996) on which his scores fell in the low–dependent range (standard score = 20). He could demonstrate how to contact the police over the phone and via his Medical Alert button. He was also able to identify safe ways of responding to some situations (e.g., turning the gas off and calling the gas company if he smelled an odor). However, in most cases, his responses to various questions regarding emergency situations were vague even with considerable cueing. At times, he seemed to make a joke in response to an interview question, but he was then unable to come up with the correct answer. For example, when asked what he would do if he had a pain in his chest and on his left side and he was having trouble breathing, he first stated, "Call an eye doctor." After the question was repeated, he said, "I would holler 'Doctor, Doctor!' and run for the hospital." He was unable to provide information about his own health or strategies for remembering to take his medications. He also lacked awareness about methods for contacting his medical providers.

Findings

In this case, we determined that Mr. Young lacked capacity to live independently. On his prior neuropsychological evaluation, he demonstrated severe impairments in executive functioning and learning and memory and mild impairments in processing speed, working memory, and semantic fluency, and these impairments are affecting his ability to carry out daily tasks. He exhibited self-neglect that was unable to be sufficiently remedied with supports that APS had put in place (e.g., he would accept but not actually eat home-delivered meals). He had poor insight into his pattern of self-neglect, including his poor hygiene, the dilapidated conditions of his home, and his inability to provide for his general welfare. Of particular concern were his lack of insight regarding his daily needs, his inability to carry out the behaviors to meet these needs (e.g., medication adherence), his history of being financially exploited, his inability to problem solve when faced with safety-related issues (e.g., being locked out of his home), and his lack of appreciation for the risks of his current living situation. Given his limited insight about the level of his cognitive and functional impairments, we determined that he lacked capacity to determine the level of support he required in the home. Therefore, if long-term care (LTC) placement were ultimately to be needed, we recommended that his health care agent should make that determination. Given the risks related to his medication adherence and his inability to problem solve around issues related to safety, we felt that additional in-home supports would be insufficient. Instead, we recommended that an alternative living arrangement with additional supervision should be considered. We recommended that his health care proxy should be activated for all but the most basic of health care decisions. He clearly stated that he would want his niece's assistance with medical decisions, which is consistent with his advance directive documentation. We felt it was unlikely that he could retain important information from his providers. We recommended that his niece or another surrogate accompany him to all medical appointments. If the Mr. Young's niece was not willing or able to serve in this capacity, then we felt guardianship would be appropriate. Although we did not formally assess his capacity to manage his financial affairs, he had been financially exploited, and his lack of knowledge about his finances suggested that he should have assistance managing his finances. He agreed to have his niece take over this duty.

Interventions and Supports

We provided feedback about our findings in written and verbal format, reviewing our recommendations at subsequent visits to support his understanding and retention. On some occasions he agreed that he needed more help, and other days when he felt better he believed that he was doing just fine on his own. We met with the APS caseworker at the agency to develop a plan, and then enlisted the niece in helping to guide care decisions going forward. The niece benefitted from regular coaching visits from the team's social worker around applying for Medicaid benefits on his behalf and other paperwork that was new to her. As we continued to provide in-home care until the guardianship was finalized (9 months after the capacity evaluation), it was important to support each other within the team around this challenging situation and to set realistic treatment goals with him and his niece. He continued to functionally decline over this time period, and although he welcomed the help in the home, he was not always aware or organized enough to answer the door. With his and the niece's agreement, a lockbox was installed in his home by APS to provide his regular homemakers access to the home to provide more frequent care to him. Other instrumental supports that helped mitigate some risk were home safety interventions provided by the occupational therapist, and his primary care provider minimizing his medication list as much as possible (as he was typically not taking his pills unless someone was in the room to coach him). Other social service interventions directed at addressing his self-neglect, such as home-delivered meals, were inadequate without the 24-hour supervision he required.

Outcome

Despite additional supports being put in place, the issue of self-neglect was not fully resolved, leaving APS to pursue guardianship because he lacked capacity for independent living. We worked closely with them, Mr. Young, and his niece for several months. Before the guardianship hearing, his protective service worker and our team met with his court-appointed attorney advocate at his home. The advocate interviewed us and Mr. Young and said his impression was that guardianship was not needed. This seemed unbelievable to us but could be consistent with the attorney's role in representing the client in a hearing, and perhaps also reflected the benefits of all the supports we had put in place. Nevertheless, in the context of our testing and assessment of his risk, we continued to believe he would benefit from a guardian. None of Mr. Young's three children could be reached by APS, our team, his attorney, or the niece as he was estranged from them. The niece ultimately agreed to be his guardian, and in lieu of no closer next of kin, she was appointed. At that point, the APS closed Mr. Young's case, as he had plateaued receiving in-home help and had oversight from his niece who lived 10 minutes away. Our team continued to work closely with her on things like getting him enrolled in Medicaid (anticipating LTC). The niece was not able to reverse the foreclosure, with the bank threatening repossession, so we worked with the niece to try to keep in him in the home as long as possible. Finally, he was found by police confused and naked in freezing cold, having locked himself out of his home and banging on car windows in street. He was hospitalized and ultimately placed in an LTC setting. From initial contact to placement, we had worked with him for 15 months.

CASE 2: MR. EDWARD MARTINEZ—SELF-NEGLECT, APS, CARE OF HOME

We next present an evaluation of a Hispanic man in his 80s who was never married, had no children, and was a former cook with a history of mild vascular dementia. He was referred for an evaluation of his independent living capacity by APS: They and the city's DPH had recently removed many animals from his home due to concerns about ESN and inability to provide adequate care for them. The week before the evaluation, he was notified that his home would be condemned if no improvement was made, which would leave him homeless. The caseworker at APS had developed a somewhat adversarial relationship with him as she attributed his poor adherence to their recommendations as being deliberate on his part.

The issues in this situation were whether Mr. Martinez could (a) remain in his home safely, (b) accept services to allow him to do so, (c) abide by the legal circumstances he found himself in regarding his property. Commonly in these situations, we would be looking at whether the individual understood relevant risks to his living situation and could appreciate how these risks applied to him and attempt to determine whether he could engage in functional behaviors to maintain a level of basic self-care such that he could remain in the home reasonably safely. If he were found to lack independent living capacity, we would look for additional supports to enhance his capacity and engage a health care proxy or caregiver to provide oversight. In this instance, circumstances with the board of health had already been escalated and interventions from APS had been tried and failed before our involvement. In other words, this case was relatively unique because he did not have a lot of time to remain in his home legally without major supports being added.

History

A chart review yielded relevant clinical history. He grew up in the home in which he still resided. Mr. Martinez was a high school graduate who served in the army during the Korean War. He worked for 30 years in food service and had been retired 25 years before the evaluation. He had previously been diagnosed with depressive disorder and memory loss. He had undergone two separate neuropsychological evaluations (most recently the month before the capacity evaluation), both of which were indicative of frontal and subcortical decline consistent with vascular dementia. He was referred to HBPC to augment medication management and home safety services to support his remaining in his home. Unfortunately, there were no available family or friends, either to provide collateral information or to serve as a proxy or guardian in the event that this was required.

We relied on input from other members of the team to inform the evaluation process. Before the capacity evaluation, the team's social worker was able to advocate for Mr. Martinez to help him interface with the various involved parties, which bought him some time to remain in place and helped us understand the various social–legal processes at play. Before we met with him, she was able to enlist in-home supports to reinforce his ability to live at home even if only for a short time. The team's occupational therapist performed a home safety evaluation and began installing safety devices such as grab bars to reduce the immediate risk in the environment. The nurse worked to improve his medication adherence using prefilled medication planners.

Interview, Examination, and Tests

Behavioral observations. Mr. Martinez was difficult to reach by phone and did not realize we were coming but happily let us in to meet with him. He appeared mildly disheveled with a few stains on his clothing noted. He had good energy and was eager to show us around his home. Sensory issues did not negatively affect the testing. Overall, he was friendly and easily engaged in the testing, feeling he wanted to prove what he could do.

Environmental observations. The capacity evaluation was completed on the second home visit. On the first visit the home was malodorous. Trash was on the porch and in the living spaces, unopened mail was piled haphazardly, and old newspapers were strewn about the home because he said he was saving them to donate to the local animal shelter. Between the first time we saw him and the second, he had accepted homemaking and heavy chore services and the living spaces were markedly improved. There were no obvious fall risks. He showed us how he had begun to use the pill planner prefilled by the home care nurse, which had resulted in improved adherence to his medications. His calendar was up to date with future medical appointments. He also had agreed to the help of a money manager, and his bills and other paperwork had been set aside for that person to review at their next visit. There were no animals in the home, but he did have several empty cages and fishbowls, saying he intended to one day get another pet.

Clinical interview. When asked about the clutter that had been in his home, Mr. Martinez indicated that all items in his home were meaningful to him and had a reason for being there. He recognized that he had been receiving homemaking services to help keep his house tidy, and home-delivered meals from the local elder services agency. He described his recovery from a stroke the year before, after which he subsequently lost his driver's license. He indicated that to remedy the driver's license issue, he is going to take courses to brush up on his skills behind the wheel, retake his driving test, and buy a new car as he is eager to regain some independence.

Cognitive testing. We assessed him with the Dementia Rating Scale—2 (DRS–2; Jurica, Leitten, & Mattis, 2001), on which his scores varied across domains. We noted in the report that this measure has a low ceiling and may not have fully captured milder cognitive declines. He displayed intact performance on tasks of attention, memory, and visual construction. His performance on the Conceptualization subscale was moderately impaired. He had difficulty understanding relationships among nonverbal information. Overall, his performance on the Initiation/Perseveration subscale was mildly impaired. Performance on a semantic fluency test was relatively poorer compared with others in his age group.

Functional measures. We administered three subscales of the Independent Living Scale (Managing Money, Managing Home and Transportation, Health and Safety; Loeb, 1996). He could demonstrate basic safety awareness such as what to do if he needed urgent medical help or if there was a fire in his home. He could identify whom he should call for general home maintenance or utility issues. He described being a medic in the service and that he knew how to treat a wound that would not stop bleeding. He had a basic understanding of hygiene and self-care. When asked why bathing was important, he said, "You gotta clean yourself. You'll get sores and you won't smell good." He could describe two safety precautions in the shower. He could describe why it was important to pay bills: "They'll take the house away and shut services off." We also administered the Katz ADL scale and the Lawton Instrumental Activities of Daily Living Scale: He was independent in basic ADLs such as feeding, dressing, and ambulating, although he had occasional bowel and bladder accidents. In terms of IADLs, he was not able to independently manage his finances, laundry, prepare his own meals, or do more than very light housekeeping.

Findings

We determined that Mr. Martinez retained independent living capacity with specific supports in place. In our report, we noted the following: Functionally, he may have difficulty with abstract information, particularly in the visual realm. Information presented to him should be as concrete as possible. Continued use of cues, especially for nonverbal information is warranted, including a medication planner with auditory reminder, an up-to-date calendar, and a list of important phone numbers. Although he did not seem to appreciate the full scope of his functional impairments, he was willing to accept the help offered to keep him living in his own home. His performance on the cognitive screening measure administered was not markedly different from prior neuropsychological testing. That examination suggested deficits in retrieval of nonverbal information, deficits in planning and initiating, and a hurried, impulsive style.

His understanding and appreciation of his present circumstances is somewhat incomplete. He does appear to understand who is concerned about him, generally why others are concerned, that he can no longer manage his home without supports, and that such supports are being offered to him. His basic reasoning skills are intact, and he can express his basic wishes about his care. At this time, he would like assistance staying in his home as long as he can.

We provided feedback about the results of the capacity evaluation to Mr. Martinez. Specifically, we informed him that we did not recommend pursuing guardianship at this time and that in our estimation he could continue to make his own decisions with the assistance of outside services to enhance his capacity. We told him that our recommendations stood so long as he was accepting of the supports detailed earlier, including money management, heavy chores, home care nursing, personal care, and laundry. His goal was to remain living in his home as long as he could, and at the time of the evaluation, he appeared to appreciate that accepting the offered supports were his best chance of being able to do so. We felt that, should he refuse the above interventions or not be able to follow through with their implementation, then the need for guardianship or conservatorship should be reconsidered. We emphasized that clinicians needed to understand that his cognitive impairments were driving his self-neglect and that his failure to respond to a less structured intervention up to that point should not be interpreted as disobedience or disinterest. Rather, his poor response was suggestive of a lack of appreciation for the extent of his problems and an inability to follow through with a plan on his own.

The home care social worker was also present during the evaluation, which was helpful for her to observe the process of capacity evaluation and led to her concurring with the finding of capacity. In person, he presented as more able than he seemed to be from collateral reports. In the weeks before the capacity evaluation, Mr. Martinez had begun to accept in-home services of many types, bolstering his capacity to remain in the home. If he had been unable to recognize the need for such supports despite them being available to him, we may have instead determined that he lacked capacity and recommended guardianship.

Interventions and Supports

Following the capacity evaluation, the protective services were able to increase his home services and advocate with DPH for Mr. Martinez to stay in the home. DPH was satisfied with the improvements and did not move forward with further citations or condemning the home. He expressed relief about this positive outcome and was glad to be allowed to remain living in place. It was important to communicate to DPH and his APS case manager that his initial difficulty following through with their treatment plan was not a matter of him being "obstinate" as they had assumed but instead was driven by cognitive impairment. Once they understood this, they seemed to be more flexible with him so long as progress on the living conditions was being made.

Outcome

Unfortunately, Mr. Martinez had another stroke about 3 months after this assessment, rendering him permanently unable to speak, and as a result, he ended up in an LTC setting. Because he was unable to identify a person to act as his health care agent, he ultimately ended up with a court-appointed guardian who concurred with his being placed in a LTC setting.

REFLECTION

ESN is a syndrome that may encompass psychological (e.g., depression, cognitive impairment, hoarding disorder) and environmental factors (e.g., inadequate social support). It is commonly used by geriatric health and social service providers to identify a constellation of behaviors that puts older adults at risk. When ESN is present, it may trigger an independent living capacity evaluation to guide actions by the clinical team and APS. Due to limited budgets and priorities in many jurisdictions, self-neglect cases may not be as high a priority for APS as other types of protective service referrals, such as abuse or neglect of the older adult by others. In some jurisdictions, ESN is not reportable to APS. In others, older adults with intact capacity may also be able to refuse APS involvement. In our experience and in our practice locations, the courts may be willing to allow individuals at risk of self-neglect to remain independent if there is not a clear and immediate threat to the person's life, which can lead to frustration for the clinical team and other concerned parties. Individuals who we recommend remain in the home with increased supportive services may find that such home services are not available to the extent that they need and thus may end up in a higher level of care than might be strictly necessary. Building a relationship with your local APS can be useful if these types of evaluations arise frequently in your setting. Partnering with them may provide access to services that would not otherwise be available without their involvement. For individuals who do stay in the home, we recommend continued support for involved caregivers, including resources like respite. Psychologists and other providers who perform these types of evaluations should be mindful of the role they play with the individual and avoid dual relationships whenever possible. For example, our teams are fortunate enough to have multiple psychologists so when an individual we have seen for therapy is referred for a capacity assessment, we will have another psychologist on the team perform the evaluation.

Although not a medical diagnosis per se, identifying ESN can be useful when communicating with elder service providers such as APS. ESN is associated with specific risk factors and is a useful construct that merits further study and definition. As a syndrome of late-life, ESN may be underrecognized in settings such as primary care or the emergency department where older adults are frequently treated. In addition to being able to recognize elder abuse and neglect, staff in these settings should be trained in signs of ESN and report to APS when they are mandated to do so. In geriatric care settings, an interdisciplinary team assessment and intervention approach is warranted. Consider creating a setting-specific decision tree to provide a pathway to working through challenging cases. Self-neglect is often an entrenched problem and as such can be extremely challenging for clinical teams, and for family and others. Team members or caregivers may have unrealistic expectations about the individual's ability to change this behavior or that the psychologist needs to "fix" the situation.

As a team, we often ask: How will things be different if the individual is found to lack independent living capacity? At times we conclude that nothing much will change. Instead, less restrictive interventions may make more clinical sense. When providers can build trusting relationships with individuals over time, they can evaluate the goals and values of the individual and provide care consistent with those wishes. For example, some people may be more willing to transition to an assisted living facility if it allows them to bring a cherished pet along. In many cases, interventions suited to the individuals' needs and values can help avoid a capacity evaluation altogether. Although an assisted living level of care is often what is clinically indicated, many people are unable to afford this type of setting, instead either living with continued risk of self-harm in the community or being placed in a nursing home before it is functionally necessary. Consider having a conversation with the individual and caregiver about goals of care in which the individual's long-term medical goals can be established and the care plan can be aligned with these wishes to the extent possible.

REFERENCES

American Bar Association and American Psychological Association Assessment of Capacity in Older Adults Project Working Group. (2008). *Assessment of older adults with diminished capacity: A handbook for psychologists.* Washington, DC: American Bar Association and American Psychological Association.

American Psychological Association. (2017). *Ethical principles of psychologists and code of conduct* (2002, Amended June 1, 2010 and January 1, 2017). http://www.apa.org/ethics/index.aspxcode

Beales, J. L., & Edes, T. (2009). Veteran's affairs home based primary care. *Clinical Geriatric Medicine, 25,* 149–154. http://dx.doi.org/10.1016/j.cger.2008.11.002

Burnett, J., Dyer, C. B., Halphen, J. M., Achenbaum, W. A., Green, C. E., Booker, J. G., & Diamond, P. M. (2014). Four subtypes of self-neglect in older adults: Results of a latent class analysis. *Journal of the American Geriatrics Society, 62,* 1127–1132. http://dx.doi.org/10.1111/jgs.12832

Cullum, C. M., Saine, K., Chan, L. D., Martin-Cook, K., Gray, K. F., & Weiner, M. F. (2001). Performance-based instrument to assess functional capacity in dementia: The Texas Functional Living Scale. *Neuropsychiatry, Neuropsychology, & Behavioral Neurology, 14,* 103–108.

Dong, X. Q., Simon, M., & Evans, D. (2010). Cross-sectional study of the characteristics of reported elder self-neglect in a community-dwelling population: Findings from a population-based cohort. *Gerontology, 56,* 325–334. http://dx.doi.org/10.1159/000243164

Dong, X. Q., Simon, M. A., & Evans, D. (2012). Elder self-neglect and hospitalization: Findings from the Chicago Health and Aging Project. *Journal of the American Geriatrics Society, 60,* 202–209. http://dx.doi.org/10.1111/j.1532-5415.2011.03821.x

Dong, X. Q., Simon, M. A., Fulmer, T., Mendes de Leon, C. F., Hebert, L. E., Beck, T., . . . Evans, D. A. (2011). A prospective population-based study of differences in elder self-neglect and mortality between Black and White older adults. *The Journals of Gerontology: Series A. Biological Sciences and Medical Sciences, 66,* 695–704. http://dx.doi.org/10.1093/gerona/glr053

Feng, M. C., Murphy, M. R., & Mlinac, M. (2017). Independent living capacity evaluation in home-based primary care: Considerations and outcomes of a quality improvement project. *Clinical Gerontologist, 40,* 51–62. http://dx.doi.org/10.1080/07317115.2016.1210272

Hildebrand, C., Taylor, M., & Bradway, C. (2014). Elder self-neglect: The failure of coping because of cognitive and functional impairments. *Journal of the American Association of Nurse Practitioners, 26,* 452–462. http://dx.doi.org/10.1002/2327-6924.12045

Institute on Aging. (2018). *Aging in America.* Retrieved from https://www.ioaging.org/aging-in-america

Iris, M., Conrad, K. J., & Ridings, J. (2014). Observational measure of elder self-neglect. *Journal of Elder Abuse & Neglect, 26,* 365–397. http://dx.doi.org/10.1080/08946566.2013.801818

Jurica, P. J., Leitten, C. L., & Mattis, S. (2001). *Dementia Rating Scale—2: Professional manual.* Lutz, FL: Psychological Assessment Resources.

Karlin, B. E., & Karel, M. J. (2014). National integration of mental health providers in VA home-based primary care: An innovative model for mental health care delivery with older adults. *The Gerontologist, 54,* 868–879. http://dx.doi.org/10.1092/geront/gnt142

Katz, S., Ford, A. B., Moskowitz, R. W., Jackson, B. A., & Jaffe, M. W. (1963). Studies of illness and the aged: The index of ADL, a standardized measure of biological and psychological function. *Journal of the American Medical Association, 185,* 914–919. http://dx.doi.org/10.1001/jama.1963.03060120024016

Lawton, M. P., & Brody, E. M. (1969). Assessment of older people: Self-maintaining and instrumental activities of daily living. *The Gerontologist, 9,* 179–186. http://dx.doi.org/10.1093/geront/9.3_Part_1.179

Loeb, P. A. (1996). *Independent Living Scales*. San Antonio, TX: The Psychological Corporation.

Mlinac, M. E., & Feng, M. C. (2016). Assessment of activities of daily living, self-care and independence. *Archives of Clinical Neuropsychology, 31*, 506–516. http://dx.doi.org/10.1093/arclin/acw049

Moon, A., Lawson, K., Carpiac, M., & Spaziano, E. (2006). Elder abuse and neglect among veterans in Greater Los Angeles: Prevalence, types, and intervention outcomes. *Journal of Gerontological Social Work, 46*, 187–204. http://dx.doi.org/10.1300/J083v46n03_11

Mosqueda, L., & Dong, X. (2011). Elder abuse and self-neglect: "I don't care anything about going to the doctor, to be honest. . . ." *Journal of the American Medical Association, 306*, 532–540. http://dx.doi.org/10.1001/jama.2011.1085

Naik, A. D., Kunik, M. E., Cassidy, K. R., Nair, J., & Coverdale, J. (2010). Assessing safe and independent living in vulnerable older adults: Perspectives of professionals who conduct home assessments. *Journal of the American Board of Family Medicine, 23*, 614–621. http://dx.doi.org/10.3122/jabfm.2010.05.090065

National Center for Elder Abuse. (2019). *Types of abuse*. Alhambra, CA: Author. Retrieved from https://ncea.acl.gov/Suspect-Abuse/Abuse-Types.aspx#self

National Conference of Commissioners on Uniform State Laws. (2017). *Uniform Guardianship, Conservatorship, and Other Protective Arrangements Act*. Chicago, IL: Author.

Pavlou, M. P., & Lachs, M. S. (2008). Self-neglect in older adults: A primer for clinicians. *Journal of General Internal Medicine, 23*, 1841–1846. http://dx.doi.org/10.1007/s11606-008-0717-7

Spensley, C. (2008). The role of social isolation of elders in recidivism of self-neglect cases at San Francisco Adult Protective Services. *Journal of Abuse and Neglect, 20*, 43–61. http://dx.doi.org/10.1300/J084v20ti01_03

Zeiss, A. M., & Karlin, B. E. (2008). Integrating mental health and primary care services in the Department of Veteran Affairs Health Care System. *Journal of Clinical Psychology in Medical Settings, 15*, 73–78. http://dx.doi.org/10.1007/s10880-008-9100-4

8

Assessment of Testamentary Capacity

Daniel C. Marson

KEY POINTS

- The *right of testation* refers to an adult's freedom to choose how their property and other possessions will be disposed of according to their will. For a will to be valid, the testator (the person making the will) must have testamentary capacity (TC) at the time that the will is executed, which is a legal judgment made by attorneys, judges, and juries.
- Although legal requirements for TC vary across state jurisdictions, four general legal criteria have been identified. Testators must (a) know what a will is, (b) have knowledge of their potential heirs, (c) have knowledge of the nature and extent of their assets, and (d) have a general plan under the will for distribution of assets to heirs.
- Some clinical evaluations of TC are *prospective* and are conducted close in time to a living testator's execution of a will. Other clinical evaluations of TC are *retrospective* and usually involve a clinician being asked, by an attorney or court, to determine whether a now-deceased testator had TC at the time of an earlier will execution.

http://dx.doi.org/10.1037/0000184-009
Assessing Capacities of Older Adults: A Casebook to Guide Difficult Decisions, J. Moye (Editor)

- As all clinical evaluations of TC are by their nature forensic, and clinicians need to know how to undertake such assessments. For example, the clinician needs to know the legal criteria for TC in their state jurisdiction and to have knowledge about other legal constructs that may affect their clinical assessment and TC opinions. These other legal constructs include *insane delusion, lucid interval*, and *undue influence*.

BACKGROUND TO TESTAMENTARY CAPACITY

The freedom to choose how one's property and other possessions will be disposed of after death, known as the right of *testation*, is a fundamental right under Anglo-American law (Frolik, 2001; Marson, Huthwaite, & Hebert, 2004). A key requirement of the law of testation is that a testator (person making the will) have *testamentary capacity* or *competency* (TC): "that measure of mental ability recognized in law as sufficient for the making of a will" (Frolik, 2001, p. 253). If TC is lacking at the time of execution of the will, the will is invalid and void in effect. The legal requirement of TC exists across all state jurisdictions (Marson, Huthwaite, & Hebert, 2004).

To make a valid will, the law also requires that the testator be free from *undue influence* exercised by another individual over the testator and the execution of the will (Frolik, 2001). Thus, a validly executed will may be voided by the court if it deems that the volition of the testator was in effect supplanted by an individual exercising undue influence over the testator. The legal doctrine of undue influence, which also exists across all state jurisdictions, is conceptually and analytically distinct from TC insofar as it applies in cases in which the testator possesses at least some residual level or degree of TC. Nonetheless, in the case of a will contest, these two legal issues often co-occur and intertwine (Marson et al., 2004), and clinicians may be asked to form opinions about both issues in a particular case.

Anglo-American law has strongly supported testation over intestacy (Frolik, 2001). Public policy and legal precedent have clearly favored allowing individuals to choose how their property will be distributed after death rather than leaving such decisions to state laws governing intestacy. However, despite the legal system's initial presumption supporting testation, cases challenging the validity of wills, whether on the basis of the testator's TC or undue influence, are common and in fact appear to be increasing in number (Marson et al., 2004; Nedd, 1998). This increase in will contest litigation reflects a number of factors:

- our aging society and the number of older adults with organic, psychiatric, and medical impairments that adversely affect mental capacity (Marson & Zebley, 2001),

- the breakdown of the nuclear family and increase in blended families with conflicting agendas, and
- the enormous wealth transfer ongoing between World War II and baby boomer generations (Nedd, 1998).

Legal cases involving issues of TC and undue influence frequently involve mental health professionals, such as neuropsychologists, clinical geropsychologists, and psychiatrists, serving as clinician expert witnesses. The meaning and application by attorneys and judges of legal constructs such as *testamentary capacity, undue influence, insane delusion,* and *lucid interval* can be substantially informed in particular cases by the clinical expertise and expert testimony of such professionals. The roles of these experts can vary widely, from consulting with attorneys about clients with questionable capacity, to clinically evaluating the TC of testators before will execution, to conducting postmortem retrospective evaluations of TC and the related validity of a previously executed will (sometimes called the *neuropsychological autopsy;* Greiffenstein, 1996; Marson et al., 2004). A related role is for the clinician expert to review case records for evidence of a testator's vulnerability to undue influence, or for actual indicia of undue influence, in both prospective and retrospective contexts.

The current legal requirements for TC in the United States vary to some degree from state to state, but in many states (although not all), four specific criteria or elements are recognized:

COMMON CRITERIA FOR TESTAMENTARY CAPACITY

A testator must

1. understand the nature of the testamentary act—in other words, must know what a will is;
2. understand and recollect the nature and situation of his or her property;
3. have knowledge of the persons who are the natural objects of his or her bounty; and
4. know the manner in which the disposition of the property is to occur. (Marson et al., 2004; Spar & Garb, 1992)

The way in which these elements are weighed by courts in determining the validity of a will varies across states (Frolik, 2001; Spar, Hankin, & Stodden, 1995). Some states require that the testator meet only one or two of the criteria for a will to be valid. Other states may require additional criteria; for example, that the testator understand a will, demonstrate memory of all property and potential heirs, and "hold this information in mind" while developing a plan for disposition of assets (Spar & Garb, 1992).

In addition to these four legal elements, many states require that part or all of the testator's will not be the expression of an *insane delusion*. The will must be free of "delusions or hallucinations [that] result in the person's devising his or her property in such a way which, except for the existence of the delusions or hallucinations, he or she would not have done" (California Probate Code, 1990, amended 1995). It is critical that the psychotic symptoms specifically affect issues related to the testator's TC and provisions of the will. Put differently, the will must be the product of the insane delusion. A will may be ruled valid if delusions and hallucinations are discrete, unassociated with the testator's property and potential heirs, or have seemingly little or no impact on the testator's plan for the disposition of assets (Marson et al., 2004; Walsh, Brown, Kaye, & Grigsby, 1997).

DEFINITION OF THE ISSUE

This chapter addresses the topic of clinician assessment of TC in forensic settings. As noted earlier, the act of testation is a crucial right under the law that allows a competent adult to make important decisions as to how his or her assets and wealth will be distributed after death. Society and the U.S. legal system strongly support the right of testation by invoking a legal presumption of TC (although this presumption can be rebutted) and by designating a low, or liberal, legal standard for the valid exercise of TC.

Disputed matters of TC are increasingly common in the courts and legal system. We live in an unprecedented aging society where cognitive decline and dementia in later life are highly prevalent and whose presence readily diminishes or eclipses TC and other legal and clinical capacities. Moreover, in the United States, we live in an individualistic and litigious society, with many blended families, where issues of conflicting family relationships and distribution of wealth are often addressed through capacity litigation and the legal system rather than through private and informal family discourse. As issues of TC and other legal capacities, and also undue influence, proliferate in the legal system and courts, so also grows the need for the involvement of clinicians experienced in forensic clinical assessment. In the case of TC, clinicians will be asked by attorneys, courts, and sometimes family members to conduct either a *prospective evaluation* of the TC of a living testator or a *retrospective evaluation* of the TC of a now deceased testator at an earlier time point. These clinical scenarios are discussed next.

Clinical Presentation: Prospective or Contemporaneous Evaluations of TC

In certain circumstances, an attorney, judge, or family member may request that a mental health professional assess the TC of a living testator shortly before, or contemporaneously with, his or her execution of a will. Two common scenarios underlie such a referral. The attorney or judge may have concerns about the TC of the proposed testator and therefore will seek clinical expertise and input on the issue before proceeding further. Alternatively, in cases of ongoing or anticipated family conflict, the foresighted estate planning attorney may seek to preempt, or at least prepare for, a future will contest by having his or her client undergo a TC assessment before will execution (American Bar Association/American Psychological Association [ABA/APA], 2008; Marson et al., 2004; Marson, Hebert, & Solomon, 2012).

Although not always the case, in my experience, testators who undergo prospective evaluation of TC tend to come from higher socioeconomic backgrounds, have high net worth and substantial estates, have family conflict issues present or looming, and are able to engage skilled and experienced estate planning counsel to oversee the TC assessment. Thus, prospective clinical evaluation of TC is not as common as one might expect given the apparent advantages of examining a living testator. In cases without obvious red flags, attorneys themselves often will feel comfortable about forming their own legal judgments of TC without pursuing the time and expense of engaging a clinician capacity expert.

Clinical Presentation: Retrospective Evaluations of TC

Although prospective evaluations of TC are often useful, as noted they generally arise in specialized circumstances and are thus selectively pursued by attorneys and clients. They do not represent the majority of forensic evaluations of TC. Far more frequently, neuropsychologists and other mental health professionals are called on by attorneys, the probate court, or interested family members to render *retrospective opinions* regarding the existence of TC (and also sometimes undue influence) at a previous point in time. Retrospective evaluations of TC usually arise after the death (or sometimes the incompetency) of a testator, when heirs or other interested parties contest a will on grounds that the decedent lacked TC at the time of the prior will execution (Marson et al., 2012).

Expert clinicians conduct retrospective evaluations of TC by carefully reviewing the record and obtaining, as available, *capacity relevant evidence contemporaneous with the prior will execution*. Such capacity-relevant historical evidence may include evidence of the deceased testator's reported capacity at the prior will execution and at other time points, medical and psychiatric health, cognitive and emotional abilities and everyday functioning, historical values, and other factors. The clinician then takes all of this evidence and seeks to make a retrospective judgment of TC using the operative state legal standards for TC in effect at the time of the prior will execution. In many cases, there may be ample evidence available, or decisive pieces of evidence that exist, that allow a clinician to offer a clinical forensic opinion. In some cases, there may not be sufficient contemporaneous evidence available for the clinician to offer a retrospective opinion (Marson et al., 2012).

Clinician involvement is integral to and in fact essential in retrospective cases of TC. Although attorneys and courts are empowered to determine the legal capacity of living testators, they understandably refrain from offering retrospective legal capacity judgments about deceased testators they did not previously encounter, know, or work with. In such instances, attorneys and courts instead turn to clinicians to assist with the retrospective inquiry. Through their clinical training, expert clinicians have the abilities to review complex medical, psychosocial, and legal case records and acquire the clinical and other information needed to form and furnish retrospective clinical judgments of capacity. On a daily basis throughout the United States, courts accept the TC and undue influence testimony and opinions of expert clinicians who have conducted such retrospective analyses of the prior capacity of now deceased testators. Thus, mental health professionals with capacity assessment expertise are essential to helping attorneys and courts resolve will contests complicated by the passage of time and the absence of a living testator.

CLINICAL ASSESSMENT METHODS: PROSPECTIVE AND RETROSPECTIVE

Methods for Prospective Assessment of TC

Spar and colleagues have written cogently on the topic of contemporaneous clinical assessment of TC and undue influence (Spar & Garb, 1992; Spar et al., 1995). Their clinical interview guidelines for TC, first published in 1992, continue to represent a key contribution to forensic practice in this area. The key aspects of the interview are to "assess the legal elements of TC, identify any features of the testator's personality and mental status that could affect susceptibility to undue influence, and determine the nature, extent, and general functional consequences of mental illness, if any" (Spar & Garb, 1992, pp. 171–172). The authors highlighted the importance of conducting the clinical interview in close proximity to the moment the testamentary document is executed (Marson & Hebert, 2008). Interviews conducted in close proximity to the time of testamentary document execution are more likely to be influential in court than those conducted at more distant time periods. This consideration is important because courts generally place great emphasis on the testator's mental functioning at the time of the transaction in question and recognize that individuals' mental functioning can vary at different time points (Spar et al., 1995).

A critical goal for the clinical examiner is to obtain sufficient information about the testator's property, names and relationships of potential and actual heirs, and, where possible, testamentary plans so that a contemporaneous judgment about TC can be offered. As noted earlier, this can be a difficult task if the testator's informants are limited to family members who may have personal biases and serve to profit from the clinician's opinions and testimony or when the assessment needs to be conducted on an expedited basis. An objective independent source of information regarding a testator's natural and actual heirs, as well as the nature and extent of the testator's assets and possessions, is usually essential. In some cases this information source may be the attorney who is representing the client and knowledgeable about the estate plan and who may have actually drafted the will being proposed for execution.

A videotaped recording of the TC interview with the testator may prove beneficial for documenting both the testator's TC and the lack of outside influences. However, decisions regarding videotaping the capacity interview, and the overall will execution itself, are properly those of the attorney and the client and not the clinician. From an attorney's perspective, the decision to videotape involves multiple considerations, including the effects of videotaping on the client and whether the attorney wishes to make this procedure a standard part of his or her estate planning practice.

The core inquiry of the clinician's TC interview is to inquire about and examine the testator's knowledge of the core elements of TC as set forth earlier. In doing so, it will be important and helpful for the clinician to be specifically aware and familiar with these elements as defined by the law of the state jurisdiction governing the creation and probating of the will. This legal definitional framework will allow the clinician to collect clinical evidence and form clinical forensic opinions directly relevant to the legal categories and standards to be applied by the particular court. At the same time, the clinician should be explicit in the report that such evidence and forensic opinions are clinical in nature and do not represent legal findings or opinions that are reserved to the court.

During the interview, the clinician may also wish to conduct evaluations of cognition, mood, and behavior to develop a fuller medical context for the TC analysis and opinions and any related undue influence analysis and opinions. However, the clinician must keep firmly in mind that such diagnostic, cognitive, and other related clinical information remains secondary evidence of capacity, which cannot itself determine the issue of TC (Marson et al., 2012). The core inquiry remains the clinical assessment of the functional elements constituent to TC in the specific state jurisdiction.

As part of the contemporaneous TC evaluation, an assessment of the testator's personal values about money, personal property, and finances can be useful (ABA/APA, 2008). As discussed earlier, courts invoke a low legal threshold for upholding wills and permitting legal transfer of property after death. Thus, the personal values and interests of the testator may be given weight by courts. Important information can sometimes be ascertained by reviewing prior wills of a testator, which will presumably reflect the previous application of his or her values to the assignment of property to designated heirs. A testator's radical departure from prior testamentary value patterns in a new will, without any explanatory rationale or supportive circumstances for the change, is sometimes referred to legally as an *unnatural will*. Such situations may lead courts to consider whether a testator is subject to diminished capacity or to coercion through undue influence (ABA/APA, 2008; Marson et al., 2012).

Methods for Retrospective Assessment of TC

As should be apparent, the clinical procedures and process of retrospective evaluation of TC differ substantially from those for prospective evaluation of TC. In the retrospective context, there is no living testator and thus no associated prospective clinical evaluation. Instead, as discussed earlier, the expert clinician embarks on an investigative journey into the decedent's historical medical, psychosocial, and legal record and past to obtain capacity-specific information contemporaneous with and relevant to the decedent's prior testamentary acts.

For these reasons, as noted earlier, retrospective evaluation of TC has sometimes been described as the "neuropsychological autopsy" (Greiffenstein, 1996), and neuropsychological methods and knowledge can be particularly useful for these purposes. In one of the first expositions of the retrospective method, Dr. Manfred Greiffenstein, a distinguished forensic neuropsychologist, proposed several steps for determining TC retrospectively (Greiffenstein, 1996). First, the clinician should consider whether the legal issue at hand pertains to TC or undue influence, or both. Next, the date of the legal transaction should be identified because this date will help determine the relevance of contemporaneous mental status, medical, and lay testimony evidence. This is typically the date on which the will was signed. The clinician should also identify the type of neurologic, psychiatric, or other medical conditions that the testator may have had at the time of the prior transaction; determine which, if any, cognitive abilities and emotional and everyday functions were affected, and conclude whether these circumstances may have affected the decedent's TC at the time of the prior will execution. This is done by gathering evidence of normal and abnormal cognitive, emotional, and functional behavior occurring as close as possible to the date of will execution.

A more recent and detailed approach to retrospective assessment of TC is presented in the ABA/APA (2008) capacity assessment handbook for psychologists. In the handbook chapter addressing assessment of TC (Chapter VI), a set of recommended steps for retrospective assessment of TC is presented for the evaluator. A slightly modified and expanded version of these steps is set forth in the following list.

RECOMMENDED STEPS IN CONDUCTING A RETROSPECTIVE EVALUATION OF TESTAMENTARY CAPACITY

1. Identify the operative legal standard for TC in your state jurisdiction.
2. Organize medical, legal, and other records relevant to the capacity issue. Creating a chronological timeline reflecting important medical and lay events and contacts, as well as relevant legal transactions, is essential to organizing information for the assessment.

3. Where possible and as appropriate, contact and speak with individuals who knew the decedent testator and can offer informed lay and professional judgments about mental status and capacity at the time of will execution.

4. Obtain information about the attorneys involved in the prior will execution. Who was the attorney, and what history did he or she have with the client? What was the series of professional interactions leading up to the will execution?

5. Assess for the presence and severity of a mental disorder at the time of will execution. With older adults, the most often disputed wills are those that were made or modified when an individual had a memory disorder or a diagnosed dementia. Is there evidence, through medical or other records, of a mental disorder that might affect cognitive and emotional abilities related to the elements of TC? In some cases, there may be specific cognitive or neuropsychological test information that will shed light on mental abilities relevant to TC.

6. In cases of dementia, if possible, seek to determine the stage of dementia at the time of will execution because it can significantly inform the clinical judgment of TC. A number of measures are available that can help a clinician determine dementia stage. Dementia stage, when properly determined, can be an evidentiary source that clinicians and probate courts can both use in making retrospective capacity determinations.

7. Keep in mind that the presence of a dementia or other mental disorder is not sufficient in itself to decide the retrospective capacity issue. Because the legal threshold for TC is low, some individuals with mild dementia may still be capable of making a new will, whereas patients with more advanced dementia increasingly will not be. However, every capacity matter is individual specific and—irrespective of diagnosis, cognitive impairment, and/or dementia stage—requires an analysis of the individual's mental status and condition in relation to the particular jurisdictional elements for TC.

8. Assess TC by determining whether there is clinical and other evidence in the record supporting the critical legal elements of this capacity. In some cases, it may not be possible to render such a judgment if there is insufficient evidence of the testator's cognitive, emotional, and everyday functional abilities contemporaneous with the prior will execution.

9. In addition to offering a capacity judgment, a neuropsychological expert may in some instances be well positioned to offer a retrospective opinion regarding the possible role of undue influence in will procurement. Many will contest cases involve an associated, alternative legal claim of undue influence, with the contention that even if the testator possessed residual TC, it was supplanted by the actions of a third-party influencer. (ABA/APA, 2008; Marson et al., 2012)

A number of information sources can assist the clinician expert in making a retrospective assessment of TC (Spar & Garb, 1992). These include the testator's business records, checkbook and other financial documents, and personal documents such as family films, videos, notebooks, and diaries. Medical records yield particularly useful information, including mental status and neuropsychological testing, diagnosis, level of impairment, and behavioral observations. As noted earlier, clinicians may find it useful to interview the testator's family, friends, business associates, and other involved professionals (e.g., physician, attorney, accountant, notary public) regarding the testator's cognitive and functional abilities during the time that the will was executed, as long as the existing or potential biases of different family members, professionals, and individuals and parties are adequately accounted for. In cases where there is ongoing litigation, the clinician's review of deposition testimony may serve as a valuable and informative substitute to conducting personal interviews. Ultimately, the clinician must assemble all of the information described earlier and make a clinical forensic judgment as to whether the testator had TC at the prior relevant time points.

As noted, in some cases it may not be possible to form a retrospective TC opinion or judgment if there is insufficient evidence of the testator's capacity and underlying cognitive, emotional, and functional abilities contemporaneous with the prior will execution. In such cases, it is likely that the presumption of competency would stand, insofar as there would be insufficient evidence to rebut the presumption or place it in legal question (Marson et al., 2012).

CASE EXAMPLES

The next two sections present actual clinical forensic cases of the author, modified to preserve anonymity, which illustrate practical aspects of prospective and retrospective clinical assessment of TC.[1]

Case 1. Mrs. McVey—Prospective Assessment of TC: Can Mrs. McVey Make a New Will?

I have included this case in the chapter as an interesting and somewhat atypical prospective TC referral. It is atypical because the referring party was a psychiatrist, not an attorney or a court, and because the TC assessment, despite the patient's relatively extensive history of psychiatric illness, was fairly straightforward and not complicated. However, I believe the case illustrates common procedures and processes of prospective clinical evaluation of TC.

---

[1]Although the case examples in this chapter are based on the author's real experiences, the identities of the individuals involved in these examples have been properly disguised to protect their confidentiality.

Capacity Assessment Referral

Mrs. McVey is a 76-year-old Caucasian woman with a high school education who grew up in Maine and was an only child. About 25 years ago, she inherited the family business, a successful hardware store, from her father. Her husband managed the business after her father died. Her son (Mr. Charles McVey) is now currently managing the store, although her husband also remains active in the business. Mrs. McVey's daughter (Ms. Merwin) has also worked in the family business.

At the time of the assessment, Mrs. McVey had been approached by outside investors about selling the hardware store, and there was significant family disagreement regarding the possible sale. The patient reported anxiety regarding the sale and the fact that her two adult children did not get along and disagreed about the sale of the business. Mrs. McVey described a close relationship with her adult granddaughter (Ms. Merwin's daughter) and reported frequent contact with her. Mrs. McVey stated that she does not often see her adult grandson (Mr. McVey's son) and also indicated some conflict with both her grandson and her daughter-in-law (Mr. McVey's wife).

Mrs. McVey was referred for capacity assessment by her psychiatrist, Dr. Sagert, because, in light of the pending sale of the business, she had decided to make changes to her will and wanted to ensure that her new estate planning wishes would not subsequently be challenged by other family members. Dr. Sagert recommended that she have a formal evaluation to assess her TC and referred her to neuropsychologist Dr. Jarman of the Department of Neurology at the University of Maine in Orono.

Medical Background

At the time of the assessment, Mrs. McVey was a right-handed, 76-year-old Caucasian woman with 12 years of education who was married and a small business owner. She was being followed by Dr. Sagert for treatment of anxiety and depression.

Mrs. McVey's medical and surgical history was positive for tuberculosis, hysterectomy, and hospitalization for acute bronchitis. She also reported bladder incontinence, kidney problems, diverticulitis, ulcers (which she attributed to stress regarding her children and her business), and multiple hospitalizations for tachycardia. Family medical history was reportedly positive for cancer (father), ulcers (father), and circulatory problems (mother). The patient's mother reportedly experienced cognitive changes following a motor vehicle accident.

Mrs. McVey's history was also positive for both inpatient and outpatient psychiatric treatment. She reportedly sought outpatient treatment for depression after her hysterectomy and the illnesses of her parents. Mrs. McVey also described receiving inpatient psychiatric treatment for depression after her father's death. She reportedly intentionally overdosed on sleeping pills, came close to dying, and was hospitalized for psychiatric treatment. Overall, she reported three inpatient hospitalizations including treatment for depression and for dependence on sleeping pills and pain medication.

Before seeing Dr. Sagert, Mrs. McVey had seen a different psychiatrist for many years before the latter's retirement. She has seen Dr. Sagert for depression associated with her most recent inpatient hospitalization, for her family difficulties, and her prior dependence on prescription medications.

Neuropsychological Assessment

As part of the TC evaluation, Dr. Jarman conducted a neuropsychological assessment of Mrs. McVey to develop a sufficiently broad clinical context for the specific prospective assessment of TC.

Mrs. McVey presented as nicely dressed and well groomed. She was accompanied to the evaluation by Ms. Merwin. In the interview, speech was goal oriented and responsive but mildly slurred with a hypernasal vocal quality. These speech difficulties were attributed to dentures and Mrs. McVey's history of respiratory difficulty. Affect was full. Her mood was pleasant, but she was somewhat serious and anxious.

During testing, Mrs. McVey was alert and pleasant. Some mild performance anxiety was noted, but she responded appropriately to encouragement and handled times of frustration appropriately. No expressive or receptive language difficulties were noted. There was no loss of task, cognitive rigidity, or spoiling. There were a few perseverations and intrusions. Mrs. McVey put forth a good effort throughout the testing. The current results appear to be a valid representation of her current level of cognitive and emotional functioning.

Mrs. McVey's neuropsychological test performance indicated intact functioning across cognitive domains of language, short-term memory, visuospatial construction, fine motor functioning, and overall intellectual functioning. There were isolated mild deficits in high load verbal acquisition, visual form discrimination, and mental flexibility, moderate impairment in delayed visual memory, and possible decline in attention and concentration. Mrs. McVey also demonstrated some mild difficulties in everyday functional abilities, including mild difficulties with small cash transactions and financial judgment and some insensitivity to threats to personal safety.

The interview and psychological testing also revealed adequate emotional functioning. Mrs. McVey denied current depressive symptoms during the interview and on a self-report inventory. She acknowledged anxiety surrounding the sale of her business, but this did not appear to be significantly affecting her judgment and decision-making. There was no evidence of current psychotic symptomatology, suicidal ideation, or significant psychiatric illness during the evaluation.

Clinical Assessment of TC

Mrs. McVey drove herself to the University of Maine in Orono and presented to the TC examination alone. During the course of her clinical interview, Dr. Jarman explained to Mrs. McVey that she wanted to ask her questions about her estate planning goals and proposed new will. Mrs. McVey was open to this and appropriately candid and forthright about her family situation and estate planning goals. She appeared to be objective and balanced in her assessment of the family situation and the planned estate planning changes.

Dr. Jarman asked Mrs. McVey specific questions addressing the four elements of TC (as defined and operationalized in her state jurisdiction). The patient responded appropriately, knowledgeably, and nondefensively to these questions. She defined a will as a "written document distributing the property of a person who is deceased according to their wishes." She provided a comprehensive description of her property and assets that appeared informed and accurate based on collateral information received from her daughter. Mrs. McVey also verbally listed her immediate descendants and potential and also actual beneficiaries of her proposed new will. She described her planned division of her estate into four equal shares for her husband, son, daughter, and her granddaughter (Ms. Merwin's child). She indicated that she was not planning to include her grandson (Mr. Charles McVey's child) in the will but provided a clear and reasonable explanation for this exclusion, which was based on her relationship with this grandchild.

Clinical Impression of Mrs. McVey's Cognitive and Emotional Status

Dr. Jarman's clinical impressions from the neuropsychological assessment was that her history of psychiatric illness notwithstanding, Mrs. McVey currently enjoyed overall intact cognitive and emotional functioning for age, education, and occupational attainment, with only a few isolated cognitive deficits.

Clinical Impression of Mrs. McVey's Testamentary Capacity

The key clinical impression was that Mrs. McVey demonstrated intact TC as generally defined within her state jurisdiction. In response to questions concerning the elements of TC, she provided an adequate description of a will, produced a full and reasonably accurate account of the nature and extent of her property, and knew both her potential and actual (intended) heirs under a new will. She also described a plan of disposition and produced coherent and adequate reasons for inclusion and exclusion of relations in her proposed new will and the distribution of property to designated heirs.

The neuropsychological evaluation results were consistent with and supported the finding of intact TC. As noted earlier, Mrs. McVey demonstrated overall intact cognitive functioning. Although there were some isolated cognitive deficits, these did not impact or impair the patient's TC as reflected by her intact performance in the TC clinical interview.

Finally, there was no evidence that the patient's proposed new will was the product of psychiatric symptoms linked to an *insane delusion* or *undue influence*. With respect to insane delusion, although Mrs. McVey had a fairly extensive history of psychiatric illness, her prior illness and her current anxiety symptoms were not directly related to the planning for and provisions of the proposed will. As noted, Mrs. McVey provided coherent reasons for inclusion and exclusion of relations in her proposed new will.

With respect to undue influence, Mrs. McVey presented to the examiner alone without any accompanying family member or other companion, and there was no history or indicia of either vulnerability to undue influence by another individual, or actual coercion or impaired volition. In Dr. Jarman's judgment, Mrs. McVey's prospective act of testation was very much her own decision, free of any influence or coercion by others.

Case Follow-Up

After completion of her clinical assessment in this case, Dr. Jarman provided feedback in person to Mrs. McVey and also her husband (who had not been present at the time of the assessment). Dr. Jarman explained the approach of grounding a specific assessment of her TC within the broader clinical context of a neuropsychological assessment of her cognitive and emotional functioning. Mrs. McVey expressed appreciation for this approach and also the findings of the assessment. She requested a copy of the report, which was provided after her provision of a signed release. A copy of the report was also provided to Dr. Sagert at Mrs. McVey's request.

Dr. Jarman was never contacted again by Mrs. McVey or any of her family members. Thus, Dr. Jarman does not know the outcome of Mrs. McVey's proposed estate planning and whether there ever was a will challenge by family members.

Case 2. Mrs. Chenowith—Retrospective Assessment of TC: Mrs. Chenowith Makes a New Will

I have included this case in the chapter as a fairly typical attorney-referred retrospective TC evaluation referral with an interesting outcome. The outcome is interesting because although there was ample contemporaneous information in this case to support a retrospective clinical judgment concerning TC and undue influence, the information was highly unfavorable to the retaining attorneys and clients. As a result, the case illustrates how a clinician expert's objective retrospective review and opinion can assist a retaining law firm by indicating weaknesses in their client's TC and undue influence case, which may alter the firm and client's litigation strategy. Retrospective evaluation is further discussed in APA's (2013) *Specialty Guidelines for Forensic Psychology* (Guideline 9.03: Opinions Regarding Persons Not Examined) and in APA's (2017) *Ethical Principles of Psychologists and Code of Conduct* (Standard 9.01c, Bases for Assessments).

Capacity Assessment Referral

Mrs. Rilly Chenowith was an older, widowed, and wealthy member of a prominent family in the southwestern part of the United States. During her career, Mrs. Chenowith had been a successful businesswoman who had acquired substantial personal wealth through careful and shrewd acquisition of real estate—in particular, rental properties. Other family members affectionately referred to Mrs. Chenowith as "Auntie Recluse" because of her retiring and private ways, but they also greatly respected her business and financial acumen and her financial success.

In prior estate planning during the 1980s, Mrs. Chenowith had made generous provisions in her wills for all members of her extended family, which they were aware and appreciative of. However, in 1995, she decided to make a new will, which she did not disclose to other family members. In this new will, she gave almost her entire estate to established charities for the poor and disabled in London, England, rather than to her family members. Mrs. Chenowith's family had their historical roots in England, and she had been fond of traveling to London and the United Kingdom during her lifetime.

Mrs. Chenowith died in late 1999. Shortly after her death, after the submission of her will to the local probate court, members of the family first learned to their dismay that they had been largely "disinherited," as they expressed it.

Aware that Mrs. Chenowith had developed cognitive problems in the middle 1990s, members of the Chenowith family retained legal counsel at the Big Desert law firm and brought a lawsuit in the local probate court challenging the will and the executors of the Chenowith estate on the grounds that she lacked TC at the time of the 1995 will execution. The court pleadings argued that the new will was invalid due to Mrs. Chenowith's cognitive impairment and related incompetence in June 1995 and requested that the probate court exclude the will from probate and instead approve a prior will of Mrs. Chenowith that had included Chenowith family members as heirs.

As part of their litigation strategy, the Big Desert attorneys sought clinician experts who could assist them with the retrospective issues of TC raised in the lawsuit. In February 2000, the attorneys contacted me by letter:

> Mr. Senior Attorney and I represent Alexander Chenowith, his siblings, and other disputants to the Will of Mrs. Rilly Chenowith. We would like to retain your services to determine whether, at the time she executed her Will (June 30, 1995), she possessed TC to do so, and/or whether or not the will may have been the product of undue influence. In our state a testator possesses testamentary capacity if she understands the nature of her act in making a will or a codicil thereto, knows the extent and character of her property, knows and understands the proposed disposition of her property, and knows the natural objects of her bounty.

The letter went on to describe relevant medical and legal records that the attorneys would be able to furnish as part of the record review. The letter concluded:

> We have a deadline of March 31, 2000, to designate experts in this case, so time is of the essence. If you have any questions or we can help in any way with these documents, please contact us.

Following further discussions, I was formally retained by the Big Desert law firm as a clinician expert for purposes of conducting a retrospective evaluation of Mrs. Chenowith's TC and possible vulnerability to undue influence at the time of the prior will execution on June 30, 1995.

Retrospective Case Record Review

Review of the medical and psychosocial record reflected a healthy older woman between 1990 and 1995 (ages 80–85) with relatively few medical problems other than hypertension and gastroesophageal reflux disease. Although reclusive, during this time Mrs. Chenowith continued to have occasional private social engagements with personal friends in book and dinner clubs. She also continued to be involved anonymously in local philanthropic efforts in her city. Although retired, she reportedly continued to track her financial investments and to read *The Wall Street Journal* every day.

Beginning in fall 1995, the medical record reflected the first reports by family members and friends of mild short-term memory loss in Mrs. Chenowith. By June 1996, additional cognitive and functional decline (instrumental activities of daily living) had become evident, and with Mrs. Chenowith's consent, one of her nephews began handling her financial affairs and taxes, and a niece assisted her with her medications and her pill box. In December 1996, she broke her hip. After hip replacement surgery, Mrs. Chenowith's short-term memory impairment and overall cognitive decline significantly accelerated. In January 1998, neighbors in her condo reported seeing her in the downstairs lobby alone in a confused state, uncertain as to how to return to her apartment, and the neighbors expressed concern about the risk of Mrs. Chenowith getting lost both within and outside the building. In June 1998, after family intervention, Mrs. Chenowith was admitted to a local nursing home in a "confused and demented" condition. Her death certificate in late 1999 noted both pneumonia and "advanced Alzheimer's disease" as causes of death.

As part of my record review, I also focused on legal and other information specific to Mrs. Chenowith's estate planning and will execution activities before and on June 30, 1995. Mr. Wall, the attorney who drafted her 1995 will and also presided over its execution, had produced for the case record his formal communications with Mrs. Chenowith and also his notes of their planning meetings at that time. These written communications of Mrs. Chenowith with her attorney clearly indicated her intent and plan to make marked changes to her estate plan and to redirect most of her fortune via a new will to a series of charities based in London. She expressed a clear awareness of the family implications of this major estate planning change. However, she stated that her extended family members were all relatively well off, and she strongly believed that her fortune could be put to better use supporting the poor, neglected, and disabled in the United Kingdom, "our family's historical homeland."

A review of the deposition testimony of both attorney Mr. Wall and Mrs. Chenowith's long-standing financial broker (with whom Mrs. Chenowith had a 35-year financial relationship), indicate that both the attorney and broker will offer strong professional opinions and testimony at trial that Mrs. Chenowith was cognitively intact and competent in June 1995 to make a new will.

There was little or no information in the record supporting cognitive impairment or psychiatric illness or circumstances of possible undue influence concerning Mrs. Chenowith in the January to August 1995 timeframe. As noted, mild symptoms of cognitive impairment were only first noted in fall 1995. In addition, the record was devoid of evidence of possible undue influence or an insane delusion shaping or driving Mrs. Chenowith's testamentary decision-making. As noted, Mrs. Chenowith in 1995 and previously had led an extremely private life with limited interactions with others, and there was no indication of any outside influences or individuals impacting her estate planning changes of 1995. In particular, all of the new beneficiaries of the new estate plan were charities across the Atlantic Ocean operating in the region of London, and they all subsequently reported being unaware of their beneficiary status until after Ms. Chenowith's death.

Retrospective Analysis and Capacity and Undue Influence Opinions

After completing the case record review, I assembled and analyzed evidence relevant to TC and undue influence and concluded that

1. there was sufficient evidence to offer retrospective opinions regarding Mrs. Chenowith's TC and the presence of undue influence in June 1995;
2. there was substantial evidence supporting Mrs. Chenowith having TC on June 30, 1995; and
3. there was substantial evidence supporting that Mrs. Chenowith's will execution on June 30, 1995, was not the result of undue influence or an insane delusion.

Based on the record review, it was apparent that Mrs. Chenowith likely had TC to execute a new will in June 1995, notwithstanding the dramatic alteration of heirs and distributions under the new will and the fact that a few months following the will execution she began to demonstrate early clinical signs of cognitive decline and was later diagnosed with Alzheimer's disease-type dementia. Medical, psychosocial, and legal record findings, and also general legal factors, supporting Mrs. Chenowith's TC in June 1995 were as follows:

Medical Record Findings

- Mrs. Chenowith was reportedly in very good medical health for her age in June 1995.
- Initial symptoms of cognitive decline were not reported until fall 1995, about 4 months following the will execution.

- There was no evidence of declining mental status contemporaneous with the will execution.
- There was no evidence of significant mental illness in June 1995 and no evidence that the new will was the direct product of an "insane delusion."

Psychosocial Record Findings

- Mrs. Chenowith had been a highly successful businesswoman in the area of real estate.
- At the time of the will execution, she continued to track her financial investments, read *The Wall Street Journal* on a daily basis, have private social interactions, and be quietly involved in philanthropic causes.
- There was no evidence of any interaction with another person or institution who might have exercised "undue influence" over her in making a new will.

Legal Record Findings

- Mrs. Chenowith's written communications with the attorney Mr. Wall at the time of the will preparation clearly supported her testamentary intent to make a new will, include new heirs and exclude other heirs, and provided a clear rationale for the will changes.
- Attorney Mr. Wall would testify that Mrs. Chenowith had TC on June 30, 1995, and met all the elements of the legal standard for TC in the state.
- Witnesses to the execution of the will of June 30, 1995, would testify that, in their judgment, Mrs. Chenowith had TC.
- Ms. Deal, Mrs. Chenowith's long-standing financial broker, would testify that in her opinion, Mrs. Chenowith was cognitively intact and competent on June 30, 1995, and that there was no individual influencing Mrs. Chenowith's decision-making during that period.

Legal Factors

- Mrs. Chenowith enjoyed a presumption of TC in June 1995, and there was little or no evidence in the record to rebut this presumption.
- The legal threshold for TC is low in all U.S. jurisdictions, including this state.

Taken together, the record review and retrospective analysis strongly supported a finding of intact TC on June 30, 1995.

As noted, the same evidentiary basis and retrospective review strongly supported a finding of no undue influence at the time of the will execution. The record afforded no evidence of Mrs. Chenowith's vulnerability to undue influence in June 1995, as well as no indicia of actual undue influence exerted upon Mrs. Chenowith by a third party in June 1995 or in the preceding time period.

Conference Call With Big Desert Attorneys

In early March 2000, I spoke with the referring Big Desert attorneys by conference call. I explained the retrospective review and analysis approach I had undertaken and the conclusions I had reached regarding TC and undue influence. I concluded that, based on my record review and the relevant medical, psychosocial, and legal record findings, it was my professional opinion that clinically Mrs. Chenowith likely had TC on June 30, 1995—that clinically on that date she would have met the elements of the TC legal standard in the state. I also noted the additional general legal factors that would support a finding by a court that Mrs. Chenowith legally had TC on this date. I further indicated that there was no evidence of undue influence or of an insane delusion that might support a voiding of the will despite Mrs. Chenowith possessing intact TC. Thus, I believed that the will of June 30, 1995, would likely be found to be valid by the court and that the Big Desert attorneys should consider this in their litigation approach and planning. I also noted that my clinical opinion, although not favorable to their clients' legal position, might still be helpful to the clients, should the attorneys want to inform their clients about alternative forms of dispute resolution, such as arbitration or settlement.

The response of the Big Desert attorneys during the conference call was interesting and instructive. They did not dispute or take issue with my retrospective analysis or any of my conclusions. In fact, they appeared to agree with them. They appeared most interested in using the clinical findings and opinions as leverage to persuade their clients to settle the case. I was left with the impression that the Big Desert attorneys had been aware early on of their clients' weak legal position in challenging Mrs. Chenowith's will via her TC or the presence of undue influence and had sought an external expert clinical opinion as a means of convincing their clients to settle the case.

Case Follow-Up

As is often the case in matters of forensic consultation, following the conference call I was not contacted again by the Big Desert attorneys in connection to this litigation. Thus, I do not know the outcome of the pending will contest and whether the clients decided to try to settle their claims against Mrs. Chenowith's estate.

REFLECTION

Assessment of TC is an important and growing area of forensic clinical practice in psychology. Although the scientific evidence base is still limited, there is an emerging consensus in the clinical and legal communities about the conceptual and legal elements of TC and the clinician's role and approach to their clinical assessment. This chapter has provided a conceptual overview of TC, discussed the distinction between clinical and legal assessment of TC, described prospective and retrospective approaches to clinical forensic assessment of TC, and provided an illustrative case study for each of the assessment approaches. In addition, the chapter devoted attention to important related forensic topics of undue influence and insane delusion, as these are forensic issues that clinicians are frequently called upon clinically to assess concurrently with the question of TC.

REFERENCES

American Bar Association and American Psychological Association Assessment of Capacity in Older Adults Project Working Group. (2008). *Assessment of older adults with diminished capacity: A handbook for psychologists*. Washington, DC: American Bar Association and American Psychological Association.

American Psychological Association. (2013). Specialty guidelines for forensic psychology. *American Psychologist, 68*(1), 7–19. https://www.apa.org/pubs/journals/features/forensic-psychology.pdf. http://dx.doi.org/10.1037/a0029889

American Psychological Association. (2017). *Ethical principles of psychologists and code of conduct* (2002, Amended June 1, 2010, and January 1, 2017). Retrieved from https://www.apa.org/ethics/code

California Probate Code, Section 6100.5, Chapter 79, 1990, Amended 1995.

Frolik, L. A. (2001). The strange interplay of testamentary capacity and the doctrine of undue influence. Are we protecting older testators or overriding individual preferences? *International Journal of Law and Psychiatry, 24,* 253–266. http://dx.doi.org/10.1016/S0160-2527(00)00081-9

Greiffenstein, M. (1996). The neuropsychological autopsy. *Michigan Bar Journal, 75,* 424–425.

Marson, D., & Zebley, L. (2001). The other side of the retirement years: Cognitive decline, dementia, and loss of financial capacity. *Journal of Retirement Planning, 4*(1), 30–39.

Marson, D. C., & Hebert, K. (2008). Testamentary capacity. In B. L. Cutler (Ed.), *Encyclopedia of psychology and the law* (Vol. 2, pp. 798–801). Thousand Oaks, CA: Sage. http://dx.doi.org/10.4135/9781412959537.n314

Marson, D. C., Hebert, T., & Solomon, A. C. (2012). Civil competencies in older adults with dementia: Medical decision-making capacity, financial capacity, and testamentary capacity. In G. J. Larrabee (Ed.), *Forensic neuropsychology: A scientific approach* (2nd ed., pp. 401–437). New York, NY: Oxford University Press.

Marson, D. C., Huthwaite, J. S., & Hebert, K. (2004). Testamentary capacity and undue influence in the elderly: A jurisprudent therapy perspective. *Law & Psychology Review, 28,* 71–96.

Nedd, H. (1998, July 30). Fighting over the care of aging parents: More siblings clashing over money and control. *USA Today,* p. 1A.

Spar, J. E., & Garb, A. S. (1992). Assessing competency to make a will. *The American Journal of Psychiatry, 149,* 169–174. http://dx.doi.org/10.1176/ajp.149.2.169

Spar, J. E., Hankin, M., & Stodden, A. (1995). Assessing mental capacity and susceptibility to undue influence. *Behavioral Sciences & the Law, 13,* 391–403. http://dx.doi.org/10.1002/bsl.2370130307

Walsh, A. C., Brown, B. B., Kaye, K., & Grigsby, J. (1997). *Mental capacity: Legal and medical aspects of assessment and treatment* (2nd ed.). Deerfield, IL: Clark, Boardman, & Callaghan.

III

EVOLVING ISSUES IN ASSESSING CAPACITIES

9

Assessment of Sexual Consent Capacity

Emma Katz, Rachael Spalding, Jarred V. Gallegos, and Barry Edelstein

KEY POINTS

- Capacity to consent to sexual activity is different from other types of capacity.
- Sexual consent capacity may be complicated by cognitive and functional deficits associated with psychiatric disorders, including dementia.
- There are no generally accepted legal standards to guide sexual consent capacity evaluation.
- Numerous factors must be considered when assessing sexual consent capacity, particularly in long-term care settings.

DEFINITION OF THE ISSUE

In all 50 states, engaging in sexual intercourse with a person who does not have the "mental capacity" to consent is considered a criminal offense (Buckley, 2013). Once an individual reaches the legal age of consent, which varies across states from 16 to 18 years, courts presume that he or she has requisite consent capacity (American Bar Association Commission on Law and Aging and American Psychological Association [ABA/APA], 2008). Therefore, adults are presumed to have sexual consent capacity. However,

http://dx.doi.org/10.1037/0000184-010
Assessing Capacities of Older Adults: A Casebook to Guide Difficult Decisions, J. Moye (Editor)

when determining whether a person who is of legal age to consent possesses sexual consent capacity, the decision can be far more complicated than simply calculating age. Adults who suffer from cognitive impairment, such as that resulting from a neurodegenerative disease or a traumatic brain injury, may be unable to navigate the complexities of a decision regarding sexual activity. However, few legal standards currently exist by which to assess the capacity of these individuals to consent to sex. Although most states use a functional approach that considers whether a person has the requisite ability to understand information relevant to sexual activity, courts are not guided by a standard interpretation of what constitutes such an understanding (Tang, 2015).

Certain challenges differentiate sexual consent capacity assessment from other forms of capacity assessment. The nature of sexual relationships and related decisions can be quite fluid, often made "in the moment" with little time for deliberation or the involvement of a substitute decision-maker (Syme & Steele, 2016). In addition, the nature of sexual activity can range from fairly low-risk behaviors, such as holding another person's hand, to the more complex choice of whether to engage in intercourse (see Appendix 9.1). Further exacerbating these difficulties is the paucity of relevant assessment strategies and legal standards (ABA/APA, 2008).

Questions of sexual consent capacity often arise in long-term care settings or skilled nursing facilities, where many or a majority of residents suffer from cognitive impairment (Zimmerman, Sloane, & Reed, 2014). As of 2012, 1.4 million people lived in nursing homes in the United States (Family Caregiver Alliance, 2015). In the United States, more than 85% of long-term care residents are over age 65, and more than 50% of residents suffer from Alzheimer's disease or another form of dementia (Centers for Disease Control and Prevention, 2014). Hence, this chapter focuses primarily on the assessment of sexual consent capacity in long-term care settings.

CLINICAL PRESENTATION

Survey-based research with community-dwelling older adults has found strong support for the sustained importance of sexuality and intimate relationships across the life span, contrary to ageist stereotypes of the "asexual older adult" (G. A. Doll, 2012). The majority of older adults (aged 65–80) surveyed in the National Poll on Healthy Aging (Solway, Clark, Singer, Kirch, & Malani, 2018) indicated that sex is an important part of a romantic relationship at any age (76%) and that sex is important to overall quality of life (54%). Further, 65% of respondents reported being interested in sex and 40% of respondents indicated they are currently sexually active (Solway et al., 2018). Notable benefits of resident sexual expression and activity in long-term care facilities include improved communication and sense of identity, improved mood, and increased self-esteem (G. A. Doll, 2012).

However, residents' sexual needs must also be balanced with careful consideration of each resident's ability to consent to sexual behaviors, which is further complicated by the prevalence of cognitive impairment in long-term care facilities. Although few statistics exist regarding the degree to which questions of sexual consent capacity typically occur in long-term care, we can estimate the frequency of the issues given the known occurrence of sexual behaviors in these settings. According to a recent survey with 90 nursing home administrators, nearly all of those surveyed reported sexual activity as occurring on a relatively frequent basis, including sexual acts, sexual talk, and romantic relationships between residents (G. M. Doll, 2013). An additional intricacy surrounding this issue is that long-term care facilities exist as individuals' homes; thus, questions of sexual consent capacity in these settings ultimately consider what people can or cannot do in their own private spaces.

WHAT IS SEXUAL CONSENT CAPACITY?

In the United States, each person who has reached the age of consent in a given jurisdiction is assumed to have capacity to consent to sexual relations (ABA/APA, 2008). *Sexual consent capacity* is the ability to consent voluntarily to sexual activity (Syme & Steele, 2016; Tarzia et al., 2012). It is still an unresolved clinical and ethical issue in long-term care settings and often is not addressed in aging research (Tarzia et al., 2012). Sexual consent capacity can be further influenced by cognitive and functional deficits associated with psychiatric and neurocognitive disorders. To complicate matters further, there are no generally accepted legal standards to guide sexual consent capacity evaluation and no universally accepted criteria for capacity to consent to sexual relations (Lichtenberg, 2014). Like sexual relations, there are also different levels of sexual consent capacity (Hillman, 2016; Syme & Steele, 2016).

QUESTION OF CAPACITY ARISING

The question of consent capacity may arise with a wide variety of residents and for various reasons and situations. Sexual consent capacity may be questioned due to the appointment of a guardian or conservator, adjudication of mental incompetency or incapacity (Sales, Miller, & Hall, 2005), recent history of a brain injury or stroke, presence of dementia, or changes in sexual behavior (ABA/APA, 2008). Staff, family members, and hospital administrators may all bring up capacity concerns and request that an assessment be undertaken for many reasons, including a desire to promote autonomy balanced by the desire to protect residents from harm. Psychosocial and situational factors that may lead to requests for an assessment include increased frequency of falls, memory problems, spending more time with a suspected sexual partner in private or in public, and having a history of relationships with other residents at the facility (ABA/APA, 2008; Syme & Steele, 2016). There are no published statistics regarding the frequency of how often sexual consent capacity questions arise on a national level in and out of long-term care facilities.

FAMILY AND SYSTEM ISSUES

The possibility of negative feelings or reactions by residents' relatives raises family-systems challenges for long-term care facilities, particularly in situations when the resident is cognitively impaired. Many states allow residents, legally recognized as "principals," to designate a surrogate decision-maker or grant a power of attorney to someone, who would then be legally permitted to make decisions (e.g., medical, financial) on behalf of the principal in the event that the principal lacks capacity. In situations where a resident has not appointed a power of attorney and lacks capacity, most states recognize default surrogate consent, meaning surrogate authority falls to family and friends in a defined order. Failing that, and if necessary, the court may appoint a guardian, or conservator, to make decisions on behalf of the resident. A person who had been granted a medical power of attorney or appointed as a guardian is permitted to make health-related decisions on behalf of the older adult with diminished capacity. However, no state has passed legislation giving someone who had a medical power of attorney the ability to make decisions about the sexual behaviors of another individual (Hill, 2014). In many instances, a family member, such as a spouse or adult child, is designated as the decision-maker. Conflict within the family may arise regarding who was appointed, how best to manage and assess a cognitively impaired resident's sexual decisions and which types of sexual behaviors are appropriate. Adult children may also feel jealous that their parent is giving attention to another or feel that their parent is not being loyal to a deceased partner (G. A. Doll, 2012). Adult children decision-makers can develop paternalistic attitudes toward their parent engaging in sexual activity, particularly when the resident is cognitively impaired, and seek to intervene to "protect" the resident (G. A. Doll, 2012). It is important to consider the opinions and attitudes of residents' family members, particularly the appointed decision-maker, in balance with the values and rights of the individual, when assessing sexual consent capacity. Family and health systems factors are further discussed later in the chapter.

DIAGNOSTIC STANDARDS

With the exception of developmental disabilities (Kennedy & Niederbuhl, 2001), there has been a dearth of research conducted about the relation between sexual consent capacity and diagnoses. No psychiatric diagnosis, including neurocognitive disorders such as dementia, should automatically prevent a resident from being permitted sexual expression (Hillman, 2016). However, some diagnoses may lead to concerns about capacity and the need for an evaluation of the resident's ability to consent. Residents experiencing dementia, depression, delirium, and other psychiatric disorders may present with limitations in their functional and cognitive capabilities that could potentially influence their sexual decision-making abilities (ABA/APA, 2008; Syme & Steele, 2016). Additionally, a psychiatric diagnosis is only one of many variables involved in a capacity evaluation and should not be the sole basis for a determination of incapacity. More recent guardianship laws have even removed diagnosis from legal standards, in part due to concerns about discrimination, yet it is important to consider diagnosis because it has prognostic value. There are no specific standards for the assessment of sexual consent capacity. In the next section we will discuss a framework that will assist in capacity assessments.

CLINICAL METHODS

In this section, we move from the more general consideration of issues of sexual consent capacity to consideration of the clinical assessment. We present an integrated conceptual framework that is intended to guide the assessment process. The framework incorporates elements of a comprehensive psychological assessment that are guided by the relevant legal standards.

Conceptual Framework and Related Issues

Relevant legal standards for one's jurisdiction should guide the clinical assessment of consent capacity. Unfortunately, as previously noted, there is no commonly accepted legal standard or statutory definition of capacity to consent to sexual relations that has been applied to older adults (Lyden, 2007; Syme & Steele, 2016). As a consequence, an individual could be determined to lack sexual consent capacity in one jurisdiction and not in another.

As with Hillman (2017) and Syme and Steele (2016), we advocate an integration of assessment frameworks based primarily on those proposed by Lichtenberg and Strzepek (1990) and its later modification (Lichtenberg, 2014), and the American Bar Association and American Psychological Association Assessment of Capacity in Older Adults Project Working Group (2008). The assessment is guided by three factors that are the basis for legal determination of consent capacity in most jurisdictions (Tang, 2015): knowledge and understanding needed to make the decision (e.g., risks of sexual activity to self and relationship, knowledge that others may not be able to give sexual consent), (b) reasoning (e.g., planning and problem-solving, weighing risks and benefits), and (c) voluntariness, or the ability to make and communicate a decision without undue influence or coercion. Tang (2015) noted that some jurisdictions require consideration of "evidence of disability" that can affect one's ability to consent.

The integrated framework advocated here is also guided by a consideration of a number of other factors, as discussed in the preceding text (ABA/APA, 2008; Hillman, 2017; Lichtenberg, 2014; Lichtenberg & Strzepek, 1990; Lyden, 2007; Syme & Steele, 2016; Tang, 2015), when evaluating individuals for a variety of capacity determinations. Many of these are incorporated into the consideration of the three principal legal factors noted in the previous paragraph. They include the following:

1. The functional elements of consent, or skills that are required to perform the task in question (e.g., consent or refuse to engage in sexual behavior)
2. Medical and psychiatric diagnoses that are thought to contribute to or be the cause of any functional disability that could diminish capacity
3. Cognitive functioning in general and specific cognitive skills that are deemed necessary for sexual consent capacity
4. Psychiatric or emotional factors (e.g., severe depression, delusions, disorganized thinking, mania, impulsivity, noncompliance; Moye et al., 2007) that may contribute to functional disability (e.g., through impaired judgment)
5. Individual values, beliefs, and preferences that guide personal decisions
6. Risks to the individual for engaging in sexual behavior
7. Social and environmental supports, as well as the amount of supervision necessary to lessen the risk and support limited capacity to consent (e.g., engage in low-risk sexual behavior, such as holding hands and hugging under the supervision of staff members)
8. The means to enhance the individuals' capacity to consent (For example, an individual lacking knowledge of the potential consequences of sexual behavior could be informed regarding potential risks. The individual could also be taught nonverbal cues that could suggest a potential partner's lack of interest in sexual behavior.)
9. Awareness of the relationship
10. Appreciation of the residents' and staff members' morality of a decision to engage in sexual relations

Even if one incorporates the aforementioned factors into one's assessment of sexual consent, the issue of specific criteria remains. For example, how knowledgeable does one have to be regarding the facts relevant to sexual behavior? What level of "mental capacity" is necessary? How cognitively intact does one have to be to demonstrate sexual consent capacity? What level of appreciation of the morality of a decision is necessary? The notion of limited capacity lends itself to sexual activity, as it has been with guardianships and conservatorships in many jurisdictions. That is, the criteria and threshold for sexual consent capacity could vary along a continuum of potential risk for the individual, with a higher standard being reserved for sexual activities that have the greatest risk (e.g., intercourse) and lower standards for activities with less potential risk (e.g., hugging, holding hands, kissing, fondling). Risk could then be considered in concert with the individual's functional and cognitive strengths and limitations, feasible environmental supports, and legal standards. This approach could enable staff members to minimize the risk to the individual and maximize that individual's autonomy.

Assessment Approaches

We recommend an approach to assessment that is consistent with that recommended by Syme and Steele (2016), which is an integration of approaches advocated by Lichtenberg and Strzepek (1990), Hillman (2016), Wilkins (2015), and the ABA/APA (2008) *Handbook for Assessment of Older Adults With Diminished Capacity*. This approach includes the involvement of an interdisciplinary care team and, when possible and appropriate, family members or legal guardians. Each member of the team can bring a unique disciplinary perspective on the issue, including information on the daily functioning of the individual and historical information regarding the individual's social history and values.

Review of Records

The assessment can begin with a review of medical records, with an eye to disorders or conditions that could affect cognitive functioning (e.g., neurocognitive disorder, bipolar disorder, schizophrenia) or sexual functioning (e.g., cardiovascular disease, arthritis, chronic obstructive pulmonary disease). Several physical disorders can present with symptoms of psychiatric disorders that can impair cognitive functioning (e.g., hypothyroidism may cause fatigue; depression may cause forgetfulness; cardiovascular disease may cause depression). Medication nonadherence and side effects of medication also can influence cognitive functioning (e.g., sedating effects of anticonvulsant, neuroleptic, and Parkinson's disease medications).

Clinical Interview

The assessment of sexual consent capacity often begins with an interview in which the clinician gathers information directly from the resident with the goal of addressing the previously noted three sexual consent capacity criteria: (a) knowledge–understanding, (b) reasoning skills, and (c) voluntariness–choice (Syme & Steele, 2016; Tang, 2015). The interview can range from unstructured to semistructured and can include questions regarding the resident's own sexual behavior and questions based on hypothetical scenarios. This approach is similar to that taken with several functional capacity assessment instruments (ABA/APA, 2008).

FACTORS TO CONSIDER WHEN EVALUATING SEXUAL CONSENT CAPACITY

- Does the resident possess the functional elements of consent and/or skills to consent that are required to perform the task in question (e.g., consent or refuse to engage in sexual behavior)?
- Are there any indications of medical or psychiatric diagnoses that could contribute to or be the cause of any functional disability that could diminish capacity?
- Are there any deficits in general cognitive functioning or specific cognitive skills that are deemed necessary for sexual consent capacity?
- Are there any psychiatric or emotional factors (e.g., severe depression, delusions, disorganized thinking, mania, impulsivity, noncompliance; Moye, Butz, Marson, Wood, & the ABA/APA Capacity Assessment of Older Adults Working Group, 2007) that may contribute to functional disability (e.g., through impaired judgment)?
- What are the individual's values, beliefs, and preferences that guide personal decisions?
- What are the risks to the individual for engaging in sexual behavior?
- What are the social and environmental supports that may lessen the risk and support limited capacity to consent (e.g., engage in low-risk sexual behavior, such as holding hands and hugging under the supervision of staff members)?
- What are potential means to enhance the resident's capacity to consent (e.g., education of resident the potential consequences of sexual behavior, nonverbal cues that a partner lacks interest)?
- What are the provisions of supportive decision-making (e.g., involving a third party in decision-making process)?
- To what extent are staff members and other residents aware of the relationship?
- How does the resident appreciate the morality of a decision to engage in sexual relations and the potential associated stigma?

Knowledge

Several recommendations have been made regarding the specific knowledge that one should expect an individual to have if he or she is found to have sexual consent capacity. Following are a set of knowledge factors, informed by Lyden (2007) and Hillman (2017), that may be considered.

Reasoning

The assessment of reasoning is likely the most complex element of the interview and can vary considerably depending on the level of cognitive

FACTORS TO CONSIDER WHEN ASSESSING KNOWLEDGE

- What is the specific sexual behavior in question?
- What are the risks associated with the sexual behavior or relationship (e.g., sexually transmitted diseases; pregnancy; stigma associated with the behavior; anger or rejection by staff, other residents, or family)?
- What sexual behaviors are illegal?
- What does it mean to respect the privacy of others?
- How can the resident ensure the privacy of the sexual behavior?
- Is the resident aware of personal safety?
- What is the resident's knowledge of illegality of sexual activity without a partner's consent?
- What is the resident's knowledge that some people are unable to give sexual consent?
- Is the resident aware of person, place, and time?
- What is the resident's understanding of another resident's choice to accept or reject sexual behavior?

functioning of the resident and the clinician's preferred approach to its assessment. Reasoning can be assessed both in the context of an interview and during more formal cognitive assessment. It can also be assessed in the context of scenarios presented to the resident that reflect a range of situations in which reasoning would be required. Scenarios also can be used to examine how the resident addresses issues pertaining to the other two criteria

FACTORS TO CONSIDER WHEN ASSESSING REASONING

- Does the resident understand how a partner might verbally or nonverbally say "no" to sexual advances or behavior?
- Is the resident able to differentiate reality and facts from fantasy or lies?
- Is the resident able to plan ahead and problem solve?
- Is the resident able to describe his or her decision-making process about sexual activities?
- Is the resident aware of his or her partner's feelings via verbal and non-verbal cues?
- Is the resident experiencing dementia, medication side effects, a mental disorder, a traumatic brain injury, or another condition that may impair judgment, perception, or thought processing?

discussed here (i.e., knowledge and voluntariness–choice). The following are examples of operationalizations of factors to consider when assessing reasoning, provided by Hillman (2017, p. 45).

Voluntariness

Voluntariness is considered an important element of the assessment of the capacity to consent to research (e.g., Appelbaum, Lidz, & Klitzman, 2009) and sexual behavior (e.g., Lyden, 2007) but does not appear to be a significant factor when considering capacity to consent to medical treatment. The assessment of voluntariness is essential when considering sexual consent and involves determining whether the individual has the ability to consent to sexual activity without coercion, undue persuasion, or inducements (Lyden, 2007; Moye, 2003). Assessment should be guided in part by the relevant legal standards in one's jurisdiction because what constitutes illegal influence varies across jurisdictions (ABA/APA, 2008). There are differences across jurisdictions regarding what constitutes illegal influence (Wertheimer, 2003). Tang (2015) noted that the combination of the criteria of understanding and voluntariness is the lowest threshold for sexual consent capacity used by courts. Following is a set of voluntariness factors to be considered, which are informed by Hillman (2016) and Syme and Steele (2016).

FACTORS TO CONSIDER WHEN ASSESSING VOLUNTARINESS

- Does the resident know that participation in sexual activity—or not participating—is a choice?
- Does the resident have the verbal or nonverbal ability to say "no" to unwanted activity?
- Does the resident know what to do if he or she wished to not engage in sexual intimacy?
- Is the resident able to identify and respond to unfair coercion or persuasion?
- Is the resident being influenced by promises or threats of some kind?
- Has the resident been sexually exploited or abused in the past?
- Does the resident understand what it is about the other person's behavior that they do or do not want to engage intimately?

Using these three standards helps to organize and target the assessment approach. These factors do not stand alone but are applied in the context of numerous issues discussed in the following subsections—cognitive function, psychiatric symptoms, personal values, health and family systems issues, and potential ageism—together representing a sometimes-exquisite balance between promoting rights and protecting from harm (APA, 2017).

In addition to knowledge, reasoning, and voluntariness, Syme and Steele (2016) recommend addressing other topics pertaining to sexual consent. For example, the resident's sexual relationship history could be explored with an eye to the nature and duration of the relationship(s). Also, the sexual behaviors under consideration could be explored with regard to the resident's values.

Collateral Interviews

Many of the same issues and factors addressed in the clinical interview may also be addressed via key informants, including the team members and other staff and family members whose history with and observations of the resident could inform the discussion.

Cognitive Assessment

Assessment of the cognitive underpinnings of the elements of consent capacity should be individualized but also guided by our current knowledge of the cognitive domains that enable one to meet the sexual consent capacity criteria noted described earlier. These domains of cognitive functioning might include memory, particularly auditory memory for presented information; abstraction and executive functions necessary for logical or rational consideration of the benefits and risks of the sexual activity; memory for past experiences related to the current situation; personal values, risks, and preferences; and ability to communicate a choice (cf. ABA/APA, 2008).

Emotional and Psychiatric Functioning

Emotional and psychiatric symptoms should be considered when assessing capacity, as these can impair cognitive functions that are relevant to functional disability and capacity determination. These symptoms might include, for example, disorganized thinking, hallucinations, depressed mood, impulsivity, or mania (ABA/APA, 2008, p. 595)

Consideration of Staff Issues, Biases, Facility Policies, and Family Issues

Personal attitudes toward the sexuality of nursing home residents are wide ranging across facility staff and family members (G. M. Doll, 2013; Hill, 2014). Ageism does not stop at the doors of long-term care facilities (Simpson et al., 2017). Attitudes vary from the belief that older adult sexual behavior should be precluded to the belief that residents have the right to sexual expression as long as it does not harm the individual or someone else. In addition, each discipline may have different concerns based on elements of sexual behavior (e.g., effect on family members, possible physical harm due to a sexual act, psychological consequences of engaging or refusing engagement in sexual behaviors, legal and ethical issues, ability to engage in sexual behaviors in light of physical limitations). Ideally, a meeting of an interdisciplinary team could consider the relevant issues (e.g., social worker; activities staff member; physical therapist; physician, geriatrician, or psychiatrist; occupational therapist;

certified nursing assistant; nurse; legal guardians; spouse with the authority to make decisions on behalf of the resident, health care surrogate; ABA/APA, 2008; Hillman, 2016; Lichtenberg & Strzepek, 1990). The goal might be to strike a balance between the resident's autonomy and privacy and the long-term care facility's duty to protect residents from harm.

Most nursing homes have no policy regarding sexual behavior (Hill, 2014). This creates problems for staff and residents who have no rules or guidelines for their behavior. Should staff members be permitted to hug residents? Should residents be permitted to hug each other or hold hands? What is appropriate and inappropriate is often determined on a case-by-case basis. Sadly, the simplest and least risky approach for long-term care facilities is to forbid any sexual behavior. This of course limits the personal autonomy of residents and denies them the right to sexual expression. In such an atmosphere, discussions of sexual consent capacity can be difficult if not contentious.

Common Pragmatic and Ethical Dilemmas

Due to the complexities and controversies of sexual consent capacity assessment, clinicians must consider many associated topics and potential dilemmas. At all stages of the assessment process, including before conducting the assessment, one must consider the extent to which other parties should be involved, including family members, facility administration, and ombudsmen. These individuals can provide useful information regarding the resident's sexual history and current behavior. Residents who have been determined to lack consent capacity in other areas (i.e., medical) may warrant greater inclusion of others to assist with the assessment process. However, in choosing to collaborate and share information with other people, clinicians should always be conscious of the resident's right to privacy (e.g., Health Insurance Portability and Accountability Act [HIPAA]) and consider who is legally permitted to have this information. Relatedly, clinicians must be sensitive to broader contexts of culture, religion, and family dynamics.

When selecting a time to conduct the assessment, one should evaluate the potential influence of factors that could affect the process and outcome of the assessment. Optimal performance on cognitive tasks varies across times of the day (Schmidt, Collette, Cajochen, & Peigneux, 2007). Thus, the circadian rhythms of individuals being assessed should be considered when selecting a time for the assessment. For approximately 75% of older adults, peak alertness, associated with improved performance on cognitive tasks, occurs in the morning (Schmidt, Collette, Cajochen, & Peigneux, 2007). One should at least inquire as to the time of day that the person being assessed appears to be most alert if optimal performance is desired. On a related note, sleep quality, or the lack thereof, should be addressed because poor sleep can impair performance on assessment tasks.

Following the assessment process, one must choose how best to convey the findings in a report. One should give careful consideration to the structure of the report, including how to most appropriately balance and elaborate on the various elements given the nature of the referral question. Clinicians should consider a breadth of options when providing recommendations and seek means of supporting residents' decision-making abilities whenever possible. Given the multidimensional nature of sexual behavior, capacity determination in these situations is rarely a binary judgment and can incorporate recommendations that permit various levels of physical intimacy (ABA/APA, 2008). For example, a clinician might determine that a resident has the capacity to consent to lower risk behaviors, such as holding hands or hugging, but lacks capacity for higher risk behaviors, such as full intercourse.

Other potential dilemmas during the assessment process include situations that require notification of Adult Protective Services, such as elder abuse or neglect. In these instances, the clinician should carefully consider legal and ethical guidelines to inform the course of action, and also consider HIPAA and confidentiality regarding discussion of findings with family members, staff, or other individuals. During assessment, the clinician should take a holistic approach and consider the residents' mental and physical limitations (e.g., mobility, hearing or visual impairment, mental health condition) as well as any relevant historical factors. Factors such as a history of sexual abuse (victim or perpetrator) or previous impulsive, violent, or criminal behavior should be noted.

CASE EXAMPLES

We discuss two very different case examples of individuals whose capacity to consent to sexual behavior is questioned.[1] Each case presents unique issues that require the gathering and integration of a variety of factors. For each case, we discuss how one might go about the assessment task and reach an informed conclusion regarding consent capacity.

Case 1: Esther

Background

Esther Tremlett was an 80-year old woman who had recently suffered a left hip fracture in her long-term care facility. She was a widow with three adult children, who were very involved in her care. Esther had been diagnosed with minor neurocognitive disorder due to possible Alzheimer's disease. She recently reported to multiple staff members her desire to engage in sexual relations with another resident in the nursing home. The nursing

[1]Although the case examples in this chapter are based on the authors' real experiences, the identities of the individuals involved in these examples have been properly disguised to protect their confidentiality.

home staff was concerned about her ability to consent to sexual activity due to her apparent cognitive deficits. Staff members had also reported varying attitudes about whether residents in the nursing home should be allowed to engage in sex at all. Esther had been spending increasing amounts of time with Marvin, a fellow resident who was an active member of the nursing home community and had no observed cognitive issues. Staff members were concerned for Esther's safety and well-being and worried that Marvin may be taking advantage of her.

Medical Record Review

A review of medical records revealed that Esther was recovering from a left hip fracture due to a fall in the facility. Two separate instances of Esther falling were documented in her chart. As part of her rehabilitation plan from her hip fracture, the physical therapist recommended that Esther ambulate with a walker. It was not believed that Esther lost consciousness during any of the falls, and there was no evidence of trauma to her head or neck as a result of the falls. Esther did have some bruising after the fall, as noted in her chart. She was diagnosed with a minor neurocognitive disorder about 1 year before entering the facility. She presented with poor inhibitory control and displayed deficits in her short-term memory. There was no evidence of additional psychiatric or emotional factors (e.g., paranoia, delusions), medical conditions (e.g., systemic infections), or potentially complicating comorbidities (i.e., anxiety, frontotemporal lobar degeneration) that could impair capacity.

Esther's medical records were then examined for factors that could influence her decision-making capacity. We found no evidence of any systemic infections that could impair cognitive functioning. Esther was currently taking medication for her arthritis and hypertension. These medications were reviewed to determine whether the medications themselves or their potential side effects could affect Esther's cognitive functioning or her ability to engage in sexual behavior, and no concerns were noted.

We also reviewed the results of laboratory tests for evidence of any additional complicating or contributing problems. Lab tests confirmed that Esther was not under the influence of any substances outside of her prescribed medication and did not suffer from any mineral or vitamin deficiencies. Esther did not have a reported history of cardiovascular disease, sexual dysfunction (e.g., dyspareunia), or sexually transmitted infections that would prevent a pleasant sexual experience.

Clinical Interview (Knowledge, Reasoning, Voluntariness)

We structured our clinical interview to assess three specific domains of sexual consent: Esther's knowledge, reasoning, and voluntariness related to capacity to consent to sexual activity (Hillman, 2017).

The clinical interview comprised two major parts, as described in the following sections. Throughout the interview, we also assessed Esther's abilities with regard to the functional elements of consent, including knowledge, reasoning, and voluntariness. Additionally, these functional elements were assessed in the second part of the interview through the use of hypothetical scenarios.

Esther was agreeable to the mental status exam and clinical interview and was cooperative and forthcoming throughout the assessment. She needed to be redirected several times during the interview. Esther presented to the clinical interview appropriately dressed and neatly groomed. She was alert and engaged throughout the interview. She appeared euthymic and displayed broad affect during the exam. Her speech was normal, and she responded to questions in a goal-directed manner. Esther was oriented to time, place, and location and comprehended the assessment questions presented to her. She lacked insight to the purpose of the assessment and did not understand the need to discuss her relationship with Marvin. She also could not articulate why some staff members were concerned. Esther reported that she felt happy most of the time but did report that she experienced some anxiety when thinking about the future. She denied symptoms of depression and symptoms of other anxiety disorders (e.g., panic attacks, social anxiety). There was no evidence of clinical psychopathology. Esther denied experiencing any delusions, mania, suicidal ideation, and homicidal ideation.

Knowledge. When assessing Esther's knowledge regarding different domains of sexual behaviors, Esther conveyed adequate understanding of the range of sexual activities (e.g., from hand-holding to sexual intercourse), social appropriateness (e.g., location/time to engage in sexual activities), the benefits of engaging in intercourse, and coercion by herself or others. Esther however was unable to discuss the risks of engaging in sex, specifically risks related to sexually transmitted diseases and infections. She was knowledgeable about socially appropriate time and place for engaging in sexual activity. Esther was aware of the potential consequences that could arise with nursing home staff if she begins a sexual relationship with another resident. However, she failed to recognize how the desired relationship might influence her relationship with other residents and her adult children.

Reasoning. To assess Esther's reasoning abilities, we had administered three hypothetical sexual scenarios that represented a continuum of sexual behaviors of varying risks that would allow us to observe Esther's planning, problem-solving, and appreciation of information relevant to sexual behaviors (see Appendix 9.2). Generally, Esther demonstrated poor reasoning skills with regard to weighing potential risks and benefits. For example, she was unable to provide a benefit of condom use during sexual activity. She stated that pregnancy was not a risk, and she did not discuss protection from sexually transmitted diseases or infections. Additionally, she was unable to discuss the pros and cons of discussing a sexual relationship with her family members. Esther often failed to mention any risks of sexual activities and was not able to discuss how her current physical limitations may pose challenges or consequences to sexual activity. Esther's diagnosis of minor neurocognitive disorder may have impaired her ability to remember all the details of the scenarios presented because she asked for multiple questions to be repeated throughout this section and sometimes had to be redirected when discussing specific details of the scenarios.

Voluntariness. We assessed Esther's awareness of the domain of voluntariness as it related to sexual activity by asking Esther questions regarding how to recognize coercion, exploitation, verbal and nonverbal ways to communicate saying "no" to sexual activity, sexual abuse, and how participation in sexual activity is a choice. Esther demonstrated a lack of understanding about the risks of coercion regarding voluntariness. Esther was unable to articulate ways in which a person's ability to give voluntary consent to sex might be impaired—specifically, she did not believe that medications, physical conditions, or cognitive deficits could limit a nursing home resident's ability to consent. Esther could not provide a response for what she could say or do to refuse a sexual advance from another resident. She also could not fully appreciate the significance of why attempts to induce sexual activities could be problematic.

History of sexual behaviors and values. Esther was initially hesitant to discuss her current sexual behaviors and expressed discomfort when asked to disclose what sexual behaviors she would like to engage in with Marvin. Esther endorsed that sexual intimacy in general was very important to her and that she would like to continue her current relationship with Marvin. She reported feeling somewhat lonely since moving to the nursing home and said that with her husband being gone for a number of years, she is interested in companionship. Esther expressed concern that staff and residents would judge her actions if she began a sexual relationship. She also stated that she does not want to be considered a "person with questionable moral character," which is why she discussed her desires with the staff before initiating a sexual relationship.

Collateral Interviews

We sought collateral information from staff members for the purpose of gathering more information related to Esther's ability to consent. Family members were not involved in the assessment process because Esther had not been determined to lack capacity in any domain and did not give permission to contact her children. Multiple staff members described how Esther voiced her desire to engage in sex with Marvin, which made some of them uncomfortable. There was disagreement among staff members about what sexual activity Esther should be permitted to engage in. Some staff members voiced their disapproval of Esther's sexual activities when interviewed. They were asked about Esther's decision-making abilities regarding engaging in sexual behaviors, and there was disagreement about what she would be able to understand. Observations recorded by staff members included Esther holding hands with Marvin, sitting close to Marvin in the activities room. In one instance, a nurse found Esther and Marvin alone in her room, but there was no evidence of recent sexual activity. Staff also stated that Esther refused to use her walker when ambulating around the facility because it makes her feel "like an old lady." Because Esther was ambulatory, staff noted the challenges of monitoring her behavior, which was concerning to them given the increasing amount of time Esther was spending with Marvin. We also met with Esther's physical therapist to review the potential physical risks associated with Esther engaging in sexual activity due to her hip fracture. Her physical therapist noted risks of pain when putting strain on her hip and the risk of falling given Esther's history and resistance to using a walker.

Cognitive Assessment

We administered a cognitive assessment battery to gather further information needed to assess Esther's current functioning as it is related to her ability to make sexual decisions. Cognitive assessment began with the administration of the Montreal Cognitive Assessment (Nasreddine et al., 2005). Esther's performance on this instrument was in the impaired range, with notable failures in the domains of executive functioning, attention, and memory. To assess executive functioning skills, the Controlled Oral Word Association Test (COWAT; Benton & Hamsher, 1976), Trail Making Task Parts A and B (Trails; Army Individual Test Battery, 1944), and the Executive Interview (EXIT; Royall, Mahurin, & Gray, 1992) were administered. Esther repeated several words during COWAT administration, resulting in an impaired score. Esther's performance on Trails B was impaired; she made several errors and did not appear to comprehend the number–letter sequence order. To assess memory abilities, the Hopkins Verbal Learning Test (HVLT; Brandt, 1991) and logical memory subtests of the Wechsler Memory Scale (WMS–III; Wechsler, 1997b). To assess attentional abilities, the Digit Span Forward and Backward Tests Wechsler Adult Intelligence Scale—III (Wechsler, 1997a) were administered. Her performance on digit span forward was unimpaired, but it was impaired for digit span backward. She did not appear to understand the task during backward items and instead repeated them as if still responding to digit span forward. Esther's results throughout the testing indicated significant impairment in her attention, working memory, and executive functioning abilities. Overall, Esther demonstrated difficulty recalling a variety of forms of stimulus information (e.g., single words, prose, numbers) that were presented to her, specifically having challenges with prose, and presented with impaired performance on the Trails task and EXIT, suggesting that her impaired executive functioning may have contributed to her memory deficit.

Team Discussion

The overarching concern was to assess whether and to what extent Esther had capacity to consent to engaging in sexual activity. The nursing staff at the facility were concerned that Esther lacked capacity to consent to sexual behavior due primarily to her poor inhibitory functioning, issues with ambulation, and minor neurocognitive disorder diagnosis.

Clinical Reasoning

Consideration of medical and psychiatric diagnoses. We considered Esther's medication and psychiatric diagnoses and decided that her only diagnosis that could contribute to issues regarding her capacity was her minor neurocognitive disorder and her fractured hip, which was temporary.

Consideration of functional elements. We considered whether Esther had the ability to engage in decision-making regarding sexual decisions. On the basis of hypothetical scenarios presented to Esther during the interview, Esther was able to appreciate that she had a choice regarding engaging in sexual behavior, how she could communicate that choice, and the range of sexual behaviors. However, Esther did not have reasonable insight into her current situation regarding why the need to discuss her relationship with Marvin was an issue and expressed discomfort when asked to disclose specifics in her sexual behaviors. She failed to adequately demonstrate her reasoning skills when asked to weigh potential risks and benefits of sexual engagement and showed a lack of understanding about the risks of coercion regarding voluntariness. Esther did not understand the risks and long-term consequences of sexually transmitted diseases or issues regarding coercion, which was concerning. In addition, Esther failed to acknowledge her limitations regarding her hip fracture. She did not acknowledge the increased possibility of falls without a walker or the toll it might take on her still-recovering hip. Staff members were concerned that she was pushing her limits by not using her walker to ambulate and considered this an example of Esther's poor judgment.

Consideration of cognitive skills. Esther exhibited impairment in the domains of attention, working memory, and executive functioning. There was evidence of problems with Esther's cognitive functioning based on the cognitive assessment administered and difficulties with demonstrating reasoning skills particularly with regard to potential risks of sexual behaviors.

Recommendations and Conclusion

In light of the assessment findings, we concluded that Esther had limited capacity to consent to sexual activity. More specifically, we considered sexual behaviors along a continuum of potential risk and concluded that Esther had the capacity to consent to mutual manual masturbation with another consenting resident. However, we recommended that she not be permitted to engage in penetrative penile–vaginal or penile–anal sexual intercourse due to higher physical risks of these activities. That recommendation was potentially problematic for staff because monitoring Esther would be a challenge given her independent ambulation. Our recommendations were discussed and accepted by the interdisciplinary care team. This was followed by a discussion of Esther's limitations and several practical issues. A plan was then developed to discuss the team decision with Esther and monitor Esther's social interactions more closely, specifically to reduce unsupervised private visits with other residents.

We also made recommendations for nursing home staff that could enhance Esther's decision-making capacity. Educational materials and subsequent discussion about safe sex practices, specifically the risks of sexually transmitted diseases, were provided to Esther. In those recommendations, staff members were encouraged to evaluate Esther's recall of the educational information immediately after presentation. We also recommended that Esther be provided with a list of sexual behaviors to facilitate a discussion about other sexual activity in which she could engage (see Appendix 9.3).

Case 2: Jeff

Background

Jeff Park was a fully ambulatory 72-year-old man who had resided at a nursing home facility for the past 10 years. As a young adult, he was diagnosed with bipolar I disorder. Before coming to the facility, Jeff often was nonadherent to his bipolar medication as prescribed by his psychiatrist. Jeff also had Type I diabetes, which was poorly controlled and further inhibited his ability to live independently. He was never married and had no children.

Jeff's decisional capacity came to be questioned due to problematic symptoms he experienced during manic episodes. These symptoms included increased energy and sociability, pressured speech with frequent continuous talk, hypersexual behavior, euphoria, inflated self-esteem, and decreased need for sleep. When he was experiencing a manic episode, Jeff denied that he was experiencing any problems associated with his bipolar disorder, arguing that he felt "wonderful." In recent years, Jeff had experienced four or more manic episodes annually, leading to the diagnostic specifier of bipolar I disorder "with rapid cycling."

Jeff had a long-term girlfriend of several years who also lived in the nursing home. She had capacity and did not need to be assessed at this time. When Jeff's mood was euthymic, he and his girlfriend were in a committed relationship and demonstrated a distinct preference for each other in the facility. However, when Jeff was experiencing a manic episode, he became very flirtatious with many of the female residents in the facility, some of whom often reciprocated his affections. Staff also noticed that certain women in the facility appeared to seek out Jeff for romantic purposes when he was known to be experiencing a manic episode. During these periods, Jeff was observed spending private time with other women and being physically affectionate (cuddling, hugging) with them in public. Although there was no evidence that Jeff had engaged in sexual activity with other women in the facility, staff members and his girlfriend were concerned about the extent of these encounters. The nursing home staff was wary about Jeff's capacity to consent to sexual activity in these situations because he only made advances toward other women when in a manic episode. Staff members worried that his mania inhibited his ability to appropriately weigh the risks of romantically engaging with other women, including jeopardizing his sexual health and his relationship with his girlfriend. A further complicating matter was the fact that Jeff was independently wealthy and enjoyed expressing his affection for women with gifts. Thus, staff feared that Jeff was at risk for financial exploitation by his numerous female suitors during his manic episodes.

Medical Record Review

A preliminary review of medical records revealed that Jeff was diagnosed with Type 1 diabetes 15 years earlier. In early adulthood, his primary care physician diagnosed him with bipolar I disorder. No history of other psychiatric or emotional factors (e.g., delusions, hallucinations, depressed mood, paranoia), medical conditions (e.g., systemic infections), or potentially complicating comorbidities (e.g., anxiety, frontotemporal lobar degeneration) that could potentially impair sexual consent capacity were noted.

Jeff was currently prescribed lithium for his bipolar disorder; however, he still continued to experience some manic symptoms. He was also prescribed insulin to manage his diabetes. These medications were reviewed to determine whether the medications or their potential side effects could affect Jeff's cognitive functioning or ability to engage in sexual behavior. No concerns were raised in this regard.

We also reviewed the results of various laboratory tests for evidence of any additional complicating or contributing medical problems (e.g., hypothyroidism, systemic infection). All results were within normal limits. Jeff did not have a reported history of cardiovascular disease or sexual disorders, such as dyspareunia, that would preclude a pleasant sexual experience. Importantly, Jeff had no record of or self-reported history of sexually transmitted infections or diseases. Jeff experienced an average of four manic episodes of varying duration per year, consistent with his diagnosis of bipolar I disorder with rapid cycling.

Clinical Interview

Jeff was cooperative during the clinical interview, although he required the repetition of several questions and frequent redirection to content. Jeff was assessed when he was in the midst of a manic episode. The timing of this assessment was intentional given the nature of his diagnosis and the fact that his mood is euthymic during other periods of time. There is no evidence to suggest that he lacks capacity when he is not experiencing a manic episode; therefore, the question of capacity only arises when he is experiencing a manic episode. The clinical interview comprised two major parts, as described in the following sections. In the first part, a mental status examination was conducted to determine whether Jeff was experiencing any psychiatric or emotional factors that could compromise his capacity to consent to sexual activity. In the second part, general questions regarding Jeff's values, and current and past sexual behaviors were explored, followed by the assessment of the three specific domains of sexual consent: knowledge, reasoning, and voluntariness. Much of this latter portion of the interview comprised questions pertaining to the domains in the context of scenarios. The scenarios reflected situations that Jeff was likely to encounter with regard to his sexual activities in the nursing home.

Jeff was agreeable to participating in the mental status exam and arrived at the interview dressed in brightly colored clothing. He appeared adequately groomed and alert. He was wearing strong-smelling cologne. Over the course of the examination, Jeff demonstrated psychomotor agitation (e.g., specifically fidgeting). His speech was rapid, continuous, and often tangential, as he was easily distracted throughout the interview. Jeff comprehended the questions being asked of him, although he requested that questions be repeated on several occasions. He displayed euphoria, reporting that he felt wonderful all the time, and evidenced impaired insight regarding the potential risks of making decisions during his manic episodes. He was unrealistically optimistic about his ability to successfully manage multiple romantic relationships with other women in the facility while maintaining his committed relationship with his girlfriend. There was no evidence for any additional emotional or psychiatric factors that could potentially influence consent capacity (e.g., depressed mood, delusions, hallucinations, anxiety). He was oriented to person and place but not to day or time.

Knowledge

Jeff's knowledge of many of the facets of sexuality was good. For example, he understood that sexual behaviors exist on a spectrum (i.e., ranging from hand-holding to intercourse) and was able to explain the nature of intercourse and some of the potential risks of sexual activity (e.g., sexually transmitted diseases). He also noted ways in which sexual activity is immediately beneficial for him (e.g., provides pleasure). However, he failed to appreciate the potential consequences of engaging in sexual behaviors with other women, particularly with respect to his relationship with his girlfriend. He also failed to recognize the potential consequences that could arise if other residents rejected him socially for what they might consider inappropriate or immoral behavior. He was aware that coercion by others and by himself was unacceptable and understood that there are socially appropriate locations and times for sexual activity. Jeff also was aware of the nature and necessity of consent when engaging in sexual activities and that some individuals may be unable to express consent for a variety of reasons (e.g., the influence of substances or cognitive impairment).

Reasoning

Jeff's reasoning was assessed through the administration of a series of hypothetical sexual scenarios featuring various levels of risk. These scenarios emphasized Jeff's ability to plan, problem solve, weigh risks and benefits in light of his stated values, and appreciate the importance of information relevant to sexual behaviors. Overall, Jeff demonstrated mixed to poor reasoning skills. With the exception of the least risky sexual activities (e.g., holding hands), Jeff often failed to recall important scenario information regarding the context of the sexual activities. When reminded of this information and asked to weigh the potential risks and benefits, he often failed to note more than one potential risk (e.g., getting caught by staff) and failed to consider the potential long-term consequences of his decisions in each scenario. In general, when Jeff did explain his decision-making, his stated values reflected what was most pleasing to him in the moment. Maintaining Jeff's attention during the scenario assessment was difficult, and he required frequent redirection to the task, which was likely a symptom of his current manic episode.

Voluntariness

Assessment of voluntariness revealed a lack of understanding regarding the personal risks of coercion or how his behavior might appear coercive to another person. For instance, Jeff did not fully appreciate the possibility that a partner might refuse to have sex with him and could not explain what it was about the partner's behavior that might suggest refusal or even disinterest. Moreover, he was unable to explain in sufficient detail what he could and would do in such a situation. When asked about the possibility of another person attempting to exploit him sexually, he laughed and indicated that he didn't see that as a problem. Finally, Jeff did not appreciate that there was anything he could do or say that would appear coercive or persuasive.

History of Sexual Behavior and Values

Jeff reported a long history of relationships with women, both within and outside of psychiatric and nursing facilities. Since young adulthood, he had been in several committed relationships but had never married. When queried about his interest in developing a sexual relationship with his girlfriend, Jeff indicated that being in a relationship with a woman was very important to him and that he was committed to the relationship with his girlfriend. However, Jeff stated that he was currently "living in the moment" and was enjoying the attention of multiple female residents in the facility. He reported buying candy for these women and other friends and spending considerable money at the facility concession counter. When confronted with his stated desire to maintain the relationship with his girlfriend and his "relationships" with other women in the facility, he had difficulty reconciling his stated value for a committed relationship with his girlfriend and his interest and behavior with other women while manic. He also demonstrated inconsistency with regard to his values, expressing both a desire to maintain a commitment to his girlfriend and to explore his relationships with other women.

Collateral Interviews

Multiple staff members reported observing Jeff with numerous female residents other than his identified partner during periods when he was manic. Jeff was observed engaging in behaviors such as spending private time in his room with these women and holding hands with them during activities. Staff also reported that Jeff elicits more incident reports when he is experiencing a manic episode. For instance, he had been observed viewing pornography on communal computers and was generally more argumentative with staff and resistant to medication use during these periods. Staff also voiced their concerns regarding Jeff as a potential victim of financial or sexual exploitation, given his irresponsible tendencies when he is manic. The possibility was also raised that Jeff might use his monetary resources to coerce women into engaging in sexual activity with him, which was equally alarming to staff.

Apart from nursing home staff, family members of other women in the facility had complained to staff regarding Jeff's open flirtations with their loved ones. Jeff's girlfriend had also expressed to staff her discomfort about Jeff's provocative behavior toward other residents and their provocative behavior toward him. Jeff did not give permission for our team to speak with his girlfriend as an additional source of collateral information. Jeff had no other living family members who could be targeted as collateral informants.

Cognitive Assessment

Cognitive assessment began with the administration of the Montreal Cognitive Assessment (Nasreddine et al., 2005). Performance on this instrument was in the impaired range, with notable failures in the domains of executive functioning, attention, and memory. Additional tests were administered to determine whether any cognitive deficits might be identified as potentially compromising Jeff's consent capacity.

To assess executive functioning skills, the COWAT (Benton & Hamsher, 1976), Trails A and B (Trails; Army Individual Test Battery, 1944), and the EXIT (Royall et al., 1992) were administered. Jeff's performance on most measures of executive functioning was impaired. His performance on the COWAT was impaired, in part because he repeatedly stopped to ask if he had previously provided a particular word. Performance on the Trails A and B was unimpaired, perhaps because the visual cues enabled him to maintain his attention to the task. However, elements of the other tests requiring sustained attention, particularly to stimuli presented orally, was impaired. To assess memory abilities, the HVLT–R (Benedict et al., 1998) and logical memory subtests of the WMS–III (Wechsler, 1997b) were administered. Total and delayed recall were impaired on the HVLT–R, as were percent retention and performance on the Logical Memory portion of the WMS–III. Testing of limits after initial administration of the Logical Memory stories revealed that Jeff could recall elements of the stories if small portions of the stories were tested. To assess attention and working memory, the Digit Span Forward and Backward tests from the Wechsler Adult Intelligence Scale—III (Wechsler, 1997a) were administered. Performance on both tests was impaired.

Overall, Jeff demonstrated difficulty recalling a variety of forms of stimulus information (e.g., single words, prose, numbers) that were presented to him, with impaired performance on the Digit Span Forward and Backward, suggesting that his impaired attention may have contributed to his memory deficit. Errors on his COWAT performance also suggested an attention deficit. His lack of sleep over the previous 2 days also may have contributed to impaired performance.

Team Discussion

The overarching concern in this case was to assess the extent to which Jeff had the capacity to consent to engaging in sexual activity during a manic episode. The nursing staff at the facility expressed concern that Jeff lacked capacity to consent to sexual behavior due to symptoms of impulsivity, inhibition, and hypersexuality experienced during periods of mania.

Clinical Reasoning

Consideration of medical and psychiatric disorders. We considered Jeff's medication and psychiatric diagnoses and decided that the only disorder likely contributing to his consent capacity was his bipolar disorder. The symptoms of mania appeared to be contributing substantially to Jeff's ability to attend to and retain information presented to him. In addition, the sleep deprivation associated with the manic episode was likely impairing his cognitive abilities. The observed pattern of performance suggests the memory deficit was not consistent with dementia but rather represented a problem with attention, encoding, and executive function associated with his mania.

Consideration of functional elements. We evaluated Jeff's capacity to consent to sexual behavior through an examination of his ability to demonstrate his knowledge of information necessary to make an informed decision, his reasoning ability, and his appreciation of voluntariness in sexual situations. Jeff's knowledge of sexual behaviors and issues related to sexual activity was good. Jeff demonstrated that he had a choice of engaging in sexual behavior and that he could communicate that choice. He also demonstrated the ability to weigh some risks and benefits associated with that choice. However, the risks and benefits that he identified reflected a focus on immediate consequences. Jeff did not adequately appreciate how his behaviors and actions could immediately affect others and potentially be viewed as coercive. Moreover, he failed to appreciate the potential long-term consequences associated with such choices in general and for his partner and him in particular.

The assessment of reasoning was compromised to some degree because the details of each scenario had to be repeated several times due to poor recall of the information presented. This is consistent with his impaired performance on tests of memory, with particularly notable impairments in memory for prose. This memory impairment is a limiting factor if Jeff is to be presented with new information that would be used to make future decisions.

When voluntariness was assessed, Jeff did not appear to understand how his sexual behavior could be coercive, thereby threatening the voluntariness of his partners' behaviors. Furthermore, he did not fully appreciate the potential risks and long-term consequences of sexually transmitted diseases or financial exploitation of him. He failed to acknowledge that some of his behavior could be viewed by women as unwanted advances or even assault. He also did not understand how sexually coercive behaviors might be a risk to the facility, which has a duty to protect him and other residents.

Consideration of cognitive skills. Jeff demonstrated impaired attention and short-term memory. However, the validity of most of the cognitive assessment was questioned in light of Jeff's apparent attention deficit.

Recommendations and Conclusion

Given the results of our assessment, we concluded that Jeff lacked capacity to consent to sexual activity when he was experiencing a manic episode. This conclusion posed a complication for staff because repeated assessment of sexual consent capacity was likely to be impractical. Consequently, staff members would need to be made aware of symptoms and signs of a manic episode so that appropriate direction of Jeff's sexual behavior could occur. A manic episode could be identified by staff based on Jeff's manic symptoms (e.g., increased spending of excessive amounts of money at the concession stand, wearing flamboyant clothing, pressured speech, wakefulness throughout the night and daytime, high energy). Our recommendation was discussed with the interdisciplinary team and accepted. We also made suggestions to the staff that could potentially enhance Jeff's consent capacity. First, we suggested that Jeff be taught the difference between coercive and noncoercive behavior, how certain behaviors might be viewed as potentially coercive (i.e., buying gifts for multiple female acquaintances), and the necessity of noncoercive consent before engaging in sexual activity. In addition, we recommended that staff members more carefully and consistently monitor Jeff's behavior during manic episodes when he is in the presence of other women and encourage these women to contact staff if they feel uncomfortable with Jeff's behavior. Staff was also urged to observe how women in the facility may be encouraging Jeff's advances, whether intentionally or unintentionally. Finally, we suggested that Jeff be encouraged to consider appointing a financial power of attorney to reduce risk of financial exploitation during his manic episodes.

REFLECTIONS

The case of Esther illustrated challenges to the assessment of sexual consent capacity. The most notable challenge was in determining the level of risk associated with a continuum of sexual activities and their associated risks. We first determined Esther's understanding of the risk associated with each type of sexual behavior. Because Esther failed to understand the risks involved with vaginal or anal intercourse, we decided that a limited sexual consent capacity determination would be appropriate. We believed that this would maximize Esther's rights to sexual expression and minimize the potential risks to her and the facility. In considering limited capacity, we also took into consideration the potential staff burden and varying staff attitudes associated with monitoring a resident's sexual behavior. We also acknowledged the transient nature of Esther's physical limitations due to her hip fracture and that monitoring her activity would likely become more burdensome as her fracture healed and she became more ambulatory. Finally, we noted that as Esther's cognitive impairment become more severe, her capacity would need to be reconsidered.

The case of Jeff also illustrated several challenges to the assessment of sexual consent capacity. The most notable challenge was the assessment of fluctuating capacity of Jeff due largely to his bipolar disorder and recurrent manic episodes. Approximately four times each year, Jeff experienced manic episodes that called into question his capacity during those periods. Fluctuating capacity is not peculiar to bipolar I disorder and can be associated with various disorders, both psychiatric (e.g., depressive disorder, neurocognitive disorder) and medical (e.g., urinary tract infection). The associated question is: When should one assess capacity? Capacity is a relative term, and the underlying pathology that can lead to incapacitation rarely occurs instantly. This issue can be discussed with a team, and criteria can be established for the signs and symptoms that would signal the need for capacity assessment and for the restoration of rights if capacity is withdrawn. A second challenge in the assessment of Jeff was the significant attention deficit, which required the interpretation of cognitive test results to be considered in light of the potential influence of inattention on test performance. Ordinarily, we would use the results of such cognitive testing to assist in understanding the functional deficits revealed in the functional assessment (ABA/APA, 2008). We were reminded of the admonition not to make capacity judgments solely on the basis of cognitive testing (ABA/APA, 2008), which could lead to an unreliable capacity determination at best. Consequently, Jeff's performance on tests of functional abilities formed the principal basis for our capacity determination.

LONG-TERM RECOMMENDATIONS

The assessment of sexual consent capacity, particularly for older adults, is in its infancy. The assessment of capacity is typically guided by legal standards; however, there are no generally accepted criteria or legal standards for capacity to consent to sexual relations. Legal standards for various other forms of capacity vary across jurisdictions; however, there is some agreement on the "tests" for some forms of capacity (e.g., Roth, Meisel, & Lidz, 1977). At this point, there is some agreement on the three sexual consent criteria we previously discussed (e.g., knowledge, reasoning, voluntariness) that could be used as a starting point for the development of recommendations for legal standards. This is a perfect time to urge the legal profession to develop such recommendations because most states have no sexual consent legal standards. Even improving existing laws (Syme, Lichtenberg, & Moye, 2016) would provide much-needed guidance for the assessment of sexual consent capacity.

Standardized sexual consent capacity assessment instruments, similar to those currently available for other types of capacity (e.g., medical consent, financial), are needed. A decision tree and worksheet based on the conceptual model advanced by Syme and Steele (2016) and Hillman (2016), much like those provided in the ABA/APA (2008) handbook, would be helpful for guiding assessment even if legal standards are not immediately forthcoming.

Nursing homes should have policies addressing resident rights regarding sexual behavior, such as that used at The Hebrew Home at Riverdale (2013) in New York, and policies regarding how problems associated with sexual behavior should be established as well. These policies could guide staff training and potentially allay fears of fines or loss of licensure by state and federal regulators for failing to protect residents from sexual abuse.

To preserve personal autonomy and rights to sexual expression while limiting risks to individuals and nursing facilities, limited capacity determinations should be considered. More specifically, certain types of low-risk sexual activities might be permitted rather than ruling out all forms of sexual expression.

Finally, a durable power of attorney for sexual consent could be created that, in theory, would address issues of sexuality (Hill, 2014). Complementary advance directives also could be drafted to provide more details to guide sexual decisions (Hill, 2014).

APPENDIX 9.1
SEXUAL CONSENT CAPACITY INTERVIEW QUESTIONS

Knowledge

1. Sexual behavior in question?

____

____

2. Risk of sexual behavior?

____

____

3. Illegality of sexual behaviors?

____

____

4. Respect for privacy of others?

____

____

5. Ensure privacy of sexual behavior?

6. Aware of personal safety?

7. Aware of illegality of sexual activity without a partner's consent?

8. Aware how some people are unable to give sexual consent?

9. Orientated to person, place, and time?

10. Understands choice to accept or reject sexual behavior?

Reasoning

1. Understanding of refusal by other person?

2. Differentiates reality and facts from fantasy or lies?

3. Able to plan ahead and problem solve?

4. Able to describe decision-making process about sexual activities?

5. Aware of partner's feelings?

6. Presence of condition that may impair thought process?

Voluntariness

1. Knows that participation in sexual activity is a choice?

2. Able to refuse unwanted activity?

3. Able to refuse engaging in sexual intimacy?

4. Able to identify and respond to coercion?

5. Influenced by promises or threats?

6. History of sexual exploitation or abuse?

7. Understands partner's ability to refuse

APPENDIX 9.2
HYPOTHETICAL SEXUAL SCENARIOS

Now I am going to tell you a few stories. After I finish each story, I am going to ask you some questions about the story.

In this first story, Jessie and Sharon are two residents at a nursing home. Jessie and Sharon like spending time together. Often Jessie meets Sharon at her room to walk together to the activities hall. Jessie has expressed interest in wanting to hold Sharon's hand while sitting together during mealtimes or watching television in the common room.

1. What are the potential risks that Sharon should consider when deciding whether to hold hands with Jessie?
2. What are the potential benefits that Sharon should consider when deciding to hold hands or not to hold hands?
3. What could Sharon do if she does not want to hold hands with Jessie?

4. How does Sharon weigh the risks and benefits of deciding whether to hold hands with Jessie? What personal values and experiences should she consider in this decision?

In the next story, Steven and Pearl are two residents at a nursing home. During movie night, Steven and Pearl kiss and cuddle on the couch in the common room. After the movie, Pearl is thinking about asking Steven to accompany her back to her room to continue kissing.

1. What are the potential risks that Pearl should consider when deciding whether to invite Steven back to her room?
2. What are the potential benefits that Pearl should consider when deciding to whether invite Steven back to her room?
3. How would Pearl know if Steven did not want to accompany her back to her room?
4. How does Pearl weigh the risks and benefits of inviting Steven to her room? What personal values and experiences should she consider in this decision?

Finally, Gary and Bea are two residents at a nursing home. Gary and Bea have been spending a lot of time together and are thinking about taking their relationship to the next level. One night Gary tells Bea he would like to have sex with her.

1. What are the potential risks that Bea should consider when deciding whether to have sex with Gary?
2. What are the potential benefits that Bea should consider when deciding whether to have sex with Gary?
3. What should Bea do if she does not want to have sex with Gary?
4. How does Bea make the decision to engage in sexual relations with Gary? How would she weigh the risks and benefits of deciding whether to have sex with Gary? What personal values and experiences should she consider in this decision?

APPENDIX 9.3
CONTINUUM OF SEXUAL BEHAVIORS

Hand-holding
Hugging
Kissing on cheek
Kissing on lips
Kissing with tongue
Touching leg
Touching buttocks

Touching breasts
Touching crotch area
Giving oral sex
Receiving oral sex
Intercourse (having sex)

REFERENCES

American Bar Association and American Psychological Association Assessment of Capacity in Older Adults Project Working Group. (2008). *Assessment of older adults with diminished capacity: A handbook for psychologists*. Washington, DC: American Bar Association and American Psychological Association.

American Psychological Association. (2017). *Ethical principles of psychologists and code of conduct* (2002, Amended June 1, 2010 and January 1, 2017). Washington, DC: American Psychological Association.

Appelbaum, P. S., Lidz, C. W., & Klitzman, R. (2009). Voluntariness of consent to research: A preliminary empirical investigation. *IRB: Ethics & Human Research, 31*, 10–14.

Army Individual Test Battery. (1944). *Manual of directions and scoring*. Washington, DC: War Department, Adjutant General's Office.

Benedict, R. H. B., Schretlen, D. S., Groninger, L., & Brandt, J. (1998). Hopkins Verbal Learning Test—Revised: Normative data and analysis of inter-form and test–retest reliability. *Clinical Neuropsychologist, 12*, 43–55. http://dx.doi.org/10.1076/clin.12.1.43.1726

Benton, A. L., & Hamsher, K. (1976). *Manual for Multilingual Aphasia Examination*. Iowa City: University of Iowa.

Brandt, J. (1991). The Hopkins Verbal Learning Test: Development of a new memory test with six equivalent forms. *Clinical Neuropsychologist, 5*, 125–142. http://dx.doi.org/10.1080/13854049108403297

Buckley, P. F. (Ed.). (2013). *Sexuality and serious mental illness*. New York, NY: Routledge.

Centers for Disease Control and Prevention. (2014). *Long-term care providers and users in the United States*. Retrieved from https://www.cdc.gov/nchs/data/series/sr_03/sr03_038.pdf

Doll, G. A. (2012). *Sexuality and long-term care: Understanding and supporting the needs of older adults*. Baltimore, MD: Health Professions Press.

Doll, G. M. (2013). Sexuality in nursing homes: Practice and policy. *Journal of Gerontological Nursing, 39*(7), 30–37. http://dx.doi.org/10.3928/00989134-20130418-01

Family Caregiver Alliance. (2015). *Selected long-term care statistics*. Retrieved from https://www.caregiver.org/selected-long-term-care-statistics

Hebrew Home at Riverdale. (2013). *Policies and procedures concerning sexual expression at The Hebrew Home at Riverdale*. Retrieved from https://ltcombudsman.org/uploads/files/issues/Sexual_Expression_PP-Hebrew_Home.pdf

Hill, E. (2014). We'll always have Shady Pines: Surrogate decision-making tools for preserving sexual autonomy in elderly nursing home residents. *William & Mary Journal of Women and the Law, 20*, 469–490.

Hillman, J. (2016). Sexual consent capacity among older adults in long term care: An approach to assessment. *Journal of Gerontology & Geriatric Research, 5*(5), 10–12. http://dx.doi.org/10.4172/2167-7182.1000346

Hillman, J. (2017). Sexual consent capacity: Ethical issues and challenges in long-term care. *Clinical Gerontologist, 40*(1), 43–50. http://dx.doi.org/10.1080/07317115.2016.1185488

Kennedy, C. H., & Niederbuhl, J. (2001). Establishing criteria for sexual consent capacity. *American Journal of Mental Retardation, 106,* 503–510. http://dx.doi.org/10.1352/0895-8017(2001)106<0503:ECFSCC>2.0.CO;2

Lichtenberg, P. A. (2014). Sexuality and physical intimacy in long-term care. *Occupational Therapy in Health Care, 28*(1), 42–50. http://dx.doi.org/10.3109/07380577.2013.865858

Lichtenberg, P. A., & Strzepek, D. M. (1990). Assessments of institutionalized dementia patients' competencies to participate in intimate relationships. *The Gerontologist, 30,* 117–120. http://dx.doi.org/10.1093/geront/30.1.117

Lyden, M. (2007). Assessment of sexual consent capacity. *Sexuality and Disability, 25*(1), 3–20. http://dx.doi.org/10.1007/s11195-006-9028-2

Moye, J. (2003). Guardianship and conservatorship. In T. Grisso (Ed.), *Evaluating competencies: Forensic assessments and instruments* (2nd ed., pp. 391–460). New York, NY: Kluwer Academic.

Moye, J., Butz, S. W., Marson, D. C., Wood, E., & the ABA/APA Capacity Assessment of Older Adults Working Group. (2007). A conceptual model and assessment template for capacity evaluation in adult guardianship. *The Gerontologist, 47,* 591–603. http://dx.doi.org/10.1093/geront/47.5.591

Nasreddine, Z. S., Phillips, N. A., Bédirian, V., Charbonneau, S., Whitehead, V., Collin, I., . . . Chertkow, H. (2005). The Montreal Cognitive Assessment, MoCA: A brief screening tool for mild cognitive impairment. *Journal of the American Geriatrics Society, 53,* 695–699. http://dx.doi.org/10.1111/j.1532-5415.2005.53221.x

Roth, L. H., Meisel, A., & Lidz, C. W. (1977). Tests of competency to consent to treatment. *The American Journal of Psychiatry, 134,* 279–284. http://dx.doi.org/10.1176/ajp.134.3.279

Royall, D. R., Mahurin, R. K., & Gray, K. F. (1992). Bedside assessment of executive cognitive impairment: The executive interview. *Journal of the American Geriatrics Society, 40,* 1221–1226. http://dx.doi.org/10.1111/j.1532-5415.1992.tb03646.x

Sales, B. D., Miller, M. O., & Hall, S. R. (2005). *Laws affecting clinical practice.* Washington, DC: American Psychological Association. http://dx.doi.org/10.1037/11218-000

Schmidt, C., Collette, F., Cajochen, C., & Peigneux, P. (2007). A time to think: Circadian rhythms in human cognition. *Cognitive Neuropsychology, 24,* 755–789. http://dx.doi.org/10.1080/02643290701754158

Simpson, P., Horne, M., Brown, L. J. E., Wilson, C. B., Dickinson, T., & Torkington, K. (2017). Old(er) care home residents and sexual/intimate citizenship. *Ageing & Society, 37,* 243–265. http://dx.doi.org/10.1017/S0144686X15001105

Solway, E., Clark, S., Singer, D., Kirch, M., & Malani, P. (2018, May 3). *Let's talk about sex: National poll on healthy aging.* Retrieved from https://www.healthyagingpoll.org/sites/default/files/2018-05/NPHA-Sexual-Health-Report_050118_final2.pdf

Syme, M. L., Lichtenberg, P., & Moye, J. (2016). Recommendations for sexual expression management in long-term care: A qualitative needs assessment. *Journal of Advanced Nursing, 72,* 2457–2467. http://dx.doi.org/10.1111/jan.13005

Syme, M. L., & Steele, D. (2016). Sexual consent capacity assessment with older adults. *Archives of Clinical Neuropsychology, 31,* 495–505. http://dx.doi.org/10.1093/arclin/acw046

Tang, S. (2015). When yes might mean no: Standardizing state criteria to evaluate the capacity to consent to sexual activity for elderly with neurocognitive disorders. *The Elder Law Journal, 22,* 449–490.

Tarzia, L., Fetherstonhaugh, D., & Bauer, M. (2012). Dementia, sexuality and consent in residential aged care facilities. *Journal of Medical Ethics, 38,* 609–613. http://dx.doi.org/10.1136/medethics-2011-100453

Wechsler, D. (1997a). *WAIS–III Wechsler Adult Intelligence Scale* (3rd ed.). San Antonio, TX: The Psychological Corporation.

Wechsler, D. (1997b). *WMS–III Wechsler Memory Scale* (3rd ed.). San Antonio, TX: The Psychological Corporation.

Wertheimer, A. (2003). *Consent to sexual relations* (Cambridge Studies in Philosophy and Law). Cambridge, England: Cambridge University Press.

Wilkins, J. M. (2015). More than capacity: Alternatives for sexual decision making for individuals with dementia. *The Gerontologist, 55,* 716–723. http://dx.doi.org/10.1093/geront/gnv098

Zimmerman, S., Sloane, P. D., & Reed, D. (2014). Dementia prevalence and care in assisted living. *Health Affairs, 33,* 658–666. http://dx.doi.org/10.1377/hlthaff.2013.1255

10

Assessment of Capacity in Medical Aid in Dying

Brian D. Carpenter and C. Caroline Merz

KEY POINTS

- Capacity evaluations for medical aid in dying are required only if a physician who has received a request for a lethal prescription suspects a patient's judgment may be impaired.
- Although no empirically based instruments or protocols are available to evaluate capacity in the context of medical aid in dying, clinicians can reasonably adapt instruments used in other capacity contexts and can rely on guidelines constructed recently by state psychological associations and hospitals.
- The ultimate question for the mental health professional is: Does the patient have the capacity to request a prescription to take by themselves to end their life?
- As in other contexts, capacity is based on four standards the patient must demonstrate: understanding, appreciation, reasoning, and the ability to communicate a choice.
- Data for evaluating capacity can come from multiple sources, including the patient, care partners, medical providers, medical records, and previous expressions of the patient's values and preferences (e.g., advance directives).

http://dx.doi.org/10.1037/0000184-011
Assessing Capacities of Older Adults: A Casebook to Guide Difficult Decisions, J. Moye (Editor)

- The final, written capacity determination should state directly whether the patient has capacity to request medical aid in dying, at the particular moment of evaluation, and acknowledge that capacity for that decision could fluctuate as health status changes.

DEFINITION OF THE ISSUE

Medical aid in dying (MAID) occurs when an individual asks a physician to write a prescription for lethal medication they can take to end their life. Where MAID is currently legal in the United States, the individual must be over age 18, mentally capable, and have a terminal illness with less than 6 months to live. The individual's terminal condition and prognosis must be independently confirmed by two physicians, and in most locations, the patient must make multiple verbal or written requests (or both) separated by several days. Once the physician has provided the written prescription, the individual must administer it without assistance from other people.

MAID is sometimes also referred to as *physician aid in dying* or *physician-assisted death* or *suicide*. MAID is distinct from related concepts such as *euthanasia*, in which a physician actively administers a lethal dose of medication at the request of the patient, and *voluntary stopping of eating and drinking* (VSED), which a patient initiates to hasten death intentionally. MAID is currently legal by legislation in nine U.S. states and territories (California, Colorado, District of Columbia, Hawaii, Maine, New Jersey, Oregon, Washington, and Vermont) and by state Supreme Court ruling in Montana. MAID and other methods of voluntarily ending life have been legal longer in other countries, such as Switzerland, the Netherlands, and Colombia. For a review of current MAID and related practices in the United States, Canada, and Europe, see a summary by Emanuel, Onwuteaka-Philipsen, Urwin, and Cohen (2016), although we caution readers that the legal landscape is changing rapidly.

As noted earlier, individuals qualify for MAID if they meet certain criteria, including having the capacity to request the prescription from their physician. According to statute, if physicians suspect that a patient may not be capable of making and communicating an informed health care decision for MAID, they are required to refer the patient to a mental health provider for an evaluation. To establish capacity, licensed psychologists, along with psychiatrists and other mental health professionals (depending on the location), must determine that a psychiatric or psychological illness is not causing impaired judgment.

Before turning to the clinical issues that arise in a capacity evaluation for MAID, we first highlight the context in which MAID requests typically unfold. That context is broad compared with what might be encountered in more narrow capacity situations, such as making a choice about a circumscribed

FIGURE 10.1. The Multilevel Context in Which Medical Aid in Dying Requests Unfold

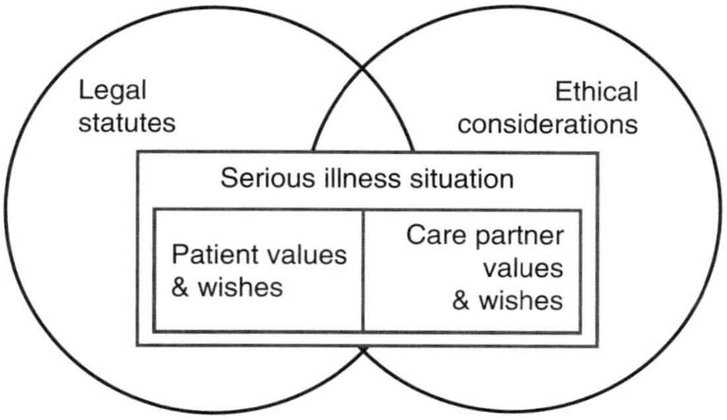

surgical or pharmacological intervention, because the outcome of MAID is dramatic (i.e., a person dies) and because its practice involves many other individuals and institutions (e.g., family members, health care providers and organizations, and state legislatures who decide whether it is legal).

Figure 10.1 depicts the broad context in which MAID requests are positioned. MAID requests have influences and implications at several levels. Serious and complex ethical issues arise when allowing people to end their lives, and the extensive legal requirements for MAID are a reflection of that seriousness. In practice, of course, MAID is the choice of an individual—an individual with a serious, life-limiting illness. The choice to end life via MAID occurs within the context of these individuals' experience of serious illness: the course of their illness, their symptoms, the treatments they have tried or refused, their prognosis, and their previous experience with illness, in themselves and observed in others. The choice for MAID also emerges from their personal values regarding the meaning of life, idiosyncratic definitions of quality of life, and personal wishes about how the end of their life will transpire. Such individuals are often (although not always) experiencing their illness alongside family members and other care partners, who have their own values, beliefs, and wishes. In sum, MAID occurs within a rich set of interrelated histories and beliefs.

CONSTITUENCIES INVOLVED IN THE PRACTICE

In this section, we discuss the characteristics of patients who may request MAID and how these vary across jurisdictions. We also describe the roles of other stakeholders in the process, including family and caregivers, health care providers, health systems, and insurers.

People Requesting MAID

Locations vary in their reporting requirements about MAID, and the policy is relatively new in most states, which means that characteristics of the people who request MAID are scarce. Summarizing the data that do exist, MAID is requested by proportionally very few people among all those with terminal illness in the locations where it is legal, and the number of people referred for a mental health evaluation is a very small proportion of that very small number. As examples, in 2017, in Oregon 218 prescriptions were written for people requesting MAID and five of those were referred for mental health evaluation (Oregon Health Authority, 2018). In Washington, 212 prescriptions were written and four people were referred for a mental health evaluation (Washington State Department of Health, 2018). Of note, neither state reports the number of people who were denied a prescription after their evaluation.

The majority of people who make use of MAID are over 65 years old, White, and their most common underlying terminal illness is cancer, followed by amyotrophic lateral sclerosis. Few data exist documenting the voices of actual patients requesting and participating in MAID. One study with 56 patients in Oregon revealed that their primary reasons for requesting MAID were to enhance their sense of control over their death and avoid dependence on others (Ganzini, Goy, & Dobscha, 2009). Furthermore, patients reported being more motivated to request MAID due to worries about symptoms they could experience in the future, not symptoms they were experiencing at the time of the request.

Family and Care Partners

Family members, friends, and other care partners are often involved when a person is dying. Their attitude toward MAID, their knowledge about the practice, and even their awareness of the patient's interest in MAID may vary. In many locations, the physician writing the MAID prescription can ask that the patient inform family members about the prescription request, although patients are not under any obligation to do so. When they do speak to their family, there is the potential for conflict if there is a difference of opinion about MAID's appropriateness, timing, or morality, although anecdotal reports suggest these conflicts are rare. Mental health professionals asked to conduct a capacity evaluation may be interested in speaking with family and care partners to gain their perspective in matters related to the patient's capacity. In some cases, that might be possible, in others not, depending on availability and permission granted by the patient. As with other health care decisions, it is patients who have final say (assuming they have capacity).

Health Care Providers

Health care providers involved with the MAID process include a physician responsible for the care of the patient's underlying illness, an independent consulting physician who must verify the patient's clinical status, a mental health provider if there is a question about capacity, and, if a prescription is written, a pharmacist to fill it. In the two states that track and release data on the length of the relationship between the patient and their attending physician (Oregon and Washington), there is wide variability (1 week to 38 years in Oregon, less than 25 weeks to 1 year or more in Washington). No formal training is required to help physicians prepare to address MAID requests, although educational modules are posted on some states' Department of Health websites (e.g., https://dchealth.dc.gov/page/death-dignity-act-2016). Given that MAID is an opt-in system for participation and no health care providers are required to participate in the practice, physicians can inform requesting patients that they do not write MAID prescriptions, although they should provide patients with information on where they might be able to access the service.

Health Systems

In all jurisdictions where it is legal, individual health care institutions can decide whether they will offer MAID. Thus, hospitals and medical centers must create institution-specific policies and procedures about how they will provide access to MAID and, if they do not, how they will nonetheless handle inquiries and requests. Institutional policies vary and may sometimes employ enhanced requirements for participation in MAID—for example, a mandatory mental health evaluation for all patients.

Insurers

Because there is no federal law permitting MAID, federal insurance programs such as Medicare and the Department of Veterans Affairs do not cover MAID costs. In contrast, most private health insurance providers do cover costs associated with MAID because it is an established medical practice that meets the standard of care (Grube & Cardenas, 2017). Reimbursement for provider visits associated with MAID are generally covered just like other medical visits. This holds true for the capacity assessment by a mental health professional. Laws stipulate that MAID participants have their underlying illness (the terminal illness that qualified them for MAID) listed as the cause of death on their death certificate. Therefore, participation in MAID does not affect death benefits.

CLINICAL METHODS

Various considerations are unique to MAID in the clinical setting, including ethical concerns and assessing capacity requirements. We describe steps in such a capacity evaluation, as well as pragmatic considerations.

Ethical Framework

Several elements of the American Psychological Association's (APA's; 2017) *Ethical Principles of Psychologists and Code of Conduct* are relevant to MAID. Broad principles of beneficence, nonmaleficence, responsibility, justice, and respect for dignity come into play as psychologists evaluate requests for MAID with individuals who are vulnerable due to their medical circumstances, pursuing an option that is ethically complex and still socially controversial. More directly, psychologists conducting MAID evaluations can find guidance in ethical standards regarding boundaries of competence, multiple relationships, confidentiality, and various assessment stipulations. For our specific discussion of capacity evaluations and MAID, we have adopted the Framework for Ethical Deliberation and Decision-Making in Public Health (Public Health Agency of Canada, 2017). As outlined in Table 10.1, this framework embraces four core ethical dimensions, and we have outlined implications of these dimensions for the actors directly involved in MAID and for the larger community. The framework also offers several procedural considerations which, when followed, could help build trust in MAID policies, enhance their legitimacy, and ensure effective implementation.

TABLE 10.1. Framework for Capacity Decisions in Medical Aid in Dying (MAID)

Ethical dimensions	
Respect for persons—recognition that all people have unconditional worth and value and therefore deserve consideration and respect	People with serious illness who have an interest in or request MAID deserve to have their concerns listened to and addressed, without judgment or stigmatization, just as the perspective of their care partners deserve their own attention and consideration.
	Autonomy is typically a foundation for this respect, but autonomy is not supreme. For example, a patient's right to request MAID (in locations where it is legal) does not command health care professionals to participate in the practice if it violates their personal or professional values. That includes mental health professionals asked to perform an evaluation.
Beneficence and nonmaleficence—obligation to promote the well-being of others, partnered with an obligation to avoid causing harm	MAID has the potential to promote well-being by giving individuals some control over the timing and circumstance of their death.
	At the same time, the practice should only be undertaken when there is no evidence of coercion or undue pressure.
Trust—confidence in the reliability, integrity, and good will of others and institutions	People seeking MAID need to have trust in the individuals from whom they seek information and assistance and faith that the practice follows procedures designed to protect their interests, monitored by public health officials.
	Health care professionals who assist people seeking MAID need to believe that they are protected by the law and institutions with oversight of the practice.
	Public trust in MAID is developed when officials are transparent in how the practice is administered, who uses it, and in outcomes, thereby creating a need for accessible, timely information about the policy and its practice.

TABLE 10.1. Framework for Capacity Decisions in Medical Aid in Dying (MAID) (*Continued*)

Justice—treating all people equally	Information about MAID should be available to all, and access should be available as long as individuals fulfill requirements, regardless of their personal characteristics or circumstances. At the same time, MAID should not be actively promoted in ways that might signal that some people or groups are less valued or respected.
Procedural considerations	
Accountability	Individuals who conduct MAID capacity evaluations have an obligation to be properly trained and to function free from bias and preordained judgments.
Inclusiveness	A MAID capacity evaluation includes input from both persons seeking MAID and their care partners (with the permission of the patient), with respect for the information and perspective provided by all parties and opportunities for all to offer support or opposition, as they like.
Responsibility	Mental health professionals have the legal authority to make judgments about an individual's capacity to request MAID. They also have the duty to act independently from the influence of others and the responsibility to follow professional standards in their work.
Responsiveness	Capacity judgments should be reconsidered as new information is made available, and all stakeholders should have the opportunity to voice their concerns regarding final decisions.
Transparency	Persons requesting MAID have the right to timely, complete information about the outcome of an evaluation, the reason for the decision, and what criteria were applied.

Note. Data from the Public Health Agency of Canada (2017).

Intersection of Standards for Capacity and Legal Statutes

In this chapter, we rely on a previously articulated set of standards for determining capacity, outlined by a joint publication of the American Bar Association (ABA) and the APA (2008) and consistent with a well-accepted formulation of capacity requirements (Grisso & Appelbaum, 1998).

Later in the chapter, we explain what questions might be asked to establish each of those four standards when a person has requested MAID. First, however, it is worth examining how those standards are reflected in the statutes that call for capacity evaluations.

As of September 2019, the nine locations in the United States where MAID is legal per statute are California (End of Life Option Act of 2015), Colorado

Standards for Determining Capacity

1. Does the individual have an *understanding* of the facts of the situation?
2. Does the individual have an *appreciation* for what the request means for him or her?
3. Can the individual *reason* about his or her circumstances and choices?
4. Can the individual *express a choice* about what is desired?

(Colorado End-of-Life Options Act of 2016), the District of Columbia (Death With Dignity Act of 2016), Hawaii (Our Care Our Choice Act of 2018), Maine (Maine Death With Dignity Act of 2019), New Jersey (Medical Aid in Dying for the Terminally Ill Act of 2009), Oregon (Oregon Death With Dignity Act of 1997), Vermont (Patient Choice and Control at End of Life Act of 2013), and Washington (Washington Death With Dignity Act of 2009). In Montana, MAID has not been codified into state law, but the state Supreme Court ruled that nothing in state law prohibits a physician from honoring a terminally ill, mentally competent patient's request to have a medication to hasten their death. No requirements for establishing mental competency have been established (*Baxter v. Montana*, 2009).

A careful reading of the statutes reveals that the legislation in each location defines the focus of the capacity question slightly differently: The patient is "not suffering from a psychiatric or psychological disorder or depression causing impaired judgment" (Maine, New Jersey, Oregon, and Washington), the patient is "capable and did not have impaired judgment" (Vermont), "the individual has the capacity to make medical decisions and is not suffering from impaired judgment due to a mental disorder" (California), "the individual is mentally capable and making an informed decision" (Colorado), "patient has the ability to make and communicate health care decisions to health care providers" (District of Columbia). How do these statutes map onto the four capacity standards? Not always explicitly, but in our opinion, consistently with well-accepted formulations of capacity (ABA/APA, 2008; Grisso & Appelbaum, 1998).

When statutes refer to an individual's "ability to make decisions," this seems to encapsulate both the individuals' ability to understand their situation and reason through their rationale for choosing MAID. Consequently, a written capacity evaluation could address that element of a statute by referencing an individual's cognitive impairments, level of insight, and the absence of coherent logic to his statements. The following is an example:

> The patient's ability to make decisions is impaired because he does not understand that his physicians believe the trajectory of his congestive heart failure is

> unpredictable and the disease may result in his death, though the timing is not certain. In addition, when reasoning about his request for MAID, he cannot formulate questions for his health care team to gather information, and he cannot remember basic facts about his medical situation. When asked to list the pros and cons of choosing MAID, he offers vague, imprecise statements.

When statutes mention "impaired judgment," that seems most aligned with the individual's ability to appreciate the personal implications of choosing MAID. A written capacity evaluation could address that element of a statute by referencing the individual's ability to reference personal values and the values of others as a foundation for his choice. For example,

> The patient has intact judgment as demonstrated by his ability to explain why he is considering MAID and how that option is consistent with the importance of autonomy and independence he has held throughout his life. In addition, his judgment reflects his ability to understand the opinion of his wife and children, that they have some ambivalence about his decision but have agreed to support him.

And when statutes reference an individual's ability to "communicate" a decision, it relates to the ability to express a choice, relaying their wish to their health care provider. In their evaluation, the mental health professional could address this element with a statement such as the following:

> Further evidence that the patient is not capable of choosing MAID is demonstrated by his inability to express his choice. At the time of the first evaluation he changed his opinion several times when asked to state whether he wanted MAID, and at the second appointment he was too somnolent and disoriented to speak or write.

When statutes refer to the presence of a psychiatric or psychological disorder, it is always to ensure that the disorder is not causing "impaired judgment," which we addressed earlier. (As a point of precision, some statutes reference depression individually, although it is, of course, a psychiatric/psychological disorder.) The written capacity evaluation should address the presence or absence of any disorder (e.g., "The patient has some mild symptoms of depression but they are not sufficient in number or severity to represent a psychological disorder such as major depressive disorder") and its impact on judgment (e.g., "The patient's long-standing obsessive-compulsive disorder and illness anxiety disorder interfere with his ability to reason about pain and its management, formulate treatment choices that are backed up by comprehensible arguments, and consider options other than MAID").

Steps in the Capacity Assessment

Capacity evaluations in cases of requests for MAID represent an emerging area of mental health practice, with few guidelines for providers, and none that have been empirically validated as of this writing. Clinicians are crafting best practices in response to a rapid evolution of public opinion, ethical and practice debates, and a shifting legislative landscape. For this chapter, we have synthesized several efforts to articulate what a sound capacity evaluation might look like in this situation. These include an early set of standards crafted by Werth and colleagues (2000), guidelines constructed by the California Psychological Association (California Psychological Association End of Life Option Act Work Group, 2017), and the Washington State Psychological Association (2009) to help professionals in those states, a recent brief published by the American Academy of Hospice and Palliative Medicine (n.d.), and a standardized protocol developed by the Department of Psychiatry at the University of California, San Francisco Medical Center (Bourgeois et al., 2018). The issue continues to evolve, however, and readers should understand that this chapter will likely need updating as public policy and professional opinion moves forward.

When evaluating the capacity for making a MAID request, mental health professionals can review and adapt materials that exist for assessing capacity in other clinical situations. Although there are no standardized, validated tools to assess capacity in this particular situation (and no instruments validated with a normative group of terminally ill patients), the overarching issues are similar. The capacity to request a life-ending prescription is parallel to agreeing to take any kind of medication, receive a treatment, or undertake a medical procedure. However, the consequences are more certain and more final, and the request originates with the patient rather than the clinician. Still, the underlying features of informed consent that a patient must demonstrate are the same.

Several pragmatic considerations are important. Because these kinds of evaluations are, by definition, conducted with patients who have serious, life-limiting illness, mental health professionals should consider possible constraints on the patient's time and energy. Patients are likely to be quite ill, and some may have limited tolerance for lengthy conversations. Mental health professionals should strive to maximize the patient's involvement and ability to participate fully in the assessment. That means coordinating the timing of conversations to coincide with the patient's optimal energy level, symptom control, and appointment schedule. It also involves having conversations in a setting that is quiet and private to the extent possible and making sure that the patient has access to eyeglasses, hearing aids, and communication aids. Frequent breaks might be needed. Other efforts to support the individual's decision-making could include providing information both verbally and in writing to reduce the demand on memory, repeating information as needed, and probing for comprehension to ensure understanding. Finally, efforts should be undertaken to ensure that the individual trusts the evaluator and feels assured that this professional can represent his or her interests. If the individual requesting MAID does not have faith in the mental health professional's motives or experience, referral to a different clinician should be offered.

The following are steps in the capacity evaluation:

STEPS IN THE CAPACITY EVALUATION

Step 1: Physician initiates the capacity referral.
Step 2: Mental health professional considers his or her own qualifications.
Step 3: Mental health professional interviews the individual making the request.
Step 4: Review medical records.
Step 5: Gather information from other sources.
Step 6: Determine capacity and summarize findings.
Step 7: Complete required documentation and communicate findings.

Step 1: Physician initiates the capacity referral. Patients are referred to a mental health professional when their physician has some question about whether the patient requesting MAID has a mental illness or other condition that impairs judgment (specific requirements for referral vary by location). In reality, physicians making the referral have diverse levels of expertise in making that determination. Some physicians may err on the side of caution and refer any patient with the slightest suggestion of impaired judgment; upon evaluation, some of these cases will turn out to be "false positives" (i.e., patient's capacity turns out not to be impaired despite the physician's initial doubts) and some will turn out to be "true positives" (i.e., patient capacity is impaired). In other situations, the physician may refer because the clinical picture is genuinely muddy, and the skill of the mental health professional is needed to make a capacity determination. All this is to say that mental health professionals can expect to see patients who are clearly impaired, patients whose impairment is subtle and complex, and patients who are not impaired but nonetheless deserve the same thorough evaluation as all patients. We also recommend that mental health professionals provide feedback to referring physicians, using the results of their evaluation to educate physicians about capacity determinations and help them hone their skills in identifying patients whose judgment may be questionable.

Step 2: Mental health professional considers their own qualifications. Before agreeing to and undertaking this kind of capacity assessment, a mental health professional should consider whether she has the requisite attitudes, knowledge, and skills to undertake the evaluation. Table 10.2 outlines questions for clinicians.

Step 3: Mental health professional interviews the individual making the request. At the beginning of a conversation with the patient, the mental health professional should gain consent to conduct the evaluation. Consent should involve explaining the purpose of the assessment and the process, including how and with whom results will be shared and the risks associated with agreeing to the evaluation, which includes the possibility that the evaluation may result in a

TABLE 10.2. Questions Mental Health Professionals Should Consider Before Agreeing to Conduct a Medical Aid in Dying Capacity Evaluation

Self-assessment question	Responses that would affirm ability to conduct the evaluation
Do I have the appropriate credentials, knowledge, and skills to conduct the assessment?	Licensed psychiatrist or psychologist (in Vermont, also social worker). Knowledgeable about mental health in the context of serious illness, issues in evaluating thoughts of self-harm versus a desire for hastened death, and approaches and tools in evaluating capacity. Training and experience conducting capacity evaluations.
To the extent possible given the circumstances, am I free of any other professional or personal relationships with the patient?	Have not conducted prior assessments or psychotherapy with the patient or member of the patient's family. Have no other personal relationship with the patient or member of the patient's family. In some circumstances when prior professional and current personal relationships are unavoidable (e.g., rural settings with few other providers available), the mental health professional takes steps to minimize the influence of these other relationships by seeking consultation and input from other providers.
Can I be objective in my assessment, considering my beliefs and values about related issues?	Make the effort to reflect on and understand own attitudes about living with serious illness, quality of life, autonomy, suicide, and thoughts about dying and death, among other relevant issues. Be aware of research that has documented biases in clinical judgment making based on factors that include, but are not limited to, gender, racial concordance, and liking of patients. Strive to remain objective when conducting the capacity evaluation by continuously evaluating the impact of own attitudes on judgments and decisions. Seek consultation and corroboration from another mental health professional to affirm objectivity, to the extent possible.

determination that the individual does not have capacity to request MAID. The mental health professional should also gain permission to talk with other relevant people (e.g., family, friends, health care providers), gain permission to review additional information (e.g., medical records, advance directives), and answer any questions the patient may have prior to beginning.

In the process of talking with the individual making the request, in addition to establishing the individual's capacity, a related consideration has to do with whether the person is making the request for MAID freely, without coercion by other people. This element of a patient's decision is related to, but distinct from, other factors that could more obviously impair capacity, such as cognitive limitations. Nonetheless, the mental health professional should be attuned to any indication that the patient feels pressure to choose

MAID. Real or perceived coercion could be based in family dynamics (e.g., an adult child with culturally sanctioned authority), influence (e.g., a domineering, demanding spouse), and circumstances (e.g., a patient believes the financial resources required for his care impose a burden on his family). Pressure to end one's life could also come from more systemic influences, such as social and cultural beliefs regarding the "value" of different kinds of lives (e.g., people with disabilities). Indeed, some authors have suggested that when people have spent their entire life bombarded by messages about their lesser value, they are inherently unable to make a rational choice to end their life (see Gill, 1999).

In the process of asking individuals about their choice to pursue MAID, it is important to inquire about several other topics related to this choice. These include *spiritual and faith beliefs* that might be part of the patient's deliberations; *cultural, racial, and ethnic identities* that might be important in how the patient views herself and her circumstances; and other *individual characteristics* (sexual identity, ability status, socioeconomic resources) that could have an impact on how the patient weighs her options.

Again, the overarching goal of the evaluation is to determine whether the individual has capacity to request MAID; that is, whether the person fulfills the four standards for capacity (i.e., understanding, appreciation, reasoning, communication). In Table 10.3, we outline potential questions that can help a mental health professional establish capacity based on the four standards (ABA/APA, 2008; Grisso & Appelbaum, 1998). Note that many of these questions go well beyond the discrete request for MAID and assess an individual's understanding and appreciation for related features of the situation, as suggested in other recommendations for assessing MAID requests.

Psychological testing with standardized instruments may help the mental health professional identify symptoms that could affect capacity, measure their severity in a relatively objective manner, and support clinical opinion with standardized tools. These instruments include screening tools (e.g., Montreal Cognitive Assessment, Nasreddine et al., 2005), Patient Health Questionnaire (PHQ–9; Kroenke, Spitzer, & Williams, 2001), diagnostic interviews for mental disorders (e.g., Diagnostic Interview for Anxiety, Mood, and OCD and Related Neuropsychiatric Disorders; Tolin et al., 2018; Structured Clinical Interview for *DSM–5* Disorders; First, Williams, Karg, & Spitzer, 2015), discrete neuropsychological tests or batteries (e.g., Halstead–Reitan Neuropsychological Battery; Reitan, 1985), and instruments specifically designed to assess capacity (e.g., Assessment of the Capacity to Consent to Treatment; Moye et al., 2007; MacArthur Competency Assessment Tool; Grisso & Appelbaum, 1998). A more extensive list of consent instruments, along with their psychometric properties (when available) appears in the capacity handbook compiled by the ABA/APA (2008), specifically Appendices B through E. Mental health professionals are encouraged to use these instruments with caution because none were developed or normed specifically for people with serious illness at the end of life.

TABLE 10.3. Topic Areas for Exploration to Determine Capacity

Capacity standard	Areas of inquiry
Do individuals have an *understanding* of the facts of the situation?	Do patients know their medical diagnoses? Do patients understand the implications of those diagnoses and what they mean for their health and functioning moving forward?
	Do patients know their prognosis? How long are they expected to live if they continue treatment, pursue alternative treatments, stop treatment, withdraw life-sustaining treatments, etc.? What is the likely trajectory of patients' condition and symptoms over that time? What can they expect to experience as the end of life approaches?
	Do patients know what approaches are available to help manage their symptoms, including pain, constipation, nausea, dyspnea, and other physical symptoms, and also anxiety and emotional distress?
	Are patients aware of resources available to them, which could include health care services, home care and support services, spiritual resources, financial support, transportation, and housing options?
	Do patients understand the logistics of obtaining and using a medical aid in dying (MAID) prescription? What are their financial and logistical responsibilities? What will happen if they take the medication? What will happen if they do not?
Do individuals have an *appreciation* for what the requests mean for them?	Can patients describe why they have considered MAID as an option? What is it about the circumstances that make MAID appealing? What do patients hope to address or avoid with the option? Could such issues be addressed or avoided through other means?
	How is patients' choice consistent with the values they have held throughout their life? What do they believe about quality versus quantity of life for themselves? Are there states they would consider "worse than death"? If the request for MAID seems inconsistent with prior values, how do patients explain their change of mind?
	Are patients experiencing acute psychiatric symptoms (e.g., delusions, hallucinations, severe depression-related cognitive distortions) that interfere with the ability to comprehend alternatives to MAID or MAID's consequences?
	Are patients aware of the attitudes and opinions of other people involved in their situation? Do they understand what the healthcare team has recommended? Do they know what important family members and friends think? Can they understand why these people might support or oppose their choice?
	Can patients describe how this choice is consistent with their values and preferences?

TABLE 10.3. Topic Areas for Exploration to Determine Capacity (*Continued*)

Capacity standard	Areas of inquiry
Can individuals *reason* about their circumstances and choices?	Do patients have the ability to absorb, remember, and comprehend information provided by health care team members and care partners? Do they have impairments in memory, attention, comprehension, executive function, or other cognitive abilities that interfere with reasoning? Can patients formulate well-reasoned questions to gather additional information? Can patients think through arguments and opinions, weighing pros and cons? Can patients state explanations for their decisions and choices that emerge logically from their thinking through of the situation?
Can individuals *express a choice* about what is desired?	Can patients communicate their preference, in writing, verbally, or in some other form? Is that same decision confirmed over time, both within the course of the evaluation and, ideally, separated by hours or days, if practical to assess? (Some statutes demand that patients make their request on at least two occasions, in most cases separated by 15–20 days.)

Note. Data from ABA/APA (2008) and Grisso and Appelbaum (1998).

An important note in this consideration of psychopathology: The presence of emotional distress (e.g., sadness, worthlessness, guilt, worry, fear) or a psychiatric syndrome does not in and of itself mean a patient lacks the capacity to choose MAID. Psychological disorders can interfere with judgment and reasoning when a patient's symptoms are so intense, severe, and persistent that they limit attention, concentration, and memory and when they inhibit rational consideration of alternatives, options, and arguments. However, some patients can experience emotional distress and yet still present a cogent case for why they are interested in MAID. Consider some of the examples in Table 10.4.

Step 4: Review medical records. Reviewed with the patient's permission, medical records can provide another source of information that corroborates reports from other people regarding the patient's clinical situation, treatment history and options, and previous conversations about end-of-life wishes. Professionals knowledgeable about pharmacology might also find a medication list useful to rule out the potential influence of medication side effects on cognitive functions.

Step 5: Gather information from other sources. Conversations with the patient's *health care providers* can provide information about the patient's clinical status; expected prognosis; treatments initiated, stopped, considered but not initiated, and initiated but not stopped; synopsis of previous conversations about MAID; and opinions about the patient's capacity. With careful questioning of

TABLE 10.4. Examples of Responses to Interview Questions and What They Could Imply About Capacity

Sample interview question	Response more likely to raise questions about capacity	Response less likely to raise questions about capacity
"Tell me about your medical situation. What about it has prompted you to think about asking for the prescription to end your life?"	*"Well, the doctors say they don't know for sure what's going on and what's left to try, so I'm maybe thinking this is the end of the road, and I don't have any choice."* Unclear whether patient understands their medical situation and what they have been told by their health care providers. Not an immediate indication of incapacity, but patient could use more education to see if they can gain understanding.	*"Well, they've tried all the chemotherapy and radiation options that are available, and I really don't want to try any experimental medications at this point. I want to leave this life under my own terms, how I want, and this seems like the best option to achieve that."* Patient appears to comprehend the lack of further treatment options and expresses a clear reason why medical aid in dying (MAID) is considered an option.
"I noticed that you filled out an advance directive, a living will, several years ago, and in that document, you said you wanted to receive all medical interventions possible if you were ever very sick. Your choice for this prescription seems different than what you were thinking back then. Can you tell me about that change in your opinion?"	*"I just think God takes you when it's your time. And I don't really understand all that paperwork. I filled out a lot of things, and I just know I want my savings to go to my daughter and my house to go to my son."* Patient makes vague reference to a religious belief but not in direct relation to care preferences. Also appears to confuse advance directive with other documents. Further inquiry about his logic would be advisable.	*"I filled that out years ago, when I was still healthy and I hadn't gone through all that I have. Back then I didn't know how bad a person could feel, how sick and uncomfortable. And I didn't know that the treatments can make you feel just as bad as the illness, or even worse. It's too bad, but now I know that medical treatments don't always work and can be pretty awful. So, my opinion has changed, and now I think there comes a point when you can do too much."* Patient acknowledges change in beliefs and articulates a clear, reasonable foundation for that change, consistent with his experience.
"Over the last 2 weeks, how often have you been bothered by thoughts that you would be better off dead, or of hurting yourself?"	*"All the time. I wake up at night afraid, crying, feeling so guilty at all I'm putting my family through. I'm exhausted, can't really concentrate, and I just know they're all stressed out and can't take much more. It would be better for them if I wasn't around anymore, if I just went to sleep and didn't wake up."* Patient's reasoning may be clouded by extreme fatigue or based on unfounded assumptions about the experience and opinions of family members. Wish to die is vague and passive rather than a clear, affirmative choice.	*"I'm thinking about the end of my life often. It's real, and I know it's going to happen. There's nothing I can do to avoid that. Sure, there are times when I really struggle, usually first thing in the morning. But not every day. And I still have bright spots in my days, seeing my family, listening to my music. But the hard parts are coming more often, and I want to end this while I still have the ability to do so."* Thoughts of death would be expected given the situation and patient realizes it. Thoughts of death do not appear to dominate the patient's thinking in a way that interferes with her ability to have positive experiences. Clear reason for choice is articulated.

other providers, mental health professionals may be able to glean some information about the patient's abilities relevant to capacity (i.e., understanding, appreciation, reasoning, communication).

Given their history with the patient, *family members, friends, and others* may be helpful in determining the extent to which the patient's request is consistent with historically expressed values and preferences. Previous conversations with the patient, either formal (e.g., while completing an advance directive) or informal (e.g., past dinner conversations or comments about a relative or case in the news), may provide insights into the patient's long-standing opinion about medical interventions and quality of life. On the basis of their recent interactions with the patient, these individuals can also provide information (albeit subjective) about the patient's psychological state, cognitive abilities, and the reasoning behind the request for MAID.

Some patients may have completed an *advance directive* outlining their preferences for end-of-life care (e.g., Five Wishes document, state-specific advance directive form, physician orders for life-sustaining treatment). Although these documents are unlikely to mention MAID specifically, they can provide a window into the patient's thinking about end-of-life care and whether the request for MAID is consistent with previously expressed opinions.

Step 6: Determine capacity and summarize findings. When writing a summary of findings, the mental health professional should assemble all information and analyze that information for consistency. Although professionals may have more or less certainty about a patient's capacity, the ultimate determination is dichotomous: The patient either does or does not have capacity to request MAID. However, in some cases the outcome may genuinely be unclear, and the mental health professional should be willing to accept that ambiguity, document reasons for it, and offer recommendations about what interventions (e.g., time, treatment) may be useful in clarifying the situation.

Throughout this process, one challenge for the evaluator is to keep in mind the distinction between what patients are choosing for themselves and what evaluators might want for themselves if they were in a similar situation. This requires self-awareness and an active mental questioning of oneself to note one's own attitude about MAID, setting that attitude aside, and focusing instead on what the patient is asking and how she is explaining it. A request for MAID may not be what the mental health professional would want, but that is beside the point; and if mental health professionals are unable to set aside their own beliefs, they are not in a position to conduct an objective assessment. Ultimately, it is not the choice to request medication that is the focus of the evaluation, but the *process of how* the patient came to that choice which reflects capacity.

Step 7: Complete required documentation and communicate findings. Locations vary in terms of the exact information that must appear in the capacity report, and some require completion of a specific form. A written summary of the evaluation should be provided to the patient and, with their permission, any power of attorney or guardian and relevant health care professionals.

Pragmatic Considerations

In addition to the issues outlined in the preceding text, mental health professionals might consider several other practicalities. First, all current laws ask the physician who has been asked for medication to "request" that patients tell family about their request—a recommendation to the patient, not a requirement. That could complicate the capacity evaluation if the patient chooses not to tell family and yet the mental health professional would like to speak with them. In most situations, the mental health professional should be able to assess a patient's capacity without talking with family, but if the professional feels the family has key information, talking with the patient about the reason for not disclosing his or her request can, at the very least, reveal something about the patient's logic and reasoning.

Second, in some patients, capacity may fluctuate *after* the mental health assessment has taken place but *before* the patient self-administers the medication. Therefore, in theory a patient could be rereferred. The consulting mental health professional may not be involved in the patient's care long enough to see these changes but should document its possibility and affirm the patient's capacity at the time of evaluation.

Third, at the time of this writing, MAID is requested by a relatively small number of patients each year, and an even smaller number of them are referred for a mental health assessment. Most mental health professionals are unlikely to gain frequent experience with this type of case. Similarly, the number of clinicians who have expertise conducting this kind of capacity evaluation is limited, as are opportunities for training. State professional organizations may be one source for information and consultation.

Fourth, professionals may encounter inconsistency between federal and state policies about MAID. For example, employees affiliated with the Veterans Health Administration (e.g., VA hospitals and clinics) are limited in what they can discuss about MAID with patients and how they may be involved in MAID cases because MAID is legal or illegal on a state-by-state basis. Therefore, professionals should educate themselves about both federal and state regulations and requirements.

A final, important recommendation is for mental health professionals to consider the impact on conducting these capacity evaluations on their work and emotional lives. Having a reputation in the professional community as someone who is prepared and willing to conduct MAID evaluations can be double-edged. Professionals (and patients) may be grateful to find someone with this expertise, but other colleagues who oppose the policy might judge the professional negatively. As in other ethically challenging situations, mental health professionals should also respect the emotional investment required in this work. They will encounter patients in extreme situations facing imminent mortality, care partners grieving and distressed in their own ways, and clinicians trying to identify and achieve an imperfect balance of quality and quantity of life for their patients. The mental health professional will have her own feelings about the situation and will need to stay attuned to those feelings and grounded in her professional responsibilities.

CASE EXAMPLE: MS. LOPATA

The case that follows presents one example of how a request for MAID might come about, the multiple parties involved in the patient's care and choice, and how a mental health professional might approach evaluating the patient's capacity and sharing feedback. The postscript to the case introduces additional complexities that could affect the process and outcome of MAID capacity evaluations.

Presentation

Ms. Melanie Lopata is a 63-year-old, married woman with Stage 4 appendiceal cancer.[1] A long-time resident of Vermont, Ms. Lopata has requested a prescription to end of her life under the Vermont Patient Choice and Control at the End of Life statute. Both her oncologist and a consulting physician, relatively new to the MAID process, had concerns about whether Ms. Lopata's emotional state was interfering with her judgment, and they referred her to Dr. Gordon, a licensed psychologist, for a mental health evaluation to determine her capacity to make this medical decision for herself.

History

Ms. Lopata has been married to her husband for 34 years and has two grown children, a son and a daughter, both in their 30s. Both of her children live nearby, and her daughter has two children. Ms. Lopata had begun planning retirement from her career as a high school math teacher, looking forward to this transition, when she turned 65. Her cancer was first detected 2 years ago, and shortly after diagnosis, she had cytoreductive surgery, followed by aggressive chemotherapy for 8 months. She responded well and experienced a return to health for 6 months, but she then developed ascites with severe bloating and abdominal pain. Investigation revealed that her cancer had recurred. She underwent three more rounds of chemotherapy, including a Phase 1 clinical trial (which precluded her admission to hospice) with limited benefit. Currently, she has periods of vomiting and significant edema in her lower extremities. She spends most of her time in bed and requires assistance

[1]The case example is not based on any one individual but rather an amalgamation of characteristics and experiences across many people, assembled for teaching purposes in this chapter. In the process, the identities of individuals have been disguised to protect their confidentiality.

with most activities of daily living. A palliative care consultation was requested, and the team recommended several adjustments to her medications for symptom management.

Ms. Lopata was recently admitted to the hospital because of an abdominal blockage, and her cancer has advanced rapidly. According to her physicians, Ms. Lopata's prognosis is not good, and their consensus is that she is likely to die within 6 months. A family meeting was offered, and Ms. Lopata agreed to let her husband attend but not her children. At that meeting, her medical team offered the option of placing a venting gastrostomy tube and starting total parenteral nutrition. The risks and benefits of that intervention were discussed, along with estimates about prognosis and the likely trajectory of her illness. Ms. Lopata became very emotional and tearful during the discussion. The palliative care social worker interceded, helped to calm her, and attempted to discuss goals of care, but Ms. Lopata became even more emotional, and the meeting was concluded.

The next day Ms. Lopata asked to speak to her physician. She said that given her limited treatment options, the expected rapid progression of her cancer, and her severe physical discomfort, she wanted her physician to write her a prescription to end her life. Although her physician thought she expressed clear reasons for her request, Ms. Lopata sobbed during the conversation and seemed very depressed to the physician, who had little training in mental health issues, worried that what he was hearing amounted to suicidal ideation. The physician also acknowledged that he had doubts himself about the ethics of MAID. Consequently, the physician referred Ms. Lopata for evaluation at the same time that he referred her to another physician to evaluate her request, as required by Vermont law.

Interview, Examination, and Tests

Dr. Gordon received a telephone call from Ms. Lopata's husband and, recognizing the time sensitivity of the referral, scheduled an appointment with her the next day in the hospital. Dr. Gordon explained the purpose of the evaluation, an outline of the information he would gather, and to whom results would be communicated. Ms. Lopata had no questions and signed the necessary consent and release of information forms. Her husband also gave Dr. Gordon a copy of her advance directive, which she had executed 2 years earlier. Using resources from the California and Washington State Psychological Association as a guide, Dr. Gordon conducted a lengthy interview with Ms. Lopata and, separately, with her husband, during which he inquired about her illness, treatments, prognosis, her personal and social history, vision for her future, and her request for MAID. Dr. Gordon also administered the PHQ–9. In the process, and as he listened to Ms. Lopata's responses to his questions, Dr. Gordon had in the back of his mind the four key elements of capacity (i.e., understanding, appreciation, reasoning, communication) he would need to comment on when making his final evaluation.

Dr. Gordon also spoke with Ms. Lopata's physician to learn more about her clinical situation.

Findings

Ms. Lopata scored 10 on the PHQ–9 but endorsed only three symptoms to the level of severity that they could possibly be considered indicative of a mood disorder: insomnia, fatigue, and poor appetite. These symptoms had been long-standing, had not changed recently, and according to her physician, were likely due to Ms. Lopata's underlying illness and treatments. The fourth depressive symptom that she endorsed, thoughts of being better off dead, she said occurred several days over the past 2 weeks. Upon further questioning, Ms. Lopata explained to Dr. Gordon that she was concerned about the pain and discomfort she had been experiencing, the possibility that it could go uncontrolled, and the distress she felt her ongoing suffering could cause her family members. She acknowledged feeling sad about her situation and foreshortened future, describing tearfully the future events in her family's lives she would not witness. But she further explained that she did not "think of MAID as suicide really, but a way to leave this life when I'm ready, on my own terms. I'm going to die anyway. It's just a matter of when and how."

Ms. Lopata provided a detailed and accurate history of her illness and treatments, consistent with what Dr. Gordon had learned from her physician. She could explain the nature of her illness, the treatment options available to her, and the reasons she was not interested in prolonging her life with these interventions. These reasons were concordant with the preferences and values she had expressed on her written advance directive. Knowledgeable about palliative care and hospice and their focus on symptom management, she nonetheless said she had requested MAID to "preserve some control over my body; so little has been in my control over the last few months, and I want this [MAID] to take back my life, even if that means to decide when it ends." Although sad about leaving her husband and children, Ms. Lopata said she had talked with them about her choice and felt they respected her wishes (her husband confirmed this). She understood that her choice would be difficult for them and that they would grieve significantly after she died, yet she believed that managing the timing of her death would enable her to have the kind of death that would limit their sorrow and perhaps create a death that would be a model for how to die in a dignified manner.

Throughout the conversation, in Dr. Gordon's professional opinion Ms. Lopata demonstrated the capacity to choose MAID. She was knowledgeable about her clinical situation (demonstrated *understanding*), could explain how her choice would affect the trajectory of her illness and speculate on its impact on her own psychological health and that of her family (*appreciation*), functioned with intact cognitive abilities (*reasoning*), and was able to express her choice independently and consistently. Although sad, Ms. Lopata's emotional state was not indicative of a mood disorder, and her desire for MAID reflected less of a desire for self-harm and more a wish for self-determination.

Supports

Dr. Gordon made several adjustments to optimize Ms. Lopata's participation in the evaluation. Because she was in a shared room in the hospital, Dr. Gordon found a small meeting room down the hall that would be quiet and private. He also made sure to visit Ms. Lopata in the early afternoon, right after she finished lunch, the time of day her husband said she was most alert and her symptoms seemed best managed. At the start of the evaluation, Dr. Gordon made sure Ms. Lopata had received her pain medication, had used the bathroom, and was feeling comfortable. Ms. Lopata preferred to stay in bed for the conversation, so Dr. Gordon conducted the evaluation bedside and provided large-print materials and a writing board on which Ms. Lopata could review papers and take notes if she wished. At one particularly emotional point in the evaluation, Dr. Gordon asked if Ms. Lopata would like to take a break, and he left her alone for a moment and returned with a glass of water, pacing the evaluation and showing respect of the difficulty of the conversation. At the close of the evaluation, with her permission, Dr. Gordon brought in her husband, reviewed his findings, answered their questions, and told the couple what he planned to convey to the medical team.

Interventions and Dispositions

Dr. Gordon prepared a written summary of his evaluation, had it scanned into Ms. Lopata's medical record, and spoke with her physician by telephone to explain the rationale for his findings.

Outcome

Ms. Lopata decided to forgo further treatment and was discharged home with hospice the next day. She received a prescription of lethal medications from her physician, which she filled at her usual pharmacy, and she kept the pills in her bedside table at home. The hospice team made several visits to her home in the ensuing days and despite best efforts, her physical symptoms continued to cause great discomfort. She had several days of relatively good health, spent with her husband and children at home, but her symptoms worsened, and one evening she gathered her family around her and took the lethal medication. She died later that evening, surrounded by her family, with the hospice nurse and social worker nearby for support. Dr. Gordon later learned about her death from her physician.

Postscript

Although objective data are sparse, anecdotal reports suggest that most people who request MAID do have capacity and receive the prescription they request (National Academies of Sciences, Engineering, and Medicine, 2018). Still, each case is unique and can include a variety of complexities. For example, despite her capacity to request and implement MAID, Ms. Lopata would have faced additional ethical and practical challenges if her husband or one of her children had been adamantly opposed to her request, perhaps even contesting Dr. Gordon's evaluation. Their opposition might not change Dr. Gordon's conclusions, but it certainly would complicate the situation for everyone involved. In another version of this case, Ms. Lopata might have endorsed more symptoms of depression on the PHQ–9, making it possible that depression was clouding her judgment. Had she expressed a more rigid belief that she was burdening her family contrary to their statements otherwise, reported excessive guilt that she was responsible for the situation, and made repeated statements that implied a profound hopelessness about the ability of her medical providers to manage her symptoms despite their success in the past, Dr. Gordon might have had reservations about her judgment. Less coherent and organized statements about the reason for her request and its significance for her care and impact on her family also might have raised questions for Dr. Gordon about her insight and reasoning. In all these possibilities, Dr. Gordon might have reached a different conclusion, with different implications for how he could communicate his decision to Ms. Lopata, her family, and her medical team.

REFLECTION

MAID has been long to evolve as public policy in the United States, and consequently, the role that health care providers play in the process has itself emerged somewhat piecemeal, particularly the role of mental health professionals evaluating capacity. Procedures and guidelines vary from state to state and institution to institution, and even then, they are sometimes quite general in what they recommend or imprecise in what they require. Therefore, mental health professionals who are interested in participating in MAID must largely educate themselves and rely on frequent consultation with other providers who may have more experience. Patients at the end of life who request MAID are at a critical point in their illness—indeed, their life—and careful, comprehensive, and objective professional services convey respect for their experience.

Over the past several years, public support for MAID has grown, and the practice has become legal in more locations, suggesting that professional organizations representing mental health professionals will need to address training and implementation more systematically. In the meantime, this chapter may be one resource that mental health professionals can use to guide their practice in this sensitive area.

REFERENCES

American Academy of Hospice and Palliative Medicine. (n.d.). *Advisory brief: Guidance on responding to requests for physician-assisted dying*. Retrieved from http://aahpm.org/positions/padbrief

American Bar Association and American Psychological Association Assessment of Capacity in Older Adults Project Working Group. (2008). *Assessment of older adults with diminished capacity: A handbook for psychologists*. Washington, DC: American Bar Association and American Psychological Association.

American Psychological Association. (2017). *Ethical principles of psychologists and code of conduct* (2002, Amended June 1, 2010 and January 1, 2017). Washington, DC: American Psychological Association.

Baxter v. Montana, MT DA 09-0051 2009 MT 449 (MT Supr. Ct. 2009).

Bourgeois, J. A., Mariano, M. T., Wilkins, J. M., Brendel, R. W., Kaplan, L., & Ganzini, L. (2018). Physician-assisted death psychiatric assessment: A standardized protocol to conform to the California End of Life Option Act. *Psychosomatics, 59*, 441–451. Advance online publication. http://dx.doi.org/10.1016/j.psym.2018.02.003

California Psychological Association End of Life Option Act Work Group. (July 14, 2017). *California's End of Life Option Act: CPA guidance for psychologists*. Sacramento: California Psychological Association. https://cdn.ymaws.com/www.cpapsych.org/resource/resmgr/DPA/EndOfLifeOptionAct.pdf

Colorado End-of-Life Options Act Article 48 of Title 25, C.R.S. (2016).

Death with Dignity Act, WA Statute c 70, s 245 RCW (2009).

Emanuel, E. J., Onwuteaka-Philipsen, B. D., Urwin, J. W., & Cohen, J. (2016). Attitudes and practices of euthanasia and physician-assisted suicide in the United States, Canada, and Europe. *Journal of the American Medical Association, 316*, 79–90. http://dx.doi.org/10.1001/jama.2016.8499

End of Life Option Act ABX2-15 (AB-15). (2015).

First, M. B., Williams, J. B. W., Karg, R. S., & Spitzer, R. L. (2015). *Structured Clinical Interview for DSM-5 Disorders, Clinician Version (SCID–5–CV)*. Arlington, VA: American Psychiatric Association.

Ganzini, L., Goy, E. R., & Dobscha, S. K. (2009). Oregonians' reasons for requesting physician aid in dying. *Archives of Internal Medicine, 169*, 489–492. http://dx.doi.org/10.1001/archinternmed.2008.579

Gill, C. J. (1999). The false autonomy of forced choice: Rationalizing suicide for persons with disabilities. In J. L. Werth, Jr. (Ed.), *Contemporary perspectives on rational suicide* (pp. 171–180). Philadelphia, PA: Brunner/Mazel.

Grisso, T., & Appelbaum, P. S. (1998). *Assessing competence to consent to treatment*. New York, NY: Oxford University Press.

Grube, D., & Cardenas, A. (2017). Insurance coverage and aid-in-dying medication costs. *JAMA Oncology, 3*, 1137.

Kroenke, K., Spitzer, R. L., & Williams, J. B. (2001). The PHQ–9: Validity of a brief depression severity measure. *Journal of General Internal Medicine, 16*, 606–613. http://dx.doi.org/10.1046/j.1525-1497.2001.016009606.x

Maine Death With Dignity Act Sec. 1. 22 MRSA c. 418 (2019).

Medical Aid in Dying for the Terminally Ill Act, N.J. Stat. Ann. 26:16-1, et. seq. (2009).

Moye, J., Karel, M. J., Edelstein, B., Hicken, B., Armesto, J. C., & Gurrera, R. J. (2007). Assessment of capacity to consent to treatment: Current research, the "ACCT" approach, future directions. *Clinical Gerontologist, 31*, 37–66. http://dx.doi.org/10.1080/07317110802072140

Nasreddine, Z. S., Phillips, N. A., Bédirian, V., Charbonneau, S., Whitehead, V., Collin, I., . . . Chertkow, H. (2005). The Montreal Cognitive Assessment, MoCA: A brief screening tool for mild cognitive impairment. *Journal of the American Geriatrics Society, 53*, 695–699. http://dx.doi.org/10.1111/j.1532-5415.2005.53221.x

National Academies of Sciences, Engineering, and Medicine. (2018). *Physician-assisted death: Scanning the landscape: Proceedings of a workshop*. Washington, DC: The National Academies Press. http://dx.doi.org/https://doi.org/10.17226/25131

Oregon Death with Dignity Act, OR Statute c 127, s 800-995 (1994, revised 2019).

Oregon Health Authority. (2018). *Oregon death with dignity act, data summary 2017* (Oregon Health Authority Report No. 8579). Retrieved from https://www.oregon.gov/oha/PH/PROVIDERPARTNERRESOURCES/EVALUATIONRESEARCH/DEATHWITHDIGNITYACT/Documents/year20.pdf

Our Care, Our Choice Act, HI Statute Act 2, SLH (2018).

Patient Choice and Control at End of Life 18 V.S.A Chapter 113. (2018).

Public Health Agency of Canada. (2017). *Framework for ethical deliberation and decision-making in public health: A tool for public health practitioners, policy makers and decision-makers*. Ottawa, Canada: Minister of Health.

Reitan, R. M. (1985). *Halstead–Reitan Neuropsychological Test Battery: Theory and clinical interpretation*. Tucson, AZ: Reitan Neuropsychology.

Tolin, D. F., Gilliam, C., Wootton, B. M., Bowe, W., Bragdon, L. B., Davis, E., . . . Hallion, L. S. (2018). Psychometric properties of a structured diagnostic interview for *DSM–5* anxiety, mood, and obsessive compulsive and related disorders. *Assessment, 25,* 3–13. http://dx.doi.org/10.1177/1073191116638410

Washington State Department of Health. (2018). *Washington State 2017 Death With Dignity Act report.* Retrieved from https://www.doh.wa.gov/Portals/1/Documents/Pubs/422-109-DeathWithDignityAct2017.pdf

Washington State Psychological Association. (June 3, 2009). *The Washington Death With Dignity Act: WSPA guidelines for mental health professionals.* https://endoflifewa.org/wp-content/uploads/2014/08/WSPA-DWD_Guidelines_6-3-09.pdf

Werth, J. L., Jr., Benjamin, G. A. H., & Farrenkopf, T. (2000). Requests for physician-assisted death: Guidelines for assessing mental capacity and impaired judgment. *Psychology, Public Policy, and Law, 6,* 348–372. http://dx.doi.org/10.1037/1076-8971.6.2.348

IV

NEGOTIATING CHALLENGES WITH FAMILIES AND SURROGATES

11

Working With Surrogates Who May Lack Capacity or Be Unfit

Kate L. M. Hinrichs and Ronald W. Smith

KEY POINTS

- People have a right to appoint a health care agent (HCA) of their choosing and usually maintain the capacity to do so, while potentially lacking other capacities such as medical decision-making.
- Sometimes a selected HCA is a poor or dangerous choice or later is revealed to be an inadequate HCA through demonstrated behaviors or by losing capacity themselves.
- Maintenance of a patient's autonomy is generally considered paramount, and overriding individuals' autonomy related to their HCA selection should only be done when there are clear and significant safety concerns.
- When the HCA's appropriateness comes into question, we must use evidence beyond a clinical interview to determine whether the HCA is a sufficiently unsafe choice to allow overriding autonomy.

DEFINITION OF THE ISSUE

Regardless of the capacity being assessed, it is critical to know whether patients have engaged in advance care planning and chosen an HCA to act as their surrogate decision-maker should they someday lack capacity. In general,

http://dx.doi.org/10.1037/0000184-012
Assessing Capacities of Older Adults: A Casebook to Guide Difficult Decisions, J. Moye (Editor)

patients have the right to appoint an HCA of their choosing. Capacity to appoint an HCA is a relatively low-threshold decision and generally consists of patients' ability to explain the role of an HCA and to be able to consistently name a chosen trusted other as their HCA (American Bar Association & American Psychological Association [ABA/APA], 2008, p. 51). Unlike making medical decisions or living safely independently, the appointment of an HCA is typically considered a low-risk, high-benefit decision. Thus, it is possible for patients to lack the capacity to make medical or discharge decisions, while retaining the capacity to name an HCA.

During capacity assessments, appointed HCAs can sometimes serve the role of providing collateral information during the evaluation of a patient because they often know the individual well. However, they often become more involved when preparing for next steps in care if the patient is found to lack capacity and the HCA is formally activated. Commonly, at the completion of a medical or independent living capacity evaluation when the patient lacks capacity, feedback will be given to both the patient and their HCA. The goal of this feedback is to alert the HCA that the patient lacks capacity and to ensure that the HCA understands they are being activated by a medical provider as the surrogate decision-maker for the patient. Providers then go on to consult the HCA for all future care decisions, continuing to engage the patient to the extent possible.

Generally, the maintenance of a patient's autonomy in choosing an HCA is considered paramount, although in rare cases a selected HCA's appropriateness or capability to act as a surrogate may come into question. The HCA may be such a sufficiently poor or dangerous choice that the capacity of the patient to even name this person as an HCA is called into question (e.g., choosing an HCA who is known to be abusive or incapacitated). Other times, the suitability of an HCA does not come into question until much later (e.g., when a previously appropriate HCA loses capacity over time). It can be challenging when in the course of providing health care to an identified patient, the decision-making capacity or appropriateness of a named or proposed HCA is questioned because these agents are rarely the subjects of our capacity evaluations and are typically not under our health care. However, in circumstances in which there are clear and significant safety concerns for the patient, it may be necessary to undertake the delicate matter of overriding a patient's choice of HCA. In these cases, we must use evidence beyond a clinical interview to determine whether the HCA is a sufficiently unsafe choice to permit overriding autonomy. These situations can cause ethical dilemmas and clinical challenges for health care teams and providers.

In this chapter, we address the challenging clinical and ethical issues that arise when it is suspected that an HCA may lack capacity or is an unfit choice to make decisions on behalf of the patient. We discuss ways of navigating these challenges when HCAs are not the targets of capacity evaluations and address issues that may affect HCA decision-making, as well as situations in which proposed HCAs are abusive. Information is provided via two cases demonstrating how such issues were addressed. We also discuss potential paths to ensuring the safety of the patient when HCAs are incapable or inappropriate and a new surrogate is needed.

CLINICAL PRESENTATION

The topic of HCAs lacking capacity or being an inappropriate choice to make decisions on behalf of a patient who lacks capacity has not been thoroughly studied. Thus, accurate statistics on the prevalence of the challenges discussed in this chapter are not available. However, data related to older adults and their family situations in general may help us better understand where a scenario involving an inappropriate HCA or an HCA who lacks capacity might occur.

Living Alone

Approximately one third of community-dwelling older adults (or 11 million people) in the United States live alone, with older women living alone at about twice the rate of older men (West, Cole, Goodkind, & He, 2014). This suggests that many older patients are without partners and are likely to list one of their adult children, or another relative, as an HCA. Because the HCA may not live with or care for the patient, knowledge of the patient's health or health care wishes may be limited.

No HCA or Advance Directive

Many older adults have no HCA named. Studies have also found that approximately half of adults over age 60 do not have advance directives completed (AARP, 2008; Pew Research Center, 2006). These percentages differ by setting, with 28% of home health care patients, 65% of nursing home residents, and 88% of hospice patients having advance directives on record (Jones, Moss, & Harris-Kojetin, 2011). Terminal or severe illnesses have little effect on increasing the prevalence of an advance directive, with less than 50% of these patients having one in place (Kass-Bartelmes, 2003). This can leave next of kin in the unpleasant situation of having to guess what the patient would have wanted with regard to medical interventions and who should make those decisions. Black et al. (2009) outlined two assumptions related to health care decisions being made by HCAs. These are (a) that patients have preferences about treatment in future hypothetical situations and (b) that HCAs can ascertain from patients what their goals for care and treatment preferences are. Unfortunately, we know that both of these are often untrue. Previous studies show that HCAs' knowledge of patient health care wishes and their subsequent decision-making is often varied and complex due to factors such as patients being generic in their directives or not talking about falling ill at all (Carrese, Mullaney, Faden, & Finucane, 2002; Gamble, McDonald, & Lichstein, 1991; Hines et al., 2001; Hopp, 2000).

Characteristics of HCAs

Several studies have examined patient and HCA dyads to learn more about who HCAs are and the types of decisions they make. In a study of 123 HCAs who made at least one major decision for a patient with dementia in a nursing home, the HCAs were a mean age of 57 years, 63% female, 93% White, and 76% married. Seventy-four percent of HCAs were the patient's child, whereas other HCAs were spouses (9.8%), nieces or nephews (7.3%), siblings (2.4%), grandchildren (0.8%), or legal guardians (3.3%). Thirty-five percent of HCAs had lived with the patient before nursing home admission. HCAs had been listed as the health care proxy for an average of 7.3 years (Givens, Kiely, Carey, & Mitchell, 2009). A second study by Torke and colleagues (2014) researched older adults who had been hospitalized for at least 48 hours to determine how many required an HCA to make decisions for them. Of 1,083 older adults, 23% of patients required the HCA to make all their decisions, while 24.4% of patients made decisions jointly with their HCA. HCAs were daughters (58.9%), sons (25%), or spouses (20.6%).

Incidence of Dementia

It has been estimated that in the United States, between 4 and 5 million older adults (or 13.9%) have some form of dementia. These prevalence estimates increase with a person's age: approximately 5% of older adults aged 71 to 79 have dementia, increasing to 24% of older adults aged 80 to 89 years and 37% of older adults aged 90 and older. Alzheimer's disease accounted for about 70% of these dementias (Plassman et al., 2007). More recent studies indicate that higher levels of education and better control of risk factors related to health conditions may have resulted in a decline in prevalence to approximately 8% of older adults over 65 (Langa et al., 2017). Estimates show the prevalence of dementia increasing in the next few decades due to an increase in the proportion of older adults in the population. Such increases will lead to many older adults with dementia needing surrogate decision-makers, as well as some surrogate decision-makers having dementia. Although rare, there is some evidence that having a spouse with dementia can lead to cognitive changes and increase the risk for incidence of cognitive impairment. Norton and colleagues (2010) studied 2,112 married couples over 65 years old and followed them a median of 3.3 years, finding 229 cases of dementia incidence. Of those 229 cases, 34 spouses (or 14.8%) also had incidence of dementia during the course of the study. The study determined that having a spouse with dementia incidence resulted in 6 times increase in the partner's risk of dementia incidence.

Types of Decisions HCAs Make

When an HCA is activated, they might be asked to weigh in on any number of medical decisions for the patient in question, including where that person will go after the hospitalization. Givens and colleagues (2009) found that common decisions for HCAs in nursing homes included feeding problems, treating infections, and pain management. Torke and colleagues (2014) found that within the hospital setting, most HCA decisions were related to life-sustaining treatment (code status), surgeries and procedures, and discharge planning.

Difficulty Being an HCA

Serving as an HCA is often a more difficult role than people anticipate. One study found that the HCAs of persons with dementia ($n = 28$) felt unprepared for their role as a decision-maker. This was largely due to their limited understanding of the trajectory of dementia, being uncomfortable with end-of-life care or having little experience with death, and not having substantive communication with health care professionals (Gessert, Forbes, & Bern-Klug, 2001). The study also noted that even when patients had filled out an advanced care directive, the values and goals were sometimes generic, which made specific decisions difficult to make on their behalf.

Unbefriended

It is estimated that 4% of older adults living in long-term care (LTC) settings are classified as "unbefriended" (Karp & Wood, 2004). The American Geriatrics Society defined an unbefriended older adult patient as (a) lacking decisional capacity; (b) having no advanced directives; and (c) lacking family, friends, or legally authorized surrogate (Farrell et al., 2017). Cases in which an older adult is unbefriended can present patients and treatment teams with unique challenges before making treatment decisions, including determining patient values and goals and searching the patient history thoroughly for potential unconventional surrogate decision-makers. See the article by Farrell and colleagues (2017) for a position statement on unbefriended older adults that features clinical recommendations. Situations in which adults have no or limited decision-makers are often associated with extended length of stay and delays in treatment across a wide variety of health care settings (Farrell et al., 2017).

DIAGNOSTIC STANDARDS AND DILEMMAS

Several contributors might make a patient's chosen HCA a less than optimal choice from the beginning. In other instances, the patient's chosen heath care agent may become a poor choice over time due to an emerging impairment. Although there is no research specific to this issue, we combine our clinical experiences in consideration of the research reviewed in the preceding section to set forth some leading factors related to this issue. Although HCAs are not the focus of an assessment because they are not the focus of clinical care and often not under the care of the same providers, clinical teams often become aware of these factors when trying to engage the HCA in decision-making, as well as through reports from front-line staff members who observe the HCA during family visits.

What follows describes contributors that may affect an HCA's capacity to make decisions on behalf of the patient; factors that may contribute to a HCA being a poor, or unsafe, choice to make decisions on behalf of the patient; and ethical and practical dilemmas that arise when an HCA lacks capacity or is an unsafe choice. Later, we discuss methods of addressing these dilemmas and also illustrate them in case examples.

IMPORTANT CONSIDERATIONS WHEN ASSESSING HCAs' CAPACITIES

Reasons an HCA may lack capacity to make a decision for the principal

- Cognitive impairment/dementia
- Substance use
- Severe mental illness
- Medical illness

Reasons an HCA may be an inappropriate choice

- Current or recent substance abuse
- History of physical abuse
- History of financial abuse
- History of conflict with the patient
- The HCA is not in close proximity
- The HCA is unable to be contacted or does not respond to request for decisions
- The HCA has little understanding of illness or the care that may be necessary and does not attempt to engage with the treatment team

Dilemmas involved when the HCA lacks capacity or is an inappropriate choice

- Autonomy versus safety of the patient who lacks capacity
- HCA is not the focus of the original capacity evaluation
- We cannot make diagnostic statements about HCAs we have not evaluated
- Preemptive or proactive versus retroactive measures (taking steps early to prevent a poor HCA from being able to make decisions versus waiting for the HCA to demonstrate poor decisions [to the risk of the patient])

CLINICAL METHODS

Conceptual Framework

To guide the course of action in managing ethical dilemmas related to HCAs who may not be appropriate, it is helpful to apply a conceptual framework.

One such framework for working through ethical dilemmas involving older adults and decision-making was put forward by Karel (2011). The standards for ethical practice in geropsychology focus on providers' understanding and knowledge of four competencies: tension among safety and autonomy, decision-making capacity, HCA decision-making, and legal resources to protect older adults. The framework allows the provider using it to clarify and consider the issues, relevant parties, decision-making authority, and the pros and cons of options before implementing a plan. The following box provides detailed framework components.

FRAMEWORK FOR ETHICAL DILEMMAS

1. Clarify the ethical issue. What is the dilemma?
2. Clarify who are the relevant stakeholders and each of their values, goals, and interests.
3. Clarify decision-making authority. Who has the right to make the decision in a particular situation?
4. Consider all ethically justifiable options and their pros and cons for each stakeholder.
5. Implement the plan, evaluate, and reevaluate. (Karel, 2011)

Assessment Approaches

Step 1: Clarify the ethical issue. What is the dilemma? The pressing ethical issue in these sorts of capacity cases is often the tension between patients' autonomy to choose their own HCA, who may lack capacity themselves or be an unsafe or dangerous choice, and protecting patients' safety from the consequences of the poor decision-making, inappropriate or dangerous behavior, or poor understanding of care needs. Patients generally have the right to choose their HCA, and overriding their autonomy can be clinically, legally, and ethically challenging.

Step 2: Clarify who are the relevant stakeholders and each of their values, goals, and interests. The stakeholders involved commonly include the patient, the chosen HCA, and the health care providers or medical teams. Patients may have shared their values or goals through documents such as an advance directive or a living will. They may also have verbalized their values and goals to their appointed HCA. It is important to clarify the values and goals of the HCA and whether these values and goals align with the patient's previously stated goals. Further, health care providers often hold values and goals of ensuring patient safety sometimes at the expense of autonomy.

Step 3: Clarify decision-making authority. Who has the right to make the decision in a particular situation? The chosen HCA will hold decision-making authority once a patient is found to lack capacity to make decisions. However, if an HCA demonstrates poor decision-making or lacks capacity, the health care provider is faced with the difficult decision of whether to override this authority. This can be particularly challenging because of the need to show clear evidence of poor decision-making or the potential for unsafe or dangerous decisions.

Step 4: Consider all ethically justifiable options and their pros and cons for each stakeholder. If you suspect a proposed HCA may be an inappropriate choice, or that an existing HCA may no longer have the capacity for the role, you must closely examine the options:

- Consult with the team.
- Search for indications that the HCA is unsafe through any evidence that is available to you, such as police reports highlighting abuse, clinical evidence of inability to keep a patient healthy or safe (e.g., via repeat admissions, weight loss, injury).
- Is there enough evidence to question the capacity of an HCA?
- Is there an alternate HCA available?
- Is there a need to apply for guardianship to ensure patient safety?

Step 5: Implement the plan, evaluate, and reevaluate. Under certain scenarios, you may know an HCA has cognitive impairment but may not have sufficient evidence that this would preclude the individual from serving as an HCA. In fact, it is possible for HCAs with some level of cognitive impairment to still serve as a reasonable HCA (e.g., consenting for low-risk–high-benefit medical procedures, making decisions that closely follow expressed wishes from an advance directive or living will, making low-risk decisions that align with the recommendations of the medical team). There may also be situations in which you suspect an HCA is significantly impaired but you do not have evidence that this individual's decision-making would actually harm the patient. In this case, the plan may be able to wait and allow the HCA to make decisions that provide evidence of your concerns, justifying the removal of the HCA from the role (e.g., the decisions they made led to harm of the patient). In this case, the team must search for alternate surrogate decision-makers or consider filing for guardianship of the patient. They will need to consider all ethically justifiable alternatives to the named HCA to protect the patient.

Common Pragmatic and Ethical Dilemmas

Whenever the question of impeding a patient's right to name an HCA or of removing a named HCA arises, there are several important issues to consider. Without question, this process is fraught for the medical teams and should only be undertaken when serious concerns for harm to the patient are at play with no obvious and practical alternative. If these conditions are met, then the evaluator and team may begin the complex process of determining next steps to ensure patient safety. To accomplish this, teams may need to gather information in myriad ways or work with other professionals outside the team.

Speaking With Family, or Others, While Respecting HIPAA

When conducting an evaluation of capacity, you will often want to acquire collateral information. This is best obtained from people who know the patient well. In ideal circumstances the patient will consent (or at a minimum, assent) to the evaluator reaching out to family, friends, or other health care providers for such information. A signed release of information (ROI) is strongly preferred. In the occasional case when patients do not provide permission to speak with others in their life, you may have few options for collateral information. One option may be to obtain information from existing records (e.g., medical, legal, adult protective). Another option (if the patient is sufficiently incapacitated) might be to speak with the HCA, next-of-kin, or other trusted person who can be located. In these cases, if you are not speaking to the activated HCA or if there is no clear HCA to activate yet, you need to be careful about what information you share while gathering relevant data. In particular, you might be conservative or vague about revealing medical or mental health diagnoses, or other sensitive or protected information, to the extent possible. For example, a phone call to an extended family member might begin with "Hello, I am Dr. Jones calling from the City Hospital about your uncle, Bill Smith. He is not able to give us much information about [insert what you need to determine—functioning, living, health], and we are hoping you could help us. What can you tell me about his previous [functioning, living, health]?" You will want to protect the patient's privacy as much as possible, while learning what you can to inform the evaluation and your recommendations to the team.

Working With Counsel, Courts, Adult Protective Services, or Police

When collaborating with professionals beyond your usual team, you may run into additional challenges in that each of you may be bound by different sets of rules, ethical guidelines (e.g., APA's, 2017, *Ethical Principles of Psychologists and Code of Conduct*), or even laws. You may also see the cases through different lenses and thus have different priorities for action regarding the case. Local counsel for your health care system may be helpful in determining what legal options exist for you and for the patient, and they can guide you in ensuring you are not making inappropriate disclosures of the patient's information. They and the courts can help determine whether guardianship is a necessary step and how to proceed. Adult protective services may have useful information about how the patient was functioning in the community and may be able to help mitigate risk after discharge by supplying home or community services to the patient to bolster their functional capacity. Police or law enforcement may hold important information about prior domestic incidents or other legal troubles involving the patient. At times such information is essential (e.g., there is an active restraining order against a named HCA; the proposed HCA has previously assaulted or harmed the patient; there is a history of physical, sexual, or financial abuses against or involving the patient). Whenever you are interfacing with other disciplines or agencies, it is important to be respectful of the bounds of what they can legally and ethically share, while doing your best to work together for the good of the patient.

Getting Outside Records and Reviewing "Inside" Records (If Working in a Health Care System)

As noted earlier, there are times we need or want to involve other disciplines or agencies to obtain all the necessary information to make a determination of capacity. In these cases, you must decide whether the information you will obtain is truly essential to your evaluation. For example, would the information potentially change your determination or recommendations? If so, it will be worth the difficulty of acquiring the outside records or information. In these cases, a signed release of information may be required, even if the patient is known to lack capacity (e.g., local law enforcement might require a signed ROI to release police reports). Other times, some agencies will be able to work with you based on your report that the patient is incapacitated (e.g., adult protective services may be willing to discuss resources for discharge planning or open investigations of theirs involving the patient). It can also be useful to speak with others within your agency who might have knowledge of the patient and their family (e.g., primary care provider, social workers). In all cases, it is important to think through how, or if, additional information will aid you in making your evaluation and recommendations.

When Such Assessments Are Not Useful or Appropriate

Complex and detailed evaluations of capacity are not always necessary or appropriate. Similarly, it is not often necessary or appropriate to dig into a patient or family's social or legal histories when activating an HCA. For example, a team would not consider removing an HCA simply because the HCA disagreed with the team, chose not to follow the recommendations of the team, or made a decision that might not perfectly align with the patient's previously held wishes. Rather, it is always an exception to the norm when this sort of complex evaluation is needed and discussed, and the path of prohibiting or removing an HCA is reserved only for times when there is concern for significant danger or harm to the patient.

Alternate Framework

Of note, a second potential framework is offered in an article by Smith, Fedel, and Heitman (2017), which discusses the dilemmas present specifically when an activated HCA is suspected to be incapacitated. We present this framework as a helpful option for readers to use in addition or as a supplement to the Karel (2011) framework. The Smith et al. framework is more specific to the situation of an HCA who may lack capacity and guides teams to understand when legal action, such as pursuing guardianship, may be necessary. Smith and colleagues acknowledged the difficulty for staff in both being unable to formally evaluate the capacity of the HCA and of taking steps to remove an HCA. They suggested a framework for informally analyzing the capacity of the HCA based on their decisions and the reasons given for those decisions. They recommended the two-pronged "Not Unreasonable Standard" approach by Rhodes and Holzman (2004), which looks at (a) *reasons given for decisions* and (b) *the outcomes that are expected from those decisions*.

According to Smith et al. (2017), the following considerations should be kept in mind when an HCA is suspected to be incapacitated:

1. the ability to receive information (from the team);
2. the ability to understand information, including risks and benefits;
3. the ability to evaluate information using the patient's own values; and
4. the ability to make a decision that is in the patient's best interest and to give reasons that others can understand regarding that decision.

Smith and colleagues (2017) recommended using an informed consent lens and considering the HCA's abilities with the following components: (a) *the ability to receive information*; (b) *the ability to understand information, including risks and benefits*; (c) *the ability to evaluate information using the patient's own values*; and (d) *the ability to make a decision that is in the patient's best interests and to give reasons that others can understand regarding the decision* (p. 285, emphasis added). Regarding the last point, the authors discussed three types of reasons given:

EXAMINATION OF REASONS

1. reasons no one could reasonably refuse (antibiotic for an infection, stitches for a lacerated artery);
2. reasons that reasonable people could prioritize differently (weighing whether to continue chemotherapy when the outcome is uncertain); and
3. reasons that other reasonable people could refuse (Jehovah's Witness refusing a blood transfusion). In this case, values often weigh heavily into the reason given. (Smith et al., 2017)

The second prong of the framework analyzes the outcomes of the decision or reason given. The authors suggested three categories:

EXAMINATION OF OUTCOMES

1. treatment being beneficial where it is unreasonable to refuse it,
2. treatment being optional with more than one reasonable choice, and
3. treatment having no significant benefit where palliation is preferable. (Smith et al., 2017)

Smith and colleagues (2017) gave examples to suggest when it might make sense to proceed with legal action, considering this as a last resort due to length of time and cost. The threshold for action is when, based on the HCA's decisions, harm is likely to come to the patient and the reasons for those decisions do not appear to be in line with the patient's values and are personal to the HCA. This framework holds great utility for fostering team discussions of the practical issues surrounding the reasons given for decisions and the outcomes that may result from the decision when it is suspected that an HCA may be incapacitated. We opted to apply the Karel (2011) framework to our cases because we are not only discussing potentially incapacitated HCAs but also potentially unfit ones.

CASE EXAMPLES

Here we describe two complex cases to illustrate the challenging clinical and ethical issues that can arise when it is suspected that an HCA may lack capacity or be an unfit choice to make decisions on behalf of the patient.[1] We discuss ways of navigating these challenges and address issues that may affect HCA decision-making, as well as situations in which proposed HCAs are abusive. We also discuss potential paths to ensuring the safety of the patient when HCAs are incapable or inappropriate and a new surrogate is needed.

Case 1: Mr. Frank Barnes

Presentation

Increasingly psychologists are functioning as integrated members of medical care teams. As an integrated psychologist in a rehabilitation and LTC service, I (KLMH) often receive consults to evaluate decision-making capacity. In this case, I received a consult for a veteran, Mr. Barnes, who had been admitted to our rehabilitation unit for completion of health insurance paperwork with the goal of eventual placement in LTC. Mr. Barnes initially presented to the emergency department for evaluation of his hand after apparently being physically abused by his adult daughter. Mr. Barnes was highly educated but had suspected cognitive impairment. The consult request I received stated: "Please evaluate for capacity to make HC decisions, as well as naming health care proxy." After discussing the case further with the team, it seemed Mr. Barnes wanted to rescind his existing advance directive and change his HCA from one daughter to another, who was recently suspected of assaulting him (further family information is provided later in the case example).

[1]Although the case examples in this chapter are based on the authors' real experiences, the identities of the individuals involved in these examples have been properly disguised to protect their confidentiality.

Analysis and Reflection on Presentation

In this case, the nature of the referral questions immediately raised red flags given the suspected elder abuse. It was clear that the issue about changing the HCA was most pressing because there were no health decisions that needed to be made imminently. It was also clear that this issue was causing the medical team distress. Some members of the team raised the point that we rarely find someone so incapacitated that he or she cannot name an HCA, while others did not believe a person who had abused her own father could really have his best interests at heart to serve as an HCA. So, although we were asked to weigh in on various capacity issues (naming an HCA and medical decision-making), these would be complicated by the desire of the patient to name a potentially dangerous person as his HCA. Although it is not typically the role of an evaluator to vet a potential HCA, we felt we had a duty as mandated reporters of elder abuse and under APA (2017) ethical principles of protecting persons from harm to explore this issue because we had received concerning information about this potential HCA via the medical record. For this case, the results of cognitive or capacity assessment are presented, along with discussion of issues related to the evaluator's responsibility to include information about the chosen HCA into the assessment of capacity, what to do when patients desire to name an unsafe HCA, the complications of working with family members who have been accused of elder abuse, and the evaluator's role in balancing the protection of vulnerable elders from harm with protection of the individual's right to make unsafe choices.

History

Mr. Barnes was a 90-year-old, widowed, White male veteran. He was college educated and a retired clergyman. His medical history is notable for hypertension, hyperlipidemia, and a bypass procedure due to heart disease. He presented with suspected cognitive impairment (e.g., could not recall where he had attended college or what he studied there) and an inability to live independently (per the medical record, he had abandoned his home and was living in his daughter Trish's low-income apartment with her, which was in violation of the state regulations under financial qualifications and legal occupancy rules). He was admitted to our care for completion of insurance paperwork and eventual placement in community LTC in the setting of advanced illness and decreased self-care. Specifically, he was not eligible for community-based LTC to be paid for by the Department of Veterans Affairs (VA) and so required an application to Medicaid for coverage; an LTC facility would not accept him until this application was completed. Mr. Barnes was initially admitted to the hospital from the emergency department for workup of an injured hand after an apparent incident of physical abuse by his daughter Trish. Of note, he had been treated in the hospital for similar issues a month before, but he left the hospital against medical advice to return to Trish's home. This information was found in a review of the electronic medical record.

Regarding family makeup, per both the medical record and the clinical interview, Mr. Barnes was widowed and had fathered five children with his wife (two sons and three daughters). One son was deceased, and one daughter lived out of state and was not involved in her father's life. His son Victor, who was part owner of the home Mr. Barnes had previously lived in and abandoned, was currently embattled with his father in court over the pending sale of the home. His daughter Cathy was the documented HCA, per an advance directive that had been completed about 8 years earlier. Mr. Barnes has said he would like to rescind this document and claimed Cathy wouldn't answer his phone calls. According to Mr. Barnes, Cathy and Victor were aligned with each other, and they were "against" their sister Trish. Mr. Barnes desired to name Trish as his HCA. Of note, Trish had been documented in the medical record as having been physically abusive toward her father when he has lived with her, both recently and in the past. Trish occasionally visited her father in the hospital and reported a desire to be involved in his life; Mr. Barnes said he wanted her to be involved. Trish was observed bringing her father foods he likes; she was also overheard yelling at him on several occasions.

Given that the majority of the information about the suspected elder abuse in this case came from our electronic medical record, we wanted some clarity on what had really transpired between Mr. Barnes and his daughter. This felt important because we did not want to make any moves to limit this patient's autonomy based solely on hearsay or chart-lore, as he made his desire for her involvement clear. Further, we found the clinical interview limited because Mr. Barnes was able to state that his daughter had in fact hit him "with a cane," but he tended to downplay the severity of these incidents and was unable to clarify when or how often any abuses occurred. Thus, we undertook the steps of obtaining legal information directly from local law enforcement. Thankfully, Mr. Barnes agreed to sign a release of information for us to contact local police to gather data about the past incidents between he and Trish. The police were able to send us copies of incident reports detailing the arrests and charges against Trish from the previous year. They also shared that there had been a previous restraining order against Trish about 5 years earlier, also related to assaulting and abusing her elderly father. Police and protective services did not provide any evidence of abuse or financial exploitation by other adult children or anyone else in his life. Of note, Mr. Barnes did not initially give permission for the health care team to contact family members. Thus, before any evaluation and findings about his capacity and in light of the elder abuse described by Mr. Barnes, we respected his rights in this matter.

Interview, Examination, and Tests

Previous assessment and imaging. A year before the current evaluation, Mr. Barnes had been referred for neuropsychological assessment because he was noted by his primary care provider to be forgetful and repeating himself often. Testing at that time revealed impairments in executing functioning (processing speed, inhibition, working memory) and memory (encoding, retrieval, recognition). Around the same time, he was referred for imaging, and a computed tomographic scan of the head showed mild general atrophic change and mild ischemic change, as well as significant medial temporal (hippocampal) atrophy. When paired with cognitive testing, it appeared likely he had a major neurocognitive disorder of the Alzheimer's type.

Current cognitive screening. Montreal Cognitive Assessment (MoCA) fell in the impaired range with a total score of 19 out of 30. Item scores were as follows:

- Visuospatial/Executive—4/5
- Naming—3/3
- Attention—4/6
- Language—1/3
- Abstraction—1/2
- Delayed Recall—0/5
- Orientation—6/6

Health Care Decision-Making Assessment

With regard to the Healthcare Decision-Making component of the Hopemont Capacity Assessment Interview (Staats & Edelstein, 1995), Mr. Barnes's responses were often perseverative, tangential, vague, and nonspecific to the questions being asked. His performance indicated inconsistent understanding of risks and limited health care decision-making abilities. Domain scores were as follows:

- Definitions—4/6
- Memory—17/18
- Understanding Benefits—4/4
- Understanding Risks—5/8
- Decision-Making—2/6
- Understanding the condition (Scenario 1)—12/20
- Understanding the condition (scenario 2)—20/20

Assessing Capacity to Appoint an HCA

With visual cues (large print handouts) Mr. Barnes was able to state back that the advance directive form would allow him to describe the kind of health care he would like to receive. However, he was unable to recall or state back that this form allowed him to name an HCA. In fact, during early meetings, he said he wanted to think more about whether to name an HCA. He did not appreciate that he had already completed an advance directive years before and named his daughter Cathy as his HCA. On a later date, he expressed understanding of the need to name an HCA but again had no appreciation that he had already done this. When discussing people who might make a suitable HCA, Mr. Barnes ruled out both Cathy and Victor, stating that Trish was his best choice despite their history of "physical altercations." His rationale hinged on the fact that Trish visited him in the hospital and his anger with Victor and Cathy over the sale of his home.

Consultation With Peers

As an early-career psychologist, this complex case left me feeling in over my head. I spent a lot of time talking with the medical team and social worker about how to proceed. I also conferred with other local geropsychologists about the capacity portion of the case, the ethical challenges, and the concerns about the "chosen" HCA who seemed an unsafe choice. This process helped clarify my thinking.

Findings

Consistent with previous testing and history, Mr. Barnes carries a diagnosis of major neurocognitive disorder, likely of the Alzheimer's type. Regarding his capacity to change his HCA, although Mr. Barnes could express a choice (Trish), his reasoning regarding the choice of Trish was so poor and unsafe that it served to further draw his capacity into question. I concluded that he could not change his HCA at that time. Thus, his daughter Cathy would remain his HCA, per his existing advance directive.

Regarding his capacity to make health decisions, Mr. Barnes was not consistently able to appreciate risks and showed limited ability to weigh risks and benefits to make health care decisions. He was found to lack capacity to independently make most medical decisions. Therefore, his HCA needed to be activated.

Analysis and Reflection on Findings

To organize my thoughts about this case, it was helpful to apply Karel's (2011) framework.

Step 1: Clarify the ethical issue. What is the dilemma? In this case, the primary dilemma centered around balancing the protection of vulnerable elders from harm with protection of the individual's right to make unsafe choices (APA, 2017). Specifically, Mr. Barnes desired to rescind a previous advance directive and change his HCA to his daughter Trish, who had been arrested for assaulting him on multiple occasions.

Step 2: Clarify who are the relevant stakeholders and each of their values, goals, and interests. Stakeholders in this case included Mr. Barnes and his medical team. Mr. Barnes's values seemed to include maintenance of a relationship with his daughter Trish and a desire for autonomy. The medical team's primary value was for the safety of this vulnerable elder. Their goal was to maintain safety while trying to move forward with eventual discharge to LTC.

Step 3: Clarify decision-making authority. Who has the right to make the decision in a particular situation? It was determined that Mr. Barnes was not able to identify risks of his choice of HCA sufficiently, weigh risks and benefits of his choice of HCA, or appreciate any risk of potential harm to himself as a result of this choice. Therefore, he was not able to change his HCA and his daughter Cathy would remain the designee, per a previous advance directive.

Step 4: Consider all ethically justifiable options and their pros and cons for each stakeholder. In this case, options included allowing Mr. Barnes to change his

HCA to Trish or not allowing this and keeping his existing HCA in place. Permitting the change in HCA may have been most respectful of his autonomy. However, risks to his safety were apparent based on this daughter's history of assaulting her father on several occasions. She had also been allowing him to live in her apartment with her despite it not being permitted by housing regulations, so it was unclear whether she would have been able to navigate making safe discharge decisions for her father. To restrict Mr. Barnes from being able to change his HCA meant we were more likely to keep him safe from harm, but perhaps at the expense of his autonomy. This course also kept him from returning to his daughter Trish's apartment to live, as we next sought to work with his current HCA to facilitate LTC placement in the community.

Step 5: Implement the plan, evaluate, and reevaluate. We worked to make the assessment findings and recommendations (discussed subsequently) clear to the care teams and to Mr. Barnes and his family with the goal of maximizing his safety, while still allowing him visits with his daughter Trish, per his wishes.

Interventions and Dispositions

Recommendations.

- Activate the HCA.
- Given this finding, we were able to pursue contact with Cathy to determine whether she was willing and able to act as HCA.
- If Cathy was willing and able, she would be consulted to make health care decisions for her father. If she was not, a guardian might be needed. Trish was not a safe or appropriate option.
- Seek a fiduciary or representative payee to manage Mr. Barnes's financial affairs.
- Work with HCA and the fiduciary to seek appropriate LTC placement for Mr. Barnes.

Outcome. The medical team repeatedly contacted Cathy to see whether she would be willing and able to serve as the HCA for her father. Throughout this time, the team social worker had been consulting with VA legal counsel about various aspects of this case. A VA fiduciary was also applied for to manage Mr. Barnes's VA income. Until these issues (HCA and fiduciary) were resolved, there was no ability to move forward with community LTC placement because Mr. Barnes needed both a payor source and someone to sign him into a facility. After some months, both the daughter Cathy and the son Victor formally declined to get involved with their father's care. In considering all aspects of his care, the team decided not to pursue a community LTC placement but rather to transfer Mr. Barnes to VA LTC. During the time he received care in the VA, his daughter Trish was permitted to visit (per her father's request) but was required to check in and out with staff to minimize risk of harm. Eventually she was required to have only supervised visits with her father due to her persistent pattern of abusive behaviors toward Mr. Barnes (e.g., yelling at him, demanding money, berating him and the staff). In the end, Mr. Barnes received high-quality LTC, and we were able to minimize risk of harm from his daughter.

Case 2: Mr. Jerome Kane

Presentation

This case is unique in that we were never actually consulted for any evaluation of the patient himself. The patient in question, Mr. Kane, was a 90-year-old man with unmistakable and significant cognitive and functional impairments. The team agreed that Mr. Kane should clearly have his HCA activated. Unfortunately, he never completed an advance directive, so there was some uncertainty about who would serve in this role. He did have his current wife, Jeannie, listed as his next-of-kin and emergency contact; by VA policy, this meant she would be in line to serve as his surrogate decision-maker within the VA system (default surrogate). However, it seemed the team had concerns about her ability to serve as the HCA because there were suspicions that she may also have serious cognitive impairment. Despite this concern, Mr. Kane was consistent in wanting his wife involved, and Jeannie was consistent in her desire to bring her husband home with her. We were brought into this case via team discussions regarding Mr. Kane's discharge plan, who should be contacted to make decisions on his behalf, and whether his wife would be able to meet his needs at home. For this case, the history and clinical picture are presented, along with discussion of issues related to identifying a surrogate when there is no formal advance directive, what steps to take when you suspect a surrogate may also be incapacitated, and the evaluator's role in balancing the protection of vulnerable elders from harm with protection of the individual's right to make potentially unsafe choices.

Analysis and Reflection on Presentation

In this case, the lack of a referral question per se led to us operating in a consultant role to the team, rather than in the typical role of evaluator. The pressing issue here was whether the team had any ethical or legal right to question the role of the wife as the default surrogate or HCA. The idea of her as the HCA was causing the medical team distress; they worried about her desire to take her husband home because they questioned her ability to meet his care needs. There was suspicion that she was so cognitively impaired that she could not see her own limitations. On the other hand, several members of the team pointed out that they could imagine also wanting to care for their spouse despite limitations, and they also wondered if it was our place to question the wife's abilities because she was not our patient. It was the impression of the team that it can be difficult to remove a family member from the role of HCA without clear evidence of harm to the patient. So we were asked to weigh in on the ethical and legal issue of whether concerns were great enough to warrant taking the extreme step of removing the wife from the HCA role. Of note, Mr. Kane wanted his wife involved; however, he was not able to understand his own care needs or her limitations. Although it is not typical for a care team to vet an HCA, we felt we had a duty to explore this issue because we had concerns about this HCA from the medical record and through interactions team members had experienced with the wife. Thus, we began the process of trying to examine risk factors to determine whether Jeannie was truly a dangerous HCA or simply a less than ideal one.

History

Mr. Kane's most recent admission began when his wife was hospitalized for a bone infection, and he was simultaneously admitted to an observation bed at the same hospital in the setting of inability to care for himself without his wife at home. This hospital diagnosed Mr. Kane with likely "delirium on top of dementia" and sent him to the VA for care. At the VA, Mr. Kane was admitted with "mild confusion" and sent to a VA LTC unit for an emergency respite stay. He was observed to be oriented to self only and had no medical complaints beyond chronic hypertension.

Mr. Kane was a 90-year-old, African American man born and raised in the Deep South. He had an eighth-grade education, was a retired mechanic, and was the last surviving sibling from a family of 10 children. He was previously married and had a daughter and son from that marriage, but he maintained little to no contact with them. He had been married to his current wife, Jeannie, for at least 10 years, and he was reliant on her for many aspects of his care. According to the medical record, Mr. Kane's memory difficulties were long-standing but fairly well managed in the context of a supportive home environment. It seems his wife had managed most household affairs since they married (e.g., bills, cooking, laundry); Mr. Kane continued to garden and do basic home repairs, and he appeared content. Unfortunately, whenever Jeannie was hospitalized, Mr. Kane was also hospitalized because he was not able to manage in her absence. It was in these times that the severity of his cognitive impairment became obvious.

Before the current admission, Mr. Kane was referred to a VA Geriatrics Clinic for evaluation of his cognitive functioning. They ordered an MRI and performed a cognitive screener. On screening (MoCA), he scored 9 out of 30 (with 1 point added for education) with primary deficits in the areas of learning and memory. This clinic diagnosed Mr. Kane with "vascular dementia; with moderate subcortical white matter disease, moderate atrophy" noting that the history, cognitive screen, and brain imaging were consistent with a vascular dementia in the setting of long-standing, poorly controlled hypertension. They noted that mixed Alzheimer's disease and vascular dementia was also possible.

On admission to our unit, it was clear that Mr. Kane could not make his own medical decisions and required an activated HCA to serve in this role. He had not completed a formal advance directive, which meant we turned to the VA hierarchy for surrogate decision-makers. As the spouse, Jeannie would be the default surrogate and HCA for VA purposes. Unfortunately, Jeannie was initially difficult to reach because of her own medical needs. She had recently had toes amputated and was in a rehab facility. She and Mr. Kane spoke almost daily by phone while admitted in separate facilities. After about 2 months in our care, Jeannie called Mr. Kane's social worker to let her know that although she was still in rehab, she intended to move home soon with her husband. During this time, the VA social worker did attempt to reach Mr. Kane's only other known next-of-kin, his estranged daughter, but the provided phone number was disconnected; neither Mr. and Mrs. Kane nor their niece had up-to-date numbers, and she was not listed in phone directories.

A few weeks later, we received a call from the rehab facility where Jeannie was getting care. They shared that she was not progressing well in rehab and might require LTC. Jeannie was unable to feel her lower extremities and could not do stairs without the assistance of at least two other people. Despite this, Jeannie has told them she planned on returning home with her husband. The rehab facility arranged for a family meeting with Jeannie and both care teams. In this meeting, neither team recommended discharge home, and both teams offered to work together to try and place Jeannie and Mr. Kane into the same LTC facility. Unfortunately, Jeannie disagreed with this recommendation and insisted she would only discharge to their home. Both care teams suggested that to discharge home, they would recommend extensive in-home services, and the teams agreed to work together to maximize home services for this couple. Again, Jeannie disagreed that she or her husband would need any assistance at home, and she would not agree to referrals for in-home services.

The next week, Jeannie called the VA social worker, informing her that she intended to pick up her husband to bring him home in a few days. After this call, the VA social worker called Jeannie's rehab facility to discuss discharge planning. That facility shared that they had found Jeannie to "lack capacity" and recommended LTC placement for her. They were not clear about what specific capacities they felt Jeannie lacked and were unable to share written reports or documentation with us. Of note, Jeannie's HCA was her adult son Jack from a previous marriage, who lived out of state and provided no instrumental supports to Jeannie or Mr. Kane. When the rehab facility found Jeannie to lack capacity, they activated her HCA. Jack agreed that despite concerns from the team, his mother could return to living independently in her own home without additional support services. Essentially, he deferred his decision-making authority back to his mother.

At this point, the VA care team felt stuck and was not sure what to do. Being separated was causing both Mr. Kane and Jeannie distress. Mr. Kane wanted to go home and be with his wife, and his wife wanted the same. Unfortunately, it did not seem that either of them were able to identify possible risks with that plan and Jeannie was not willing to accept any additional in-home services that might bolster her capacity to care for her husband at home. Mr. Kane could not really participate beyond saying he wanted to be home with Jeannie. He required 24-hour supervision due to his cognitive impairment. We had reports that Jeannie "lacked capacity" and that she was physically unable to get around without assistance. It was our strong suspicion that she would not be able to meet her husband's care needs at home without assistance. However, her HCA was deferring to her and was planning to allow her to return to independent living without assistance. She would be discharged home the following week.

Interview, Examination, and Tests

Given the urgency of knowing Jeannie could show up within days to bring Mr. Kane home, our team discussed the options we felt existed to us at that time. We agreed on the following steps:

1. Mr. Kane could not be discharged to the care of his wife until there was a safe(r) plan in place.
2. Because Jeannie was not our patient, we could unfortunately not assess her capacity directly. Thus, we would rely on a compilation of the available information to guide our thinking.
3. We would place a consult to our health care system's ethics committee to seek guidance.
4. If after ethics consultation, it was determined that Mr. Kane could be discharged home with Jeannie, we would need to make a referral to adult protective services for suspected self-neglect.

Ethics Consult

Our local ethics committee responded to our request by interviewing our team to better understand the concerns and dilemma, and they facilitated a helpful discussion with our team. We discussed the reported assessment of Jeannie as lacking decision-making capacity during her recent admission to a rehab facility and her leaving that facility against medical advice. This raised important concerns regarding the safety of our patient if he were to return home to this caretaker. Given that decision-making capacity is context specific and may change over time, we all agreed that an assessment of whether a person lacks capacity to make a particular decision about one's own health care, in and of itself, does not ethically preclude that person from being a caretaker of a patient with dementia, particularly with supportive services in place that could bolster functional capacities. In this case, there were several concerns beyond Jeannie's decision-making capacity, such as her mobility, that also raised concerns. The ethics consultants highlighted for us their guidance that the medical team's ethical obligation in this case was to make a thorough safety assessment of the patient's discharge plan to home under his wife's care, using all available sources of information. This was to include conversations we'd had with the rehab facility, conversations with Mr. Kane and Jeannie, as well as any other relevant information we could obtain. We discussed the possibility of using adult protective services to help assess the home situation for safety, and we concluded that there was enough open concern for the patient's safety at home to contact elder services for assistance. Ultimately, the goal of our team was to reunite Mr. Kane and his wife while respecting their values of autonomy and independence in the safest possible way.

Family Meeting

The VA social worker was able to reach out to Jeannie and let her know we would need to meet to come up with a safe plan for Mr. Kane to leave the VA. Because Jeannie could not drive, we met by phone, and she asked her local niece, Lynnette, to join the call. On this call, the VA team discussed our worries about Mr. Kane discharging home given his great care needs (e.g., constant cueing, medication management, food preparation, and 24-hour supervision), and Jeannie's recent need for rehab herself. Initially she denied any concerns or issues saying she could handle it on her own. Thankfully, Lynnette also shared our concerns and was able to help her aunt be a bit more flexible in her thinking about the discharge plan. Ultimately, after a lengthy discussion, Jeannie agreed to the following supportive services: referrals for Meals-on-Wheels and homemaker services provided by local elder services, a referral for home-based primary care and a personal alarm system for Mr. Kane both provided by VA, and a family member would stay over for the first few nights Mr. Kane was home to ensure a safe transition. With Jeannie's agreement for services and her niece agreeing to stay with them for a few days, our social worker began making referrals to get the veteran home with his wife the next week. Of note, both the team, and the niece Lynnette continued to encourage Jeannie to think about LTC placement for her and her husband.

Discharge Home

Mr. Kane was discharged home with a plan for extensive in-home services to aid his wife in caring for him. Six days later, Lynnette called to report that her aunt Jeannie was admitted to a local hospital for dehydration. She shared that Jeannie and Mr. Kane had been found in their home with the windows and doors shut and the heat running, despite outside temps of more than 90 degrees. They had apparently refused to allow any services into their home, and no family had been permitted to stay over. Mr. Kane was brought back to the VA and found to have lost 11 pounds since he left our care 6 days earlier. In the days that followed, Lynnette informed us that her aunt would be needing surgery and she no longer felt it would be safe for Jeannie to care for Mr. Kane in their home. However, during this time, Jeannie continued to call the VA stating her desire to bring her husband home again. The team felt this discharge had served as a fork in the road and began conferring with legal counsel about the process of removing Jeannie as the HCA.

Findings

It had been clear from the beginning that Mr. Kane required a surrogate decision-maker. In the absence of an advance directive, his wife Jeannie was tasked with this role. Despite initial concerns regarding her capacity, the team worked hard to try and find a solution that would both honor Jeannie and Mr. Kane's desires to be together and also mitigate risk by providing ample in-home services to bolster her capacity to care for Mr. Kane at home. As in most capacity and risk situations, we were balancing promotion of autonomy with protection from harm and given the couple's strong desire to be together at home we prioritized autonomy with supports to the full extent possible, while trying to ensure safety (APA, 2017). This decision involved accepting some risks. Unfortunately, that plan failed, as evidenced by her hospitalization, his rapid weight loss, and her absolute refusal of all offered in-home supportive services once she had Mr. Kane home. The failed discharged then served as robust evidence of Jeannie's incapacity for serving as the surrogate decision-maker for her husband because she was unable to see her own limitations and had now shown she was unable to make choices that kept her husband safe. The sum of the evidence now led to the conclusion that Jeannie could not serve as Mr. Kane's surrogate, and another surrogate would have to be found or appointed.

Analysis and Reflection on Findings

To organize our thoughts about this case, we again apply the Karel (2011) framework presented earlier.

Step 1: Clarify the ethical issue. What is the dilemma? In this case, the primary dilemma centered around questions of the team's responsibility when a surrogate appears to no longer have capacity, and the surrogate is not under our care but is part of our care plan for the patient who is under our care. A related dilemma included trying to balance the protection of a vulnerable elder from harm while trying to honor his desire to be with his wife who no longer seems capable of safely caring for him.

Step 2: Clarify who are the relevant stakeholders and each of their values, goals, and interests. Stakeholders in this case included Mr. Kane, his wife Jeannie, and his medical team. Mr. Kane's goal was to be with his wife Jeannie. He did not understand the recommendation against going home, so it is unclear whether he strongly desired to go home or if his main value was being with his wife regardless of location. Jeannie's goal was also reunification with her husband. However, she was clear that she had a strong preference against LTC and would only settle for having Mr. Kane at home. Her values were firmly in the camp of autonomy and independence. The medical team's primary goal was to reunite Mr. Kane with his wife in a safe environment, which was thought to require LTC placement of both parties. The main value of the medical team was for the safety of this vulnerable elder, even at the cost of being with his wife (because she was not agreeing to LTC placement).

Step 3: Clarify decision-making authority. Who has the right to make the decision in a particular situation? It was determined that Mr. Kane needed a surrogate decision-maker. However, he had not completed an advance directive, and it was eventually determined that his next-of-kin (wife) also did not have capacity to make decisions on his behalf. Despite a strong desire to care for her husband at home, she was not able to identify any possible risks of doing so or appreciate any risk of potential harm to him even after a failed attempt at discharging him home to her care. Therefore, Mr. Kane was in need of a new surrogate decision-maker.

Step 4: Consider all ethically justifiable options and their pros and cons for each stakeholder. In this case, options included allowing Mr. Kane's wife Jeannie to continue serving as his surrogate decision-maker, or not allowing it and having to search for a new surrogate for him. Keeping Jeannie in place as the HCA may have been most respectful of both Mr. Kane's and his wife's autonomy and values of being together. However, serious risks existed with this option, as evidenced by the poor outcomes of the last attempt to discharge Mr. Kane home to Jeannie's care. It was clear to the team that Jeannie could not make safe decisions for her husband. However, to remove Jeannie as the HCA meant we were more likely to keep him safe from harm, but at the expense of their autonomy. This course was also rather extreme because it is unusual for a team to determine an HCA is not able to serve in this role; this course must only be considered when there is evidence of a high likelihood of harm to the principal. Further, this route had no clear end because there was no other obvious HCA available. This would keep Mr. Kane in VA care until either a new HCA could be identified or until a guardian could be appointed.

Step 5: Implement the plan, evaluate, and reevaluate. We worked to make the team's determination and recommendations clear to the care teams and to Mr. Kane's family with the goal of maximizing his safety.

Interventions and Dispositions

Following the team's final decision, the medical provider documented the need for an alternate decision-maker due to the wife's apparent incapacity, and she was removed from her role as Mr. Kane's HCA. Jeannie obviously disagreed with this finding and could not understand why her husband was being "kept" from her. Thus began the long process of identifying a new HCA for Mr. Kane. In subsequent family meetings Jeannie often involved her niece Lynnette. Lynnette revealed herself to be a very caring person who wanted to help her aunt and uncle but who also wanted to maintain a relationship with them. She had a background in social work herself and was a savvy intermediary between the team and Jeannie. However, she was also Jeannie's niece and thus not formally related to Mr. Kane.

For several months, while Jeannie was herself in a rehab facility, the team reiterated to her and Lynnette the recommendation for Mr. Kane to be placed in LTC. When Jeannie was discharged from rehab, she undertook months of attempts to again bring her husband home with her. Jeannie made demands, accused the team of racism, and complained to the mayor's office. During this time, the team continued to periodically meet with Jeannie to try and explain the situation that her husband could not come home with her, that home had not gone well, and that he now needs LTC. In the background, much work was done to try and track down other potential HCAs. Mr. Kane's daughter was eventually located when a cousin reached out to Lynette with an updated phone number for her. Mr. Kane's daughter agreed to have Jeannie's niece Lynnette serve as the point of contact and HCA for Mr. Kane, and she would serve as a secondary HCA. Lynnette then agreed to seek guardianship of Mr. Kane with the ultimate goal of placing him and Jeannie in the same LTC facility.

Outcome

Mr. Kane continued receiving care at the VA. For several months, his wife persisted in asking to take him home and in periodically having him screened for assisted living facilities. She was again hospitalized and sent to a rehab facility that was also recommending her for LTC. Lynnette began the process of becoming Mr. Kane's guardian, and the courts granted limited guardianship within a year. She was then able to begin applying for insurance that would allow her to place Mr. Kane in a non-VA LTC. Throughout this course, Mr. Kane spent more than 2 years in VA LTC until he suffered an irreversible heart failure exacerbation, and Lynnette made the decision to transfer him to a VA hospice unit for end-of-life care, where he remained until his death.

REFLECTION

It is generally accepted that people have a right to appoint a HCA of their choosing, and they usually maintain the capacity to do so even while potentially lacking other capacities. However, sometimes selected HCAs are a poor or dangerous choice or are later revealed to be inadequate for the role of HCA through demonstrated behaviors or losing capacity themselves. These cases are challenging for health care teams, and it is often unclear what responsibility, if any, the team has in intervening with chosen HCAs. Maintenance of a patient's autonomy is generally considered paramount, and overriding patients' autonomy related to their HCA selection should only be done in cases when there are clear and significant safety concerns. If the HCA's appropriateness comes into question, we must use evidence beyond a clinical interview (e.g., adult protective services or police reports, collateral info from family or other health care providers, clinical evidence of harm to the patient) to determine whether the HCA is a sufficiently unsafe choice to allow overriding autonomy. The risk of harm to the patient would need to be high, imminent, or both. To supersede someone's autonomy is always an extreme act, and it must be done so only after a careful examination of all acceptable alternatives.

LONG-TERM RECOMMENDATIONS WHEN HCAs' CAPACITIES ARE IN QUESTION

- When working with challenging or potentially unsafe HCAs, it is wise to be informed about hospital policies and state laws that might guide you (e.g., VA policy regarding hierarchy of surrogates).
- If team members are considering trying to remove an HCA, they should consider a thorough and structured discussion of the case using an ethical framework such as those presented in Karel (2011) or Rhodes and Holzman (2004).
- Psychologists in most states have a legal responsibility to protect older adults from harm via our role as mandated reporters.
- Consultation is key. These sorts of cases often require conferring with other professionals such as legal counsel or your local ethics committee to help ensure you are in compliance with the law and with ethical principles.
- Consideration of risk is crucial to determining an HCA is not appropriate. It is not enough for the HCA to disagree with the team or present a vague risk of harm. Rather, you will want to consider the likelihood of serious or imminent harm to the patient in your decision about the named or proposed HCA.

REFERENCES

AARP. (2008). *AARP Bulletin Poll. "Getting ready to go," executive summary*. Retrieved from http://assets.aarp.org/rgcenter/il/getting_ready.pdf

American Bar Association and American Psychological Association Assessment of Capacity in Older Adults Project Working Group. (2008). *Assessment of older adults with diminished capacity: A handbook for psychologists*. Washington, DC: American Bar Association and American Psychological Association.

American Psychological Association. (2017). *Ethical principles of psychologists and code of conduct* (2002, Amended June 1, 2010, and January 1, 2017). Retrieved from https://www.apa.org/ethics/code

Black, B. S., Fogarty, L. A., Phillips, H., Finucane, T., Loreck, D. J., Baker, A., . . . Rabins, P. V. (2009). Surrogate decision makers' understanding of dementia patients' prior wishes for end-of-life care. *Journal of Aging and Health, 21*, 627–650. http://dx.doi.org/10.1177/0898264309333316

Carrese, J. A., Mullaney, J. L., Faden, R. R., & Finucane, T. E. (2002). Planning for death but not serious future illness: Qualitative study of housebound elderly patients. *BMJ, 325*, 125–127. http://dx.doi.org/10.1136/bmj.325.7356.125

Farrell, T. W., Widera, E., Rosenberg, L., Rubin, C. D., Naik, A. D., Braun, U., . . . Shega, J., & the Ethics, Clinical Practice and Models of Care, and Public Policy Committees of the American Geriatrics Society. (2017). AGS position statement: Making medical treatment decisions for unbefriended older adults. *Journal of the American Geriatrics Society, 65*, 14–15. http://dx.doi.org/10.1111/jgs.14586

Gamble, E. R., McDonald, P. J., & Lichstein, P. R. (1991). Knowledge, attitudes, and behavior of elderly persons regarding living wills. *Archives of Internal Medicine, 151,* 277–280. http://dx.doi.org/10.1001/archinte.1991.00400020049011

Gessert, C. E., Forbes, S., & Bern-Klug, M. (2001). Planning end-of-life care for patients with dementia: Roles of families and health professionals. *Omega: Journal of Death and Dying, 42,* 273–291. http://dx.doi.org/10.2190/2MT2-5GYU-GXVV-95NE

Givens, J. L., Kiely, D. K., Carey, K., & Mitchell, S. L. (2009). Healthcare proxies of nursing home residents with advanced dementia: Decisions they confront and their satisfaction with decision-making. *Journal of the American Geriatrics Society, 57,* 1149–1155. http://dx.doi.org/10.1111/j.1532-5415.2009.02304.x

Hines, S. C., Glover, J. J., Babrow, A. S., Holley, J. L., Badzek, L. A., & Moss, A. H. (2001). Improving advance care planning by accommodating family preferences. *Journal of Palliative Medicine, 4,* 481–489. http://dx.doi.org/10.1089/109662101753381629

Hopp, F. P. (2000). Preferences for surrogate decision makers, informal communication, and advance directives among community-dwelling elders: Results from a national study. *The Gerontologist, 40,* 449–457. http://dx.doi.org/10.1093/geront/40.4.449

Jones, A. L., Moss, A. J., & Harris-Kojetin, L. D. (2011). *Use of advance directives in long-term care populations* (NCHS Data Brief No. 54). Hyattsville, MD: National Center for Health Statistics. Retrieved from http://www.cdc.gov/nchs/data/databriefs/db54.pdf

Karel, M. J. (2011). Ethics. In V. Molinari (Ed.), *Specialty competencies in geropsychology* (pp. 115–142). New York, NY: Oxford University Press. http://dx.doi.org/10.1093/med:psych/9780195385670.003.0009

Karp, N., & Wood, E. (2004, Spring). Incapacitated and alone: Healthcare decision making for unbefriended older people. *Human Rights Magazine, 31,* 20. Retrieved from https://www.americanbar.org/groups/crsj/publications/human_rights_magazine_home/human_rights_vol31_2004/spring2004/hr_spring04_incapacitated/

Kass-Bartelmes, B. L. (2003). Advance care planning: Preferences for care at the end of life. *Research in Action Issue, 12.* Washington, DC: U.S. Agency for Healthcare Research and Quality. Retrieved from http://www.ahrq.gov/research/endliferia/endria.htm

Langa, K. M., Larson, E. B., Crimmins, E. M., Faul, J. D., Levine, D. A., Kabeto, M. U., & Weir, D. R. (2017). A comparison of the prevalence of dementia in the United States in 2000 and 2012. *JAMA Internal Medicine, 177,* 51–58. http://dx.doi.org/10.1001/jamainternmed.2016.6807

Norton, M. C., Smith, K. R., Østbye, T., Tschanz, J. T., Corcoran, C., Schwartz, S., . . . Welsh-Bohmer, K. A., & the Cache County Investigators. (2010). Greater risk of dementia when spouse has dementia? The Cache County study. [See editorial comments by Dr. Peter P. Vitaliano, pp. 976–978]. *Journal of the American Geriatrics Society, 58,* 895–900. http://dx.doi.org/10.1111/j.1532-5415.2010.02806.x

Pew Research Center. (2006). *Strong public support for right to die: More Americans discussing—and planning—end-of-life treatment.* Retrieved from http://people-press.org/report/266/strongpublic-support-for-right-to-die

Plassman, B. L., Langa, K. M., Fisher, G. G., Heeringa, S. G., Weir, D. R., Ofstedal, M. B., . . . Wallace, R. B. (2007). Prevalence of dementia in the United States: The aging, demographics, and memory study. *Neuroepidemiology, 29,* 125–132. http://dx.doi.org/10.1159/000109998

Rhodes, R., & Holzman, I. R. (2004). The not unreasonable standard for assessment of surrogates and surrogate decisions. *Theoretical Medicine and Bioethics, 25,* 367–385. http://dx.doi.org/10.1007/s11017-004-3138-6

Smith, K. L., Fedel, P., & Heitman, J. (2017). Incapacitated surrogates: A new and increasing dilemma in hospital care. *The Journal of Clinical Ethics, 28,* 279–289.

Staats, N., & Edelstein, B. (1995, November). *Cognitive changes associated with the declining competency of older adults.* Paper presented at the Gerontological Society of America, Los Angeles.

Torke, A. M., Sachs, G. A., Helft, P. R., Montz, K., Hui, S. L., Slaven, J. E., & Callahan, C. M. (2014). Scope and outcomes of surrogate decision making among hospitalized older adults. *JAMA Internal Medicine, 174,* 370–377. http://dx.doi.org/10.1001/jamainternmed.2013.13315

West, L. A., Cole, S., Goodkind, D., & He, W. (2014). *65+ in the United States: 2010* (P-23–221). Washington, DC: U.S. Census Bureau. Retrieved from https://www.census.gov/content/dam/Census/library/publications/2014/demo/p23-212.pdf

12

Addressing Family Conflicts When Assessing Capacities

Amy E. Albright, Michelle M. Hilgeman, and Rebecca S. Allen

KEY POINTS

- Evaluations of capacities often arise in complex social contexts where families are in conflict, raising the question "who decides?"
- Sex and gender roles, birth order, cohesiveness, family size, perceived intelligence or expertise, financial contribution, employment or occupational status, household composition (e.g., single parent, blended, or grandparent led), unmarried cohabitating couples, and a host of other ever-changing factors can shape decisions from purchasing habits to rule-making to who makes legal and health care decisions (e.g., Lee & Beatty, 2002).
- Intersectional identities and positive marginality are likely to vary tremendously by cohort, as individuals and their choices are influenced across the life span by the timing of events such as cognitive status changes within a life, the historic time and place in which a life is led, the linking of individual lives with others, and an individual's own agentic decision-making (Elder, 1998).
- Family conflict can contribute to inefficient or ineffective provision of care and can precipitate or complicate an evaluation of capacities.

http://dx.doi.org/10.1037/0000184-013
Assessing Capacities of Older Adults: A Casebook to Guide Difficult Decisions, J. Moye (Editor)

For most people decisions occur in a social context. When an older adult develops difficulty with capacities, such as in the setting of dementia, decisional support is typically provided by family caregivers through informal and formal mechanisms. Often, in these supportive families, formal assessment of capacities is not needed as the family network dynamically adapts its supports. Or if an assessment of capacities is needed in late-stage dementia, the assessment is fairly straightforward as families spring to fulfill roles as health care agents under an advance directive or durable power of attorney agreement. This book does not focus on such straightforward situations, but on those in which decisional supports are challenging to implement because the family is in conflict (as well as situations in which there is no family). The purpose of this chapter is to discuss the families in conflict as a common element of the social context in the evaluation of capacities. First, we discuss the social context for decision-making. Then we discuss four issues that intersect with families in conflict and that may arise in evaluation of capacities: diversity, blended families, interpersonal violence, and disclosure. We illustrate these issues with case vignettes; the cases are not meant to illustrate "how to do" an assessment of capacities (which is the subject of previous chapters) but to bring the complexity of the social context to life. Finally, we describe an ethical framework and clinical approach for resolving these challenges.

FAMILY AS SOCIAL CONTEXT FOR HEALTH CARE AND PERSONAL DECISION-MAKING

Factors that affect an individual's decision-making within the family system have been widely studied since the 1970s (Allen & Shuster, 2002; Belch & Willis, 2006). Gender roles, birth order, cohesiveness, family size, perceived intelligence or expertise, financial contribution, employment or occupational status, household composition (e.g., single parent, blended, or grandparent led), unmarried cohabitating couples, and a host of other ever-changing factors can shape decisions from purchasing habits to rule-making to who makes legal and health care decisions (e.g., Lee & Beatty, 2002). The interplay of these issues only becomes more complicated when one individual's capacities to make decisions independently is diminished. In general, Americans define *family* as "a group of individuals who by birth, adoption, marriage, or declared commitment share deep personal connections and are mutually entitled to receive, and obligated to provide, support of various kinds" (Levine, 1990, p. 33). When capacities to make decisions are diminished due to illness or other factors, families of origin—and families of choice—are typically the first to step into that role.

Families step into this role through various mechanisms, most notably as health care agents under an advance directive, executed by persons to designate which individual, often a family member, should make a decision in a situation where they are unable to do so. In the absence of an advance directive, most states (and via policy in the U.S. Veterans Health Administration) allow "default" consent after an order of priority (e.g., spouse, children, siblings) but do not fully address how to resolve conflicts that may arise between surrogates at the same or different levels, nor do they include nontraditional proxy decision-makers such as girlfriends or boyfriends, or nieces and nephews. As noted in Chapter 1, some states are also beginning to recognize shared decision-making agreements, but with these too, it may be challenging to resolve situations in which family supporters are in conflict or when a neurocognitive disorder diminishes individuals' insight into problems with memory or judgment that seriously jeopardizes their safety or those of others.

Nevertheless, most decisional support in aging families happens more informally. Families often fulfill long-term caregiving roles, providing as much as 90% of in-home long-term care (Adelman, Tmanova, Delgado, Dion, & Lachs, 2014; Institute of Medicine, 2014). Fortunately, for many families, diminished independence occurs gradually over time (e.g., as in Alzheimer's disease, advanced cancer, AIDS), allowing for discussions about preferences and more partnered decision-making as the disease progresses. In a small but elegant study, Samsi and Manthorpe (2013) interviewed 12 dyads (one person with dementia and one caregiver) four times over 1 year to examine the experience of shared decision-making among care partners. They identified gradual transitions in decision-making. Specifically, decision-making discourse evolved over time where everyday decisions, at first, were made jointly among care partners but were made more wholly by the caregiver later. Stressors identified throughout this process involved determining their relative's decision-making capacities and weighing options regarding their values and best interests.

Edwards, Olson, Koop, and Northcott (2012) used the analogy of "dancing on the stairs" to chronicle the "inordinate efforts taken by informal caregivers to ensure that their family member would be able to live and die in the manner of his or her choosing" (p. 178), even after the person could no longer be involved in expressing their wishes. At the core of gracefully navigating the dance was the goal of maintaining the individual's control for as long as possible. The imagery of their conceptual model resonates—as the picture of what we hope to see, or as the best-case scenarios for high-functioning families across settings:

- Inviting the Dancers (seeking answers, receiving the diagnosis)
- Finding the Tune (taking stock, making lifestyle changes)
- Managing the Steps (taking the lead, cutting in)
- Finishing the Dance (controlling access, winding down, bowing out)
- The Experience of Death
- Leaving the Dance (processing, moving on, considering the future)

The landscape, however, quickly becomes more complicated when the sphere of decision-makers expands beyond the involvement of two individuals;

when transitions occur more abruptly or even unexpectedly; or when complicated family histories, competing needs, or distressed individuals join the mix. The stress of such transitions in medical or financial decision-making often engenders family conflict, even in families that have had low conflict in the past. Ethical quandaries are inevitable for clinicians (and teams) who must determine "who decides?"

Clinical Presentation

Family conflict is defined as "interpersonal tension or struggles between two or more persons (family members) whose opinions, values, needs, or expectations are opposing or incompatible" (Kramer, Boelk, & Auer, 2006, p. 794). It can contribute to inefficient or ineffective provision of care and is one of the most common reasons for ethics consultation in health care settings. Most often studied in palliative care and end-of-life decision-making—when the identified patient is least likely to be functioning independently—family conflict has been described as a major barrier to success in addressing end-of-life care needs by hospice teams, nurses, and physicians (Bridgman & Carr, 1998; Holst, Lundgren, Olsen, & Ishøy, 2009; Kayashima & Braun, 2001; Kramer & Yonker, 2011). It has been documented to jeopardize quality end-of-life care and to increase distress among patients and their families (Kramer, Boelk, & Auer, 2006).

When working with older adults and their families, the following potential sources of familial conflicts may arise (some of these are illustrated in the four case vignettes that follow):

- Autonomy versus safety of the patient and family member (Cases 1, 2, and 3)
  - Driving cessation priorities (e.g., dignity/independence, potential for harm)
  - Independence in financial decisions (e.g., making "bad" purchases, gambling online, giving money away)
  - Freedom of movement (e.g., to lock or unlock the doors; when to supervise or discontinue work in the carpentry shed out back?)
  - Differences in perceived risk around safety concerns (e.g., need for supervision, retaining firearms and their storage) (Case 1)
- Changes to the patient's role or identity (Cases 2 and 4)
- Accusations of neglect, exploitation, or sequestration of the person with diminished capacities (Cases 1, 2, and 3)
- Geographic proximity or distance of family members (Case 2)
- Grief responses of both the patient and family member (Cases 1 and 2)
- Mediation of communication pathways (Case 2)

- Financial practicalities and allocation of resources (Cases 1, 2, and 3)
  - Potential conflicts of interest (e.g., when life-sustaining treatment decisions are made in the context of a family or spouse that is dependent on a service connection or social security check for basic needs).
- Trust of health care system and providers (Cases 1, 3, and 4)
- Family adjustment to health care advocacy role (Case 1 and 3)
- Making medical decisions when patient wishes are unknown (Case 3)
  - Pain treatment priorities (e.g., comfort, sedation, lucidity, "dependence")
  - Decisions counter to medical advice (e.g., forgoing treatment, futile tests and treatments)
- Considerations of culture and diversity (Case 1 and 4)

These conflicts listed are not limited solely to the older adult; they may frequently involve ways in which individuals interact within a dynamic family system or health care or legal setting. When working with older adults and their families, it is important to be aware of which party is the identified client—the individual, a family member, an attorney, or an agency—and to convey that during informed consent processes (Standard 9.03 of the American Psychological Association's [APA's; 2017] *Ethical Principles of Psychologists and Code of Conduct*). For example, in the case of assessment of capacity to appoint a durable power of attorney, a mental health professional may be required to interact with multiple family members. Moreover, the mental health professional may be working under a contract with a legal firm or service and therefore hold obligations to this service that may be at odds with the desires of the individual and family (Bush, Allen, & Molinari, 2017). In these cases, clear and early identification of the client is critical for the provider, the older adult, the family, and the agency(ies) through which services are being provided. For example, in a recent case, a legal services attorney group within a local university-affiliated Elder Law Clinic was our client. They asked us to determine an older adult's capacities to (a) revoke a power of attorney for finances and (b) live independently. The evaluation resulted in a determination that the individual did not retain capacities to revoke durable power of attorney or to live independently. Although this information was needed and useful for the Elder Law Clinic to provide legal services, it was not to the liking of the older adult, who desired to regain autonomy.

Inevitably, clinicians working in the area of the assessment of capacities will encounter families experiencing distress. A primary source of distress is a diagnosis of an illness that affects individual capacities, such as dementia, and the caregiving role (Blieszner & Roberto, 2010; McIlvane, Popa, Robinson, Houseweart, & Haley, 2008). In addition, family distress may include presentations involving factors such as the following:

- multiple marriages, involvement or lack of involvement of adult stepchildren;

- estranged families, divorced spouses (e.g., serving as health care proxies; he said–she said conflicts);
- current or past psychopathology or substance abuse;
- current or past physical, sexual, or emotional abuse or neglect (e.g., resentment as a potential risk factor for abuse, or unavailability of health care proxies who know the older adult's wishes);
- legal disputes between family members (e.g., restraining orders);
- financial dependence or exploitation;
- newly formed romantic relationships; and
- complex caregiving contexts with multiple people receiving care from the same caregiver (e.g., mother, dependent child(ren), unbefriended elderly neighbor).

It should again be noted that these conflicts may involve the older adult or family members. Even if the older adult does not appear to be directly involved, such conflicts may influence family decision-making and subsequent care. Parks and colleagues (2011) conducted telephone interviews with 202 community-dwelling, cognitively intact older adults (mean age = 78.9 years) and their identified health care proxies (mean age = 59.6 years) to examine the impact of family conflict on accuracy in end-of-life treatment decisions. Their results showed that elder–proxy relationships with more family conflict were marked by lower accuracy or agreement when trying to predict what the older adult would have wanted. They also found that overall, spousal proxies were more accurate than adult children. There was not an interaction between proxy–relationship type and level of conflict on accuracy of decisions (Parks et al., 2011).

DIVERSITY AS SOCIAL CONTEXT IN THE EVALUATION OF CAPACITIES

Families are one aspect of social identity. Diversity factors intersect with family factors to define a person's identity but may also place them at risk for health disparities. Health disparities increase morbidity and risk of mortality and also reduce the ability to achieve optimal health outcomes among disadvantaged groups, including people of color, those with low education and income, and rural-dwelling individuals (Centers for Disease Control and Prevention, 2013); this is compounded within the context of changing cognitive abilities. The intersection of family structure with race, ethnicity, socioeconomic status, gender identity, sexual orientation, ability status, religious beliefs, and geographic place of residence may expose individuals with greater combinations of low social status identities to significantly more stigma and discrimination, even among individuals in legal contexts such as forensic examiners and jury members (Cox, Stanziani, Coffey, & deLacy, 2018; Stanziani, Cox, & Coffey, 2018). Intersectionality theory (Bauer, 2014; Bowleg, 2012; Earnshaw et al., 2018) posits that distinct social identities work together simultaneously and dynamically to influence self-identity and experiences within society (Cole, 2009; Collins, 2000; Crenshaw, 1991), including changes that may take place in aging families during changes in cognitive abilities of one member and resultant care transitions. Discrimination, stigma and health disparities are not exclusive to individual social categories, but rather involve the intersections of multiple identities. Therefore, the experience of a rural, Christian, African American, mother–daughter dyad in the Deep South engaged in care transitions in which the mother's capacities may be in question is likely to be quite different from that of a non-Hispanic White, agnostic, married, heterosexual couple in a large metropolitan city in the northeast in which the wife's capacities may be in question.

In addition to the aforementioned factors, individuals holding minority identities such as lesbian, gay, bisexual, transgender, and queer (LGBTQ) family systems may be challenged by discriminatory policies and practices particularly in legal or health care settings (Acquaviva, 2017), including who is considered next of kin if no advance planning documents are available containing this information (Allen, Noh, Beck, & Smith, 2016). However, individuals self-identifying as members of such minority groups may also experience a level of social support that increases their resilience to manage such difficulties. Positive marginality exists when the individual embraces marginal identities and positions him or herself as an activist by making their outsider status explicit and known to others (Mayo, 1982; Unger, 2000). This may be particularly true for those who hold identities and social statuses based on less observable forms of marginality, including social class, religion, sexual orientation or gender identity, concealable physical disabilities, and chronic illness. Intersectional identities and positive marginality are likely to vary tremendously by cohort, as individuals and their choices are influenced across the life span by the timing of events such as cognitive status changes within a life, the historic time and place in which a life is led, the linking of individual lives with others, and an individual's own agentic decision-making (Elder, 1998). The issue of family disagreement in the setting of diversity is illustrated in the case vignette that follows. In this case and those that follow, although based on a real case, details are changed for the purposes of protecting anonymity and conveying a highly complex set of facts that typically evolved over months in a brief vignette.

Case Vignette 1: Mr. Johnson

Capacity Issue

Does Mr. Johnson have the capacity to decide where to live—namely, to live at home alone? Does he have the capacity to refuse the sale of his farm?

Social Context Issues

Mr. Johnson's wife died several years ago, and a son is acting as caregiver. However, there is conflict, and the son moves out. The son is in conflict with another son and Mr. Johnson; there are allegations of assault and abuse, some of which are substantiated. Issues of race and rurality add to social complexity.

Presentation

Mr. Robert Johnson, an 87-year-old African American man from rural Mississippi with major neurocognitive disorder (Alzheimer's disease), first came to the attention of the psychology team on a specialty geriatric psychiatry inpatient unit. Mr. Johnson was committed to this unit from the court after a domestic incident in which he wounded one of his sons, his caregiver, with a firearm. He was determined to be unable to stand trial due to dementia and was transferred to the inpatient unit for further evaluation and to determine a plan of care. The team was concerned about discharging him home alone given his level of dementia and declining functioning and judgment (described later in the vignette). His son, although recovered from the gunshot, no longer wishes to function as his caregiver, nor could other family. Home services (e.g., home health aide, chore service, meals on wheels) were limited in his rural area, and Mr. Johnson also refuses these. The team recommended placement in a setting with supervision, such as an adult foster home or a long-term care facility. However, without savings or income to be able to pay for this institutional care, he would need to sell his farm, and after spending these proceeds, apply for Medicaid to pay for the care. An additional complication is that he remained legally involved because of the shooting, with the criminal court also weighing in on his disposition.

History

Mr. Johnson was raised and educated in the rural Deep South during segregation, and educational resources and therefore quality were unequal in this geographic area at that time. He completed high school and worked as a farmer after graduation. He served in the U.S. Army and returned to his community following his military service, eventually purchasing a farm. Mr. Johnson was married for more than 50 years, and he and his wife had two sons. He reported a deep sense of attachment to his farm for several reasons. It was the home in which he and his wife had lived for the entirety of their marriage. In addition, in the mid-1950s he faced many obstacles in purchasing and retaining his farm as an African American, and this further added to his attachment to the land. Mr. Johnson had no legal history before the altercation with his son, which was understood to be a lapse of judgment associated with his dementia.

After the death of his wife several years earlier, one of Mr. Johnson's sons moved into the family home to act as his caretaker and assist with meals, home care, and farm care. Mr. Johnson stated that he had always had a troubled relationship with his son. Mr. Johnson alleged his son was stealing money from him, although an investigation by elder protective services could not substantiate this claim but did conclude that Mr. Johnson was at risk for financial exploitation. Mr. Johnson's son continued to live with him, and after an altercation in which his son allegedly struck him in the head, Mr. Johnson shot him with a firearm. The son stated the disagreement was an escalation related to his prompting his father to bathe.

During his time in the inpatient facility, Mr. Johnson needed prompting for bathing and meals but regularly attended group therapy sessions. Although other patients on the unit could exhibit high levels of agitation and distress, he remained calm and tolerated this environment well.

Assessment of Capacities

Mr. Johnson was assessed to determine his capacities to make decisions about where to live, along with his ability to refuse sale of his farm. Along with cognitive and functional evaluation, factors considered included his self-care at home and on the unit, impulsiveness with his son (shooting him), lack of impulsiveness on the unit, and elder protective services reports, along with consideration of his values as assessed with the Values Preferences Scale (Whitlatch, Feinberg, & Tucke, 2005) and supports available. He established rapport easily with examiners. He understood that the purpose of the testing was to determine his capacities to decide where to live and whether to sell his farm and that an outcome could include the appointment of a guardian.

Cognitive testing ranged from the low average to borderline range, with significant impairment in memory and executive function, consistent with major neurocognitive disorder. Functional assessment scores, including the Lichtenberg Financial Decision Rating Scale (Lichtenberg, 2016), were in the low–dependent range, indicating risk for financial exploitation. In the interview, Mr. Johnson could express a choice about where to live and demonstrate understanding but not appreciation or reasoning, regarding potential risks or supports needed. In particular, he did not acknowledge that he needed help with some tasks such as grocery shopping, meal preparation, home care, and farm care. He acknowledged that he had shot his son, and he expressed understanding of why this caused conflict among his relatives but was limited in his appreciation as to its impact on the caregiver relationship. He did not want to sell his home and farm and continually expressed a desire to return to his home.

Disposition

Following the domestic altercation, Mr. Johnson's son moved to Georgia, and his other son, who resided in Texas, was appointed his legal guardian (because of concerns about Mr. Johnson's capacities and need for a protective arrangement). Mr. Johnson spoke with the son and daughter-in-law in Texas several times a week and stated that he was in agreement with the appointment of the guardian. His son stated in treatment planning conferences that they would follow the recommendations of the team regarding Mr. Johnson's future care; he agreed with the suggestion to dispose of assets to support a supervised living setting to protect Mr. Johnson's safety. Mr. Johnson was in disagreement with the plan to sell the home and farm. The court following him for the criminal charge did not concur with his placement in a group home, because state regulations did not allow persons with a history of assault and battery with a dangerous weapon to reside in licensed homes.

Reflection

This case is one example of family conflict that precipitated and followed an evaluation of capacities. Numerous social factors, including race, rurality, legal involvement, and personal values, complicated disposition planning. The psychology team faced an ethical dilemma of whether to advise Mr. Johnson's son to sell his property. Although Mr. Johnson did not have the legal capacity to make decisions involving the management of property because of the guardianship, he was adamant across a span of several months that he did not wish to sell his home. Farm ownership was a core achievement and value for him, even though retaining the asset meant he could not be discharged to a supervised setting. The best course of action was unclear, which may often be the case when working with complex interactions of social, cultural, and medical factors. Although an optimal outcome may not always be possible, clinicians should seek to consider the autonomy and safety of the client and consult with colleagues as needed.

BLENDED FAMILIES AS SOCIAL CONTEXT IN THE EVALUATION OF CAPACITIES

By definition, individuals in "aging families" have been in relationships, negotiated challenges, and celebrated triumphs together for extended periods of time. Carden, Murry, Matthews, and Allen (2018) noted the changing definition of families across time and reminded us that individuals may prefer negotiating care transitions with care partners in families of choice rather than families of origin (see also Acquaviva, 2017), reflecting differences in culture and the influence of intersecting identities. When new family members join an aging family, they enter a preexisting dynamic of attachment, personality, emotion regulation, communication pattern, and interplay of values across cohorts (Qualls & Noecker, 2009; Qualls & Williams, 2013). The issue of blended families in conflict is illustrated in the following case vignette.

Case Vignette 2: Mr. Costa

Capacity Issue

Does Mr. Costa have the capacities to be a primary caregiver for his wife?

Social Context Issues

Mr. Costa and his stepson are in conflict; the stepson is preventing him from seeing his wife; issues of language as well as differing backgrounds and history add to the social complexity.

Presentation

Mr. Costa, an 83-year-old man who immigrated from Portugal and lives in the rural southern United States, was diagnosed with mild neurocognitive disorder due to vascular disease and was referred to a psychologist by a legal services group. They asked for an assessment of his capacities, specifically to serve as primary caregiver for his wife, as part of a family dispute they were addressing. For the past 6 months, Mr. Costa's wife had been living with her adult son and daughter-in-law in a house across the street from Mr. Costa. This living situation was arranged after an incident of fecal incontinence in which Mrs. Costa had refused the help of Mr. Costa and the daughter-in-law had been called in to assist.

History

Mr. and Mrs. Costa married at age 60 after the death of her first husband, with whom she had one son. They met through mutual friends during one of Mrs. Costa's yearly visits to Portugal to visit her extended family. After an extended long-distance courtship, Mr. and Mrs. Costa married, and Mr. Costa immigrated to the United States. At the time of this evaluation, they had been married for 23 years.

Mr. Costa and Mrs. Costa's son, Edgar, never formed a positive relationship. Edgar regularly remarked that Mr. Costa was not his father and was not "living up to the standards" his mother was used to in a husband. Five years ago, Mrs. Costa began to experience problems with her memory and difficulty completing household tasks, such as managing the finances and preparing meals. Three years ago, Mrs. Costa was diagnosed with Alzheimer's disease by her primary care physician. Mr. Costa became her primary caregiver, responsible for managing finances, preparing meals, and cleaning the house. He was successful with some of these but struggled with others; the house had become increasingly unkempt, and both Mr. and Mrs. Costa had lost weight. Over the previous year, Mrs. Costa's condition worsened. She began having urinary and then fecal incontinence. These were medically evaluated and attributed to her dementia; the physician made a referral for aging services (e.g., home health aide), but Mr. and Mrs. Costa refused these. While both Mr. and Mrs. Costa managed her urinary incontinence with little difficulty, neither wanted Mr. Costa to be involved with her self-care needs beyond that point, but preferred the daughter-in-law take on these responsibilities. Mr. Costa indicated to the examiners his dislike of the task and reported that Mrs. Costa stated both to him and to Edgar's wife, "That's not for my husband to do." Mr. Costa reported that after the episode of fecal incontinence in which Edgar's wife assisted, family conflict ensued, and Edgar helped his mother move across the street into his house. At the time of this evaluation, Mr. Costa only had contact with his wife when she happened to be sitting on the front porch of Edgar's house. She would call to her husband to ask why he was not visiting her and did not want to see her. Edgar stated he was not welcome in the house and prevented him from coming on the porch, in the house, or having physical contact with Mrs. Costa. Mr. Costa did not want further conflict and did not feel able to resolve this situation without legal representation leading to his contact with legal services.

Assessment of Capacities

Mr. Costa was assessed to determine his capacities to care for his wife. Along with cognitive and psychological evaluation, factors considered included the history of care at home, along with his values and supports available. Mr. Costa arrived on time and was well groomed and motivated to put forth his best effort on both days of the assessment. Notably, Mr. Costa's first language was Portuguese, so he performed some tasks more slowly due to translating instructions for himself from English to Portuguese to respond appropriately; thus, timed tasks were not used in the assessment. Additionally, Mr. Costa displayed heightened emotional responses throughout the evaluation, becoming tearful at several points as he described his situation and his desire to see his wife. These factors must be taken into consideration in the interpretation of findings. He understood that the purpose of the testing was to determine his capacities to serve as primary caregiver.

Cognitive testing ranged in the low average to borderline range, with significant impairment in attention and memory but intact visuospatial–constructional skills. The overall cognitive assessment was consistent with mild neurocognitive disorder. His scores on the depression and anxiety scales indicated clinically significant levels of depression and anxiety. Functional assessment scores indicated that he was capable of understanding problematic situations, generating solutions, and making a clear choice about how to handle a problematic situation in general, but he did not always recognize limitations. In the interview, he recognized that he sometimes "screamed or yelled" at Mrs. Costa, becoming angry when she would mistakenly call him by her first husband's first name. He stated that he was unable to assist her with all of her toileting and felt overwhelmed with being her caregiver. He expressed some relief that his daughter-in-law was now functioning in that role but wanted to be able to visit his wife.

Disposition

Ultimately, Mr. Costa's capacities to provide care for his wife, as the primary caregiver in a community setting, were determined to be insufficient for her safety. Of particular concern were his incipient cognitive difficulties, his inability to assist Mrs. Costa with all her needs, the decline in their health and home, and his reluctance to accept in-home services. Recommendations included treatment for depression and anxiety, encouragement to accept in-home services, and continued work with legal services. The legal service agency established a mediation plan during which the goal was to establish a visitation arrangement. However, the family remained in conflict, and the son and daughter-in-law refused mediation. At the time of this writing, legal services were considering other legal options.

Reflection

This case is another example of family conflict that precipitated an evaluation of capacities, which also identified a previously unrecognized neurocognitive disorder in Mr. Costa. The team faced an ethical dilemma in feeling limited in their ability to resolve the family conflict with long standing family animosity. This case engendered compassion for Mr. Costa and self-reflection regarding boundaries of professional roles. Here again, the best course of action was unclear, particularly given that the son, Edgar, refused the suggested mediation. As stated in Case 1, a clear resolution and optimal outcome may not always be possible when capacity evaluation takes place within the context of family conflict. As psychologists, clinicians should seek to consider the autonomy and safety of the client and consult with colleagues as needed.

INTERPERSONAL VIOLENCE IN FAMILIES AS SOCIAL CONTEXT IN THE EVALUATION OF CAPACITIES

Interpersonal violence affects aging families as well as younger families and arises in the evaluation of capacities in several ways. In some situations, a new episode of interpersonal violence is perpetrated by a person whose capacities are in question, as in the first case vignette. In other situations, interpersonal violence is perpetrated toward the person with a neurocognitive or neuropsychiatric illness. Also, historical interpersonal violence may influence a family's approach to supports. One to two percent of older adults experience physical interpersonal violence based on elder abuse reports or survey data (Acierno et al., 2010; Miszkurka, Steensma, & Phillips, 2016), whereas 4% to 6% of experience physical violence from a family member during their lifetime (Miszkurka et al., 2016). Exposure to violence across the life span is associated with poorer physical and mental health and predicts current risk for violence (Bonomi et al., 2006; Walsh et al., 2007).

Case Vignette 3: Mr. Roman

Capacity Issue

Mr. Roman had previously been evaluated for dementia. A physician determined that he lacked the capacity for health care decisions. His wife was acting as his health care agent under his advance directive.

Social Context Issue

There was a history of interpersonal violence by Mr. Roman toward Mrs. Roman, and a recent episode prompted a referral for a capacity assessment.

Presentation and History

Mr. Charles Roman, a 74-year-old non-Hispanic White man with mild neurocognitive disorder due to Lewy body disease first came to the attention of the psychologist when he and his wife were referred to a telephone-based caregiver support program. Mr. Roman and Mrs. Roman had been married 28 years and had no children. It was a second marriage for both; neither had children from their first marriage. The couple had a conflictual relationship that periodically escalated into interpersonal violence by Mr. Roman toward Mrs. Roman. Later in life, after he developed a neurocognitive disorder, she became his caregiver. Recently, Mr. Roman grabbed and choked Mrs. Roman during an episode in the middle of the night, but she was able to escape and call the police.

Assessment

Before the referral to the caregiver support program, Mr. Roman had a dementia evaluation consisting of physical examination, laboratory testing, brain imaging, and neuropsychological testing. Taken together, these confirmed mild neurocognitive disorder due to Lewy body disease with executive impairments, visual hallucinations, and parkinsonian symptoms. During a recent primary care visit, the physician opined that Mr. Roman lacked the capacity for health care decision-making and activated Mrs. Roman as the health care agent. When referred to the caregiver support program before the choking episode, Mr. Roman had a vague understanding and appreciation of the purpose of the program: "To help us so I can stay at home." Mrs. Roman reported significant caregiver burden, as well as significant symptoms of anxiety and depression.

Disposition

After the choking incident, we learned that the wife had moved her husband into an assisted living facility. She reported that she was not comfortable sleeping under the same roof as him and moved him into a reputable (and expensive) care facility. Although the caregiver support program is designed to continue to provide support during such transitions, Mrs. Roman declined further participation, citing that she was finished with caregiving.

Reflection

As a team, there had been several peculiarities during our work with this family that were notable but not alarming. For example, the wife, who was highly educated and had worked in the medical field, asked after each session about how details related to his symptoms and diagnosis were being documented in his medical record. She circled back to this after each contact, wanting a copy of the neuropsychological report as soon as it was available. As a clinical team, we appreciate that advocacy is important in health care, and yet something about her quick decision to move her husband into a care facility within the span of a week seemed to be consistent with early heightened awareness in our collective clinical intuition. As a team, we knew little about the family's financial resources or family constellation and discussed whether our perceptions of her quick decision to move him out of their home were unfairly shaped by the fact that this was his second wife or that he was always calm and independent in interactions with our team. We found ourselves questioning whether we had done enough (or too much) to educate her about the probable course of his disease, consequences of behavioral disturbance, and the need to plan for potential moves into a supportive living environment. Yet we also wondered whether we had undervalued the impact of the interpersonal violence, the fear and danger she experienced, and the past conflict in the relationship.

DISCLOSURE WITHIN FAMILIES AS SOCIAL CONTEXT IN THE EVALUATION OF CAPACITIES

As with any assessment, deciding how much information to place in the older adult's medical record or report can be a potential ethical dilemma because others within the health care system may have access to included information (Bhe, Summers, Pakyurek, Soulier, & Ferranti, 2015; Richards, 2009). When working within the family system, this ethical dilemma may become particularly salient because others, in their role as agent under an advance directive, may gain access to confidential information that the older adult may prefer to keep private. For example, the APA Ethics Code states that behavioral health providers must create records of their professional services to meet institutional requirements and ensure accuracy of billing (Section 6: Record Keeping and Fees; APA, 2017), which is confidential (Section 4: Privacy and Confidentiality; APA, 2017). However, family members could later gain access to these records (i.e., through guardianship or durable power of attorney) and learn information that the older adult did not wish to share with them. Including information about the family system or specific individuals other than the identified older adult can also be problematic. For example, it may appear necessary to describe some sensitive information in your report or other formal records, such as (a) concerns about undue influence or elder abuse, (b) information about family members who were interviewed during the assessment, or (c) diagnostic information about someone other than the identified older adult (e.g., when a spouse has a medical or psychiatric condition that affects their capacities to provide care for the identified older adult or creates stress for the older adult). However, the clinician should keep in mind that including such information without explicit consent of those affected may result in unintentionally disclosing protected health information to unintended parties (e.g., if an adult son with a power of attorney gains access to his father's medical records and learns about his stepmother's diagnoses from your report).

Behavioral health providers should be aware of the potential impact of family conflict on the necessity of the information included in medical records. Simply documenting an encounter with a mental health professional may alert others to the fact that the older adult is receiving psychiatric services (Richards, 2009); although this is often unavoidable, specific details should be kept to a minimum to protect the privacy of the older adult. The issue of disclosure is illustrated in the case vignette that follows, which also harkens back to diversity issues, specifically LGBTQ issues, identified earlier.

Case Vignette 4: Mr. Fraser

Capacity Issue

There was not a current concern for Mr. Fraser's capacities, but a recent stroke raised the specter of concern about neurocognitive vulnerability should he have a second stroke.

Social Context Issues

Mr. Fraser requested that information not be shared with his family; he had some dependence and disagreement with his son; and issues of gender identity and geographic setting add to social complexity.

Presentation and History

Mr. Marty Fraser, a 68-year-old Caucasian individual with a history of depression and recent stroke who lived with his son in the Deep South, was referred to a psychologist in the emergency department. Mr. Fraser's case arose after he called local emergency services while experiencing suicidal ideation without plan or intent. Mr. Fraser had attempted suicide by hanging several years previously. During the current crisis, he shared with emergency responders that he secretly identified as a transgender woman. This was not recognized by his family members, and Mr. Fraser did wish to disclose it to them. He chose to continue using masculine pronouns because he was not out about his status and to avoid stigma in his community (masculine pronouns are used here as well, to reflect this stated preference). Mr. Fraser waited to call 911 until he was sure that his son, with whom he resided, was not home. His son was providing some support with self and home care subsequent to Mr. Fraser's recent stroke and was designated by Mr. Fraser to be his health care agent in his advance directive in the event of future incapacities. However, Mr. Fraser's son openly expressed animosity toward LGBTQ individuals. Identity-related distress played a large role in the maintenance of Mr. Fraser's depressive symptomatology, and this was directly related to his previous suicide attempt.

Assessment

Mr. Fraser was assessed to determine his level of suicide risk and potential need for psychiatric hospitalization. He shared that he had been receiving psychotherapy for several years from a therapist within the same medical system. Along with a clinical interview, mental status examination, depression scale, and cognitive screen, factors considered included his history of self-harm and engagement in treatment. The assessment found a moderate degree of depression but not imminent danger of self-harm; mental status and cognitive screening was within normal limits. The psychologist determined he did not require or meet criteria for psychiatric hospitalization. Following the assessment, he was amenable to completing a safety plan and scheduling an emergency appointment with his behavioral health provider for the next morning.

Disposition

At the end of this encounter, the consulting psychologist needed to document the interaction and safety plan in Mr. Fraser's medical record. Information about his gender identity was documented in his psychiatric record (with his permission), which was restricted within the electronic health record, but emergency records were not restricted. Given the stigma that Mr. Fraser might face, as well as his reluctance to disclose this information to others, the psychologist chose to exclude details of Mr. Fraser's gender identity from the encounter note.

Reflection

This situation created an ethical dilemma for the psychologist. His diagnoses of depression and gender dysphoria were directly relevant to his presenting issues and his previous suicide attempt. His recent stroke and dependence on his son for some care, along with conflict with his son, elevate a level of concern about disclosure. Similarly, if his capacities to reveal or conceal his female gender identity are diminished in the future, the information that this was a lifetime preference may be critical for treating this individual with respect and dignity near the end of life (Acquaviva, 2017). If the psychologist had chosen to include this information, there may have been serious repercussions, particularly as medical records are not necessarily designed to incorporate this information (Deutsch et al., 2013). Given Mr. Fraser's age and vascular risk factors, he might eventually find himself in a situation in which another individual, such as his son, was granted access to his medical records as his health care agent under his advance directive.

Additionally, this case raised general concerns for the psychologist about the cultural context of disclosing this information—in relation not only to the family conflict but also the geographical context. Although gender identity is considered private health information and is protected under HIPAA laws, Mr. Fraser resides in a state where protections for transgender individuals are not included in state antidiscrimination laws. Thus, if this protected health information was disclosed by a member of the health care team, consequences could be significant for Mr. Fraser. At this time, in Mr. Fraser's locale, it is still legal for individuals like Mr. Fraser to be denied housing or fired from employment based on gender identity. It is hoped that highly trained and experienced medical staff would continue to treat Mr. Fraser with respect; this unfortunately cannot be assumed. In sum, to exclude the information may deprive health care providers of critical information for managing his risk and providing culturally competent care. In contrast, to include the information risks disclosure in the future to the son and potentially to others who might discriminate against him. Here too, the way forward is not entirely clear.

Conceptual Approach

The balance of autonomy and beneficence while working with older families is a core ethical conflict in clinical gerontology (Bush, Allen, Heck, & Moye, 2015; Bush et al., 2017) and psychology (APA, 2017). The CORE–OPT framework (see Exhibit 12.1; Bush et al., 2017) and the core tasks of Caregiver Family Therapy (see Exhibit 12.2; Qualls, 2008; Qualls & Noecker, 2009; Qualls & Williams, 2013) are two conceptual models that can be combined to navigate families in conflict.

First, the clinician must clarify the ethical issue (e.g., autonomy vs. beneficent responsibility) and use clear and understandable terms to describe the need for an evaluation of capacities to the family (e.g., etiology and social and environmental context; see Exhibit 12.2: Task 1, Goal 1).

Second, the clinician must acknowledge obligations owed to stakeholders, particularly when services are delivered to or through organizations (e.g., a skilled nursing facility, an attorney or an elder law clinic). In the CORE–OPT ethical framework, this also necessitates thorough identification of resources and the need to examine personal beliefs and values (e.g., the relative value of autonomy vs. beneficent responsibility may vary across professional ethics codes and practices). Knowledge of resources within the family and community also supports shared decision-making and supported autonomy, addressing Task 2 and Goals 3 and 4 of Caregiver Family Therapy (see Exhibit 12.2).

EXHIBIT 12.1

CORE–OPT: Model for Ethical Decision-Making in Geropsychology

Clarify the ethical issue
Obligations owed to stakeholders
Resources (ethical and legal)
Examine personal beliefs and values
Options, solutions, and consequences
Put plan into practice
Take stock, evaluate outcome, and revise as needed

Note. Data from Bush et al. (2017).

EXHIBIT 12.2

Caregiver Family Therapy

Therapy is organized around three core tasks:

1. clearly describing the caregiving situation in terms of etiology and social and environmental context,
2. renegotiating roles and responsibilities to maximize systemic functioning, and
3. facilitating the needs of all members within the caregiving family system.

The four goals of caregiver family therapy are to

1. empower families to make decisions that balance safety risks to the person with diminished capacity with the highest potential level of autonomy for that person;
2. assist caregivers in achieving substantive and subjective support in relation to the family as a whole through healthy negotiation of family transitions;
3. facilitate the needs and growth of all family members according to family values; and
4. maximize quality of life for the older adult, caregiver(s), and other family members throughout the process of role transitions.

Note. Data from Qualls and Noecker (2009).

Third, the options, solutions, and consequences must be considered. For example, the choice of measures to include in an assessment of capacities depends on available options, and each choice will produce certain consequences. For example, in the rural southeast, some African American older adults likely completed less than an elementary education (as in the case vignettes), and the quality of education in segregated schools for these cohorts must bring into question the utility of standardized assessment instruments such as the Montreal Cognitive Assessment (Bernstein, Lacritz, Barlow, Weiner, & DeFina, 2011; Hilgeman et al., 2019; Nasreddine et al., 2005), Saint Louis University Mental Status Examination (Tariq et al., 2006), or Repeatable Battery for the Assessment of Neuropsychological Status (Randolph, Tierney, Mohr, & Chase, 1998) when used as part of an evaluation of capacities.

Fourth, the clinician must put the plan into practice by conducting the assessment of capacities and carefully scoring instruments and interpreting results within the current social and environmental context, as well as the history of the individual and his or her family. This addresses the third task and Goals 3 and 4 of Caregiver Family Therapy (see Exhibit 12.2). The final step in conducting an assessment of capacities when a family is in conflict is to take stock, evaluate the outcome, and revise as needed such that the recommendations regarding capacities, cognitive supports, and optimal family functioning within the report truly facilitate the needs of all members of the family system and maximize their quality of life (see Exhibit 12.2).

Assessment Approach

Capacities depend on the decision context (American Bar Association and American Psychological Association Assessment of Capacity in Older Adults Project Working Group [ABA/APA], 2008). What, exactly, is the concern or care transition that is necessitating the evaluation of decisional capacities? Is it the specific capacity in question related to independent living, the capacity to consent to medical treatment (Moye & Marson, 2007; Moye, Marson, & Edelstein, 2013) or capacity to engage in financial decision-making (Lichtenberg, 2016; Lichtenberg, Ficker, & Rahman-Filipiak, 2016; Lichtenberg, Stoltman, Ficker, Iris, & Mast, 2015)? Older adults with neurocognitive disorders are at increased risk for grave financial mismanagement, scams, and theft, sometimes at the hands of family members (Boyle et al., 2013; Lichtenberg, 2016; Lichtenberg et al., 2015, 2016). As with neuropsychological and personality assessment, instruments used as part of an assessment of capacities must be chosen based on knowledge of very clear referral questions and an accurate understanding of the role of proxy decision-makers or potential decision-makers in the life of the older adult (ABA/APA, 2008; Allen & Shuster, 2002; Moye, Marson, & Edelstein, 2013).

Research and resources on the assessment of capacities are growing; however, the gold standard reference for psychologists remains the ABA/APA (2008) *Handbook on Assessment of Older Adults With Diminished Capacity*. This handbook provides guidance, resources, and references for assessing medical, functional, sexual consent, financial, testamentary, driving, and independent living capacities, as well as how to determine the presence of undue influence and how to work with attorneys and within the court system. Given this chapter's focus on families in conflict, in Table 12.1 we note some instruments that may be useful within the context of families in conflict in which an assessment of capacities is needed. Additionally, there are numerous tools for assessing values, including those for older adults with multimorbidity who converge on certain values as important in maintaining quality of life after illness (Naik, Martin, Moye, & Karel, 2016).

When families are in conflict, assessing for undue influence, abuse, or exploitation is one of the most important components of in the assessment of capacities (ABA/APA, 2008; Lichtenberg et al., 2016; Marson, 2016; Moye & Braun, 2007; Moye, Marson, & Edelstein, 2013). Individuals with diminished capacities and living with conflictual family dynamics are at risk of succumbing to undue social influence of others in their "support" network. Conditions include a sense of isolation and dependency, as well as feelings of powerlessness, fear, and vulnerability. Chapter 7 of the ABA/APA (2008) handbook reviews four undue influence models. Additionally, prior research indicates that cognitive ability and rate of cognitive change predict transitions in financial decision-making (Boyle et al., 2013; Lichtenberg et al., 2016), a time of potential vulnerability and exploitation for older adults with diminished capacities. However, clinicians assessing the financial capacities of an older individual within a family in potential conflict must be wary of their own assumptions and biases regarding what constitutes undue influence and exploitation (Bush et al., 2017). Hsu and Willis (2013) found that in healthy and well-functioning couples in which one partner experienced diminished financial capacities, 33% chose the person with cognitive deficits to be the one primarily responsible for family finances.

TABLE 12.1. Assessments for Families in Conflict

Measures to consider for families in conflict	Use and details	Comment
Decisional Conflict Scale (O'Connor, 1995)	Five domains: 1. Uncertainty—clarity of choice 2. Informed—awareness of options, benefits, risks 3. Values clarity—knowledge of personal preferences 4. Support—resources available 5. Effective decision-making	Widely used in advance care planning-focused research studies as an outcome measure
Lichtenberg Financial Decision Rating Scale (Lichtenberg, Ficker, & Rahman-Filipiak, 2016)	Person-centered approach to assessing capacity to make financial decisions, and its relationship to self-reported cases of financial exploitation	Used in research studies and clinical practice Used in situations in which a family member may be exerting undue influence or, more problematically, perpetrating financial exploitation
Measure of Family Conflict Regarding Care Decisions (Parks et al., 2011)	Generates a Family Conflict Score (0–36) by calculating the mean product of "importance" ratings for each care decision on the level of "disagreement" for each decision-maker on a 0- to 6-point scale	Used in research
Values Preferences Scale (Whitlatch, Feinberg, & Tucke, 2005)	For use in both research and practice settings, this 24-item scale assesses the everyday care values and preferences of persons with cognitive impairment and the perceptions of family caregivers about their relative's values and preferences	Used in research studies and clinical practice
Zarit Burden Interview (Zarit, Reever, & Bach-Peterson, 1980)	Assesses personal strain and role strain associated with providing care, often called *caregiver burden* Scale length ranges from a four-item screening tool to the original 29-item version.	Widely used in research and clinical practice

Seeking Ethics Consultation

Mental health professionals should be aware of and familiar with mandatory reporting guidelines, but many cases arise in which family conflict and ethical dilemmas are present but not reportable. For example, in the context of the family system, there may be conflicts among family members who are responsible for making health care decisions on behalf of a loved one. This may become particularly complicated in the case of nontraditional families, which may include multicultural families, whose members may not be physically present to consult with the medical team (Gallagher-Thompson, 2006); families of choice (Carden et al., 2018); and blended families (Moye & Marson, 2007).

A particularly salient ethical dilemma that may emerge in the context of family decision-making is whether an older adult should be informed of diagnostic and prognostic information. Within the United States, it is a default component of ethical practice that information about diagnoses be disclosed (Standard 9.10: Explaining Assessment Results; APA, 2017). However, this varies greatly as a function of culture, and it may be more or less acceptable in different cultures to withhold this information from the older adult (Ni & Alræk, 2017). In these cases, the provider should attempt to ascertain the wishes of individual families rather than make assumptions based on observed identities (Halli-Tierney, Albright, Dragan, Lippe, & Allen, 2018). However, in the case of family conflict, it may be useful to pursue an ethics consultation through a health care institution or, if that is not available, through peer consultation.

REFLECTION AND CONCLUSIONS

Family conflict and its ramifications for both clinical care and medicolegal decision-making are unavoidable in legal and health care decision-making. As a provider, you may encounter ambiguous or discordant cases like the ones described in this chapter across a variety of professional roles—embedded interprofessional treatment team member; as an outside consultant; in capacity assessment service; or as an ethics team member, researcher, or expert witness, for example—where you must make a recommendation on *who should decide*?

Strong evidence supports the association between the existence of written advance care planning documents and reduced distress, decreased decision-making discomfort, and overall improved quality of dying across care settings (e.g., Vandervoort et al., 2014). When working with older adults who still possess some capacities to be involved in formal care planning—as is often the case in mild to moderate stages of dementia—educating persons to execute an advance directive and financial power of attorney documents should be a high priority. Many families may not know that identifying a health care proxy is often still possible even after capacities to execute a living will or make complex health care decisions have been lost. In these situations, when conflicts arise, interventions such as caregiver family therapy (CFT) may facilitate healthy family functioning (Qualls, 2008; Qualls & Noecker, 2009; Qualls & Williams, 2013). Clinical gerontologists and other health care providers must reflect on their roles and responsibilities in providing person-centered and ethical practice. As the case vignettes in this chapter have illustrated, aspects of this practice include cultural competency and cultural humility. Working with older families in conflict is challenging but also rewarding, providing opportunities for cultural competence. The intersection of race, ethnicity, socioeconomic status, gender identity, sexual orientation, ability status, religious beliefs, and geographic place of residence may expose individuals with greater combinations of low social status identities to significantly more stigma and discrimination. The dynamic interplay of such characteristics influences how health and mental health providers must interact with families in conflict when one individual is experiencing diminished capacities.

REFERENCES

Acierno, R., Hernandez, M. A., Amstadter, A. B., Resnick, H. S., Steve, K., Muzzy, W., & Kilpatrick, D. G. (2010). Prevalence and correlates of emotional, physical, sexual, and financial abuse and potential neglect in the United States: The National Elder Mistreatment Study. *American Journal of Public Health, 100,* 292–297. http://dx.doi.org/10.2105/AJPH.2009.163089

Acquaviva, K. D. (2017). *LGBTQ-inclusive hospice and palliative care.* New York, NY: Harrington Park Press. http://dx.doi.org/10.17312/harringtonparkpress/2017.03lgbtqihpc

Adelman, R. D., Tmanova, L. L., Delgado, D., Dion, S., & Lachs, M. S. (2014). Caregiver burden: A clinical review. *Journal of the American Medical Association, 311,* 1052–1060. http://dx.doi.org/10.1001/jama.2014.304

Allen, R. S., Noh, H., Beck, L. N., & Smith, L. J. (2016). Caring for individuals near the end of life. In L. D. Burgio, J. E. Gaugler, & M. M. Hilgeman (Eds.), *The spectrum of family caregiving for adults and elders with chronic illness* (pp. 142–172). New York, NY: Oxford University Press. http://dx.doi.org/10.1093/med:psych/9780199828036.003.0006

Allen, R. S., & Shuster, J. L., Jr. (2002). The role of proxies in treatment decisions: Evaluating functional capacity to consent to end-of-life treatments within a family context. *Behavioral Sciences & the Law, 20,* 235–252. http://dx.doi.org/10.1002/bsl.484

American Bar Association and American Psychological Association Assessment of Capacity in Older Adults Project Working Group. (2008). *Assessment of older adults with diminished capacity: A handbook for psychologists.* Washington, DC: American Bar Association and American Psychological Association.

American Psychological Association. (2017). *Ethical principles of psychologists and code of conduct* (2002, Amended June 1, 2010, and January 1, 2017). Retrieved from http://www.apa.org/ethics/code/index.aspx

Bauer, G. R. (2014). Incorporating intersectionality theory into population health research methodology: Challenges and the potential to advance health equity. *Social Science & Medicine, 110,* 10–17. http://dx.doi.org/10.1016/j.socscimed.2014.03.022

Belch, M. A., & Willis, L. A. (2006). Family decision at the turn of the century: Has the changing structure of households impacted the family decision-making process? *Journal of Consumer Behaviour, 2*(2), 111–124. http://dx.doi.org/10.1002/cb.94

Bernstein, I. H., Lacritz, L., Barlow, C. E., Weiner, M. F., & DeFina, L. F. (2011). Psychometric evaluation of the Montreal Cognitive Assessment (MoCA) in three diverse samples. *The Clinical Neuropsychologist, 25,* 119–126. http://dx.doi.org/10.1080/13854046.2010.533196

Bhe, E., Summers, S., Pakyurek, M., Soulier, M., & Ferranti, J. (2015). Outpatient psychiatric documentation use by primary care physicians following de-sensitization in the electronic medical record. *Academic Psychiatry, 39,* 639–644. http://dx.doi.org/10.1007/s40596-014-0201-0

Blieszner, R., & Roberto, K. A. (2010). Care partner responses to the onset of mild cognitive impairment. *The Gerontologist, 50,* 11–22. http://dx.doi.org/10.1093/geront/gnp068

Bonomi, A. E., Thompson, R. S., Anderson, M., Reid, R. J., Carrell, D., Dimer, J. A., & Rivara, F. P. (2006). Intimate partner violence and women's physical, mental, and social functioning. *American Journal of Preventive Medicine, 30,* 458–466. http://dx.doi.org/10.1016/j.amepre.2006.01.015

Bowleg, L. (2012). The problem with the phrase *women and minorities:* Intersectionality—an important theoretical framework for public health. *American Journal of Public Health, 102,* 1267–1273. http://dx.doi.org/10.2105/AJPH.2012.300750

Boyle, P. A., Yu, L., Wilson, R. S., Segawa, E., Buchman, A. S., & Bennett, D. A. (2013). Cognitive decline impairs financial and health literacy among community-based older persons without dementia. *Psychology and Aging, 28,* 614–624. http://dx.doi.org/10.1037/a0033103

Bridgman, H., & Carr, E. (1998). Providing family care in hospital. *Nursing Times, 94,* 44–47.

Bush, S. S., Allen, R. S., Heck, A. L., & Moye, J. (2015). Ethical issues in geropsychology: Clinical and forensic perspectives. *Psychological Injury and Law, 8,* 348–356. http://dx.doi.org/10.1007/s12207-015-9242-2

Bush, S. S., Allen, R. S., & Molinari, V. (2017). *Ethical practice in geropsychology.* Washington, DC: American Psychological Association. http://dx.doi.org/10.1037/0000010-000

Carden, K. D., Murry, K. J., Matthews, L. H., & Allen, R. S. (2018). Cultural diversity and intersectionality in the end-of-life experience. In R. S. Allen, B. D. Carpenter, & M. K. Eichorst (Eds.), *Perspectives on behavioural interventions in palliative and end-of-life care. Aging and mental health research series* (pp. 112–140). Abingdon, England, and New York, NY: Routledge. http://dx.doi.org/10.4324/9781315212265-6

Centers for Disease Control and Prevention. (2013). CDC health disparities and inequalities report—United States 2013. *MMWR 62*(Suppl. 3). Retrieved from https://www.cdc.gov/mmwr/pdf/other/su6203.pdf

Cole, E. R. (2009). Intersectionality and research in psychology. *American Psychologist, 64,* 170–180. http://dx.doi.org/10.1037/a0014564

Collins, P. H. (2000). *Black feminist thought: Knowledge, consciousness, and the politics of empowerment.* New York, NY: Routledge.

Cox, J., Stanziani, M. R., Coffey, C. A., & deLacy, R. D. (2018). LGB Q&A: An investigation of the influence of sexual orientation on professional practice among LGBQ-affiliated forensic mental health professionals. *Professional Psychology: Research and Practice, 49,* 255–263. http://dx.doi.org/10.1037/pro0000196

Crenshaw, K. (1991). Mapping the margins: Intersectionality, identity politics, and violence against women of color. *Stanford Law Review, 43,* 1241–1299. http://dx.doi.org/10.2307/1229039

Deutsch, M. B., Green, J., Keatley, J., Mayer, G., Hastings, J., Hall, A. M., . . . Wolf-Gould, C., & the World Professional Association for Transgender Health EMR Working Group. (2013). Electronic medical records and the transgender patient: Recommendations from the World Professional Association for Transgender Health

EMR Working Group. *Journal of the American Medical Informatics Association, 20,* 700–703. http://dx.doi.org/10.1136/amiajnl-2012-001472

Earnshaw, V. A., Rosenthal, L., Gilstad-Hayden, K., Carroll-Scott, A., Kershaw, T. S., Santilli, A., & Ickovics, J. R. (2018). Intersectional experiences of discrimination in a low-resource urban community: An exploratory latent class analysis. *Journal of Community & Applied Social Psychology, 28,* 80–93. http://dx.doi.org/10.1002/casp.2342

Edwards, S. B., Olson, K., Koop, P. M., & Northcott, H. C. (2012). Patient and family caregiver decision making in the context of advanced cancer. *Cancer Nursing, 35,* 178–186. http://dx.doi.org/10.1097/NCC.0b013e31822786f6

Elder, G. H., Jr. (1998). The life course as developmental theory. *Child Development, 69*(1), 1–12. http://dx.doi.org/10.1111/j.1467-8624.1998.tb06128.x

Gallagher-Thompson, D. (2006). The family as the unit of assessment and treatment in work with ethnically diverse older adults with dementia. In G. Yeo & D. Gallagher-Thompson (Eds.), *Ethnicity and the dementias* (2nd ed., pp. 119–124). New York, NY: Routledge.

Halli-Tierney, A., Albright, A., Dragan, D., Lippe, M., & Allen, R. S. (2018). Ethical issues in palliative and end-of-life care. In R. S. Allen, B. D. Carpenter, & M. K. Eichorst (Eds.), *Perspectives on palliative and end-of-life care: Disease, social, and cultural context* (pp. 91–118). Abingdon, England, and New York, NY: Routledge. http://dx.doi.org/10.4324/9780429489259-5

Hilgeman, M. M., Boozer, E. M., Snow, A. L., Allen, R. S., & Davis, L. L. (2019). Use of the Montreal Cognitive Assessment (MoCA) in a rural outreach program for military veterans. *Journal of Rural Social Sciences, 34*(2), Article 2. Retrieved from https://egrove.olemiss.edu/jrss/vol34/iss2/2

Holst, L., Lundgren, M., Olsen, L., & Ishøy, T. (2009). Dire deadlines: Coping with dysfunctional family dynamics in an end-of-life care setting. *International Journal of Palliative Nursing, 15,* 34–41. http://dx.doi.org/10.12968/ijpn.2009.15.1.37951

Hsu, J. W., & Willis, R. (2013). Dementia risk and financial decision making by older households: The impact of information. *Journal of Human Capital, 2013*(4), 45.

Institute of Medicine. (2014). *Dying in America: Improving quality and honoring preferences near the end of life.* Washington, DC: The National Academies Press.

Kayashima, R., & Braun, K. L. (2001). Barriers to good end-of-life care: A physician survey. *Hawaii Medical Journal, 60,* 40–44.

Kramer, B. J., Boelk, A. Z., & Auer, C. (2006). Family conflict at the end of life: Lessons learned in a model program for vulnerable older adults. *Journal of Palliative Medicine, 9,* 791–801. http://dx.doi.org/10.1089/jpm.2006.9.791

Kramer, B. J., & Yonker, J. A. (2011). Perceived success in addressing end-of-life care needs of low-income elders and their families: What has family conflict got to do with it? *Journal of Pain and Symptom Management, 41*(1), 35–48. http://dx.doi.org/10.1016/j.jpainsymman.2010.04.017

Lee, C. K. C., & Beatty, S. E. (2002). Family structure and influence in family decision making. *Journal of Consumer Marketing, 19,* 24–41. http://dx.doi.org/10.1108/07363760210414934

Levine, C. (1990). AIDS and changing concepts of family. *Milbank Quarterly, 68*(Suppl. 1), 33–58. http://dx.doi.org/10.2307/3350175

Lichtenberg, P. A. (2016). Financial exploitation, financial capacity, and Alzheimer's disease. *American Psychologist, 71,* 312–320. http://dx.doi.org/10.1037/a0040192

Lichtenberg, P. A., Ficker, L. J., & Rahman-Filipiak, A. (2016). Financial decision-making abilities and financial exploitation in older African Americans: Preliminary validity evidence for the Lichtenberg Financial Decision Rating Scale (LFDRS). *Journal of Elder Abuse & Neglect, 28,* 14–33. http://dx.doi.org/10.1080/08946566.2015.1078760

Lichtenberg, P. A., Stoltman, J., Ficker, L. J., Iris, M., & Mast, B. (2015). A person-centered approach to financial capacity assessment: Preliminary development of a new rating scale. *Clinical Gerontologist, 38,* 49–67. http://dx.doi.org/10.1080/07317115.2014.970318

Marson, D. (2016). Conceptual models and guidelines for clinical assessment of financial capacity. *Archives of Clinical Neuropsychology, 31,* 541–553. http://dx.doi.org/10.1093/arclin/acw052

Mayo, C. (1982). Training for positive marginality. In L. Bickman (Ed.), *Applied social psychology annual* (Vol. 3, pp. 57–73). Beverly Hills, CA: Sage.

McIlvane, J. M., Popa, M. A., Robinson, B., Houseweart, K., & Haley, W. E. (2008). Perceptions of illness, coping, and well-being in persons with mild cognitive impairment and their care partners. *Alzheimer Disease and Associated Disorders, 22,* 284–292. http://dx.doi.org/10.1097/WAD.0b013e318169d714

Miszkurka, M., Steensma, C., & Phillips, S. P. (2016). Correlates of partner and family violence among older Canadians: A life-course approach. *Health Promotion and Chronic Disease Prevention in Canada: Research, Policy and Practice, 36*(3), 45–53. http://dx.doi.org/10.24095/hpcdp.36.3.01

Moye, J., & Braun, M. (2007). Assessment of medical consent capacity and independent living. *Changes in decision-making capacity in older adults: Assessment and intervention,* 205–236.

Moye, J., & Marson, D. C. (2007). Assessment of decision-making capacity in older adults: An emerging area of practice and research. *The Journals of Gerontology: Series B. Psychological Sciences and Social Sciences, 62,* P3–P11. http://dx.doi.org/10.1093/geronb/62.1.P3

Moye, J., Marson, D. C., & Edelstein, B. (2013). Assessment of capacity in an aging society. *American Psychologist, 68,* 158–171. http://dx.doi.org/10.1037/a0032159

Naik, A. D., Martin, L. A., Moye, J., & Karel, M. J. (2016). Health values and treatment goals of older, multimorbid adults facing life-threatening illness. *Journal of the American Geriatrics Society, 64,* 625–631. http://dx.doi.org/10.1111/jgs.14027

Nasreddine, Z. S., Phillips, N. A., Bédirian, V., Charbonneau, S., Whitehead, V., Collin, I., . . . Chertkow, H. (2005). The Montreal Cognitive Assessment, MoCA: A brief screening tool for mild cognitive impairment. *Journal of the American Geriatrics Society, 53,* 695–699. http://dx.doi.org/10.1111/j.1532-5415.2005.53221.x

Ni, Y. H., & Alræk, T. (2017). What circumstances lead to non-disclosure of cancer-related information in China? A qualitative study. *Supportive Care in Cancer, 25,* 811–816. http://dx.doi.org/10.1007/s00520-016-3464-z

O'Connor, A. M. (1995). Validation of a decisional conflict scale. *Medical Decision Making, 15*(1), 25–30. http://dx.doi.org/10.1177/0272989X9501500105

Parks, S. M., Winter, L., Santana, A. J., Parker, B., Diamond, J. J., Rose, M., & Myers, R. E. (2011). Family factors in end-of-life decision-making: Family conflict and proxy relationship. *Journal of Palliative Medicine, 14,* 179–184. http://dx.doi.org/10.1089/jpm.2010.0353

Qualls, S. H. (2008). Caregiver family therapy. In K. Laidlaw & B. Knight (Eds.), *Handbook of emotional disorders in later life* (pp. 183–210). New York, NY: Oxford University Press. http://dx.doi.org/10.1093/med:psych/9780198569459.003.0008

Qualls, S. H., & Noecker, T. L. (2009). Caregiver family therapy for conflicted families. In S. H. Qualls & S. H. Zarit (Eds.), *Aging families and caregiving* (pp. 155–188). Hoboken, NJ: Wiley.

Qualls, S. H., & Williams, A. A. (2013). *Caregiver family therapy: Empowering families to meet the challenges of aging.* Washington, DC: American Psychological Association. http://dx.doi.org/10.1037/13943-000

Randolph, C., Tierney, M. C., Mohr, E., & Chase, T. N. (1998). The Repeatable Battery for the Assessment of Neuropsychological Status (RBANS): Preliminary clinical validity. *Journal of Clinical and Experimental Neuropsychology, 20,* 310–319. http://dx.doi.org/10.1076/jcen.20.3.310.823

Richards, M. M. (2009). Electronic medical records: Confidentiality issues in the time of HIPAA. *Professional Psychology: Research and Practice, 40,* 550–556. http://dx.doi.org/10.1037/a0016853

Samsi, K., & Manthorpe, J. (2013). Everyday decision-making in dementia: Findings from a longitudinal interview study of people with dementia and family carers. *International Psychogeriatrics, 25,* 949–961. http://dx.doi.org/10.1017/S1041610213000306

Stanziani, M., Cox, J., & Coffey, C. A. (2018). Adding insult to injury: Sex, sexual orientation, and juror decision-making in a case of intimate partner violence. *Journal of Homosexuality, 65,* 1325–1350. http://dx.doi.org/10.1080/00918369.2017.1374066

Tariq, S. H., Tumosa, N., Chibnall, J. T., Perry, M. H., III, & Morley, J. E. (2006). Comparison of the Saint Louis University Mental Status Examination and the Mini-Mental State Examination for detecting dementia and mild neurocognitive disorder—A pilot study. *The American Journal of Geriatric Psychiatry, 14,* 900–910. http://dx.doi.org/10.1097/01.JGP.0000221510.33817.86

Unger, R. W. (2000). Outsiders inside: Positive marginality and social change. *Journal of Social Issues, 56,* 163–179. http://dx.doi.org/10.1111/0022-4537.00158

Vandervoort, A., Houttekier, D., Vander Stichele, R., van der Steen, J. T., & Van den Block, L. (2014). Quality of dying in nursing home residents dying with dementia: Does advanced care planning matter? A nationwide postmortem study. *PLoS ONE, 9,* e91130. http://dx.doi.org/10.1371/journal.pone.0091130

Walsh, C. A., Ploeg, J., Lohfeld, L., Horne, J., MacMillan, H., & Lai, D. (2007). Violence across the lifespan: Interconnections among forms of abuse as described by marginalized Canadian elders and their care-givers. *British Journal of Social Work, 37,* 491–514. http://dx.doi.org/10.1093/bjsw/bcm022

Whitlatch, C. J., Feinberg, L. F., & Tucke, S. S. (2005). Measuring the values and preferences for everyday care of persons with cognitive impairment and their family caregivers. *The Gerontologist, 45,* 370–380. http://dx.doi.org/10.1093/geront/45.3.370

Zarit, S. H., Reever, K. E., & Bach-Peterson, J. (1980). Relatives of the impaired elderly: Correlates of feelings of burden. *The Gerontologist, 20,* 649–655. http://dx.doi.org/10.1093/geront/20.6.649

INDEX

A

B

C

V

W

Z

ABOUT THE EDITOR

Jennifer Moye, PhD, is a professor of psychology in the Department of Psychiatry at Harvard Medical School and the associate director of education and evaluation for the New England Geriatric Research Education and Clinical Center at the VA Boston Healthcare System and the Bedford VA Medical Center. She received her doctorate from the University of Minnesota in 1992. She is the editor in chief of *Clinical Gerontologist.* Dr. Moye's main research interests concern capacity, guardianship, and adjustment to medical illness in older adults, especially in the setting of late reemergent post-traumatic stress disorder, as well as geriatrics and gerontology education.